Cosimo Arrichiello was born in Secondigliano, a small
town near Naples, where the struggle for existence was
precarious and even dramatic. As the Fascists seized
power, their dictatorial policy not only aggravated the
people's living conditions, but also proved to be fatal.
When Cosimo was twenty he had to do his military
service while his country was at war, which he writes
about in this book. At the end of the War, ashamed and
depressed by the defeat and destruction of his beloved
country, he emigrated, hoping to find a land where he
could settle down and live happily ever after, but this
proved to be elusive, because as he moved from one
country to another, he found himself faced with new
confrontations and challenges. He lived in Jakarta for
four years, but the local political instability led him to
emigrate to Australia, where he spent fifteen years. He
worked hard there and studied at night in order to gain
some academic qualifications. In 1966 he decided to leave
Australia for London, where he worked as an accounts
clerk and afterwards joined the civil service. He loved
being in London because of the various cultural activities
and opportunities it had to offer. Now retired, he lives in
London and is still writing.

ITALIAN HEARTBREAK

Life Under Mussolini

Cosimo Arrichiello

The Book Guild Ltd
Sussex, England

First published in Great Britain in 2004 by
The Book Guild Ltd
25 High Street
Lewes, East Sussex
BN7 2LU

Typesetting in Times by
Keyboard Services, Luton, Bedfordshire

Printed in Great Britain by
CPI, Bath

A catalogue record for this book is available from
The British Library

ISBN 1 85776 764 0

This book is a picture about life, and what may befall us as we travel through time and space, hoping that at the end of our earthly journey, we will get reunited with our Maker.

I dedicate this book to Uncle Cosimo
who died towards the end of the Great War
at the age of eighteen.
Often, when I think of him,
I can almost envisage being him
at the front and getting killed.
Frequently during my life,
I have been haunted by a strange feeling
of being Uncle's reincarnation.

With reference to Part Five

After the Italian Armistice, 8 September 1943, the Italian Army refused to cooperate with the Germans who had occupied our country, and so it was ordered to disband.

Being a disbanded soldier in Northern Italy and unable to go home, I wandered for a few days through the countryside. A farmer gave me hospitality and, in exchange for that, I helped him on the farm. I had to stay there until the end of the war in May 1945.

Many events took place in nearby towns and villages while I lived in that area, so part of my narrative is concerned with them. To conceal the identity of persons involved and the localities, I have changed their names.

The setting, which at the beginning was comparatively peaceful, later became a scene of dramatic developments.

I have dealt with events which occurred in the forties, and most of the protagonists are no longer living.

CONTENTS

CONTENTS

Part Two: A year in France

Part Three: Preparation for War

Part Four: Army Experiences

Part Five: Country Life

xiii

Part Six: Returning Home

List of Illustrations

Floor plan diagram of Secondigliano is at the end of Chapter 7.

Diagrams of the Sacred Hearts and of a confraternity in procession are at the end of Chapter 18.

The photos of my relatives and a few illustrations listed below are between pages 140 and 141 in the following order:

5th

Our patron saints: Cosma and Damiano

6th

Immaculate Conception in the Chapel of the Sacred Hearts
Venerable Gaetano Errico, founder of the Missionaries of the
Sacred Hearts

Views of Secondigliano and photos of the author between pages
300 and 301.

The views of Secondigliano were extracted from the book
Secondigliano da Documenti Inediti, by Father Salvatore Loffredo.

Preface

This book is about my experiences in the years before the Second World War, during the war and a few months after it. It deals with twenty-seven years of my eventful life: my childhood; Fascist indoctrination; one year I spent in France (1937–38); military service; the fall of Mussolini on 25 July 1943, and the disbandment of the Italian Army after 8 September 1943; my being stranded for about twenty months in Northern Italy; my return home at the end of the war; and my journey to the island of Java in 1947.

It is the result of almost six painstaking years devoted to writing and to studying reference books relevant to that period to check up on dates and other details.

I was born in Secondigliano, a small town on the outskirts of Naples, in June 1920. About two years later, Mussolini, unelected, was allowed to form a government, and so the Fascist era began.

I am eighty now and, if my health doesn't fail me, I would like to write about the four years I spent in Indonesia (1947–51), followed by fifteen years in Australia (1951–66) and thirty-four years in London (1966–2000), where I am still living.

I did not like Indonesia because of its climate and political instability. My life in Australia was extremely hard and I was earning just enough to survive. I worked during the day and went to evening school to complete my higher education. Although I had a few friends there, I felt rather lonely, so during 1966, I went back to Italy. I spent a couple of months there, but as it was hard to get a job, I decided to go to London. I arrived there in 1966, worked as an accounts clerk for a few years, and later in the civil service. I retired at sixty-five, but since then I have always been active. I enrolled at an adult education college to learn to write short stories and poetry.

Coming from a large, and by no means rich, family of eleven children, I wasn't spoiled and in my adult life, when I was left on my own, I always had to strive hard to earn my living and to graft for whatever I wanted to achieve.

The Italy of 2000 is a democratic country and is regarded as the seventh richest country in the world. The people live well. Most of them own the house or flat in which they live and a car; they enjoy all modern amenities, a fair national health service, state pension and social welfare. Moreover there are good schools and facilities for promising students.

The country has not quite achieved political stability yet, on account of the existence of too many political parties and the corruption which seems to be rampant.

Many pensioners of Italian origin would like to go back home, but they fear that they would be unable to survive financially, and would prefer stronger government.

Often I wonder how a country like Italy can be in such a predicament. It is a country with a great history and culture which has largely contributed to the development of Western civilisation. There has never been any lack of intelligence, skill and inspiration; what is needed now is determination, perseverance and cooperation to put things in order and make the country worthy of the respect it deserves in Europe and throughout the world.

My views concerning events in Italy during the Second World War reflect my personal experiences. I did feel, when I was a child and later a teenager, the impact of being systematically brainwashed by the Fascist propaganda, which made me believe that we Italians were invincible; that we, heirs of those great Roman soldiers, would reconquer our lost Empire. However, when our military campaigns started going wrong during the Second World War, I personally resented it very much, was dismayed, disillusioned, and broken-hearted at the thought that we were going to lose the war.

I am grateful to Mr Sidney Fagan, Mr Graham Bird and Dr Peter Ball for reading my manuscripts and making helpful comments.

PART ONE
CHILDHOOD AND ADOLESCENCE

1

My grandparents and my parents. My birth.
Father goes to France

My grandfather, Saverio Arrichiello, and my grandmother, Carmela Russo, were poor. They brought eight children into this world: five girls and three boys. The entire family was cooped up in two ground-floor rooms at 8, Via Arco, in a small, poor, country town called Secondigliano, on the outskirts of Naples.

Most people had large families – and yet at that time there was no such thing as social security benefits or old age pensions. These were privileges that only retired teachers, bankers, civil servants and other government employees enjoyed.

My grandfather was a fishmonger; he had a stall in the main square, *Piazza Municipio* (Town Hall Square). This was how he provided a crust of bread for his large family.

My father, Giovanni Arrichiello (John), was the third child of the family. He spent three years at primary school. He was probably unwilling to go any further, or perhaps his father thought that the boy had had enough education and so he sent him to be a shoemaker's apprentice. Giovanni became a high-class shoemaker and went into partnership with signor Furlone, who ran a small shoe factory in the vicinity of Capodichino military airport. However, competition was very stiff, so Giovanni and his associate had to strive hard to carry on.

Giovanni eventually met a pretty girl, Anna Saccone, and fell in love with her. She was not in love with him. Besides, Giovanni was two or three centimetres shorter than her and she would have preferred someone taller.

Anna came from a poor family of four children. She had two sisters, Concetta and Annunziata, and a brother called Vincent. Concetta was about two years older than Anna, and Annunziata was

3

two years younger. Vincent was probably older than Anna. He worked as a builder's labourer, but died, possibly of consumption, before he was twenty.

Anna lost her mother before she was ten. Her father married again, but Anna's stepmother, who had a daughter of her own, was not too kind to Anna. She stopped sending her to school and sent her instead to work as a hairdresser's assistant. Although Anna was intelligent, lively and willing to learn, she was deprived of the opportunity of a basic education.

Anna blossomed into an attractive girl and had several suitors, one of them being Gennaro Barbato, a barber who emigrated to the USA in 1910. Gennaro set up a barber's shop in Chicago and afterwards wrote to Anna asking her to marry him. Anna was not interested in going to the USA but her sister Concetta was, so it was arranged that she would marry Gennaro by proxy and go in Anna's place.

On several occasions Giovanni proposed to Anna, but she always refused, thinking him not good enough for her. Giovanni would not take no for an answer, so he insistently asked until, out of pity, she accepted. They got married in 1913; he was twenty-six and she was twenty-three. Being a little shorter than her, he had a new pair of shoes with thick heels made specially for the wedding, to gratify his vanity. They went to live in a large room on the third floor at 2, Vico Primo Censi, a section of our town where the poorest people lived.

Having formed an alliance with France and Britain, in May 1915 Italy joined the war against Austria-Hungary and Germany. My parents had already had two children, Carmen and Saverio, by the time Father went to war. My mother received some form of government subsistence which was worth next to nothing, while my father was risking his life for his country. How could Mother pay the rent for her room and bring up her two children on such a pittance? So when her stepmother died, which was before the end of the war, Mother gave up her accommodation and went to live in a cheap bedsitter situated on the ground floor in the courtyard where her father lived.

My grandfather was not entirely on his own when his second wife died, as Annunziata, Mother's single youngest sister, was living with him. Annunziata, however, was working as a maidservant, so she did not have time to look after her widowed father.

4

Grandfather was pleased to have Mother living nearby and taking care of him. As he was still working as a coachman, they managed between them to keep the wolf from the door.

The First World War was a disaster for Italy, especially with our bloody retreat from Caporetto in October 1917. Father went through this tragic upheaval and saw some of his comrades reduced to pulp by enemy artillery. He saved his life by the skin of his teeth, and being in a state of shock, he was sent home on short leave. While Father was at home, he did not waste his time. He made Mother pregnant once again, and in 1918 she gave birth to my brother Vince.

Father and Uncle Pascal were demobilised at the end of 1918. They came back to their homes, but Father's youngest brother, Uncle Cosimo, was killed in action just before the end of the war.

Since there was no work, Uncle Pascal emigrated to France. He was eight years younger than Father and quite an accomplished soldier. He had become sergeant-major during the war. One day while on patrol he had surprised and captured an Austrian detachment, as they were taking a rest and relieving themselves in a bushy area, and was decorated for this achievement.

The French welcomed the Italian immigrants, especially those who had been fighting side by side with them during the war. Uncle Pascal was young, handsome and intelligent, but he had not learned a trade. What could he do in France? He contrived to earn a living doing what hundreds of Neapolitans were doing; that is being a door-to-door salesman, selling suiting material. He loved living and working in Normandy, and French women liked Uncle Pascal, the young handsome heart-throb Italian, so they bought whatever he had for sale, perhaps just to help him to make a living. Quite a number of his affectionate women customers even shared their beds with him! Uncle Pascal – in no time, it seemed – did quite well financially, so he was able to send remittances back to his parents. He even bought a one-bedroom ground-floor flat for them, so that they did not have to pay rent.

Aware that Uncle Pascal was doing so well in France, Father decided to go there too. After all, he was hardly making a living with his shoe business. Life in Italy after the war was a nightmare: the cost of living had soared; there were millions of unemployed; there was a lot of discontent, strikes and political instability. The situation seemed to be worsening from day to day.

5

I was born in June 1920. A few months later, Father, with Uncle's financial help, went to Normandy to try his luck. But since he could not speak French, what could he do? To find an easy way out, he, like his brother Pascal, became a door-to-door salesman, an activity which did not call for either skill or knowledge of the language. Neapolitans were very good at gesticulating with their hands and making themselves understood, in any case.

To influence potential customers and induce them to buy, Father used to tell them that he had been fighting the Germans at Verdun. This usually aroused a feeling of patriotism in his prospective customers, and made them disposed to part with a few banknotes to help an ex-comrade.

Father was quickly doing very well; he was making money, sending some home regularly and coming home for a month or longer every year, usually at Christmas or at Easter. Every time he came home he made Mother pregnant. He spent the evenings playing cards at the businessmen's club where he invariably lost a certain amount of money before returning to France.

Father lodged at small hotels. In the evenings he socialised with Neapolitans he met at coffee-houses. Whenever he wanted a woman, he sought her at a brothel. This was the kind of life that most of the Neapolitan door-to-door salesmen lived in France.

2

Fascism in power. Nicola – quite a character

I can remember as far back as the age of two. Saverio, Vince and I slept in a double bed. When Father was away, my sister Carmen slept with Mother or in a makeshift bed: two boards and a pallet supported by four chairs. We had to use a chamber pot which Mother emptied in the morning into the courtyard's toilet. This was used by all who lived in the courtyard. At this stage there were six of us in all – four children and our parents – and we had to use our bedsitter for every need. It was poverty indeed.

One day, I think it was in 1922, while I was sitting on a chair in the courtyard, I saw an airship – probably a Zeppelin – in our blue sky. What a sight! This huge, strange thing floating in the air made quite an impression on me.

From the courtyard entrance, later the same year, I saw a column of Fascists passing by. They were marching north along Corso Umberto Primo. It could have been 28 October, when columns of Fascists from many regions of Italy marched on Rome. It was at this time that our King, Vittorio Emanuele III, to avoid a confrontation, entrusted Mussolini with the task of forming a new government.

Our door-keeper, Nicola (Nick), was quite a character. He, with his wife and their little boy, lived in a room on the ground floor opposite our bedsitter. Nicola's duties were to keep our staircase and courtyard clean and tidy, to be on guard for intruders, to shut the entrance to the building at eleven or midnight, and open it early in the morning. The proprietor, signor Russo, was a notary and lived on the second floor. He went to his office in Naples every morning and came back in the evening. Since the building we lived in was small, all that Nicola received for being a door-keeper was his free lodging and an occasional tip when a tenant came home after midnight. As the door was already shut at that hour, Nicola had to get up from his cosy bed, walk to the door, open it and let the tenant in.

Having two mouths to feed, Nicola, every morning, left his wife in charge and caught the tram which took him to a small town a few kilometres away. He knocked at doors and told the occupants that he was an ex-serviceman. He showed them war medals which he had bought at some market stall. Moreover he told them that he was unemployed and had to feed his family. When he came home from his begging errand, his wife got busy frying or roasting. The smell of cooking permeated the courtyard and made our mouths water. We could not afford meat and had only a morsel of it perhaps once a week. Nicola and his family gorged themselves on meat or fish every day and washed it down with a few glasses of red wine. We knew more or less what he was up to, but he never divulged the secret or the source of his comparative prosperity.

Signor Russo was afraid to go upstairs when he came home from his office later than usual. As the stairs were badly lit by gaslight and he seemed to fear that the place was haunted, he would ask Nicola to accompany him, and on such occasions he would tip him. At times he would perhaps be ashamed of his cowardice and would say to himself: Why should I be afraid of going upstairs alone? Why should I be afraid of ghosts? They can't be as bad as people, can they?

Having said this he boldly attempted to climb the stairs alone. Nicola was not pleased with signor Russo's act of courage. Should he overcome his fear, then Nicola would lose the tips. To prevent this, while brave signor Russo was going upstairs alone, Nicola contrived to cause some noise such as swishing bats, falling objects, shrieking, moaning, groaning and so on. This was too much for our valiant signor who, being terrified, would shout hysterically: 'Nicola! Nicola! Help! Help!'

Nicola, who had hidden somewhere nearby, would then go to his rescue. Showing much concern and solicitude he would run upstairs and downstairs, but would not find anything wrong.

'Are you sure, signor, that you heard some noise?'

'I'm not deaf, you know,' the other would answer.

'I can't find anything,' Nicola would say with a perplexed look on his face.

'Well, it doesn't matter,' signor Russo would say, shrugging his shoulders and going to his flat escorted by the cunning caretaker.

These incidents certainly taught signor Russo a lesson. From that time on he insisted on Nicola escorting him upstairs whenever it was dark, and Nicola would of course be grateful for the tips he received.

3

We move to a one-bedroom flat. My kindergarten education

My mother got pregnant every year and my brother Antonio was born in 1921, Giuseppe in 1922, my sister Maria in 1924 and Fortuna in 1925; so in a few years there were eight children in our family. Our bedsitter accommodation was overcrowded; we badly needed a larger home. Since Father was doing well in France, we could afford to rent a one-bedroom flat on the first floor just across the road, and we moved in towards the end of 1924. Our new bedroom had enough space for two double beds, but we always needed an extra one, especially when Father was at home.

We had a large kitchen which we used as a dining room and, at night, as a bedroom. We managed somehow to erect a makeshift bed which we dismantled in the morning and put away. For the first time we could also enjoy the luxury of having our own toilet, which was situated in a secluded corner of our kitchen and had a view of the garden at the back of our flat. Living in a flat represented a distinct improvement in our standard of living.

Mother was very busy – she had to take care of eight children who needed a lot of attention. Having so much on her hands, she could not find time to visit and gossip with her old cronies; however, she soon made friends with people living next door, or elsewhere in the building. We were living in a flat with a self-contained toilet, and this made us feel respectable.

Thank goodness Mother no longer had to carry our chamber-pot ceremoniously through the courtyard as she had in previous years. Now that we could rent a flat with an indoor toilet, some people thought that we were well-to-do. But of course we weren't. Things were certainly better for us, but we were still poor in real terms. For instance, we could afford meat only once a week.

Our new friends did not address Mother by her first name, but with a certain deference; they called her signora Arrichiello. This undoubtedly indicated that we were getting on socially.

At this time, my elder sister Carmen was about eleven. She helped with the chores and was my mother's deputy. My brother Saverio was about nine, Vince seven, and I five. Carmen, Saverio and Vince went to primary school. I was attending some kind of private kindergarten located in Via Lungo del Ponte. The mistress running the school was called Donna Virgilia Quinto. She seemed to have quite a good reputation. She had two sisters helping her: a younger one, Erminia, and an older one, called Mariuccia (Little Mary). Erminia had some teaching qualifications, while Mariuccia was just a helping hand and mostly did menial tasks. The girls had a brother, Vincenzo, who was away most of the time in Shanghai or some other Far Eastern city. He seemed to be engaged in some kind of selling activity. He came back home for a while, spent a month or more with his three spinster sisters, and then away he went again.

The school comprised two rooms on the ground floor, a fairly large room and a small one. The large room was used as a kindergarten and could accommodate about sixty children. The small room could hold no more than thirty, and was used for coaching those who were having difficulties with their primary school. Donna Virgilia packed as many children as she could into her school as more children meant a higher income, of course. My mother paid ten or fifteen lire a month to send me there. She took me to school every morning. My sister brought me lunch between midday and one o'clock, and returned about four in the afternoon to take me home. The other children and I were herded into the large room where there were individual stools along the walls. The purpose of going to kindergarten was to learn something, but while we were there no attempt was made to teach anything at all; we were left to our own devices. Cooped up there with nothing else to do, I had to mix with children of different backgrounds. Most of them came from poor homes and some had rough manners. There was absolutely nothing to learn, so to pass the time we shouted, swore and played rowdy games.

After a couple of weeks I made friends with a number of boys with whom I frequently exchanged insults. We teased each other, played at being members of political parties: Fascists, Socialists,

11

Communists, and so on, and clashed boisterously. When we grew tired of doing this we caught flies, squeezed their bottoms, and then inserted small strips of paper and let them fly away. It became daily practice for my naughty mates to show me their willies, and I, not to be outdone, showed them mine. We let them grow stiff and then compared their sizes. Having nothing more worthwhile to do we indulged in these foolish and vulgar pastimes. What a travesty of education! I was only learning how to be a wild boy.

Donna Virgilia, her sisters and brother had their midday meal on the desk in our classroom. They sat around that makeshift table, ate macaroni or minestrone, and chatted animatedly. These elderly spinsters, quite unaware of us, sat at the table with open legs which showed us part of their fleshy thighs and knickers. Such a display attracted our attention, of course. We mischievous boys stared at those fleshy thighs, hoping to discover something more intimate which women are usually loath to display.

Those thighs triggered off erotic fantasies in us. Often one boy would teasingly ask another: 'Have you ever heard your parents' bed vibrating at night? When it does it means that your parents are banging.'

The other boy, a little irritated or offended, might reply: 'And what about your parents? Without their banging, you wouldn't be here, would you?'

I must have gone to that kindergarten for about two years and the only useful thing I learned was the alphabet. What a high price was paid for this! It cost Mother a small fortune to send me there, and I grew into a savage boy whom she found hard to control.

One event associated with my kindergarten years is worth remembering. During the month of May each boy and girl took a candle and a small bunch of white lilies to Our Lady of the Rosary. We wore our best clothes: boys in shorts, white socks, embroidered shirts and bow-ties, with carefully combed hair; girls with long hair and ringlets wore white dresses – a symbol of purity – with white socks, shoes and gloves. They were adorned with blue and white ribbons and they looked like angels.

Our mistress, Donna Virgilia, a confirmed spinster in her forties, was tallish, a little corpulent and had a long face which was beginning to grow wrinkled. She lined us in threes. We were in a line about thirty metres long. Donna Virgilia and her younger sister Erminia proudly led us in a parade through the main streets of our town. As we moved along we sang hymns or praises to Our Lady of the Rosary. The lilies we carried undulated slightly; we must have seemed like a mobile garden. People from ground-floor flats or double-room homes poured into the streets and boisterously exclaimed: '*I nostri bambini! I nostri bambini stanno passando. Su sbrigatevi, andiamo a vederli. Vedete! Vedete! Come sono belli; sembrano degli angioletti.*' (Our children! Our children are passing by. Hurry up, let us go and have a look at them. Look! Look! How lovely they are; they look like little angels.)

Other people clustered on their balconies and they too joyously hailed the parade. A civic guard, the only one we had in our small town, gesticulated pompously and looked like a colossus as he swaggeringly stopped the traffic to allow us to pass by. People who had lined the streets felt the touch of our vibrating youth and vitality. Old folk, especially those riddled with infirmities, were overjoyed to see us. Some of them shed a few tears. We reminded them of the days of their youth when they were strong, good-looking and healthy, and full of zest for life.

4

*Our traditional patron saints' dinner. I have an
accident. Secondigliano in the late twenties*

Every year, towards the end of September, we had our patron
saints' – Cosma and Damiano – celebration. And on such occasions
most people managed somehow to have something extra to eat or
to prepare some special or traditional dish. Now that we were much
better off than in previous years, we could afford meat twice a
week. We did not have a lot of it – only one kilo of meat on
Sundays for the whole family of eight children, plus Grandfather,
Mother's father, who dined with us on Sundays. During the week
we had perhaps half a kilo of meat, or instead ate fresh anchovy or
sardines which were much cheaper than meat.

At the feast of our patron saints, Mother prepared our traditional
dish of *bucatini* (thick hollow spaghetti) with meatballs, then she
killed a young rooster and cooked it in tomato sauce.

Once, a week or so before the feast, Mother bought a beautiful
elegant rooster. I was about six at the time and I fell in love with
him at first sight. I fed him and, regardless of the complaints of the
people living next door, I loved to hear him crow. I became so fond
of him, in fact, that I hoped Mother would let me keep him for a
pet. However, on the Saturday before the feast, while I was visiting
Grandfather, Mother killed the rooster and prepared it for cooking.
When I came back home the rooster was missing; immediately I
became suspicious. Mother was looking sad. She told me that while
I was away the rooster had broken loose and had been run over by
a horse and gig. He had been so badly mutilated that she had to
put him out of his misery. I cried and cried pitifully for quite a
while afterwards. To soothe me, Mother promised that she was
going to buy me something I liked the following day.

My eldest brother Saverio, about four years older than me,

14

happened to be gluttonous where chicken was concerned, so when we had dinner at our saints' Sunday feast he wolfed down his portion, licked his plate, smacked his lips and looked forward to a second helping, which unfortunately for him was not available. He knew that I was upset about the killing of the rooster and, naturally, I was not inclined to eat my portion of chicken. However, greedy Saverio had set his eyes on it, his mouth was watering, devouring my portion of chicken in anticipation. In spite of my mother's insistent pleas to eat the chicken she had set before me – a delicacy that we rarely had – I stubbornly refused.

She tried and tried to convince me by saying: 'Cosimino (little Cosimo), if you eat that piece of chicken you will grow into a tall and strong man.'

I was flattered. I *did* want to be a tall and strong man like Samson in the Bible. Mother almost persuaded me to eat the chicken.

My brother Saverio was not pleased; he wanted it for himself, so he called out jokingly: 'Cosimino, don't eat it. If you do, the rooster will crow in your belly.' This remark finally put me off. Mother was cross with Saverio but he had cleverly achieved his purpose. Mother put the uneaten portion of chicken aside somewhere near the stove, hoping that I would have it later. Saverio, however, contrived to make it disappear and then blamed the cat belonging to the people living next door.

My brothers Saverio and Vince, being a few years older than me, always treated me as their little brother which I strongly resented. They went out to play with their own chums and did not want to take me. I too wanted to go out but, because I was a small boy, Mother wouldn't let me go on my own; she was afraid of the traffic and trams on our main road. It was always a busy road with many types of vehicle, especially heavy lorries and trailers coming from the industrial areas of North Italy and going towards the South.

My brothers were usually allowed to go to the cinema once a week. The admission charge for the cheapest seats was only fifty cents. They went to see cowboy movies in which one of the main actors was Tom Mix. He seemed to be an invincible hero – ever ready to punish the villains and to come to the rescue of a pretty girl in the nick of time!

15

Other popular film stars were: Charlie Chaplin, Ridolin, Fatty Arbuckle, Buster Keaton and Harold Lloyd. Any time my brothers went to the cinema they had to take me with them, otherwise Mother would not let them go. They were often reluctant to take me with them when they went out to play on a piece of waste land known as *Fosso Del Lupo* (Wolf's Ditch); we used it mainly to play football. At other times we transformed it into a battleground and threw stones at gangs.

We had no public toilets in our town. Some men used our playground to relieve themselves alongside its walls. Street urchins and ragamuffins went there to masturbate, and prostitutes to do business at night.

Late one afternoon in 1926, my brothers were going out somewhere. They had no intention of taking me with them and tried to run away by stealth. I saw them and ran after them, but they had already shut the door. I could see them through the glazed panels; they were outside grinning mockingly as they held the handle firmly to keep me inside. I shouted angrily at them, kicked at the door and beat the palm of my left hand against a panel. Suddenly the glass shattered and my left forearm went through it. In doing so, a jagged piece of glass lacerated my forearm, causing a nasty wound about three inches long. I was bleeding profusely. I was shocked: the sight of my blood terrified me. I screamed hysterically, attracting the attention of our neighbours who hurried to the scene. My mother was having a chat with someone in our courtyard and as soon as she heard me she rushed towards the house.

Seeing me badly hurt she yelled: '*Mammamia! Mio Dio! Mio Dio!*' (Dear me! My God! My God!) and didn't know what to do.

Neighbours who had gathered there suggested: 'Signora Arrichiello, let us take the boy to the *Pronto Soccorso!*' (first aid).

The first aid room was between 300 and 400 metres from our home. It was located on the ground floor of our *Municipio* (Town Hall). A male nurse by name of Salabella was in charge of it.

Signor Salabella had been a regular low-ranking marshal during the Great War, which is a title in the Italian Army, one grade below second lieutenant. However, people now addressed him as Marshal Salabella. He was a bachelor in his fifties, and rather short and stout. He liked a few glasses of wine and as a result was always a little tipsy. I don't think he was well paid. In any case he must have spent a good part of his salary on wine, which had obviously become part of his staple diet.

Soon after the accident, Mother wrapped my wounded forearm in a make-do bandage, seized me firmly in her arms and ran all the way to the first aid room. Some of our neighbours accompanied us. A few inquisitive boys and girls followed. Accidents in our small town always created a certain stir, something to talk about.

Marshal Salabella had a throaty, raucous voice. This was probably due to the fatty snacks he ate and the amount of wine he consumed. His white coat was none too clean and his breath smelled of wine and tobacco.

He examined my wound, cleaned it and said to reassure Mother: 'The wound is not too bad; there is nothing to worry about.' Having said this, he applied some tincture of iodine which stung me so acutely that it made me scream. He bandaged my forearm and afterwards we walked back home. Having a bandaged forearm made me feel important; as if I were a hero of the Great War. I became the centre of attention; everybody was asking Mother what had happened to me.

My brothers, who had been the cause of the accident, could not avoid Mother's fury and she beat them with a stick. On hearing the whacks and my brothers' yells of anguish, I felt that I was being vindicated. As a further punishment, they were not allowed to go to the cinema for one month. Afterwards, as I was on the mend, nobody must upset me – else they would have to reckon with Mother! My brothers tried hard to be kind to me now, so I quickly forgave them.

Eventually, after a month or more, the wound healed, but I was left with an ugly scar – all because Marshal Salabella did not exactly know what he was doing. The wound needed to be stitched, and if Marshal Salabella could not do it himself, he should have told Mother to take me to the hospital in the city. Even now, any time I look at my scar it reminds me of Marshal Salabella's incompetence. I am not angry with him, though; most probably the poor chap died from cirrhosis of the liver.

When the accident occurred, my elder sister Carmen – the eldest in our family – was about twelve. She went to primary school every morning and returned by twelve-thirty. She was thoroughly reliable and obedient. Carmen at this age was slender and had fair hair cut in a fringe. A pretty girl, she had thin black eyebrows and kind, sensitive grey eyes. She had a few female companions, and played and went to Mass with them.

Carmen was entrusted with the keys of the cupboard where we kept our bread, pasta, lard, cheese, eggs, olives, raisins, olive oil, bottled tomatoes, coffee, sugar and so on. She also had access to the drawers where Mother kept the jewels which Father had bought for her and was in charge of our finances. Whenever Mother needed money for our daily shopping, she asked Carmen to go and fetch it. Carmen gave a verbal account of how much money we had left till the end of the month when our father's next remittance was due to arrive. Mother was an excellent parent, but she developed the bad habit of overstepping her spending limit. By the end of the month she often had to pawn some of her jewels in order to make ends meet.

Sometimes during a moment of distraction, Carmen would leave the keys of our larder around the house, and if Saverio and Vince happened to be at home, they would pounce on the keys, open the food cupboard and help themselves to bread and cheese or some other delicacy. After a while Carmen became suspicious, so she once set a trap. She deliberately left her keys somewhere where the would-be thieves could easily spot them. As they opened the food cupboard and were trying to help themselves, Carmen appeared with the broom in her hand and chased them round the house.

When they opened the front door and ran out Carmen pursued them with her broom. A few minutes later the culprits would approach her with their tails between their legs and beseech her not to report them to Mother, else Mother would not allow them to go to the cinema. They tried to bribe Carmen by promising her that they were going to wash our tiled floors for her, a job she did at least once a week. They also promised that they would run errands for her and help her with arithmetic, which Carmen was finding hard to follow. She was having difficulty in learning long division. Carmen usually agreed with their suggestions, so Saverio and Vince got away with it relatively lightly.

Mother was not in the habit of making a list prior to going out shopping. Frequently she forgot to buy garlic, parsley, celery, stamps, writing paper and so on. Whenever this occurred and Mother was running short of something, if Saverio and Vince were not at home, she would ask Carmen to go out and buy whatever was required.

18

Mother's unmethodical way of shopping proved to be quite a nuisance, and Carmen or Saverio and Vince were kept busy running out every now and then to buy items she had forgotten. When I was older I also had to go on these unnecessary shopping errands – sometimes as many as two or three times a day.

In one way or another we all have our faults. I certainly excuse my mother's shortcomings. She came from a very poor family. Her mother died when she was still a little girl. Her father was an illiterate coachman. Her stepmother could not care less. Who then could have taught Mother methodical housekeeping? In the town where we lived, perhaps half the population had more or less the same underprivileged upbringing as Mother.

By the late twenties, Secondigliano had not changed very much since the end of the nineteenth century. A few blocks of flats had been built on both sides of the main road with the money that emigrants had earned in South America. Of course, we now had the electric tram passing through and connecting Naples city to a number of neighbouring towns. The cinema was quite a revelation for the majority of our population, who knew little or nothing of what went on beyond the boundary of our small town. Our town was still surrounded by countryside, which was owned by small farmers who lived precariously. There were no secondary school facilities and no industries whatsoever. Eighty per cent or more of the parents could not afford the tram fare to send their children to secondary schools in the city. They had no choice but to send them to learn a trade. As we had no trade schools, parents had to beg artisans to accept their children as apprentices. They would not get paid until they had acquired some skill. The trades that children could learn were tailoring, shoemaking, carpentry, hairdressing and so on.

As the number of artisans by far exceeded the demands for them, there was stiff competition, which meant that they had to work hard and cheaply in order to survive.

We did not have a market-place, so fruit and vegetable vendors and other traders came mainly from the nearby countryside and small towns. Every day they poured into the town with their horse- or donkey-drawn carts, formed a mobile market and caused a great deal of hullabaloo.

19

They moved slowly through the streets and alleys, and every few metres they stopped and shouted about their merchandise at the tops of their voices: 'Aubergines and peppers', 'Cauliflowers, broccoli, new potatoes', 'Fresh figs', 'Melon full of fire' (they meant that the water melons inside were as red as fire). There were also a number of traders who displayed their goods as they stepped from door to door.

As the vendors approached, women came out of their homes and did their shopping in the street. Others preferred doing theirs from their first, second or third-floor balconies. Then a lot of shouting and haggling followed from every direction. Holding a long rope in their hands, women let down their baskets, which were almost as big as buckets. The vendors placed the goods in the baskets and the women pulled them up. If the goods were satisfactory the transaction was concluded. If not, they were returned and this would send vendors into a fury; they would curse their difficult customers for having rejected the merchandise. Unfortunately, at that time, such was the way of doing business; if a vendor lost his temper, shoppers would have nothing to do with him.

American movies of the 'Roaring Twenties' were dazzling and stimulating; they showed that most people in America were rather well-to-do. They lived in splendid modern houses and drove luxurious motor cars. There were elegant shops, hotels, glamorous women and a life of comfort and ease where fortunes could be made overnight, seemingly without effort, and millionaires would light their cigars with banknotes.

Our gullible people were no doubt greatly influenced by such movies; they wanted to go abroad, where the streets seemed to be paved with gold. They could not foresee the difficulties: the language barrier, strange environments, climatic and cultural differences and so on. They did not realise that these obstacles could not be overcome without a certain degree of determination and fortitude.

A number of people emigrated every year. There were those who, by working extremely hard and being thrifty, saved enough money and came back home. They bought their houses and perhaps a business and possibly lived happily ever after. Other emigrants married local girls, started their families there, and that was the end of them as far as we were concerned. The unlucky ones did not succeed, so they regretfully came back home and were no better off

20

than they had been before they ventured abroad.

The victims of emigration were those who, lured by the dream of becoming rich, discovered that foreign lands, after all, were not paved with gold. They were clearly disillusioned. Being without friends and unable to communicate, they were poorer than when they were in their native land, where they could at least speak their own language and enjoy the company of their friends. Stranded, unaided, in some foreign land, with no money to buy their passage back, perhaps they became ill or died in poverty and were buried in some common or forgotten grave.

5

Fascist indoctrination

In 1927 I started my first year of primary school. The campaign of Fascist indoctrination throughout Italy was in full swing, with Blackshirt propaganda in the press, cinema, education and anything else affecting the life of our country. The Fascist attitude was: 'If you are not with us, you are against us,' which left us no choice but to do as we were told. Even schoolchildren were compelled to join the Fascist Party. Parents had to pay five lire subscription for each child they sent to school. Five lire then was equivalent to half a day's pay for an unskilled worker who had to work no less than ten hours a day, six days a week.

There were at least forty boys or girls in each classroom. The teacher's desk faced the pupils. On the wall behind the desk hung two portraits: King Vittorio Emanuele III on the right and Benito Mussolini (*Il Duce*) on the left, with a crucifix between them. Some classrooms even had a portrait of the Pope.

Before the lesson began we said the daily prayer, followed by one or two Fascist songs. These invariably ended with the Roman salute and shouts of: '*Viva Il Duce!*' (Long live *Il Duce!*)

Our schools could not cope with the increase in the numbers of pupils. We badly needed extra classrooms, so our schooling was limited to three and a half hours each day. Some children went to morning school from nine to twelve-thirty; others to afternoon school from one to four-thirty.

At that time most parents were prolific, a practice that the Fascists encouraged; it would help to make the country stronger by increasing the number of 'bayonets' in case of war.

The church was absolutely against abortion, so practically every pregnancy meant a new baby. Having sex for procreation was not sinful, so this gave some parents a good excuse for indulging in it.

Although the Fascists encouraged procreation, they did not provide any kind of assistance to parents who had large families. What did the Fascists expect? How could our poor country grow stronger when our children were undernourished?

In those years there was no such thing as the old-age pension, nor any kind of social welfare, and when they were old, parents had to rely for support on their grown-up children.

Poor children were usually brought up on a staple diet of bread, pasta, minestrone, sardines, a few eggs, a little cheese and perhaps a microscopic portion of meat once a week. When parents could afford to buy this, each member of the family received his portion, and there was no second helping. Nobody was at risk of getting indigestion from having eaten too much! Though this was perhaps possible at Christmas and on Easter Sunday.

Before they went to school, children usually breakfasted on brewed roasted barley with a little milk and sugar. White coffee was a luxury, since coffee was expensive. Unfortunately the poorest parents could not even provide brewed barley for breakfast, so their children had a piece of bread with a little lard spread on it. If the bread was stale, they soaked it under a tap before eating it. These children did not always have a hot meal every day.

A tourist said on one occasion after observing a porter soaking a chunk of bread under one of the taps at Naples station, 'By gosh! Italians are very clean. Look at that chap there, he washes the bread before eating it!' What the tourist did not realise was that 'that chap' had not earned even a few cents to buy a little cheese, so he was having the piece of soaked bread for his lunch.

The Fascists wanted to build a nation of strong and healthy children, so they insisted that all those who went to school must do some physical exercise once or twice a week. As we did not have a gymnasium, we used the school courtyard for our physical exercises. All we did there was march to and fro like soldiers on parade.

Those undernourished schoolmates of mine were, understandably, not too keen on physical exercise. It made them hungrier, a hunger that they could not appease, even when they went back home.

Some parents made extra sacrifices to please their children. They squeezed a few lire out of their income to provide them with Fascist uniforms. Children loved being little soldiers and drilling for parades. On Sunday mornings they often marched at the beat of drums through our town and proudly followed Italian and Fascist banners.

Il Duce's mottoes, in large letters, were displayed in our classrooms, offices and in the square of our town; it was impossible to avoid them.

Il Duce, it seemed, was in the process of becoming very famous, a great leader to be obeyed at all costs. He expected his adherents, and indeed all the Italian people, to conform to his motto – *Credere! Obbedire! Combattere!* (Believe! Obey! Fight!)

Our textbooks were full of Fascist propaganda and informed us of all the good deeds that *Il Duce* was doing for our country. The intention, of course, was to arouse our national awareness and identity. There was a lot of stress on the achievements of the great Romans, Italian artists, composers, inventors, pioneers and so on, who had largely contributed to the making of Western Civilisation.

Even if we had wanted to, we could not avoid the endless pressure of Fascist propaganda. This, reinforced by *Il Duce*'s inflammatory speeches, inflated our egos, made us feel great, supercilious and even arrogant. *Il Duce*'s ways and sayings made quite an impact, especially on us – students and adolescents – who were easy prey to this Fascist propaganda. Brainwashed as we were and being too young, we could not understand the problems of our hard-pressed parents. They wanted something more substantial – a better standard of living – than those frivolous and clownish displays.

We were indoctrinated to regard ourselves as the heirs of those heroic legionnaires who had fought for the mighty Roman Empire. Guided by *Il Duce*, who seemed to believe that he was the reincarnation of Julius Caesar, we would march as *Il Duce* said: *fino in fondo!* (till the end!), presumably until we had reconquered our Roman Empire. Fascist songs drummed this message into us again and again.

Il Duce was spending a fortune on lavish Fascist propaganda at home and abroad. But could we afford it? Millions of Italians were unemployed. Those who were employed had to accept whatever wages or salaries they could get, and be grateful. Those who protested about their miserable working conditions were regarded as subversives, enemies of the Fascist cause and *persona non grata*.

The Fascists employed quite a number of well-educated people who wore flamboyant uniforms and boosted the Fascist campaign.

This heightening of our national awareness and ambition to conquer made France, Britain and other countries suspicious of us. What was *Il Duce* up to? This growing distrust of Italy proved to be very harmful to our economy. Countries which had once been friendly with Italy stopped doing business with us. Economic sanctions were applied against Italy by the League of Nations in 1935. Consequently thousands of workers lost their jobs.

What good was nationalism doing us when we were losing friends, had no freedom of speech, no security and had to toil hard for our basic necessities? Our people, generally speaking, would have preferred less vainglory, at least one square meal a day and a future for their children.

Remaining healthy under the Fascist regime was a privilege affordable only to the well-to-do. Tuberculosis was rampant and we had almost no sanatoria to treat the disease. In spite of our appalling conditions, many stupid people still shouted: '*Viva Il Duce!*'

6

*We move to a flat in Palazzo De Rosa. Mother gives
birth to twins. We move to a larger flat near the
Chapel of the Sacred Hearts*

Between 1925 and 1927 Mother had a chance to rest from her
annual pregnancies, because Father had embarked on a long voyage
to try his luck in South America. He visited El Salvador, Guatemala
and Venezuela. He did very well in Venezuela, but when he came
back home he learned to his dismay that the bank in which he had
deposited his South American earnings had gone bankrupt. This
was a severe blow which affected him for a while, but he was a
resilient man and did not make a tragedy of this financial set-back.

We badly needed at least a two-bedroom flat, so in May 1927 we
moved to a new apartment on the first floor of a building known as
Patazzo De Rosa, situated next to the Tripoli Cinema. It was built
in the early twenties and was flooded with light when the sun was
shining.

This flat seemed brand-new to us and was very clean and
spacious. We had two fairly large bedrooms, a dining-room, kitchen
and toilet. At the back we had a terrace with a view of the
countryside. Compared to our previous homes it seemed like
paradise. Each bedroom had a balcony looking out on to the main
road, Corso Umberto Primo, which used to be part of the Appian
Way of Ancient Rome. This road swarmed with traffic all day long,
and to a certain extent even at night.

Mother and my sister Carmen used to sit and relax on our
balconies during the warm seasons when the chores had been done.
They watched people passing by on the footpaths below and made
comments about them. During summer evenings, Mother often used
to buy a couple of watermelons from a cart passing by, which we
ate with great relish.

Although Father provided us with basic necessities, the fact that he was away for so long made him seem almost like a stranger. I do not think that any one of us had a chance to form a link of affection with him. All he did whenever he came home was to make Mother pregnant and then run away. Mother, bless her, was always with us. Although she had had very little education and was always with child, she had to worry about our schooling, health and whatever else we needed. She was strong and had perhaps inherited the strength of her father, who had outlived his two wives by several years. She never complained, and accepted her role with a sense of duty and fulfilment.

Three or four months after we moved into the new apartment, Father embarked for Iraq and probably Iran. He did not stay long in these Muslim countries and moved on to the southern hemisphere, to the island of Java. He had been told that Java would be a promising country for his business.

In January 1928 Mother gave birth to twins, a boy and a girl, who were named Damiano and Immacolata. We were now a family of ten children: five boys and five girls.

We loved our new flat, and were surprised and angered when our landlord gave us notice to quit. He needed the accommodation for his daughter who was engaged to get married, the flat being part of her dowry. Mother, in particular, was not happy at the thought of leaving the place. She knew it would be difficult to find an apartment as good as that. However, although she resented having to move, she resigned herself to it and looked around for a new home. After a while she found a large flat on the second floor at 54, Via Arco, and we moved there in May 1929. We now had three double bedrooms, a large dining-room and kitchen. Every room, including the kitchen, had a balcony looking on to Via Gaetano Errico. The flat was located in an old building showing signs of decay. The advantage of being there was that we lived about fifty metres away from the state schools and ten metres from the Chapel of the Sacred Hearts.

The disadvantages were enormous, almost alarming. We missed the view of the countryside from our previous flat. We were living in a poor section of the town next to the slum area, and had to rub shoulders with uncouth people and beggars. This was a serious situation that Mother had not anticipated; it was a hindrance to our education and the development of good manners in us as children.

In this part of the town several families lived in one room on the ground floor next to the street.

There was a shop nearby selling bread, pasta, olive oil and delicatessen products. The shopkeeper, signor Orano, had a family of six and lived in two bedrooms above the shop. He was courteous to his customers and only too eager to serve them. His wife, no longer attractive, reflected years of toil and neglect. Having to bring up a large family with their meagre means was quite a trial. Now she was squat and flabby, and she helped in the shop when her husband was too busy; otherwise she did the cooking and some sporadic chores.

Because of the competition from nearby shops, Orano and his wife were compelled to slave away in their shop from 7.00 a.m. till late at night. In summer they worked even longer. They had no meal breaks, not even on Sundays, when customers would pop in at any time of day. If the shopkeeper and his family were having their midday meal and a customer came in, he would stop eating, leave the table and serve him. Customers never seemed to respect business hours; after all nobody had taught them to do so. The shopkeeper could not afford to say: 'Sorry, Sir, it is my mealtime. Please come back later.'

Customers seldom bought more than two things at a time. Had they been sent away, they would no doubt have done their shopping elsewhere.

The shopkeeper had to keep his customers sweet. He needed endless patience, especially with those who were in the habit of bargaining, or who bought little or nothing. Some only went to his shop hoping for a chance to gossip.

The shopkeeper's eldest son was learning to be a barber. The rest of the family helped in the shop.

One of his sons, about my age, was nicknamed 'Ciotto' (Neapolitan term for 'little fat boy') and was no longer going to school. It would seem that he had completed just two of the normal five years at primary school. His father must have thought that Ciotto already had enough education to face the world of our small town. He used the boy mainly to send on errands.

At other times, Ciotto would play rough games in the courtyard. He was wild-looking, and his hair was so closely cropped that one could see several scars, sustained no doubt from stone-throwing episodes – for he often engaged in gang warfare.

28

He was about nine, but of average height, with a short forehead, dark eyes and a pale round face. He dressed almost in rags.

We were living on the second floor, which was also the top floor. Whenever I went downstairs I had to pass through the courtyard and could not avoid him. At the beginning, I did not like him at all, because he was too vulgar, rough and a bully. I resented being bullied by him and was not too keen to have a fight with such a wild, tough and dirty-looking boy. However, as I had nobody else to play with in that new environment, I ventured to play with him sometimes. In spite of my mother's disapproval, I gradually became Ciotto's best friend.

He soon started showing me the ropes of flooring an opponent. We practised in the courtyard. At times I even succeeded in pinning his shoulders to the ground. He did not like it; he would not be convinced that I could beat him, so he challenged me repeatedly until he succeeded in pinning *me* to the ground, thereby restoring his reputation of being my master.

Playing with Ciotto as I did, I acquired a vocabulary of foul swear words which enabled me to qualify as a street urchin. Soon I was behaving like him and I started bullying my younger brothers and sisters. I became wild, almost a terror in my family. Mother was desperate; she wanted to send me to an institution where I could be tamed. She deeply regretted having gone to live in that appalling tenement.

My brothers Saverio and Vince were also influenced by the new environment, but not as much as I was, for they too had to adapt themselves to whatever kind of friends they could find in those surroundings.

Living near the chapel, we were able to participate in various church events and festivities. We made the acquaintance of the missionary fathers and started going to catechism.

7

Ciotto's influence – quite an education. Going to catechism. The building of the Chapel and College of the Sacred Hearts

Having become Ciotto's disciple, I could not help getting involved in his mischief, so I also had to dare and fight. He always asked me to accompany him on his errands. I went with him if I had nothing better to do. When we were together we yearned to put into practice our fighting prowess. Often we deliberately provoked boys whom we met in the streets. If they were as cocky and daring as we were, there ensued a confrontation which in many cases resulted in a fight.

I always went through the expected ritual prior to a fight. I would start by threatening the boy I had dared, saying: 'Boy oh boy, get out of the way, go home, before I give you a sound thrashing and a bleeding nose!' If my opponent had no heart to fight, he would be intimidated and retreat meekly. This gave me something to boast about, a kind of victory. If he was tough, he would ignore my threats and even reciprocate them.

The next step was for me to touch the tip of his nose with one of my thumbs. He would then retaliate – either pushing me back or throwing a punch. Soon we would be engaged in a fist fight or a wrestling match. I would try to floor and immobilise him by pinning his shoulders to the ground. If I succeeded, I had won the fight. If my adversary was too rough though, he would not easily accept defeat and the fight would go on until someone watching or a passer-by intervened and separated us; or perhaps the fight would end with a black eye or a bleeding nose.

I am still sorry today that I once – egged on by my supporters – delivered too many punches to an almost defenceless opponent. A few weeks after this I was very sorry indeed; I thought that I might easily have killed the boy – all because of the influence of my street urchin companions. About a year later, when we moved to a better environment and I had grown a little more civilised, I endeavoured to make friends with the boy I had fought. I tried to be very gentle with him, and even used my pocket money to buy him some sweets. My conscience drove me to such bribery.

Of course, when I fought, I was not always the winner. Occasionally I would get a bloody nose myself and a few stinging blows to my chin. These set-backs, incidentally, did not deter me from engaging in other fisticuffs!

Besides the fights, as a result of Ciotto's influence I became involved in quite a number of other mischievous activities. For instance, one day he and I were going on one of his errands through the streets where the poorest people lived. Suddenly we saw a frisky white kitten in a sunny courtyard. We wanted to steal it, but the kitten ran away into a large ground-floor house which had its doors wide open. It ran under a tall, majestic-looking double bed. The room was clean and tidy and contained a wardrobe, dressing-table, table, chest of drawers and a few chairs. Its occupants were not there. Maybe they were having a chat with one of their neighbours.

As he chased the kitten, Ciotto dived under the bed and I reluctantly followed him. The lively kitten, however, eluded us and darted outside again. While we were in the room, Ciotto was tempted to open some drawers, presumably with the intention of stealing something. I was still under the bed and frightened. While he was busily searching through the drawers, a stout middle-aged woman suddenly appeared on the threshold. 'Thieves! Thieves! Thieves!' she shouted.

Fortunately there was another door which had been left ajar and gave access to the adjacent street. Ciotto and I ran for our lives; my heart was pounding against my ribs. The woman's hysterical shouts created pandemonium in the street. Neighbours rushed out of their houses, wanting to know what was happening. Was it an earthquake? Some people even tried to chase us, but we had already covered a certain distance and were still running. We did not stop until we were well away from that troubled thoroughfare.

A couple of days after that particular exploit, we heard that the people involved had associated this happening with certain numbers. You see, some people in Naples are very superstitious and link things that happen with numbers in the lottery. For instance, 'thieves' were equated with the number sixty, 'room' with the number fifty-four, 'shouting woman' with the number eighty-four, 'fear' with ninety, and 'people trying to assist the women' with the number sixty-six. People put these numbers together: 60, 54, 84, 90, 66, and gambled on the lottery, or *giuoco del lotto* as we called it.

The remarkable thing is that on the Saturday after our adventure in that woman's home, all the people who had used those five numbers to gamble on the lotto won some money. Ciotto and I had been a godsend to them; we must have seemed like agents of Divine Providence.

As we were living near the chapel, my brothers, Saverio and Vince, took me to catechism, or to play in the chapel's courtyard. The catechism gave us something to do, even if we did not take it seriously. For us it was just a chance to go out and meet other boys.

We addressed our catechism tutors as prefects. I still remember a few of them: Napolano, Longo, Pellegrino, Poerio and Salerno. Not only were they excellent tutors, but when they narrated Bible stories they made them so interesting that we were always eager to listen.

Gaetano Errico, the founder of the Missionaries of the Sacred Hearts, was born in Secondigliano in 1791. In the early 1820s he was a priest who said Mass in the local parish church of Saints Cosma and Damiano. Later, he decided to build the Chapel and College of the Sacred Hearts.

The building of the chapel began in 1827 and was completed by 1830. It was large enough to hold more than 300 people. In 1830 the building of the college also started.

Father Gaetano had a Madonna – the Immaculate Conception – especially made for the chapel, but Gaetano was very hard to please. The face of the Madonna was not to his liking, so he had it made again. Still he was not pleased, and altogether he had it made seventeen times until he was satisfied with it. This definitive Madonna was installed in the chapel on 9 December 1830, and has been there ever since.

The college was built beside the chapel. At the back were the living quarters, which could accommodate fifty or more missionary students and a large courtyard.

The famous Italian military leader, Giuseppe Garibaldi, had a grudge against the Pope, who always sought French protection to prevent Rome being taken by him and united with Italy. So when Garibaldi freed Naples from Bourbon domination, he confiscated part of some of the church buildings and used them as schools. Half of the College of the Sacred Hearts underwent the same treatment, as did many other church buildings elsewhere.

Garibaldi was really a blessing in disguise. Since the government was unable to provide state schools following the unification of Italy, the confiscation of part of the church buildings enabled thousands of Italians to benefit from free state education.

Father Gaetano Errico, whom the townsfolk and peasants addressed as *O supriore* (the priest in charge of the chapel and college), was a saintly man; a true man of faith. Energetic and full of initiative, he was held in high esteem. Many people, in spite of their poverty, helped him as much as they could. The building of the chapel and the college was made possible by donations. Father Gaetano died in 1860. At the beginning of the twentieth century he was recognised for his work and devotion, so the Church conferred on him the title of *Venerable*.

Most students came from farming areas where living conditions were appalling. I suspect that many peasant boys chose to become missionaries – training cost them nothing – to escape from their miserable living conditions. Being at home, they had to work like slaves all their lives. Choosing instead to become missionaries, they had the chance to study, to become ordained priests and to be sent to South America. All these prospects were, of course, far more interesting than being farm-hands in their poverty-stricken rural areas.

During my boyhood the college was only half the size it had once been. Attached to the chapel, it had three storeys which included the living quarters. The second half, occupied by the state school, was separated from the first half by the courtyard. The state school had only a ground floor and first floor.

Other boys and I played in the courtyard before going to catechism. We played football or chased one another and thoroughly enjoyed ourselves. However, when some real urchins joined in, our games became too rough and would often end in a fight.

The college, school and courtyard shared the same entrance in the Via Dante. The kindergarten, some classrooms, toilets and the schoolmaster's office were on the ground floor; the rest of the classrooms were on the first floor. There were about twenty classrooms in all, used morning and afternoon for teaching boys and girls.

The courtyard was at the disposal of the school during term time, but after school and during the holidays, the college used it as a playground for their students and for boys going to catechism.

During the Great War, the part of the building previously allocated to the state school was used as a military hospital.

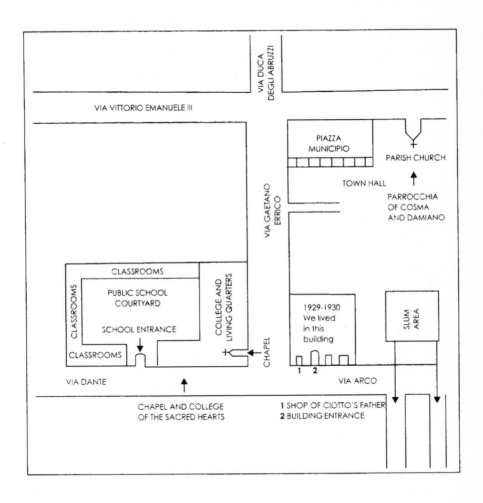

8

Saverio needs a new coat. He wants to become a priest
and enters the College of the Sacred Hearts.
Mother gives me a good hiding

A few weeks before Christmas 1928, my eldest brother Saverio was
almost twelve. He was about five feet tall, of slender build and had
brown eyes and black hair with a left parting. He badly needed an
overcoat, so Mother bought some dark brown cloth and had one
made to measure. The tailor delivered the overcoat on the morning
of Christmas Eve. Mother had hardly any money left for Christmas
shopping. If she paid the tailor's bill – about a hundred lire – she
would have no money to spend for Christmas. On the other hand,
the tailor was a poor man who had to pay his assistant and feed his
family.

Mother was extremely worried. She pondered for a while, but at
last resolved to put her trust in the hands of the Lord and paid the
tailor's bill.

My brother looked very elegant in his new overcoat, but we
didn't care a damn about this; we were angry and dejected at the
prospect of having to do without our traditional Christmas dinners
and jollities.

Mother could not bear our sadness. She sat down in front of the
image of the Madonna with beads in her hands and recited the
rosary. As a result, she probably had one of her Divine Inspirations.
Suddenly she got up. She had a radiant look on her face. She
shouted: 'Carmen, quick! Quick! Fetch my overcoat!' My sister
promptly did as she was told. Mother walked to her bedroom, took
out a key and opened a drawer. In the recess of the drawer was a
box containing her jewels and her father-in-law's gold pocket watch
attached to a gold chain. She placed the watch and chain in her
handbag and, without saying much, she left. She rushed to a pawn

shop about half a kilometre away and came back two hours later. She waved some banknotes at us, a gesture that we jubilantly applauded. We thanked God for Mother's Divine Inspiration – we were going to have a really merry Christmas!

Mother felt greatly relieved at having taken the right decision. This clearly showed that the Lord, in time of need, had not abandoned us. The devil, however, always tries to creep in to spoil our joy and harmony. Later during the day Mother felt a little uneasy at having pawned Grandfather's watch and chain. She said to herself: Suppose that my father-in-law wants to wear his watch and chain at Christmas? What am I going to say? This would put me in a very awkward situation. This thought troubled her, so she retired to her bedroom once again, sat in front of the image of the Madonna and prayed: 'Please most holy Mother, forgive me for asking your help twice today. Do not let my father-in-law desire to wear his watch and chain during the Christmas holidays. They are with the pawnbroker, and I won't be able to get them till after the festivities.'

We were extremely excited when Mother went out to do the Christmas shopping. Half a dozen or so of us volunteered to accompany her, helping to carry parcels and imagining their contents, which we relished in anticipation. Perhaps the Lord was amused as He looked down at us from above?

My brother Saverio, having finished five years of primary school and two years of preliminary school before joining the secondary school, expressed his desire to join the college and become a missionary. Whether he had a vocation or not, it was hard to say. Perhaps he thought that by becoming a missionary he would achieve something; a position of some authority and respect.

Before entering the college, my brother was still going to school. He attended church services regularly and went to catechism. He did not seem to have any other interest. There were no opportunities for anybody in that godforsaken town, except for rich people who had some initiative.

Going to church every day, my brother became an addict. Could this be his vocation? Having obtained my parents' and the college authorities' consent, in October 1929, he entered the college and began his missionary career. We were allowed to visit him once a month.

During the first year he was happy, but in the second year he began to get restless, especially when he saw girls in the streets. The students would go out walking with one of the missionaries, and had been told to lower their eyes whenever they saw a girl, but Saverio could never stop himself eyeing a girl and assessing her feminine attractions; after the walk he would return to the college with his feelings deliciously aroused. Eventually, he came to the conclusion that he was not destined for the priesthood!

My brother Vince and I were just plodding along, in the academic sense, at our primary school. Vince, two years older than me, was doing his fourth year, while I was still doing my second, which I had to repeat on account of being too distracted and not doing my homework. Having too much freedom, and keeping Ciotto's company, caused my academic achievements to suffer drastically. I also grew so undisciplined that I was of serious concern to my mother. What could she do? Whether she liked it or not, she had to put up with me. She could not afford to send me to a boarding school or elsewhere, where I could have come in contact with well-behaved boys and become civilised.

My problem was basically due to the wretched environment in which we were living; it could have been solved easily if we had moved away and gone to live in a better place.

Mother had endless patience, especially with me, but she had to look after ten of us. If I drove her to the limit, then I could not avoid her punishment. She locked all the doors that gave access to the outside, so I could not escape. With the help of my sister Carmen, and a scourge in her hand, she chased me all over the flat. I fled in panic as she brandished it, seeking refuge anywhere in the hope of escaping her blows.

Mother's scourge, by the way, was a wicker carpet-beater which resembled an extra large tennis racket. She used to say: '*Mazze e panelle fanno e figlie belle*' – in other words, smacking and bread make good children.

I yelled hysterically as Mother chased me, and invariably dived under her double bed. This tactic did not always protect me though, for if she was really determined to give me a sound beating then she and my sister undid the bed, removed the mattresses and the boards supporting them, and caught me. I was cornered then and exposed to her stinging blows, which I tried to fend off – usually unsuccessfully! Having given vent to her rage, she would relent and walk away with a sense of satisfaction, leaving me a poor disconsolate heap in the corner, crying and licking my bruised knuckles.

'I enjoyed it, I enjoyed it,' she would shout as if she had been at a banquet. Her words aggravated my misery, making me feel forlorn, with no one to protect or comfort me.

A few minutes after Mother had thrashed me, my sister Carmen would come round (of course, my mother had sent her) to assess my cuts and bruises. Mother's blows never hurt me badly. Even when furious, she exercised a measure of restraint. She maintained that an occasional flogging, or any other kind of punishment, was necessary to prevent anarchy and restore order at home.

Whenever I was naughty, Mother would send me to bed without supper. Later, when she had gone to bed, my sister Carmen would come by stealth and feed me. This again was a tacit arrangement between Mother and my sister. Mother played the part of being harsh and intransigent; my sister Carmen played the part of peacemaker and a good Samaritan.

9

The college cook – a wicked man

Mother always begged Vince to take me with him when he went out, so that I would not be left in Ciotto's company. Vince had made some good friends, but he was reluctant to comply with Mother's wish; perhaps he did not want the responsibility of taking care of me. Besides, he and his friends were flirting with some girls they had met while they were attending the chapel services. When Vince and I went to catechism, he left me playing with the other boys in the college courtyard.

Going to catechism, listening to Bible stories and participating in the chapel services made me feel heavenly – almost an angel – but as soon as I was in Ciotto's company I'm afraid I became a devil again.

The missionary fathers employed a chef whose name was also Vincent. He was in his late thirties and rather tall. He had black hair, combed from front to back, black eyes, whiskers and a pale complexion. They also employed a couple of lay brothers who did menial tasks.

The kitchen and refectory were on the first floor; so were the cook's, sexton's and lay brothers' accommodation. Each of them had his own room.

When a lay brother needed assistance, he looked for one or two idle boys whom he found playing in the courtyard or on the footpath outside the entrance of the chapel. He used these boys to carry parcels or even to pull a small cart, which could be hired for a few cents, when they had many items to carry. At the end of the errand, the lay brother tipped each boy who had assisted him with a half loaf of bread and a generous slice of *provolone* cheese. The hungry boys gobbled up their fare with great relish.

Often a boy of nine or ten was asked to carry something to the kitchen, or to fetch a tray with a pot of coffee and one or more cups. The coffee was usually offered to a visiting priest after he had celebrated the Mass, to a visiting preacher, or to distinguished callers.

When the boy went to the kitchen and nobody was around except the cook, the latter, under the pretence of being playful, rubbed his prickly beard against the boy's face. At first the boy thought that the cook was doing it for fun. The boy concerned would always be given something to eat by the cook, so he would seek another opportunity to go to the kitchen. Bit by bit, the cook would change his tactics, after a while kissing the boy as passionately as a lover. Perhaps the boy was shy and confused, but being bribed with bread and cheese or bread and salami, he did not remonstrate. Next time the boy went there, the cook became bolder; he smuggled the boy to his room nearby and assaulted him.

There was a boy called Aldo whom I had met while I was playing in the courtyard. He was on over-friendly terms with the cook, and never seemed to run short of bread and cheese, salami and other delicacies. I suspected that some kind of hanky-panky was afoot. Since Aldo was a clever boy, he shared the food with a couple of his close friends, so that they kept silent, and the affair stayed more or less hush-hush.

I had seen some detective movies that puzzled and fascinated me and made me inquisitive. As a result, I wanted to find out what was going on between Aldo and the cook. On a few occasions, when Aldo went to the kitchen, I secretly followed him. I peeped through the kitchen door or the keyhole when Aldo was in the cook's room, and could clearly see them in compromising positions.

Being a catechism student, I was shocked that such acts of indecency were taking place in that religious environment. The missionary fathers were very strict; they observed the clausura (enclosure rules) which did not allow women into their living quarters. Yet the cook, who was supposed to be an upright man, was abusing the boy's trust. The fathers did not suspect that they had a wicked cook preparing their meals and endangering their reputation. I did not breathe a word to anybody. I did not want to stir up trouble as I was afraid of causing a scandal and having to face the consequences. Also I did not want to harm Aldo, who came from a poor family, or to upset his parents.

If a boy had been raped he did not fully realise that he had been

41

the victim of a serious crime. Besides, he was afraid of telling his parents; he feared that they would give him a sound hiding. And later, perhaps, everybody might get to know what had befallen him, and some might jump to the conclusion that he was a *finocchio* (gay).

If the parents of a raped boy had sued the villain, it would have cost a great deal, and they would have had to wait at least a year before the case came to court.

Some unpredictable parents, confronted with a case of rape in their family, were liable to lash out and hit the offender severely. Many bystanders would have applauded such punishment, even if the offender had been murdered.

10

*My primary school and Father's operation. We move
back to Palazzo De Rosa*

In 1929 I was in my second year of primary school. My teacher's
name was Purchio. Some of the parents who were illiterate could
not remember or pronounce his name properly. When they were
talking about him and tried to mention his name, they ended up by
calling him Professor 'Pidocchio'. Consequently we nicknamed him
Professor Pidocchio. *Pidocchio* means louse, so whenever someone
mentioned this nickname, people would laugh out loud.

Professor Pidocchio was in his fifties. He was tall, skinny, bald
and had a swirly black moustache. With his pallid complexion, he
looked as if he was in need of a substantial meal. He was so
pathetic as a man that I always felt sorry for him.

As a teacher, he did not command authority – in fact, I was not
impressed at all. When we annoyed him, he pinched our arms,
which left black bruises on our skins.

Professor Pidocchio had a colleague of about the same
age whose name was Mandolino. At the end of their afternoon
classes, Professor Pidocchio and Professor Mandolino – both
bachelors – walked together to the tram stop, for they both lived in
the city. Often before catching the tram they stopped at a wine
shop, had a snack and a couple of glasses of wine. I imagine that,
as they were getting on in years, they were looking forward to
Ÿtheir state pensions, a privilege that all government employees
enjoyed.

Being a pupil of Professor Pidocchio was fun. He had a thin,
piercing voice and resembled Ben Turpin, one of the comical
characters of the silent movies. Professor Pidocchio taught us how
to spell, read and master basic numeracy.

At the end of the school year I was promoted to the third year.

I regretfully had to say goodbye to Professor Pidocchio, for he taught only the first two years of primary school. I left him with mixed feelings of sadness and affection.

In September 1930 I joined the third year. I was not a good pupil, because my father was far from home and my mother too busy to supervise homework. There was nobody who could control and help to educate me. My poor mother, with such a large family, was supposed to keep an eye on all of us. But she had so much to do that she really could not cope without my sister's help. Carmen was a jewel; she kept our large flat very clean. She mopped the tiled floors of our three double bedrooms and our large dining-room once a week. The floor of our large kitchen, with so much cooking and washing to be done, had to be mopped every day. Besides that there was the laundry, mending, ironing, sewing buttons and so many other tasks to be done. With ten lively children living there, our flat used to get dirty and untidy, and Mother could not afford to hire a domestic help.

I went to school at one o'clock and came back home after four-thirty. So there were only three and a half hours of daily schooling from Monday to Saturday. There were about forty boys in my class. My teacher, signor Del Mastro, was in his thirties, tall, slim and bald. He looked austere and showed little mercy when we annoyed him. He would not hesitate to use the cane which he called 'remedy'. The cane was like a wide ruler, and signor Del Mastro used to deliver stinging blows on the palms of our hands which made us wince and grimace.

In spite of his fierceness with the cane, he was an excellent teacher. I used to get very absorbed whenever he taught us Roman history; he made me feel proud of our Roman ancestors and their achievements.

Signor Del Mastro often had his lunch in class. He ate bread and cheese, or bread and mozzarella, while he kept us busy doing some exercise or other. He also smoked a few cigarettes while he gave lessons.

Unfortunately, whenever he absented himself from the class, even for five minutes, the black sheep in the class would start rioting. Objects would be sent flying and insults would be hurled around the classroom. Those who held a grudge against our teacher would take his hat and swish it like a flying saucer from one side of the classroom to the other. Needless to say, I was not a mere spectator and though I was not the ringleader, I was borne along by the riotous behaviour and joined in the turmoil.

The schoolmate sitting near me was a gentle and good-looking boy called Renato Maiella. His father was an accountant and he had a very beautiful mother. Renato looked like her. He had curly chestnut hair, thin eyebrows, brown eyes, a small nose, high cheekbones and a peachy complexion. He wore dark and very short trousers well above his knees, showing off his round and well-shaped legs. His thighs were presumably a replica of his mother's. He always wore white shirts and was the cleanest and best-dressed boy in our classroom. I was very attracted by his looks and by the shape of his body; he looked more like a girl than a boy. I was curious about his thighs and touched them to reassure myself – they were as hard as marble. I jokingly said that he was my girlfriend and occasionally I gave him a kiss on his peachy, marble-looking cheeks, but without sexual intent; I was still too young for that.

Renato and I were just good chums, and I chivalrously assumed the role of protecting him. Any boy who dared to annoy him would have to reckon with me.

One of our schoolmates, Leo, was skinny and much taller than me. On a number of occasions Leo had met Renato in the street and bullied him. I was sorry for Renato and so one day I challenged Leo to a fight at the end of the lesson. A number of our schoolmates gathered outside the school entrance and were eager to watch the battle. Leo and I stood face to face and poised for action.

'Will you apologise to Renato for having bullied him?' I demanded.

'No, no fear! ... Why should I?' Leo replied.

We started pushing each other. Then I seized him by the lapels of his jacket and threw myself back on the roadway. As I did so, I quickly placed my right knee against Leo's chest and flung him back in a somersault. He fell on his back; before he had time to recover I rolled over on him and, using all my strength, pinned his shoulders down. As I did so, our schoolmates acclaimed me as the victor, which made me feel very cocky. I then released Leo, but he did not try to fight me again – indeed, he was very glad to go. From then on, nobody in our class dared to bully Renato.

In the whole school, there were only a few boys and girls whose parents were professional people. To hear that one's father was a physician, pharmacist, lawyer or teacher made a certain impression on boys and girls whose parents were just working people. We thought that children of professional parents were made of better stuff and that it was an honour for most of us to rub shoulders with them. Even our teachers were class-conscious; they treated these children of professional people with a certain deference.

Living near the slums, one could almost forget that there was a Fascist regime in Italy. Most people were poor, illiterate, had no radio, and so they did not take an interest in politics. They had always been poor. They had no time or mental energy to devote to anything except keeping the wolf from their door.

Those who went to school were subject to a certain degree of Fascist indoctrination, mainly through the textbooks. They were aware of the Fascist regime, but not really impressed. How could they be? Under the Mussolini government they were poorer than ever. The extreme right-wing propaganda could not help to improve their living conditions, so people looked with suspicion at the Fascist regime and its clownish displays. At the same time they were afraid and disorganised; they could not oppose the Fascists and, after all, *Il Duce* had silenced all his political opponents.

Among the population of our small town, which in the early twenties numbered about 6,000, perhaps only one per cent were staunch Fascist supporters. Most of these were given privileged positions in the towns and wore their black shirts to show their party allegiance. Others tried to gain prestige from belonging to the party but, if anything, the misery of our people was aggravated by all their self-seeking. The Fascists wanted our downtrodden people to back their party and *Il Duce*. They wanted them to produce lots of children – but for what? To be future warriors in their wars? They wanted us to be proud – but how could we be proud of the malnutrition and diseases rampant in our towns? How could we possibly accept these miseries with contentment? In spite of these afflictions, they wanted to make us the new Romans who were supposed to reconquer our lost Empire of about 1,500 years ago. They wanted us to conform to *Il Duce*'s motto: *Libro e moschetto fascista perfetto*! (Book and rifle make a perfect Fascist!)

Of course, we could afford to go to primary school which cost almost nothing – but only a few of us went to secondary school, which was far from our town. Whatever progress we had made at primary school, it was not followed up, so our knowledge became rusty. Besides, there were no public libraries – so how could we learn and become *Fascista perfetto*?

Another drawback was that most of our weapons were antiquated, fit only for the scrap heap, so how could we fight a modern war and have the chance to reconquer our lost Empire? *Il Duce*'s mottoes were no doubt impressive, but like any other empty vessel, they just made a lot of noise.

During 1930 Mother received news from Father that he had had a kidney disorder, had undergone an operation and was recovering. He was also extremely worried, for he mistrusted the person who was keeping an eye on his business. Father's illness was a matter of serious concern for us, for he was our only source of sustenance; how could we manage if he was sick and unable to work? The money he sent us every month was the equivalent of, or even better than, the salary of a senior government employee.

Mother had always put her trust, especially in an emergency, in Divine Providence and in all the saints. When she was confronted with a serious situation – an illness in the family, for instance – she lit candles in front of our printed image of Saint Antony of Padua and of the Immaculate Conception. She said the rosary every day, took the photo of the sick member of our family to the chapel and pinned it to the hem of the Madonna's dress.

As soon as Mother received the bad news, she made a solemn vow to Saint Antony of Padua. She trusted that the saint would help to speed up Father's recovery. One day she wore a cowl, as monks do, and white socks, and jogged about ten kilometres to the sanctuary of Saint Antony of Padua in Afragola, a nearby town. She donated 500 lire to the sanctuary, which was almost the equivalent of a month's salary for a teacher. It was money than Father had sent especially as a donation to his favourite saint who had guided, as Father said, the surgeon's hand while he was performing the operation. Mother also went to Mass with the express intention of hastening Father's healing and she received communion.

In the summer of the same year, Father came home to convalesce. He was still shocked from the operation, down-hearted and weak. Mother needed a lot of patience to cheer him up, until he was well again; then he began arguing and quarrelling with her as he had

47

always done when he came home from abroad. We were pleased about this, for if he had the energy to quarrel with Mother, it meant that he was strong again!

As we had not particularly enjoyed living near the slums, and my parents were well aware of their influence on us, they decided to look for a flat in Corso Umberto Primo, where the best class of people lived. So towards the end of 1930 we moved back to Palazzo De Rosa, near the Cinema Tripoli, but this time on the second floor.

We all were happy with the change. I started making new friends by frequenting a Fascist youth club every Sunday morning, for there was nothing else to do. Now that I lived some distance from Ciotto's house, I did not see him so often and his influence on me subsided. I still had my schoolmates and the friends I had made by going to catechism – my good Christian friends.

At the beginning of 1931, Father left for Rouen, France. He did not feel strong enough to go back to Java and cope with its climate. He went to Rouen to assist his younger brother Pascal for a while, who had married a French girl and had a business there. Probably Father did not see any possibility of making a living there, for France was getting too crowded with all kinds of people flooding in. The only advantage of being in France was that he was not too far away from us. But having been used for a number of years to brilliant tropical sunshine, he did not particularly enjoy the chilly northern climate of Rouen.

Before going to France, he made sure that while he was away Mother had plenty to do – and consequently she was pregnant once again; another of the Lord's blessings, as people called it. Any newly born child was considered a Lord's blessing, even if it seemed to impoverish the family concerned.

11

*I have another accident. Saverio leaves the College
of the Sacred Hearts*

We usually had our main meal at 1.00 p.m. My school hours were between 1.00 p.m. and 4.30 p.m., so I had to leave home by 12.30 p.m. Before going to school I had a snack consisting of a chunk of bread soaked in the water in which the haricot beans were cooking, with a trickle of olive oil and a pinch of salt and oregano. If I had been playing with my mates in the morning, I was very hungry and so I relished my frugal pre-school meal. At that time all the food we ate was organically grown, so haricot beans tasted of beans and olive oil tasted of olives. When I could not get this snack, my mother or my sister gave me a tomato or an omelette sandwich. After this less filling meal, I was supposed to go to school and learn.

My mother came from a poor and illiterate family and had not the faintest idea about the science of nutrition. She and many other people of our town had probably never heard about protein, vitamins and minerals. For them, eating meant that when they were hungry they had to put some food into their stomachs; anything would do as long as they appeased their hunger. Mother did not know that if her children were not fed properly they would find it difficult to learn. Of course it was not easy to provide for a large family like ours satisfactorily on our limited income.

More often than not I arrived at the school entrance a quarter of an hour or so early. Girls and boys would already be waiting to be admitted. While we were waiting, we played boisterously and teased and jostled one another. But one day in February 1931, while I was playing roughly with my schoolmates, I slipped on a patch of wet paving. A housewife living in a nearby ground-floor room had emptied a bucketful of water outside her door. As I fell,

49

one of the large wheels of a horse-drawn cart ran over my legs between my knees and ankles. I was lucky because the cart was moving very slowly and carrying nothing, otherwise it would have crushed my legs completely.

I screamed hysterically, not so much from the pain, but from the shock and the fear of having lost my legs as I thought. My poor mother must have received the news telepathically, for a few minutes after the accident she appeared on the scene as if from nowhere. She was barefoot and her long hair cascaded over her shoulders. Very likely she learned the news while she was combing her hair in front of the mirror. She had stopped doing this at once, kicked off her slippers and dashed towards the school about half a kilometre away from our home.

As I lay in the road, shocked and terror-stricken, I had a vision of the Madonna. She was like the statue I had seen in the chapel. She stretched out her arms and gently lifted me up from where I lay. As she did so all my pain and fear went. I realised then that the Madonna was my own mother, and that I was safely in her arms. She ran home with me as fast as she could, praying all the while.

She should have taken me to hospital in the city, but she didn't. Why not? Was she under the spell of Divine Guidance? Somebody suggested that she should send for a middle-aged woman called Forturella who was an expert herbalist. This lady came at once and examined my badly bruised and swollen legs. Having ascertained that there was no fracture, she resolved to apply some herbal poultices prepared on the marble top of our kitchen table. She bandaged my legs and put them to rest horizontally on a chair in front of where I was sitting. After a week or ten days of herbal treatment, thanks to God and my mother's prayers, I could walk again. It had indeed been a miraculous recovery.

A couple of months after the accident in which I almost lost my legs, I was involved in an incident of a different kind. There was a schoolgirl about my age whose name was Giuseppina Carbonelli. She went to an afternoon class for girls, while I went to an afternoon class for boys. I saw her every day, either on her way to school or at the school entrance. She had long blonde hair parted in the middle, grey or blue eyes, and a face resembling an angel portrayed in the paintings of the great masters. When it was cold, she wore a white lambswool coat. She made me blush every time I met her face to face, and my heart would go 'pit-a-pat'. Was she aware of it? I never spoke to her and I was too shy to approach her. But when I was with my friends I boasted that she was my girlfriend. I wanted them to know this, so that nobody among them would claim her for himself.

Most of the time when I went to school I was in the company of a chum whose name was Sabato (Saturday). Sabato was in the third year of primary school. He was a rough boy, but not as bad as Ciotto. Sabato and I often noticed Giuseppina on her way to school, as she usually walked just in front of us. Sabato once dared me: 'Look, that's Giuseppina in front. If she's your girlfriend, run and overtake her and kiss her. If you're afraid of doing it, I'll do it. Then she'll be *my* girlfriend!'

'You must be joking,' I said. 'Men don't kiss women in the street. I know it's done in American movies, but we don't do it here; it would create a scandal!'

'I have got you,' Sabato said, 'you're afraid. I don't think she's your girlfriend at all, and if I kiss her, then she'll be *mine*.'

'You must be mad!' I shouted. 'You can't do that.'

'Can't I? Can't I? I'll show you.'

Having said that, Sabato ran, overtook Giuseppina, seized her and kissed her on the cheek.

I could not believe my eyes. Having kissed Giuseppina, Sabato fled, for the girl was shocked and started crying. Some passers-by were appalled and indignant, but they couldn't catch and punish him. He had disappeared.

Giuseppina was still in tears when she reached school and reported the attack to the schoolmaster. He promptly carried out some investigations and soon found out who the culprit was.

Sabato tried to excuse himself by involving me. He said that it was I who had dared him to kiss the girl, and that I had told him that she was my sweetheart, and since I did not have the courage to do the kissing myself, I had urged him to do it for me.

I tried to defend myself, but the schoolmaster had made up his mind that I was implicated and resolved to take disciplinary action. Sabato and I were suspended from school for three days. I was furious at what Sabato had done and could not forgive him. Consequently our friendship came to an end.

I was extremely sorry about Giuseppina. I still loved her, of course – who knew what she thought of me now? The romance I had hoped for was over. I was heartbroken!

In 1934 or 1935, Giuseppina and her mother went to London, where her Italian father lived. He had an antiques business there. Two or three years later mother and daughter came back home, for they could not adapt to the weather and the English way of life. After her return, Giuseppina married a businessman about ten years older than herself.

At the end of May 1931, my brother Saverio left the college, where he had spent nineteen months, and came home. It happened so suddenly that we were surprised. The missionary priest, Father Cristoforo Di Donna, asked to see Mother and said to her: 'It's about Saverio. I'm afraid he must leave the college because he hasn't sufficient vocation to become a priest. It's better for him to spend a few months at home. Later, if he really wants to become a priest, he can always come back to the college and resume his studies.'

Father Cristoforo was a truly spiritual man. He was in charge of the missionary students and had years of experience. He could discern that Saverio was finding it hard to cope with the rigorous training required for the priesthood.

Saverio's weakness consisted of his fondness for women. As I have mentioned already, whenever he and his fellow theological students were taken out for their weekly walks, they had to pass through the streets of our town to get to the countryside. Saverio, alas, could not keep his eyes off the girls, especially the ones who had sex appeal.

No doubt quite a number of the other students were in the same boat. However, unlike my brother, they were not prepared to give up their chance to become priests. They were willing to make the necessary sacrifice for their career in the Church. Somehow they contrived to be exemplary students – to convince or fool their spiritual Father, Cristoforo Di Donna, that they had the qualities demanded for the priesthood. They were perhaps able to prevent or suppress the allure of the flesh by means of additional prayers.

Saverio's advantage, compared with that of a number of his college mates, was that he could come home, live with us and decide what he really wanted to do in life.

Although we were not rich, our standard of living was higher than that of many others in our town. So if he withdrew from the college, he certainly would not suffer hardship. Here at home, Saverio could sort himself out about his future. With Father's financial help, he could either carry on studying for academic qualifications or become a businessman.

It so happened that it took Saverio a little time to get adjusted to home life again. We were glad to have him with us, of course, for he amused us with the jokes he had learned at college.

After a little while he began to study for a secondary school examination which was taking place the following summer. Unfortunately when he sat for the examination he failed, because he had not spent enough time in preparation.

My brother's college studies were not recognised by the educational authorities and they had no academic value. It was therefore necessary for him to obtain some state school qualifications if he wanted to get a job or go to university in Naples.

My elder brother Vince was doing his first year of secondary school. As there was no such school in Secondigliano, secondary school students had to travel by tram to Naples. Paying the fare was costly for us, and for many others who were no better off.

Vince loved playing with his schoolmates and was not a serious student, so, not surprisingly, he was not promoted to the second year. Mother was not happy with his school results; nevertheless, the following autumn she gave Saverio and Vince a second chance. Saverio, with the assistance of an old teacher, studied privately, thus the money we were supposed to spend on his tram fare helped to pay for his private tuition. Regrettably, Saverio and Vince found it hard to make the effort. Perseverance, alas, was not their strong point. In consequence, they did not get very far with their studies.

12

Mother gives birth to her eleventh child. Our
Christmas, New Year and Epiphany celebrations

On 2 November 1931, Mother gave birth to her eleventh child: a baby girl she named Teresa. In spite of this extra mouth to feed, Father did not increase his remittance, so we had to adapt as best we could.

As Father was not doing very well in France, he did not come home the following Christmas, so we spent the festive season by ourselves as we had already done on a number of occasions.

Although Father couldn't come home, the Christmas spirit was with us. There was the joy of saving a few coins to buy additional little figures for our rather elaborate crib; the making of the crib itself was an exciting task. The joviality of Christmas was very dear to us: the decoration of the shops, pipers playing carols, street vendors shouting at the tops of their voices and the hustle and bustle of shoppers. Even the poorest people, who did not know where their next meal would come from, lived in anticipation. They had a glimmer of hope that Father Christmas – or better still, the Divine Father – would not fail to provide for them.

On Christmas Eve the pipers, whom we called *Zampognari*, came into our home and played a tune called 'Novena' in front of our crib. This well-loved traditional tune had words which told of the birth of baby Jesus.

Our two pipers, Peppe and Doni, came from villages in the Abruzzi mountains. They were rather tall and stout, dressed in typical peasant robes, and wore short cloaks and soft felt hats similar to the Tyrolean kind.

Their legs and feet were wrapped in cloth fastened with criss-cross straps. Their faces were weather-beaten and their cheeks almost as red as plum tomatoes. They came to stay in our town a couple of weeks before Christmas and visited houses every day, where they played the 'Novena'. They lodged at a cheap *osteria* (inn), ate solid food and drank plenty of red wine. On Christmas Eve, the last day of their mission or service, they received, I think, five lire head and in some cases a supply of food and wine.

Mother's father, a widower, used to have dinner with us on Christmas Eve. There were thirteen of us, including Grandfather. We sat at a long table and ate meatless dishes. Being Roman Catholic, we were not allowed to eat meat on the day before Christmas.

Vince, as usual, was boisterous, garrulous and greedy. He always wanted to be the centre of attention, to be heard and to have the lion's share of everything, so we nicknamed him *Ciotolone* (big bowl), by which we meant 'greedy boy'.

At the end of dinner, we remained sitting at the table till late. We read letters and poems which we had written at school before the Christmas recess. They celebrated the Nativity and included promises to our parents that we were going to be good, obedient and affectionate. At the end of such a performance, we expected to receive our Christmas presents, or at least to be tipped. Having a few coins jingling in our pockets gave us the feeling of opulence. How nice it was to know that we could use our money exactly as we liked!

My younger brothers and sisters went to bed before midnight; the older ones were allowed to play tombola until late. In the small hours the streets were deserted. Several people continued feasting throughout the night: they waited for the half past four church bells to ring, inviting them to attend the first Christmas Mass and pay their respects to the newborn babe.

Although we went to bed very late, the excitement and the unusually heavy meal made it impossible to sleep. When we heard the church bells ringing, some of us got out of bed and peered through the steamed-up glass panels of the door overlooking the main street. It was pitch dark outside and slightly foggy. My elder brothers and I got dressed, wrapped ourselves in woollies and walked towards the chapel which was lit up and crowded. The Christmas service was notable for its aroma of frankincense, and for its hearty singing and prayers; it went on for more than an hour. It then continued with a procession through the main streets of our town. As he walked along, the Father Rector, Natalino Russo, who was in charge of the chapel and college combined, held the statue of baby Jesus in his arms. This was under an ornate canopy as wide as a beach umbrella, which was held up by another priest.

The rector moved forward solemnly while several pipers followed him. They played the 'Novena' and other carols. The procession advanced slowly through crowds lined up on both sides of the street. A number of spectators held burning Bengal lights (fireworks) in their hands, contrasting brilliantly with the pitch darkness and dazzling our eyes. People from adjacent balconies saluted the procession by letting off firecrackers.

The air, laden with smoke from the firecrackers, was thick and almost unbearable. We did not care; the procession was so entrancing that we loved every moment of it. We returned home at daybreak, a little tired from not having slept sufficiently – or not at all – but we were thrilled with a heavenly joy. Besides this, we were looking forward now to the continuation of Christmas festivities, the celebration of New Year and Epiphany. What a rich time it was!

The New Year's Eve and New Year's Day celebrations were also happy events. On New Year's Eve we had a substantial dinner, played tombola, sang old songs, and the people next door joined us before midnight to exchange greetings. Occasionally we drank a couple of bottles of real champagne, though mostly we had something less expensive.

Those who could afford champagne saluted the New Year boisterously and let off firecrackers. Poorer people threw down damaged plates, cups, old chamber-pots and other breakable objects from their balconies. With so many firecrackers and other objects flying around, it was too risky for anyone to venture out in the streets at midnight. In the morning of New Year, we always learned that there had been a number of casualties, especially among those who had mishandled firecrackers. And the streets were littered with fragments of shattered objects which kept street sweepers very busy indeed.

This throwing away of old, damaged or unwanted objects also had a symbolic significance. It meant getting rid of afflictions and any other hindrances of the past year. No doubt some people imagined that by throwing away their old chamber-pots they were getting rid of the Fascists!

Soon after New Year, we children looked forward to Epiphany

on 6 January. According to Neapolitan tradition, children usually do not get their presents from Father Christmas, but from the *Befana* (an ugly old woman) who brings gifts during the night between Epiphany Eve and Epiphany Day.

When we went to bed on 5 January 1932 we all hung a sock on our bed posts. Towards midnight or later, my elder sister, disguised as the *Befana*, came around and took our empty socks away; then she filled them with sweets and other items and brought them back.

We were rewarded according to our conduct. As I was not always a good boy, my sock usually contained fewer sweets than those of my better behaved brothers and sisters. It also contained a chunk of coal, a carrot, a potato and a reprimand – a warning to me that if I continued to displease Mother I wouldn't get any presents at all at Epiphany the following year!

My elder brothers and I no longer believed in the *Befana*; we knew exactly what went on at Epiphany Eve, and who the *Befana* was, but we had to pretend that we believed in her in case we forfeited our share of sweets and presents.

On the day of Epiphany we woke up before daybreak. A number of us had hardly any sleep: we were too anxious to discover what the *Befana* had brought us. During the night we started fumbling and fingering our bulging socks, and by dawn each of us was sitting in his bed, extracting their contents. Sucking our sweets, we talked excitedly as we compared our presents.

It did not please me, of course, to find a chunk of coal, a carrot, a potato and a reprimand. My present was not too bad, however – it was better than nothing. The last present I received was a scooter, which I used on our asphalted road. If my brothers and sisters wanted to borrow it they had to beg me. After all, it was my very own property! Provided that they did not cross me in any way, they were usually allowed to use it.

13

Our traditional Easter

Easter was regarded as being almost as important as Christmas. It was the time that reminded us of the ignominious death of Christ and His glorious resurrection. It was also an occasion for many to wear new spring clothes; tailors and dressmakers were kept busy coping with orders taken long before Easter, for young and old alike loved showing off their new suits and dresses on Easter Sunday.

As Mother could not afford to buy new clothes for us, she used to say, 'Those who wear new clothes for the first time at Easter are not the sort of people I care for. It's only beggars and vulgar people who want to be admired on Easter Sunday. Nobles and refined people don't compete with the rabble and the scum.'

Comments like this made my mother seem like a snob, yet we had come up from poverty ourselves, so she had no right to be so proud. Although she was such a kind, loveable person, Mother had this little human weakness. At the time, however, I was flattered by Mother's statement; it made me feel that we were not, after all, at the very bottom of the social scale!

We looked forward to Easter just as much as we looked forward to Christmas. For one thing, the start of the school holidays preceded this event, which began with Holy Week.

On Holy Thursday we visited several churches which displayed life-sized statues of Jesus taken down from their large crucifixes. Such statues showed Jesus stretched out on a rectangular frame, representing the Holy Sepulchre. This was adorned with an abundance of fresh spring flowers, helping to give the display an odour of sanctity. To make it more dramatic, Jesus's wounds were given a touch of red paint, making them seem recently inflicted. We moved forward in a queue, kissed Jesus's feet, made an offering –

whatever we could afford – and moved on. Some people knelt and prayed for a while before they left the church.

It was customary to visit more than one church. Visitors compared the various church displays for their artistic value. While they fulfilled this religious obligation, they had the chance also to meet acquaintances and friends.

In the city of Naples there was a long, fashionable street called Via Roma. On Holy Thursday it was closed to traffic from 8.00 p.m. till 12.00 p.m. This enabled the civic dignitaries, the aristocracy and the well-to-do to parade along it on their way to visit the churches.

Via Roma was flanked by luxurious shops and hundreds of neon signs. The men were elegantly dressed, while the women wore the latest fashions and were bedecked with jewels. The perfume of eau-de-cologne, vying with the scent of carnations, permeated the air. The people parading there were the *crème de la crème* of Neapolitan society. They were in the company of their relatives and friends. They walked in groups, making a shuffling noise with the soles of their shoes along the paved street, a noise which Neapolitans called *struscio*.

The following day, Good Friday, was supposed to be a day of fasting and mourning. We went to the three o'clock church service which was called 'The Three Hours of the Agony of Jesus' – and it lasted three long agonising hours especially to those who attended only out of duty!

We went to the chapel, which was packed. The atmosphere inside was gloomy; each statue of the saints had been covered with dark linen. The main altar had disappeared. It was concealed by a huge screen, also made of linen, on which three giant crucifixes had been fixed, with Jesus and the two thieves nailed to their respective crosses. At this service we always had a guest preacher whose eloquence was able to move us to tears. As he preached, every now and then he rested for a few minutes. While he did so, a priest took over and led us in prayer. Later, the preacher continued with his passionate outpourings. When he reached the point at which Jesus was breathing his last, a handbell was rung, whereupon someone behind the screen pulled a hidden cord attached to the crucifix, causing Jesus's head to rise and fall three times. At this point some members of the congregation, already stirred by the preacher, became hysterical and wept. The preacher had to stop speaking for a moment to enable these overly affected worshippers to calm down.

Among the congregation there were those who were less susceptible than others, whom the preacher could not move to pity. They probably found him boring, so while he preached passionately, they exchanged their views about their Easter baking.

There was a local or regional tradition of making an Easter pizza and cake, and a kind of large doughnut which people called *casatiello*. Most people were not equipped with baking facilities, so if they made their own bread, pizza and cake they had to send them to the baker. The *casatiello* was not made with sugar but with pork fat, salt and pepper. It was topped with a number of eggs in their shells which were sunk deeply into the *casatiello*'s surface.

To keep us happy, Mother made a *casatiello* for each of us. She made them with one, two, three or more eggs. Saverio, Vince and I had one *casatiello* each, made with four eggs. Mother also made our traditional pizza and cake. The pizza was stuffed with eggs, ham and salami; the cake was made with boiled wheat grains, butter, cream, ricotta cheese, sugar and spice. All the baking had to be done by Holy Saturday.

Mother did her Easter shopping during Holy Week. She bought whatever she needed for our elaborate ritual Easter dinner – a feast almost as costly as the one we had at Christmas.

After the gloomy church services of the preceding three days, Holy Saturday was a day of expectancy: a joyful day indeed. The church bell had been silent for three days, but on Holy Saturday morning, after the church service of Resurrection, all the bells rang triumphantly, announcing that Jesus had risen from the dead and had entered Heaven. As the bells swung with all their might and proclaimed Christ's glory, people, regardless of where they were, fell on their knees and kissed the earth. Our hearts were suddenly filled with a joy which cannot be described – a joy experienced by every sincere Christian.

Easter Sunday was usually warm and sunny. The verdant countryside was in full bloom and the air was pure and pleasant to breathe. On Easter morning we went to Mass and communion, and had dinner at about one. Sometimes our grandparents (Father's parents) were invited to dine with us, so our long dining-table had to accommodate fifteen people, including Mother's father.

We started dinner with a blessing. Mother held a palm twig in her hand, immersed it in holy water, sprinkled a few drops over us and then said grace. We ate chicory cooked with seasoned pork sausage and bits of bacon; noodles in chicken broth; lamb with peas, onion and sliced potatoes, all baked together; sliced salami, hard boiled eggs and *provolone* cheese; stuffed pizza, salad; and *pastiera* (Easter cake). Together we drank about two litres of wine with the main dishes. After the Easter cake we drank a few drops of brandy and then had some fresh fruit, ending dinner with black coffee.

One of the main events of Easter started a couple of hours before dawn on Easter Monday, which the Italians call *Pasquetta*. Intermittently, groups of those who had made a vow (the Neapolitans called them *Fuienti* – joggers or runners) passed along our main road. Some of the joggers originated locally, while others came from nearby towns. They ran barefoot about fifteen kilometres or more to the sanctuary of the Madonna of the Arch. Men and women runners were each wrapped from neck to ankle in some sort of white linen cloth. Round their waist they wore a red sash, with another sash diagonally across their chest. As they jogged along they collected money which they offered to the sanctuary.

When they arrived and entered the church, they prostrated themselves and crawled along the nave from porch to altar. There they prayed for grace received or to be received. Later they joined a ceremony in which the statue of the miraculous Madonna was taken in procession in an atmosphere of hymns of glory, punctuated by fireworks.

Having watched the joggers passing by during the night and in the early morning, we felt a little drowsy, but we were still full of excitement for the events yet to come. Between nine o'clock and ten, Saverio, Vince and I were ready to go on our traditional Easter Monday picnic. Our elder sister gave each of us some *casatiello*, a slice of stuffed pizza and cake. We wrapped them in napkins and left home. We sauntered along for about an hour, often stopping whenever we came across groups of boisterous youths blowing their trumpets and shouting and singing joyfully.

We each used part of our pocket money to buy a trumpet (cheap ones made of cardboard or tin) and a fanciful cap, and then joined one of the groups of youths. As we moved along, we walked through a bushy area and down to a ravine called *Cavone*, where there was a small church with a miraculous Madonna. It was said that one day, while a deaf and dumb shepherd boy was pasturing his sheep in that area, the Madonna appeared, spoke to him and gave him the faculties of speech and hearing.

The *Cavone* was communal land with hillocks, walnut and hazel trees, and.a few cultivated plots. Spare patches of land were sometimes annexed – possibly illegally – by people who used them to grow their own food. We found the *Cavone* area crowded with picnickers and visitors. After a while we sat on a hillock under some hazel trees, spread our napkins on the grass and started eating. We were not really hungry; we had not yet digested the huge dinner of the previous day, so how could we be? But we felt it our duty to eat because so many other picnickers were doing so.

By being there we were just following tradition; we had to eat *casatiello* with baked eggs, slices of stuffed pizza and Easter cake. It really was a struggle, especially eating those hard eggs, which were so difficult to swallow. In fact, we needed several glasses of water to wash them down. But there was no water in that spot, so we had to buy it from itinerant water-sellers who made a brisk business out of the misery of thirsty people. A few men carried small kegs across their backs and charged ten cents for a glass of water flavoured with extract of aniseed. My stomach, burdened with the undigested food of the previous day and the food I had just eaten, seemed to be crying out for a drink of some kind, so I had to spend whatever pocket money I had left to quench my thirst.

There were groups of picnickers with basketfuls of food and drink who were making pigs of themselves. How could they do it, after their large traditional dinner of Easter Sunday? I was amazed at the amount of food they could eat; it was sheer greed. Many of them had brought gramophones, so they danced on the grass and enjoyed themselves immensely.

Mother and the rest of the family went to the *Cavone* picnic area later in the morning. They just went for a stroll, to experience the cheerful atmosphere of Easter Monday.

Those who really benefited from our endless eating and drinking festivities were the doctors and chemists. As a result of their excessive eating, a lot of people became heavily constipated. Since there was no free National Health Service, they had to pay dearly for their sins of gluttony!

14

Intimate winter evenings and Mother's reminiscences

Winters were generally not too long or very cold, except for a few days in January, when the temperature dropped below zero. We were thrilled when it snowed. We had to stay at home then, because our school had no heating facilities. We wrapped ourselves up properly, ran outside and played. We touched the snow as if it was precious, sucked it, threw snowballs at each other and made a snowman. The snow was great fun, but unfortunately it did not last long enough. Within a few hours it melted away and the enchantment of it all ended too soon for our liking. At school, however, snowfall always became a topic for discussion and homework.

In winter time, ordinary people used braziers to warm their flats. The well-to-do could afford central heating. Winter was not much of a problem for families cooped up in one room, which was often used as bedroom, eating and sitting-room, and kitchen. So many bodies in a small area made warmth, and sometimes braziers were not required in such circumstances.

As we lived in a three-bedroom flat, Mother left our brazier in the bedrooms during the day, which was of little help to us. After the evening meal, we gathered in the dining-room and sat around our brazier. Mother always wore a large red shawl around her shoulders, and every now and then she used a long metal spatula to adjust the embers and ash. We often fought for a cosier place, then took our shoes off and warmed our feet by letting them rest on the wooden frame of the brazier-stand. While we were gathered there, we discussed various events. We mentioned our neighbours, the people next door who often knocked at our door, asking Mother to lend them a cupful of salt, or sugar, or a box of matches and other items.

When Mother was in a loving and motherly mood she told us

about the good old days – her youth, her father, mother, brother and sisters – as she had already done several times on similar occasions during the previous winters. She also told us about one of her suitors called Gennaro Barbato.

'Some years before the Great War,' she used to say, 'Gennaro asked to marry me.'

Gennaro was a barber who emigrated to the USA. Being on his own, he badly needed a wife – not any wife, but a wife from the place where he was born; a wife who could speak his own language, cook the food he liked, a wife to provide him with physical and spiritual comfort. So he proposed to Mother.

Mother went on: 'I didn't want to go to America. Besides your father was courting me. He said, "If you decide to marry Gennaro I'll slash your face!" I was afraid of your father's threat, so I made up my mind and refused to marry Gennaro. The poor man was desperate, so he proposed to my elder sister Concetta. They married by proxy a week or two before she sailed for the USA.

'At that time, before the Great War, ordinary people had a strange way of doing things. For instance, if a girl decided to drop her boyfriend for a new one, and if the first one was passionately in love with her, he wouldn't release her easily. In fact he would threaten to slash her face if she rejected him.'

This kind of thing really did happen in the old days. As a matter of fact, after Mother told us this, I would sometimes notice a married woman with a disfigured face; I realised now that she too had suffered at the hands of an excessively passionate boyfriend.

We often nagged or teased Mother. We showed our disapproval for her not having married Gennaro. Had she done so, we thought that we would have been born in America, thereby being citizens of a rich nation instead of the poor Italy enslaved by *Il Duce* and his Fascists. We had seen glamorous American movies of the 'Roaring Twenties' which showed us that the standard of living of ordinary Americans was much higher than that of Italians. At that time, 1932, *Il Duce*, instead of improving our standard of living, was ruining our economy by building up the army to conquer Abyssinia. We wanted bread; he wanted to give us a new territory that could neither appease our hunger, nor provide us with medical care or with more sanatoria to fight the tuberculosis which was rife among us.

By the end of February or early March it was virtually the end of winter. Braziers were put away, the sun grew warmer and shone more frequently. Spring breathed life into us, and street vendors shouted with renewed vigour as if they had imbibed some rejuvenating elixir.

15

Mother gives Vince a good hiding. He runs away,
but returns the following day. Carmen is taken ill.
Infant mortality is high

Although we had our meals regularly at home and were better off than many people, we could not always afford the more nourishing kinds of food. This meant, of course, that we often went short of the protein necessary for bodily growth. As a result some of us did not grow as tall and robust as we might have done. In spite of this, I always seemed to have plenty of energy.

My brother Vince lacked the willpower, concentration and perseverance necessary for serious study, so he was not doing well at school. He was stronger than I was, and rather robust. He had black hair combed from front to back, grey eyes, a straight nose and was good-looking. Girls found him handsome, and he forever yearned to hug and kiss them.

Vince was sexually precocious. Any woman with a little sex appeal would turn him on. He abused himself and wasted vital energy which he could have used in studying.

He and I shared a single bed and slept head to foot. Often I felt the bed shaking during the night and knew that he was playing with his 'toy'. In the morning the sheets of our bed confirmed that he had masturbated.

Mother was surely aware of Vince's sexual precociousness and what he was up to. She must have warned him more than once about the effect that self-abuse would have on his health and study. She feared sometimes that he might molest our sisters.

I remember that one afternoon in early summer 1932, Vince, Tony and I were having a siesta on a blanket spread on the floor of our bedroom. While I was sleeping there, Tony and Vince went to a corner of the room, and there Vince showed Tony how he masturbated. It was quite a revelation and an education for my younger brother Tony. He was amazed and woke me up to tell me of the novelty. He also invited me to witness a performance and he urged Vince to do it again. Vince did it again then – just to oblige us.

Although Tony and I had not reached that stage yet, Vince's demonstration had been a discovery for Tony. It was not like that for me, for I had seen some other boys doing it. I myself had tried it, but being still too young and not having experienced an orgasm, I was not really interested. However, when I noticed a girl or woman with sex appeal, I became strangely excited – but this was as far as I got at this stage.

I think Mother was exasperated at Vince; she was itching to give him a sound hiding. On learning that he was playing truant at school, she became so furious that she thrashed him soundly. The following day Vince was all sore and sulky. After breakfast, a brew made with ground roast barley, milk, sugar and two slices of bread, Vince took some sandwiches, which my elder sister had prepared for him, and went to school. But he did not come back home in the afternoon. In the evening he was missing. Where was he? We searched the places that he usually frequented. We asked his friends, but nobody knew where he was.

We were extremely worried, especially Mother. Later, as the large church clock chimed the hour of midnight and the streets were deserted, we were still looking for him. Since it was getting very late and we were getting nowhere, we resolved to visit the local *carabinieri* (police). They, in turn, rang up their headquarters in Naples which had no news or report about Vince. The *carabinieri* told Mother to be patient, to go home and wait till the following morning for further investigations.

We went to bed, but rest for most of us was out of the question. Mother was in a sorrowful state. Anxiously we listened to every approaching footstep hoping that it was Vince returning to us, but it always turned out to be someone passing by, perhaps on the way to work. We longed for dawn; but when it came we were unable to appreciate the splendid sunrise of that summer day; anguished thoughts of our missing brother gave us no respite.

There were no public telephones, and having a private telephone was a luxury that only rich people and well-established businessmen could afford. In the hope of getting information, Mother, my brother Saverio, my grandfather (Father's father) and I all went to the police headquarters in Naples. They rang up hospitals and other places, but nobody knew anything.

In the afternoon, dejected and crestfallen, we returned home. We looked at each other gloomily and had little or nothing to say. Suddenly we heard something stirring, a mingling of voices getting nearer and louder. Some of our neighbours ran upstairs, knocked at our door and called out, 'Signora Arrichiello! Vince is here! Vince is here! He is coming; your father is bringing him.'

As we heard the news, we leaped for joy and all of us rushed downstairs to meet him. There he was, with Grandfather gripping his hand. It seemed as if he had captured a wild beast and was determined not to let it escape. Vince looked sunburned but subdued; perhaps ashamed of his foolishness. The lost lamb was returning to the fold. His clothes were crumpled and dusty, his shoes were worn out and had holes in their soles, and his feet were sore.

Mother was greatly relieved, overjoyed and weeping. She embraced Vince, crying in a warm and affectionate voice: 'Where have you been, you naughty boy? You must be very hungry!' Then she led him to our dining-room and placed bread and cheese before him. My sister quickly prepared a two-egg omelette and cooked some spaghetti for him. All of us, including Grandfather, sat around our long dining-table and nudged one another; we looked at Vince devouring food like a wolf and wondered at his appetite.

It turned out that the day after Mother had thrashed him, Vince had taken a map, intending to go to Rome instead of going to school. How could he get there? He had an omelette sandwich with him and eighty cents in his pocket. He had walked some distance and hitchhiked, but at the end of the day he had hardly covered a hundred kilometres. Being hungry and tired, no doubt he had begged for food and shelter at nearby farms.

He soon realised that staying away from home involved hardship. Lacking the necessary determination to continue his journey he turned back, longing for home, sweet home, where there was food and a comfortable bed waiting for him. Moreover, he would not have to earn his keep.

The prodigal son became the centre of attention for several days; every friend and acquaintance wanted to know about Vince's adventure. I found it ridiculous later, and very funny, to learn that

Vince's real intention was to go to Rouen in France to be with Father. After all, how could he get there – and would he not turn back and come home again after only a few kilometres? From then on, whenever Vince crossed me, I laughed at him and said, 'What a clever boy you are! Fancy you going to France with eighty cents in your pocket! My word, what a silly chump!'

After finishing primary school, Carmen had to stay at home to help Mother to look after her large family. Mother usually did the shopping and cooking, but when for one reason or another she had to be out for the whole morning, Carmen did the cooking as well. She had been trained by Mother – and what a good cook she was, especially when she prepared minestrone, pasta with fresh tomatoes, stuffed aubergines and peppers. It was food cooked with loving care. We really relished it and were always ready for a second helping. We even licked our plates and praised Carmen as we did so.

In 1932 Carmen was about eighteen. She was a good-looking, well-formed girl of average height, and had short, fair hair with a left parting. During the summer, she was suddenly taken ill. This illness developed into a persistent fever, so Mother sent for our family doctor, Antonio Di Nocera. Dr Di Nocera was well established and had a reputation of being a good physician. But it had not been so when he was a young inexperienced doctor, relying only on his medical books; in the process of gaining practical experience, it was said that he had caused a certain amount of damage to a number of unfortunate patients.

We had very few hospitals in Naples, and these were run on meagre budgets. They served a huge population and were always crowded and not very well equipped. Many newly graduated doctors did not have the chance to get enough practice in these hospitals – either that or they did not like the atmosphere. So they were eager to start their own practices, and, in doing so, would be able to earn their living.

The disadvantage of using the services of young, inexperienced doctors was that they often prescribed medicines that did more harm than good. They tried new prescriptions again and again, and by the time they found the right ones, their patients, alas, were often dead.

If patients had strong constitutions, maybe their bodies could cope with the toxic effect of misprescribed medicine and they would recover, otherwise they would be ready for the undertaker. In those days, of course, patients, rich or poor, had to pay doctors' fees as well as paying for the medicine.

In the twenties and early thirties infant mortality, especially among poor people, was staggeringly high. Although poor parents had no money to pay for doctors' fees and for medicines, they did their best to get their sick children well. They went without food in order to pay for the necessary medical expenses.

When a baby died, parents, in spite of their penury, were determined to give their child a decent funeral, and in one way or another they managed to find the money they needed. They decorated the space around the body with white linen (white being the symbol of purity). The little body was dressed in white lace and white socks. The cot was decorated with white lace too, and white ribbons and white carnations. A tray, containing large sugar-coated sweets filled with syrup, was placed at the foot of the cot. Four tall, thick, burning candles, in candle stands, were placed one on each side, at the head and at the foot of the cot.

Parents hired the services of a small white hearse, drawn by a horse, and of a priest, who blessed the tiny corpse with holy water, before it was placed into a white coffin. The baby's mother could not always contain her grief and often wept profusely. Some would even yell hysterically as the undertaker carried the coffin out of the house and placed it in the hearse.

The funeral procession was made up of relatives, friends and other mourners. As it moved forward, members of the family threw the sugar-coated sweets on to the hearse. While this was happening, a dozen or more children would turn up and scramble for any sweet that had fallen on the flagstones. Sometimes, this resulted in quite a pitched battle.

When the hearse reached the cemetery, the priest blessed the coffin once again and recited the prayer for the dead. At the end of the prayer the coffin was put away in the morgue, where it usually rested for one day before it was interred.

Such was life. In spite of the excessively lavish propaganda of the Fascists regarding the greatness of our country, they did not lift a finger to alleviate our appalling living conditions. How could we feel great when the majority of our population had to put up with untold hardships and could not complain? *Il Duce* himself came from poor parents, but now that he was in power he forgot about his poverty-stricken people. He was too busy spending our money in preparation for the Abyssinian war; a conquest which would have given us a worthless prestige and impoverished our already crippled economy. It would be the conquest of a country so far away from Italy that, should a war occur, it could not be defended. *Il Duce* did not care a damn about our living conditions; he was too busy frolicking with those beautiful women who admired his virility, and perhaps too busy courting Claretta Petacci.

Dr Di Nocera came to see Carmen and soon diagnosed typhoid fever. He said that she was very ill and needed prompt attention. He offered to treat Carmen at home, adding that, with Mother looking after her, she would get all the care necessary for a swift recovery. If he sent her to the hospital, he would not be able to predict what might happen to her.

We had a hospital in Naples where patients with infectious diseases were sent. It had a poor reputation, and people were reluctant to send their relatives there, fearing that if they did the consequences might be fatal.

Mother was prepared to do anything to get Carmen restored to health, so she agreed with the doctor to have her treated at home.

We were lucky. The people living next door, signor and signora Boezia, a middle-aged couple with a grown-up daughter, were very helpful indeed. Signora Boezia was a trained ex-nurse who used to work in a general hospital and had a lot of nursing experience. The doctor gave Mother and signora Boezia instructions, and they followed them scrupulously. Mother sealed all the doors giving access to the bedroom where Carmen was confined. We, brothers and sisters, had to keep out; only the doctor, Mother and signora Boezia could enter that bedroom. Whatever object came in touch with Carmen had to be sterilised. We were not even allowed in the kitchen, where my sister's medications were prepared.

Mother and signora Boezia, in turn, spent a few nights beside my sister's bed, hoping that her temperature would drop. At the crucial moment, Carmen was delirious. Mother and signora Boezia were continually applying bags of ice to my sister's head to keep her temperature down.

Mother lit candles in front of a print of the Madonna, and as long as Carmen was dangerously ill, she never stopped praying. She bade us to pray too, and also asked one of our priests to say a Mass for Carmen.

We were all very sad, and stopped playing rough games while our sister was so ill. We were very concerned to see the doctor coming every day and Mother and signora Boezia going to and fro and telling us nothing about our sister's condition. We feared the worst, for we loved her dearly.

Our suspense lasted for a week or longer. Thank God for the ceaseless care of Dr Di Nocera, Mother and signora Boezia, for in time Carmen made a full recovery.

Her illness had cost us a small fortune. Doctor's fees and the medicines had to be paid for. Also after her illness, Carmen had to go on a special diet to regain her strength. All these expenses had to be paid for out of the regular monthly remittance that Father sent us. If one of us was sick, Father did not send any extra money. This meant that we had to tighten our belts and eat whatever food we could afford. At such times Mother had to pawn her jewels to make ends meet. But we were prepared to make any sacrifice as long as it helped Carmen to get well and resume her role in our family.

Signora Boezia did not charge us anything for nursing Carmen. Afterwards, every now and then, she would borrow a cup of salt, sugar, olive oil and so on. We were only too glad to oblige her and did not expect her to give back the borrowed items. From then on, whenever Mother made a pizza or a cake, she also made one for the Boezia family as a token of gratitude. She now knew from personal experience that 'A friend in need is a friend indeed'.

16

*Father comes back from France and spends
Christmas with us*

Autumn of 1932 was passing uneventfully when we received the news that Father was coming home about a week before Christmas. When he arrived, he brought us some souvenirs from Normandy and three pairs of boots with wooden soles; one pair for me, one for Tony and one for Giuseppe. They were a novelty, not available at our shoe markets. They were comfortable, especially in wintertime, and kept our feet dry and warm. However, when we walked, they made a lot of noise which attracted the attention of people in the street. Soon Joe, Tony and I became well-known; people could hear us approaching by the noise of our boots.

Now that we children were growing up so fast – many of us were already in our teens – Father began thinking about our future. What were we going to do in life? Which career should we follow?

Many local people, and even those in large towns and cities, had no hope of finding jobs and improving their standard of living. They wanted to go away, emigrate, go anywhere as long as they could make a decent life.

We young people, aware of so much discontent around us, could not help being influenced by our unhappy elders. Under the Fascist regime, our country had nothing to offer except deprivation, tears, depression and untold misery. We didn't have the faintest idea of what going abroad implied, or of the hardship involved. All we could think of was emigrating to a land of plenty, a land that could give us what we badly wanted: money and fulfilment. We did not realise that people in other countries were also struggling to achieve the same things as we were. Being newcomers we would, no doubt, be regarded as foreigners and intruders. And if we did not speak the language, we would find life more difficult than it was at home.

Father spent Christmas and New Year with us. He had no intention of going back to France. Because of our Fascist regime, French people – especially the workers, who were predominantly socialists or communists – looked at us with suspicion, and no longer welcomed Italian settlers as they had done years before.

Father had been ill when he was in Java in 1930, where he underwent a kidney operation, so he was not keen on going back there. He was now considering a voyage to Guatemala, for he had heard that it was a land full of promise. He intended to take my brothers Saverio and Vince with him and start a business there. However, he met some difficulty in obtaining visas. Father did not try very hard to get them, and later he lost interest altogether. He now decided to return to Java, where he could easily make a living. In spring 1933 he sailed for Java. He told my brothers that he could not take them with him for the time being, but if Java was still a favourable place for business he would send for them at the earliest opportunity.

My brothers had set their hearts on going abroad and were bubbling over with excitement and anticipation, but now, to their great disappointment, they learned that they had months to wait, perhaps even years. Meanwhile I had finished primary school. As Vince was not a good student, Mother came to the conclusion that I would not be any better, so I was not given the chance of enrolling for secondary school, which was located in the city. Mother argued that she could not afford the tram fares, so if Saverio, Vince and I badly wanted a secondary education, we should study by helping each other. Besides, what was the good of worrying about secondary education in a country where millions of people were unemployed and left to their own devices? Emigration seemed the only way to solve our problems, the only hope of preventing us from going hungry and freeing ourselves from the Fascist oppression. It really did not matter what kind of work we did abroad, as long as it was honest and enabled us to earn our living and possibly enjoy more freedom than we did under Fascism at home.

There were some immigrants in France who lived by their wits. They set themselves up as door-to-door salesmen, but hardly knew a dozen French words and sought a quick and easy way to make money. They dressed like seamen and carried bags or bundles over their shoulders containing their merchandise. When they approached prospective buyers they said that they were seamen aboard ships anchored in the port and that they had bargains to offer. Most of the time such bargains consisted of three-metre pieces of suiting material which could be used either for men's or women's clothing. They always claimed that these were English textiles, which at that time were known to be of the best quality. If they succeeded in convincing prospective buyers and selling them their goods, they could realise 100 per cent profit or even more. Some door-to-door salesmen were no better than thieves, for they sold absolute rubbish, describing it, in sign language and the few French words they knew, as 'quality English merchandise'.

Father told us that some of these dishonest salesmen worked in teams. Often they posed as Turkish merchants, such as one sees in a bazaar. They knocked at the doors of houses or villas of well-to-do French people, trying to sell them oriental carpets. Once they had been let in, these impostors, unable to speak French, would utter a lot of gibberish that only one of them seemed capable of understanding. Thus he would translate into French, praising the quality of the carpets and saying that they were of original design, hand woven, easy to clean and would last forever. If the sale was concluded, these swindlers made a huge profit which kept them going for a few days. This gave them time to plan their next swindle.

However, when the duped customers started to vacuum their carpets, they peeled off, lost their luxurious appearance and there was not much left, except a square or oblong of dull matting. Having found out that they had been conned, they stopped dealing with door-to-door salesmen altogether. And who could blame them? Salesmen who cheated had no regular customers, so they had to move from place to place in search of new simpletons.

These men lived precariously. Being unable to speak French, they could not find work, or perhaps they just liked to be their own bosses. They lived for the day, doing whatever they chanced to, and seemed unable to free themselves from their set way of living.

17

Holidaying in Gerolomini. Cinema addiction and influence. Saverio embarks for Java

In the summer of 1933 we spent two weeks' holiday at a place called Gerolomini, which is on the outskirts of Pozzuoli and not far from Naples. Its thermal baths attracted visitors, but most of them were middle-aged or elderly people affected by rheumatism, arthritis and similar ailments.

Mother found the thermal baths refreshing and beneficial and took advantage of them while we were holidaying there. My brothers, sisters and I bathed in the sea, which was not far from our self-catering flat.

Gerolomini, as a seaside resort, was not ideal, because it had only a narrow and none-too-clean pebble beach, littered here and there with human excrement. The municipality did not provide public toilets, so no doubt some people, under the urgent pressure of nature, relieved themselves in corners of the beach or among the rocks. Perhaps fishermen at sea and irresponsible bathers also defecated in the water; for their stools, tossed by waves and breakers, often floated alongside the beach.

The sea was, in any case, heavily polluted because of nearby industrial and sewage discharge. Local authorities seemed to ignore this for fear that, if they made a fuss about it, holiday-makers might decide to stay away.

We had no idea of the harmful effects of pollution, so we were quite unconcerned. The sea close to the beach was murky, and there was flotsam scattered all over its surface. This was probably from the liners and cargo ships that we saw on the horizon entering the harbour of Naples, or sailing from it.

We were young and determined to have a lot of fun, so we dived into the oncoming breakers with great excitement. As we did so, we could not help swallowing some of the filthy water. Thanks to our Guardian Angel, however, we were not affected by the contamination.

Often my brothers and I went to the beach at 6.00 a.m. to watch the fishermen. About a dozen of them pulled the ropes of a huge net which they had set out during the night. With each yank of the ropes, they would all shout together, bringing the net with its catch nearer and nearer to the beach. As the net drew closer, we saw the lively fish, large and small, jumping and struggling as they tried to free themselves from the deadly trap. The fishermen, their bare feet in the water, rushed forward eagerly to examine their catch. When it was plentiful, they were boisterous and cheerful. When it was poor, they cursed Jesus and all his family, for had they not worked the whole night and caught next to nothing? Their lives depended on fishing and a bad catch meant a gloomy day for them and their families.

Their catch invariably ended up at the local daily market, where some of them had stalls. A number of customers went there early in the morning, for fresh fish sold out very quickly. Every morning, Mother, escorted by a half-dozen of us who volunteered to act as her porters, marched to the market. It was held on a very wide footpath off the main road alongside the beach. Here boisterous vendors shouted continually to attract customers. They sold fruit and vegetables from their horse-drawn carts.

The poor horses stood there for many hours, with nothing to do except swish their tails and twitch their skins to get rid of large, voracious flies that sucked their blood. There were also a few donkeys that occasionally protested, no doubt on account of being bored. They would unleash sonorous brays which helped to enliven the market atmosphere.

A group of young scoundrels, always ready for a lark, would often make a nuisance of themselves. If they noticed a donkey sexually aroused, they would touch its genitals with a stick. The irritated animal, offended, would then protest by kicking and braying hysterically.

There were stalls selling beachwear, domestic appliances and many other items. Selling was not always easy for these traders, because shoppers were in the habit of haggling, and Mother was not an easy customer. When she approached a stall, she examined the goods, felt them for quality and looked at the prices. Although she had already noted the price, she would deliberately ignore it and ask the vendor: 'How much are those peaches?'

'Eighty cents a kilo, signora.'

'That man over there sells them for fifty cents a kilo,' Mother would say. Mother made up stories when she did her shopping. This crafty way of hers helped her to save money for our large family.

'Did you say fifty cents?' shouted the vendor. 'Fifty cents? You must be joking, signora. They cost me more than that. This is the best quality, signora. See how big and juicy they are? I should sell them at one lira a kilo.'

'They're not as good as you say,' Mother argued. 'They won't keep. If you don't sell them today, they'll rot by tomorrow.' She added then, 'You know what I'll do? I'll give you sixty cents a kilo, all right?'

After a few days some of the vendors, by then knowing that Mother had a large family, tried to help her as much as they could. Not only that – she was, after all, a regular customer. Others, however, thought that Mother was a terror and dreaded her approach, for they knew that there was going to be a fierce war of words before they could agree over a paltry sale.

Every day, after a frugal breakfast of bread and fresh figs, my brothers, Saverio and Vince, and I went to the beach. We explored the rocks which formed a barrier between the houses and other buildings and the sea itself. We would catch a few small crabs, pull their legs off and suck them, hardly extracting any juice. Sometimes we sat on the rocks and watched the few anglers who often spent hours without catching anything.

Mother and my sisters came to the beach about eleven o'clock. They always carried with them a large basket and two shopping bags, which contained our lunch, some fruit, drinking water and a few towels.

Mother preferred her thermal baths, so she did not bathe in the sea. She sat in our deckchair in the shade of a beach umbrella which we hired daily. Between half past twelve and one o'clock we had lunch consisting of sandwiches, which we ate hungrily. We always had plenty of fruit with us. Afterwards we would splash about in the sea, sunbathe and play rough games with other boys we had met.

Mother was quick at engaging in conversation with other signore (ladies) sitting under their beach umbrellas close by. Any trivial topic could switch them on. Since they were not in the habit of reading, or had no time for it, they excelled at gossip and were inquisitive and always ready to exchange personal experiences and novelties. When not on holiday, their husbands, children, domestic tasks and everyday problems kept these housewives fully occupied, so they had no time for anything else. Perhaps they might have a casual chat with the people next door, or with their visitors, distant relatives or close friends when they bumped into them after Sunday Mass – but that was that. Usually, then, they had no opportunity for long chats – however, now that they were on the beach for a few hours, just keeping an eye on their excited children playing at the edge of the sea, they could let themselves go! Some of these housewives' chats on the beach seemed to drag on endlessly.

But one could understand it; after all, when their husbands came home after work, they were hungry and worn out. They had neither the time nor the energy for a romantic, loving conversation, such as they used to have when they were courting the young, attractive girlfriends to whom they were now married. Most of these housewives had lost their good looks and were now fat and wrinkled. Some, indeed, had been transformed into bags of flabby flesh.

Conversations at home were strictly limited to domestic affairs, and when husbands made love to them, it was merely a physical act which, in many instances, the worn-out wives no longer enjoyed. How could they, especially if they had half a dozen children to look after and had to be very careful with their limited spending money?

These housewives talking on the beach were eager to discover what went on in one another's families. In the heat of conversation, they often gave vent to their feelings and made no secret of their domestic affairs. They felt a strong urge to confide in one another without constraint, and at the end of their conversation, each had a fair idea of what went on in the other's family.

A couple of metres away from our beach umbrella was signora Pupa, with her sister and cheerful friends. She was an attractive young woman, perhaps in her early thirties. *Pupa* means 'doll' in English. Whether Pupa was her name or nickname, it's hard to say. She, her sister and her young friends spent many hours of the day under two beach umbrellas which were erected next to our own.

Signora Pupa was shapely and slender and had short dark hair parted in the middle. She had large sensitive brown eyes, a small straight nose, a voluptuous mouth and a peachy complexion. She certainly had sex appeal, and many men found her desirable.

Signora Pupa and her friends, besides bathing, passed the time chatting, telling jokes and smoking cheap cigarettes; this suggested that they were not very well off. Yet they gave the impression of being refined people by the way they spoke and acted. Perhaps they were pretending to be survivors of an impoverished nobility? Had they had the means, they obviously would have chosen a more refined holiday resort instead of Gerolomini.

At that time ordinary women did not smoke; only eccentric ones did, and those who were eager to show that they were emancipated. When signora Pupa and her friends were tired of playing cards, they would engage in conversation, discussing the news, the films they had seen, and so on. Sometimes they argued in a friendly way. She and her sister, who was also an attractive woman, sang some romantic songs. Signora Pupa had a most distinctive sensual voice and could sing like a professional. Whenever she did so, a crowd of bathers clustered round her beach umbrellas. Sometimes two or three male bathers would approach her and ask, 'Signora Pupa, will you sing for us, please?'

We wondered if signora Pupa was an actress or a film star.

One afternoon, while she and her friends were busily chatting and laughing, I wrapped myself up in my elder sister's *accappatoio* (bathrobe), which covered me completely. It looked as if I had cloaked myself in a sack. Suddenly I was seized by a spirit of mischief and rolled to and fro on the beach in the vicinity of signora Pupa and her friends. I rolled about vigorously, turned somersaults, and made weird raucous noises.

'*Cos'è! Cos'è!*' (What's that! What's that!) screamed signora Pupa and her friends as they panicked and ran away.

Mother was not scared at my antics, for she knew that I had wrapped myself up in the bathrobe, though she hadn't the faintest idea of my intentions. But when she heard the strange noises I made and saw signora Pupa and her friends fleeing in panic, she was greatly amused and couldn't stop laughing. Later, when signora Pupa and her friends returned to their beach umbrellas, she apologised for my bad behaviour. Still a little shaken, signora Pupa and her friends resumed playing cards and smoking their cheap cigarettes. I don't think that they ever forgave me for having frightened them so much!

Sometime during the holiday we had a photo taken alongside a fisherman's boat stationed on the beach. The photographer placed us in a line according to our ages. My elder sister came first, then Vince and Saverio sitting on a boat (Saverio was older than Vince); I was next, and then came Tony, Giuseppe, Mary, Fortuna, Immacolata, Damiano and Teresa.

Mother intended to send the photo to Father to remind him of the large family to whom his remittances were indispensable. Perhaps she hoped that the photograph would prick his conscience and help him to behave himself and not get hooked on one of those young, alluring Javanese girls who were only too ready to gratify the whims of Europeans.

Every day we left the beach at about 3.00 p.m. and walked home. It was still hot and sunny when we arrived, so before doing anything else, we had at least an hour's siesta. Later, Mother and my sister Carmen prepared a quick meal. Most of the time we had spaghetti with the sauce of whelks or mussels stewed in fresh tomatoes and olive oil, flavoured with garlic, basil and parsley. We usually had fried or stewed fish for the second course, with a side salad of lettuce, spring onions, celery and tomatoes, dressed with olive oil and lemon juice. We drank a litre of wine and ended the meal with fresh fruit.

Owing to the heat, there were a lot of flies buzzing around. The strong scent of soil and vegetation permeated the air. My mother and sister had to be very careful to keep the flies away and prevent them from diving into the sauce or anything else they were cooking.

Around seven o'clock we were ready for our evening stroll along the seashore. We walked about a kilometre to the city of Pozzuoli, which was part of a Greek colony founded between the seventh and sixth century BC. Later it became a Roman town known as Puteoli.

Pozzuoli had a small port. There was a daily ferry service to the islands of Ischia, Procida and other places. I think the port was used mainly by fishermen who ventured beyond the harbour. The fish of Pozzuoli were in demand for their high quality. It had a small public park, but the area near the port was infested with flies, probably because of its fishing activity. The land closest to the sea was hilly, and it was here that the villas and best buildings of the town were situated. They were surrounded by orchards, kitchen gardens, vineyards, many pine trees, shrubs and bushy spots where prickly pears grew abundantly.

We strolled to Pozzuoli every night with other holiday-makers. After all, there were no better places to go to. Tourists went to Pozzuoli to visit its Roman amphitheatre, Saint Gennaro's shrine (Saint Gennaro is the patron saint of Naples), and the nearby Solfatara, a sulphurous hot mud volcano which reaches a temperature of 160 degrees. They also travelled a few kilometres further and visited Torregaveta, Baia, Cuma and other towns originally colonised by the Greeks.

On our way home, if it was too early to retire, we would sit for an hour or two on the beach. We listened to the lulling of the waves and the water lapping against the rocks. We gazed at the phosphorescent sea with the silvery reflection of the moonlight, the lighthouses of the harbour, and contemplated the mysterious starry sky. Everything was awesome and entrancing. Fishing boats, with petrol lamps at their bows, glided silently over that seemingly oily surface. They hoped to catch octopuses, which are part of the Neapolitan diet. Octopus-catching is a job done at night. These creatures, attracted by the light of the lamps, rise to the surface and are caught in nets on the end of long poles.

We always ate a few prickly pears and a couple of refreshing melons before we went to bed. We could buy them so cheaply there.

At the back of our flat was a chain of hills which stretched for many kilometres along the coast. A steam train puffed its way towards the north of the peninsula. It emerged whistling from a tunnel and almost immediately disappeared into the next one.

Cicadas, crickets and other insects indulged in their ceaseless serenades during the night. I was enchanted by the noise they made; it never failed to lull me into deep, peaceful sleep.

Our grandfathers came in turn to visit us for the day. It was a chance in their otherwise uneventful lives to go on a journey not too far from their homes. Also it kept them in touch with us and the sea. They dined with us in our flat and relished the savoury fish of Pozzuoli.

They enjoyed the local fresh figs, too, which we had for breakfast every morning and looked forward to a few glasses of Pozzuoli wine. They were disappointed when they tasted it, thinking that it had been adulterated and was wine only by name: 'This wine has been made with the stick,' they commented. This meant that the wine shop owners, to make more profit than usual, had mixed local wine with other wines of inferior quality. Sometimes they might even add other ingredients and stir them all up with a stick.

I don't think that the few wine shops of Gerolomini did well in wintertime, when there were no holiday-makers. They had to make the most of it during the summer season and earn enough money to see them through the year. It seemed that they were prepared to resort to any expedient to exploit holiday-makers and day visitors. Since the people they exploited stayed only a few days or weeks, they didn't complain. Besides, what was the use of complaining when nobody did anything about it?

The rest of 1933 went by without any major happening. Saverio, Vince and I were still pretending to study by ourselves, but we did this in such a disorganised way that it was getting us nowhere. We badly needed a good tutor, a strong willpower and perseverance. Being young, we were exposed to all kinds of temptation. We found the cinema very stimulating and revealing. We acquired some useful knowledge, but many of the films had a corrupting tendency. Being so young, we were unable to discriminate between the films which were informative and those which were misleading. However, we soon became addicted to cinema-going.

About the beginning of March 1934, we received a letter from Father informing us that he had fixed a passage for Saverio to go to Java. Saverio was very excited; a new chapter of his life would soon begin. He would be of great help to Father, who was no longer as strong as he had been before his kidney operation. Saverio would have his chance to prove himself – to work, earn money for the first time in his life and acquire some worldly experience.

In April 1934 we went to see him off at the port of Naples, where he embarked on the five-week voyage to Java. Since Saverio did not speak any foreign languages and was on his first voyage, Father had arranged for his passage on the Italian cargo ship *Sumatra*. He knew one of the ship's stokers, whose name was Theodore. He promised to keep an eye on Saverio. The ship had to call at several ports on its way to Java, which is why it took so long to get there.

Saverio sent us cards from foreign ports. He told us that the voyage was going well and that he had made friends aboard with seamen who were cheerful fellows, always ready for a joke.

When the seamen landed for a few hours at one of the foreign ports, some of them undoubtedly went to visit prostitutes. I don't think Saverio joined those seeking the gratification of the flesh. Almost certainly, signor Theodore would have warned him to keep away from the company of lecherous seamen in search of reckless pleasure ashore.

Vince was a little disappointed that his presence in Java was not required yet. He would have liked going there, exploring the tropics and making love to Javanese girls. Unfortunately he still had to wait for some years before he was able to do so.

Meanwhile, Mussolini appeared to be putting up a good show in our country. He seemed to be boosting our economy. He encouraged art, architecture and literature – provided that these reflected a certain Fascist style or influence. He stimulated food production which was so badly needed for our fast growing population. He tried to make our civil service work efficiently and our trains run on time. He approved and financed the Pontini Marsh Reclamation Scheme. He signed the Laterano Treaty with the Vatican, making the teaching of the Roman Catholic religion compulsory in our schools. He was also building up our merchant shipping, navy, and air force. The military build-up had gone on since 1932. It was designed, of course, for the attack on Abyssinia a few years later.

Mussolini never did anything, however, to improve the workers' living conditions. The reality was that they were nothing but slaves under the Fascist regime and our system of capitalism. Although there was discontent and poverty among the workers and the middle class, some, aware of what our dictator was trying to achieve for our country, stopped hating him and were gradually converted to his cause. They hoped that one day he would really succeed in making Italy a great and prosperous country, so that all Italians, rich and poor, would benefit from his achievements.

Gullible people, brainwashed by the extravagant propaganda: '*Il Duce ha sempre ragione*' (The Duce is always right), were unable to envisage that one day, this demigod would plunge our poor Italy into a disastrous adventure.

18

Our religious celebrations

From Easter to autumn, we had three great local celebrations: Corpus Christi, the feast of the Sacred Hearts and our patron saints, Cosma and Damiano. The feast of the Sacred Hearts was the chapel's celebration, while Corpus Christi and our patron saints were the parish church's celebrations.

At the Sacred Hearts celebration, whole streets near the chapel were decorated with flags, festoons and arches. The arches were set astride the streets and contained hundreds of colourful bulbs, which were switched on soon after dusk and lasted till midnight to give a festive atmosphere.

At the patron saints' celebration, the illumination was extended to the whole town, and each celebration went on for two or three days. The streets were flanked with numerous stalls selling toys, balloons, streamers, nuts, nougat and candy. A brass band played at night on a rostrum erected on the square near the parish church.

The celebrations always attracted hundreds of visitors from nearby towns. Our streets were packed at night, and when people were tired of walking and chatting, they gathered in the brightly illuminated area, where the brass band played arias from operas and melodies by our famous composers.

There was a certain rivalry between the parish church and the chapel; each seemed to have its sphere of influence and, during their celebrations, they tried to outdo each other. They had no money, but they always found a way of raising it somehow to honour their saints. They also felt that it would give poor people the chance to join in the festivities and forget about their hardship and misery. To raise the money, the priests appointed a commission formed of reputable and influential people, who went from house to house collecting from those who were likely to contribute towards the cost of the festivities.

On such occasions we had very impressive processions: parades of statues of saints, flags, pennants and two brass bands, one at the head and the other at the tail of a procession, playing religious tunes. A procession could be about a kilometre long, and it took three quarters of an hour to pass through our streets, which were lined with a dense crowd of our townsfolk and visitors.

Each statue, depending on its weight and size, was carried on the shoulders of four or more sturdy men. A presence of *carabinieri* and constables, in their flamboyant uniforms, flanked the main section of the procession, which included the dignitaries as well as the statue of the saint for whom the procession was being made.

The main road was closed to traffic. Windows and balconies alongside the route of the procession were decorated with colourful carpets, handmade lace and flowers. The occupants of the balconies watched the procession passing by and let a rain of petals, fragrant flowers and confetti fall on the statue of the celebrated saint. Often the statue stood for a few minutes in front of a flat or a building where someone was seriously ill. Some people knelt down and prayed while the statue faced that particular building. One of the priests would bless the place, and as he did so, relatives and friends of the sick person would often be moved to tears.

Quite a number of inhabitants along the route donated banknotes, which stewards would then pin to the garments of the donors' favourite saints.

Every now and then, as the procession passed a shrine consisting of the statue of a saint – Saint Antony of Padua, a miraculous Madonna or some other saint whom local people especially worshipped – the community nearby saluted its approach with a firework display.

Some people loved having a shrine of their favourite saint, at which they could worship at any time during the day as they went about their business. They would stop for a moment, say a prayer and then walk on. They also raised money – a few coins that poor people would put in a box when they were able to do so. They could spend this money on firecrackers, whenever a procession was on.

A number of confraternities from nearby small towns were invited to participate in the processions. Each confraternity paraded with its tall triangular standard, bearing its insignia and held outstretched by two boys walking behind it. Its members dressed elegantly in black suits, white shirts, bow ties and white gloves and moved along slowly in a dignified manner after their standard. The confraternities which performed better than the others were awarded first, second and third prizes.

The celebrations culminated on the last night with a brilliant firework display which lit up the sky and eclipsed its twinkling stars.

The procession and the illuminations; the brass bands and the fireworks; the stalls selling toys, balloons, candy, doughnuts and nougat – all contributed to a thrilling event that people couldn't forget, and they eagerly looked forward to the next festivities.

Apart from religious celebrations, every year we commemorated two great national events: 24 May and 4 November – that is the start and the end of the Great War. On each of these occasions we had a parade through the town where ex-servicemen proudly displayed their medals. They gathered in town and later marched behind their flags. A brass band accompanied them through the main streets, which were adorned with the national flag. They reached a small square in front of the Town Hall and came to a halt. There a bugler played the Last Post. Later the town authorities read the names of our 'glorious fallen' embossed on a white marbled surface outside the Town Hall and placed some garlands there. The ex-servicemen would end the ceremony by singing patriotic songs and proudly marching again through the town amidst tumultuous acclamation.

The Fascists did not participate in our religious processions, for these had no political significance. However, they were welcome like anybody else to join our ceremonies and festivities. Had the Fascists had their way, they would have probably forced our saints to wear black shirts!

The Fascists were always ready to exploit any event to propagate their belief and to brainwash us. During a patriotic manifestation, there was a lot of hailing going on: Hail the King! Hail the army! Hail the ex-servicemen! The Fascists, not to be outdone, shouted: 'Hail *Il Duce*!' They tried very hard indeed to force him down our throats.

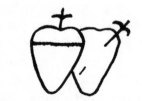

Sacred hearts of Jesus
and Mary fused together.

A standard — each confraternity
had its own insignia.

A confraternity.

19

Saverio is doing well in Java. Vince is taken ill
with pleurisy

In the autumn of 1934, we learned that Saverio was doing well in the East Indies; he seemed to have an acumen for buying and selling imported goods. This good news filled us with joy. No doubt Saverio's success lifted Father's morale, for he was no longer alone in earning money to support his large family; he could rely on Saverio now in every eventuality. Vince and I sniffed Saverio's letters, trying to detect some scent of the islands of Java, Sumatra, Borneo and Celebes, for we too hoped that one day we would be able to go to Java and feast on tropical luxuries. Often we looked at those islands in the atlas – they were so far away and fascinating.

The lands of Africa and Asia sounded so mysterious to us at that time – lands which in past centuries had not deterred European pioneers from challenging the odds and exploring them.

My brothers, the rest of our family and I were not making much academic progress. We were more interested in the lovely sunny weather, what we were going to eat, our friends, local events and what *Il Duce* had in store for us. Like thousands of other Italians we were talkative, but we had not yet acquired the habit of reading. We were not encouraged to do so because we didn't have public libraries and could not afford to buy books. Had we possessed a radio, we could have used it to a certain extent as a means of education.

Mother, being too busy with our domestic problems, could not see the advantage of having a radio for its intellectual stimulus. She could have made an effort and bought one on easy terms. As it happened, we had to wait till 1938, when Saverio decided to buy one.

We were in one of those Italian towns where worldly progress did not make an immediate impact, and because our people had no facilities to learn, they carried on living as usual: a life made up of little intrigues, gossip, argument, passion and laughter. It was just bad luck for us that we had to put up with a way of living that got us nowhere. Our future salvation lay in making an effort to tear ourselves away from that hopeless town and go where we could find work, be industrious and prosper.

During the spring of 1935, Vince was taken ill with a severe attack of pleurisy. Our family doctor charged us fifteen lire for a home visit. As Vince was very sick, the doctor suggested that he should be visited by a top chest specialist called Cicconardi, who had the necessary equipment for a thorough examination. As Dr Cicconardi was also a lecturer, people addressed him as Professor Cicconardi. His fee was 100 lire per visit.

We really couldn't afford him, but we were extremely worried about Vince's health and wanted to get him well at any cost. So one day Mother and my eldest sister, having arranged for an appointment with Dr Cicconardi, wrapped Vince up in warm clothes, hired a taxi and took him to the doctor's surgery, which was situated in a luxurious section of Naples called Parco Margherita. They arrived at the doctor's residence a few minutes early and waited in the sitting-room. Later they were ushered into the surgery.

Dr Cicconardi had a high forehead and looked very intelligent and impressive. He was a man who quickly inspired confidence.

'How old is this boy?' he asked.

'Nearly seventeen,' Mother replied.

Dr Cicconardi asked some more questions while he examined Vince. He peered at Vince's chest through his X-ray apparatus. Then he inserted a syringe into Vince's chest and extracted about half a litre of fluid.

'Just in time to save his life!' Dr Cicconardi exclaimed. 'Another week's delay and I wouldn't have been able to help him.'

He prescribed some drugs. Mother paid his fee and thanked him. Mother, my sister and Vince came back home by taxi. It had been a very expensive day indeed, but Mother didn't complain; she was glad and confident now that Vince would soon recover.

Vince had to rest in bed, in a comfortably warm and ventilated room. Two candles burned day and night in front of the prints of Saint Antony of Padua and our Lady of the Sorrows, where Mother prayed frequently for Vince's recovery.

Mother and my sister nursed him day and night with great love and devotion. They had to change his underwear when he perspired, prepare extra-nourishing meals for him and cheer him up whenever they could. They let his friends come to visit him. Later, when he got a little better, he was allowed to sit in a chair for a few hours during the day and play cards with his friends.

It took over a month of constant care to get him well. He had to visit Dr Cicconardi three times in all, which meant that Mother had to spend 300 lire for his fees. Besides this treatment, good food and medicine also cost us a lot of money. Since we lived on a limited income, we had to make sacrifices to pay for them. Whenever we were sick, Mother would disregard the cost and do anything to help us regain our health. She could find no peace until we were completely well.

20

The Abyssinian War

From about the end of 1934, the Fascists began reminding us of Italy's abortive attempt to conquer Abyssinia at the end of the nineteenth century. At that time a force of 20,000 men under the command of General Barrettieri was sent there. They had been greatly outnumbered by Abyssinian warriors and had suffered heavy losses – in fact 8,000 of our soldiers were massacred at Adowa. As a result of this disaster, Italy had to give up all hope of conquering that country.

Feeling strong and bold now, the Fascists revived the Abyssinian question. They said they wanted to avenge the deaths of those Italian 'heroes'. The Fascist campaign gradually spread throughout the whole of Italy and aroused nationalistic feelings which took people's minds away from their domestic tribulations.

The campaign continued persistently and tried to persuade us that, by conquering Abyssinia, thousands of kilometres away, we were going to enjoy a better standard of living some time in the future. Besides this, our military achievement, they said, would enhance our prestige in the eyes of other countries.

During 1935 the British and the French, especially, were determined to thwart Mussolini's ambition to conquer Abyssinia. However, he defiantly went ahead and made preparations to invade. He called to arms thousands of men in their late twenties and early thirties who had already served as conscripts.

Vast numbers of unemployed young men volunteered to join the army. They received twenty lire per day. At that time it was equivalent to the daily pay of a skilled worker. These men wore impressive uniforms and, while waiting to embark for Africa, swaggered round our towns, squandering their money in restaurants, bars, cinemas and brothels. They certainly put on a good show.

They seemed jolly, handsome, prosperous and full of vitality.

The poor wretched men who had to toil long and hard for a crust of bread envied these young, flamboyant soldiers bound for Africa. Unfortunately only those who were very fit were eligible to join them.

In the afternoon of 2 October 1935, sirens wailed all over Italy, as if we were expecting a huge air attack. Guns of warships anchored in the harbour of Naples boomed and military aircraft flew overhead. People in the streets, alarmed and surprised, scattered in all directions. These were signals that we had been warned of days and weeks previously. When this happened, Blackshirts and the rest of the Italian population were to assemble in the main squares of our towns and listen by radio to what Mussolini had to tell them.

The dictator was eloquent and full of bluster as he delivered his historic speech from the famous Venice Palace in Rome. He announced to the crowd gathered there that the Abyssinian conflict had begun, and that the economic sanctions applied against Italy would not deter him from carrying on with his great military campaign.

People had no choice but to put up with the dictator's decisions; nobody would dare to oppose him. So he decided and went ahead, fully convinced that whatever he did was right and undisputed.

About a quarter of a million soldiers were sent abroad to fight the costly Abyssinian war. Wives and mothers were seriously concerned for the safety of their husbands and sons, and they prayed fervently that the war would not end in tragedy as the Italian campaign of 1896 had done.

I was visiting some friends in Naples that day when the sirens wailed and the warships' guns boomed. I saw hundreds of people who, having stopped work, were hurrying through streets and lanes or jumping on public transport, trying to get home as quickly as possible.

I had never witnessed such an event before – it was a kind of stampede – I was awe-struck. I was fifteen when this occurred and was a member of a Fascist organisation called *Avanguardista* (avant-gardist). Soon after the wailing of the sirens, I was supposed to be wearing my *Avanguardista* uniform and playing a drum on one of the street corners of our town. The drum had been lent to me by the Fascists a couple of weeks before this day of national upheaval. I was very angry indeed because, when the alarm came, I was in Naples, and unable to play my part in that historic and dramatic hour.

I caught the tram to go home, but most of the trams were very old, only fit for the scrap heap. It was impossible to make them go fast, especially when passengers were packed in like sardines. The tram coughed, spat, got all worked up and hardly made any progress. I almost foamed with rage and frustration. How could I get home quickly, wear my black shirt and join my comrades? The tram moved along like a snail, especially when it was toiling uphill; then it had to stop several times, because its motor protested with sporadic bangs and then refused to budge.

'This bloody tram has had it,' shouted a number of exasperated passengers. 'Let's push it, otherwise we won't be able to go home.'

Besides the appalling performance of our tram, the main road was heavily congested with traffic. I could hardly control my anger. I yearned to be in uniform and play my drum, which would have made me feel important. *Il Duce* certainly needed my support, and he was telling us that the war with Abyssinia had begun.

It took the tram over an hour to get to the vicinity of my home. It reached a town called Miano and could not proceed any further. I got off and ran the kilometre or so to my home. I was gasping for breath, my chest ached, my lungs were on the verge of bursting. The main street, Corso Umberto Primo, which ran alongside our two balconies, was crammed with Blackshirts gathered behind their flags and pennants. They were still listening to *Il Duce*'s speech on the radio when I arrived at my house. Mother let me in, but she was very concerned when she noticed that I was puffing and gasping for breath like an asthmatic.

'What's the matter with you? Are you sick?' she asked.

'No, I'm not,' I replied, but I was still breathing with difficulty. 'I've been running.'

'Sit down, have a rest,' she ordered me. I obeyed.

Having rested for a minute or two, I rushed to the wardrobe, but my uniform and my drum were missing!

'The Fascists were looking for you,' Mother said, 'but you weren't here, so your brother Tony put on your uniform and took the drum with him.'

I was furious for being late and resentful towards Tony. Previously I had never allowed him to wear my uniform – he could not even touch it; but now he was swaggering in it, while I badly wanted to wear it. Still seething with rage, I rushed downstairs, went out in the street and searched for Tony in the dense crowd. After a few minutes I found him, seized him by his arm and dragged him home.

'Hurry up,' I shouted menacingly. He meekly obeyed, for he knew that when I was in a fit of temper I wouldn't hesitate to treat him roughly. I dressed up rapidly and soon felt as if I were a general or *Il Duce*'s second-in-command.

In no time I was among my comrades who were still gathered in the main street, and in unison with them I shouted, '*Viva Il Duce!*' We sang Fascist songs. Later our superiors, dressed in flamboyant uniforms, packed us into trams that took us to the city of Naples. Once there we marched for a couple of kilometres and showed our patriotic feelings by praising *Il Duce* and singing. We endeavoured to make an impression on a poor and densely populated section of Naples.

I returned home late, exhausted, hungry and with a raucous voice. I wolfed down the frugal supper which Mother had kept warm for me in the oven and then I went to bed. I dreamed of our majestic *Duce* – in his dictatorial pose – on the balcony of Venice Palace and hailed by the crowd on the square below. They boisterously acclaimed our attack on Abyssinia. Was it perhaps the first step forward towards that greatness the Fascists and *Il Duce* so badly wanted?

During the following days, weeks and months the attention of the Italians was devoted to the progress of the war. Most people seldom bought a newspaper but when there was exciting news from the front, the sales of our daily shot up dramatically. We ourselves did not buy the newspaper; we learned about the news from what we overheard by chance, or from what we could gather from newspapers on display outside newsagents' shops. Everybody, literate or illiterate, was interested in the news.

Newspaper vendors shouted at the top of their voices about our military successes such as the capture of an Abyssinian town, the surrender of a large Abyssinian Army unit and so on. Victory after victory boosted our morale. People were jubilant that our armies, under the command of Generals Badoglio and Graziani, were making great progress. Everybody, Fascist or not, became patriotic overnight. They praised the army, our generals and *Il Duce* who was the promoter of the campaign.

Wherever I went, people were enthusiastic about our victories. Students saluted every major military feat by walking out of their classrooms or university lecture halls, assembling and staging patriotic demonstrations through the main streets of our cities.

The Italians could not be indifferent – all those victories seemed too good to be true. Under this influence, patriotism mounted very high. Who could perceive or envisage that about seven years after the glorious and costly Abyssinian campaign, our patriotism and all our military achievements would end in ruins?

While our army was doing well in Abyssinia, Mussolini was overjoyed and had something to boast about. No doubt he thought that we were invincible and adequately equipped to avenge the loss of the Roman Empire about 1,500 years before.

When the Italian Army attacked Abyssinia, the League of Nations applied economic sanctions against Italy, and we had to pay in gold to get military supplies through the Suez Canal. Bearing this in mind, the Fascists organised a ritual ceremony called 'Gold to the Fatherland'. They assembled with their brass bands, flags and banners in front of the Town Halls, where married women paraded ceremoniously. As they did so, one by one, they took their gold wedding rings off their fingers and proudly donated them to the fatherland. We all applauded their patriotic gesture and were deeply touched by it. They had given to their country what was precious to them – a symbol of love, fidelity and devotion to their husbands and families. In exchange, they obtained rings made of base metal.

On 5 May 1936, after a campaign of seven months and three days, Marshal Badoglio, who had been promoted from general presumably as a reward for his victorious campaign, entered Addis Ababa triumphantly. This brought about the conclusion of the Abyssinian war. There was a great national celebration all over our country. *Il Duce* spoke again to the dense crowd amassed on the square below Venice Palace. He stated categorically: 'The Italian people have conquered an empire with their blood. They will be ready to defend it against anybody.'

After the Abyssinian war, the Fascists became more arrogant and boisterous; it looked as if they were ready to challenge the whole world. The misery of poor people increased, the cost of living went up, while wages and salaries were static. Sicknesses raged, afflicting downtrodden workers who could hardly provide themselves with basic necessities. They were supposed to look after their large families, but how could they do so without nourishing food and free medical assistance? Since they could not afford to buy good food and medical care, mortality, especially among young children and elderly people, was alarming. We had few modern hospitals; hardly any new ones were built. The conditions of our people were ignored, yet Mussolini was wasting our meagre resources on Abyssinia. We conquered a white elephant which made us feel great, but left us with empty hands; our treasury was in dire financial straits. At the end of the war it was costing us a fortune to keep an army there. Most of our colonies seemed to be nothing but liabilities, yet the Fascist propaganda made us wallow in a false glory which could only aggravate our misery.

21

Our maternal grandfather dies. A yarn about a King of Naples and a King of Spain. Dopolavoro *(after-work club)*

Towards the end of 1935 my maternal grandfather, Vincenzo Saccone, who was about seventy-seven, died. He had married twice. His first wife, Giuseppina Giacometti, died when my mother was still a little girl – not yet ten. His second wife, Caroline, who was not too gentle with my mother, died before the end of the Great War.

Grandfather was a coachman. As long as horse-drawn cabs were in demand he made a meagre living. He started work early in the morning and drove his cab to Naples, where his cab stand was to be found outside the central railway station. When he did well he used to finish work fairly early, otherwise he would knock off after eight o'clock.

In 1930 he retired, but had to depend on us for support. Mother even gave him a few coins to enable him to buy tobacco for his pipe. Since we were a large family, he must have felt that he was a burden to us, and perhaps unwanted. Had he been living on his own means, I think he would have lived longer.

Having wasted a lot of time participating in various patriotic demonstrations during the Abyssinian war, Vince and I simply had to convince Mother that we were getting on with our intermediate studies.

We were young and did not have to worry about our keep. We did not see the necessity of exerting ourselves, so any activity was subordinate to our feelings of like or dislike. We indulged ourselves, spending many hours of the day in the company of idle friends, whose future was precarious and whose company was a hindrance to our progress. Mother, busy with her chores and the rest of her large family, could not always bother or be concerned about how we passed our time, as long as we did not get involved in any mischievous practices detrimental to the dignity of our family.

At this stage, with Father's monthly remittance, we were better off than many people, so to a certain extent we were regarded as well-to-do, and I personally felt very cocky about it.

Now Vince and I and our respective friends went for long walks through the lovely countryside at the edge of our small town. Vince was about eighteen. Being two years older, he assumed that he was more knowledgeable than me! He was garrulous and very keen to express his views in an imposing manner, so whenever we were together he did the talking and I the listening. Because of his overbearing and professorial attitude, I was inhibited and reluctant to express my own views, and inclined to be taciturn. We were rather opposite characters – I was shy and somewhat introverted, he bold and extroverted. Each of us had his own friends. When we were walking with them, we indulged in idle talk; we criticised someone showing off, gossiped about the love affairs of people we knew, praised the beauty of glamorous girls and passed comments on movies we had recently seen, or on world events. Our topics of conversation were frequently mere repetitions of what we had been talking about on previous days, so we really were getting no wiser; we were just passing the time with trivial nonsense.

At midday Vince and I came back home from our walks with a good appetite; we could have devoured a donkey. Since there was no donkey available, we gobbled down our main meal which consisted of pasta or minestrone, followed by a not very convincing portion of fish, or an imperceptible piece of meat. We invariably ended our meal with some fruit of the season which, as Mother said, would help us to digest our 'substantial' repast. The evening meal consisted of sandwiches, or a chunk of bread with a meticulously thin-cut slice of cheese, or perhaps vegetable soup and maybe a sliver of liver. There was never a lack of appetite in our family. We were young and full of vim and vigour, and would have asked for a second helping, but it was not always available. Mother occasionally disregarded our financial problems and treated us to some rare delicacy; then we feasted in anticipation before the meal and savoured its taste for a long time afterwards.

We all enjoyed *pasta e fagioli* (pasta with haricot beans), which was then a very popular Neapolitan dish and very satisfying indeed.

Nowadays Italy is considered a prosperous country – a prosperity that does not always convince many older Italians – and some Neapolitans, who have progressed financially, have become snobs. They seem to have forgotten about the homely goodness of *pasta e fagioli* and have become more choosy. Now they gorge themselves with an excess of fish and meat which, no doubt, does them more harm than good.

The inconvenience of eating *pasta e fagioli* is that if the *fagioli* (beans) are not cooked properly, they will cause flatulence. Street urchins, whose main meal of the day this was, broke wind frequently and made jokes about it. In cold weather, when they huddled up together, they had the touching belief that breaking wind helped them to keep warm.

These street urchins sometimes told this story: 'One day a Neapolitan King was invited to visit Spain. Soon after a lavish court banquet given in his honour, the Spanish King started belching. After each belch, with a sense of gratification he declaimed, "Greatness of Spain!" The Neapolitan King was revolted but for politeness' sake, did not remonstrate.

'A month later the Spanish King was invited to visit Naples. The Neapolitan King invited a half-dozen street urchins to the court banquet given in his honour. The night before the banquet, the Neapolitan King fed the street urchins on *pasta e fagioli*, but the *fagioli* had deliberately not been cooked properly.

'A few hours before the banquet was due to start, the urchins were dressed in princely robes, so they looked like young illustrious aristocrats. They were taught table manners and ordered not to answer when they were spoken to, but just to smile and bow. For some reason, women were excluded from this banquet; they were feasting separately with the Queen of Naples.

'While the banquet was on, at every signal of the King of Naples, the urchins answered by breaking wind. The Spanish King was shocked and bewildered. The Neapolitan King just laughed derisively as he declaimed again and again, "Greatness of Naples!" '

Vince and I spent much time strolling through the countryside. We did not bother reading anything, except our textbooks, and when we did so, we read them grudgingly. During these rural peregrinations of ours, we wore out the soles of our shoes – which helped to keep our family cobbler busy.

We had far too many cobblers in our town. They deliberately

used poor quality leather to replace our worn-out soles, so that we would need their services frequently. Since we were a large family, we were our cobbler's best customers; he almost made a living out of us.

There was a kind of workers' recreational club called *Dopolavoro* (after-work club) which was a Fascist institution. Its membership fee was ten lire a year. The club building consisted of a four-room ground-floor flat situated on one side of Corso Umberto Primo which today is called Corso Secondigliano. It was a very busy road swarming with every kind of vehicle, especially trailers which transported goods from North to South Italy.

The members, when the weather was warm and sunny, used to sit outside the club where they chatted or watched people and the traffic passing by.

On Sundays, most of the members wore their best suits, but as they sat outside the club, their eyes were focused on elegantly dressed girls going to Mass. The girls were usually in the company of their mothers, or other members of their families. Girls of decent families never went out alone; they felt embarrassed by the stares of lustful men.

Attractive girls walking past, with long silky hair and undulating bodies, were a fascinating spectacle for those randy men. The rhythmic movement of their legs, their dancing bosoms and buttocks sent these men wild with desire.

'My word!' they would cry out, 'What bosoms! What buttocks! I would give my right arm to suckle those juicy breasts.'

If a woman was not so young, but still had some sex appeal, then these men might exclaim: 'Still good for banging!'

Those who frequented the *Dopolavoro* were mainly labourers and some unemployed men. The latter were probably supported by working members of their families. There were also a few artisans, clerks and a couple of professional men. The members passed the time playing cards, billiards, listening to the radio and talking, but they were not allowed to criticise the Fascists and *Il Duce*. The club was really just a meeting place for men who could afford nothing better.

Because of the lack of opportunities in our town, people aged prematurely and became mentally sterile. Had there been free adult

101

education, they would have had a second chance to learn, enrich their lives and the life of our country.

Generally it was unthinkable for an adult to go back to school. Since they were not used to studying, they would have found it extremely hard to read and learn, so they did not try; they were defeated by their negative attitude before they attempted any such thing as higher education. Having a large family, financial problems and being undernourished were strong deterrents, so people had neither the disposition nor the energy to acquire an education.

Vince and I, although we were not members of the club, went there to meet friends. I personally did not like that smoky place, especially in winter, when it was too cold to sit outside. Besides, it did not offer me any mental stimulus. The cinema was my greatest interest at that time.

22

La Signora *(The Lady)*

During summer we always welcomed the annual church festivities, which meant a lot to ordinary people. These traditions – processions through the town, illuminations at night, brass bands playing in the main square and fireworks – brought some joy to our poor people, whose quality of life was sad indeed and even tragic at times.

Our Sundays were distinctively different from the other days of the week; in warm weather the streets were always crowded. Some people went to Mass, others for a walk, or stopped outside coffee-houses and sipped their *cappuccini*.

The churches were invariably packed, especially for the one o'clock Mass. People went to Mass to pray, to fulfil an obligation, to meet acquaintances and friends or to admire the fashionable clothes of the well-to-do. Young men went to Mass with the intention of wooing girls.

Most of the girls a little higher up the social scale went out on Sunday mornings and on other special occasions. Prospective lovers had to be brave. If an aspiring Romeo was not bold enough to climb up to his Juliet's balcony, he might have to wait a whole week before he was able to see her again.

Occasionally, wooers ventured to serenade their would-be sweethearts. Unfortunately some of these romances came to an abrupt end when bucketfuls of water were poured over them. I knew a persistent wooer, bent at any cost on serenading a girl with whom he had fallen in love. He ended up in hospital with rifle pellets lodged in his posterior.

Walking along the narrow streets, one's nostrils would be greeted by the pungent odour of the Sunday ragout, which always made the mouth water. Sunday dinner, according to various possibilities, could be simple, sumptuous or an orgy. In some instances members of an extended family with several husbands, wives and children came together. They brought food with them, so dinner consisted of several dishes and lasted for hours.

In the afternoons and evenings people usually went for a walk, which was the cheapest kind of recreation. Often a group of teenage boys would chase a similar number of girls. Maybe one of the boys would approach a girl he found attractive and say: '*Signorina, posso farvi una preghiera?*' (Miss, excuse me, may I?)

The girl would reply: '*La preghiera la fate nella chiesa.*' (Go and find somebody else!)

The boy would say: '*La preghiera nella chiesa già l'ho fatta, ma voi che siete una madonnina la faccio anche a voi.*' (I've done that, but I want to talk to you.)

The girl, flattered and interested in what her wooer had to say, would perhaps reply: '*Impertinente! Non fate lo spasimante!*' (Oh you cheeky thing!)

The wooed girl apparently showed no interest in her pursuer, but if she really liked him, she heard what he had to tell her.

'From the first time I saw you,' the boy would say, 'I fell in love with you and have never stopped thinking of you. I've just longed for this opportunity to talk to you and ask whether you will allow me to be your special boyfriend.'

Perhaps the girl, feeling a little embarrassed, would say: 'I've never had a boyfriend. I am still too young, and my parents wouldn't like it.'

At that time, teenage girls were not permitted to have boy companions without their parents' approval. Many girls had boyfriends secretly, and perhaps their parents unofficially knew about it. They did not object if the boyfriends came from good families; there was the chance then that their daughters would eventually marry some rich or eligible young men.

One day, when I was fourteen, I plucked up courage and approached a good-looking girl of my own age whose name was Anita. As I was very shy and nervous about pouring out my romantic feelings to her, I prepared my declaration of love in advance and learned it by heart. Anita was so charmed by my words that she unhesitatingly consented to become my girlfriend. I felt as if I had captured a fortress and was a kind of Casanova, ready to win the hearts of a myriad of attractive women. My romance did not last long because my girlfriend and her family were emigrating to South America, where her father worked and decided to settle down.

On Saturdays and Sundays at that time a few prostitutes from the city hung around dark and secluded spots at the edge of the town. One of these spots was *Fosso del Lupo* (Wolf's Ditch) where the prostitutes did brisk trade.

One of the prostitutes was known as *La Signora* (The Lady). She was a middle-aged woman who looked more like a cow than the famous seductress 'Helen of Troy'.

I am still perplexed at the attitude of those men who ventured to 'bang' *La Signora*. They were probably sex-starved men who could not afford to visit brothels and badly wanted a woman. However *La Signora* was hardly a woman; she was more like a monster. She hired her body cheaply – half a lira for a massage, one lira for a banging, two lira for a double and three lira for an orgy, provided that this did not exceed half an hour. She had a luminous clock at hand, and when the time was up, she abruptly rejected her once ecstatic but now frustrated customer! Later she wiped herself down with a dirty rag and was ready for the next amorous man. Payment had to be made in advance. She pocketed the money before letting men have a taste of her honey.

Some teenagers, who were too young to be admitted to brothels and longed to experience the joy of sex, visited *La Signora*. These boys were either ignorant that they were running a great risk of catching venereal disease, or perhaps they were simply reckless.

La Signora wanted to get on with her business – her time was money – so if one of her customers was too slow to reach an orgasm, she would nag him: 'Come on, come on, *rammollito* (old man), you're too bloody slow!' This telling off certainly made such men nervous and spoiled their joyful banging.

If the unsatisfied man demanded his money back for service not rendered to his requirements, it was likely that the transaction would end in a vociferous altercation.

'If you can't do it, it isn't my bloody fault,' *La Signora* would shout. 'If you're impotent, don't waste my time; I can't help you. Go, ... see a doctor!'

'Me impotent! Me impotent! I'm not impotent!' the angry customer would shout back. 'You bloody *puttana* (prostitute), you're too rough. I can't make love when I'm under pressure; it puts me off. Now give me my money back.'

La Signora was tough, as well as crafty, and was quite accustomed to such scenes which were a normal part of her trade. But if a customer was too hot to handle, she didn't try to exasperate him, but simply let him have his way, otherwise she would have run the risk of being beaten up, and even robbed of her takings.

La Signora would do well at the weekends and, whenever she did, she usually had a rest for as long as her hard-earned money lasted.

Unchecked prostitution was risky indeed; it caused many afflictions and much misery, especially when teenagers caught gonorrhoea or syphilis. They could go to hospital for treatment, but many mistrusted hospitals and sought private treatment, which was costly. If a husband or son contracted venereal disease, it often caused untold financial hardship to the family concerned if it had a limited income, not to mention the embarrassment and shame.

Local authorities knew what was going on, but did little or nothing to get rid of the prostitutes. I would not be surprised if those who were supposed to inspect the red light area were bribed and simply let sleeping dogs lie.

I learned indirectly that my brother Vince had more than once fallen into the seductive arms of *La Signora*. I was amazed at his unexpected and reckless behaviour: how could he? How could he have made love to such a dirty tart? Didn't he know that he was playing with fire: putting his health at risk, to say nothing of the other serious consequences? Had he caught a venereal disease, it would have caused us worries, anxiety and a struggle to foot the bill.

23

Father and Saverio return from Java for a long summer holiday

The end of 1936 passed quietly. With the recent conquest of Abyssinia, 1936 had been a memorable year for *Il Duce* and Italy. He was at the helm of our country, which was still being shaken by waves of foreign opposition on account of the Abyssinian war. In spite of our staggering economic predicament after a costly war, and our arrogant and risky foreign policy, *Il Duce* seemed to be in control.

France and Britain were not pleased with his policy of expansion, but our *Duce* was adamant and proud to stick to his famous mottoes:

Me ne frego! Duro con i nemici, marceremo con gli amici fino in fondo! (I don't give a damn! Unyielding to our enemies, we shall march with our friends till the end!)

The 'end' might have meant his final aim; possibly to make Italy a great country.

We poor people disagreed with a number of *Il Duce*'s sayings. We were not as learned as he was, but we were humble and practical. We instinctively knew what was good for our country, and if we were too proud of ourselves and arrogant, this might alienate our foreign friends, cause us loss of trade and create additional unemployment.

At the beginning of 1937, we learned that my father and brother were coming home for a long holiday the following May. We were excited and looked forward to their arrival. We were anxious to know what Saverio had to tell us after three years of living in Java. We had noticed from the photos that he had sent us that he had grown into a full-blown businessman, a man of substance. He had earned and saved a good deal of money and boosted Father's capital. With our improved standard of living, we now considered ourselves to be middle-class.

We greatly admired Saverio's achievement, but were sorry for him because during 1935, while he was on a business tour in Surabaja, he had contracted typhus and lost his hair. He wrote to us saying that the Dutch clinic in which he had been hospitalised was excellent and that he had been looked after extremely well.

I remember that when we learned he had caught typhus, we were greatly concerned. Mother rushed to the Chapel of the Sacred Hearts and pinned Saverio's photo to the hem of the long and ornate dress of the Madonna (Immaculate Conception). She also went to Mass and communion every day, lit candles in front of the printed images of the saints we had at home, and recited the rosary at least twice daily.

Having a strong constitution, Saverio made a quick recovery. It was a pity that his illness left him bald.

Vince and I were impatient for the arrival of the ship in Naples. Father never told us anything of those foreign countries where he worked and earned the money he sent us. Saverio, however, would no doubt have much to tell us of his time in Java.

We all counted the days and the hours to that very moment when the ship moored up in the Port of Naples, which is right in the heart of the city.

Father sent us a telegram from Port Said. They were travelling in a Japanese ship, *Hakusan Maru*, which was expected to be delayed on account of a storm in the Mediterranean Sea.

On the appointed day, Vince, Tony and I went to the port, but we needed a permit to enter it. We were just in time to see the ship mooring up. We weren't allowed to get too close, so we stood on the tarmac about fifty metres away. Soon we caught sight of Father and Saverio, waving their handkerchiefs from the stern. Our excitement mounted high as we waved our hands about and shouted: 'Hey! Papa! Saverio!' This greeting went on for quite a while and attracted some of the bystanders' attention.

At about eleven o'clock the passengers started disembarking. Father and Saverio, followed by a porter carting their luggage, walked towards us. We joyously welcomed and hugged them. I was very glad to see Saverio, but I had no feelings of affection for my father – probably because, when he came home, he always quarrelled with Mother. He shouted angrily, smashed plates on the floor and banged doors; once he even shattered the glass panes in our dining-room cupboard. Such scenes terrorised us, and we children could not help absorbing the force of his fury – how could I love a father like that?

Having welcomed him and Saverio, we walked together towards the exit gate of the port. A customs officer made a quick inspection of the luggage, which included a trunk. This contained about sixty pounds of Dutch East Indies crystalline sugar and a few pounds of aromatic tea. Father told the officer that he had a large family of eleven children, and that the stuff he had brought from Java was for personal use. The officer was trying to be difficult. Father silenced him by putting a banknote in his hand, whereupon he shut the trunk, marked it with a piece of chalk and let us go.

Father hailed a taxi, and with the help of the driver we placed some of the luggage in the car and the rest on top. There was hardly any room left for the five of us; but badly cramped though we were, we somehow managed to survive the journey! The taxi drove for a while through the busy and noisy city streets, and then towards our destination which was about five kilometres from the port.

At that time, only a very few of our townsfolk had ever had the chance of travelling in a taxi. This was regarded as a luxury that only the well-to-do could afford. So when the taxi came closer to our home and the driver blew the horn repeatedly as he drove into the courtyard, it caused quite a stir. A hen and her chicks scuttled away cackling, a dog barked, a couple of donkeys brayed and our neighbours poured out of their flats to see what the fuss was about. Had some important person just arrived?

The taxi came to a halt near the staircase and we alighted. All the eyes of our neighbours were focused on us. Vince, Tony and I were aware of being the centre of attention, and we could not help feeling flattered and conceited.

Long before the taxi arrived, Mother, my two younger brothers and five sisters were on the lookout from our two balconies; as soon as they saw the taxi entering the courtyard, they became extremely excited. Exultantly, they all rushed downstairs to welcome Father and Saverio.

'*Ehi, come state? State bene? Siete stanchi? Avete fatto un buon viaggio? Ci avevano detti che il mare era agitato, e noi eravamo un po preoccupati. Venite, venite sopra, vi abbiamo fatto una bella pizza e melenzane alla Parmigiana.*'

(Hey, how are you? Are you well? Are you tired? Have you travelled well? The shipping company told us that the sea was rough, and so we were a bit worried about it. Come, come upstairs, we've prepared a delicious pizza and some aubergines with Parmesan cheese.)

After all the greetings and welcoming fuss, the taxi driver helped us to carry the heavy trunk to the second floor. Mother tipped him with a delicious slice of pizza and a glass of wine.

Father and Saverio had been away several years, and now we were able to sit together at our long dining-table and feast on the dinner that Mother and my sister had prepared. We couldn't keep our eyes off Father, and especially Saverio, now that they were among us once again.

Later, Father and Saverio started unpacking their luggage. We clustered around them, full of curiosity and expectation. We imagined that at any moment some kind of Javanese deity or monster would spring up from their suitcases. What we sensed instead was presumably the scent of stale tropical air which smelled like rotten eggs, as they removed clothes and various objects from the luggage. There were some small carved Javanese statues, Bali's colourful batiks, a small black elephant figure probably bought in Ceylon (Sri Lanka), a brass bell, a small brass gong and an elegant ten-by-six-inch mother-of-pearl box from Singapore. Moreover, there were many white Japanese silk pyjamas, a few Oriental silk kimonos and a dozen pairs of white jackets and trousers made of drill material.

Now that we had a plentiful supply of tea and sugar that Father had brought from Java, we soon began drinking two or three cups a day, which we found delicious and refreshing; we were unknowingly acquiring an Oriental and an English habit. Having drunk tea for a few weeks, we felt less like Neapolitans and a little more like the English, so we began to address each other as 'Mr and Mrs So-and-So', or 'My Lord and My Lady', followed by English names we had heard at the movies.

We even started offering tea to our visitors. This would have enabled us to save money, for coffee was very expensive. Unfortunately they were shocked at the novelty when they tasted it. 'What's this? What's this?' they shouted. We then had to soothe our disgusted visitors with strong cups of coffee!

These visitors of ours soon started gossiping; they told their

110

friends that we were going nuts and described their experience of tasting 'the awful stuff', as they called it.

One of them remarked: 'The English drink three or four cups of tea a day.'

'Do they?' said his friend, a little puzzled.

'Perhaps drinking tea teaches them how to be stoical.'

'Stoical? No wonder, with their gloomy weather and tea-drinking they must be very stoical indeed.'

After our visitors' reaction to tea, we learned to be cautious before offering others tea instead of coffee.

One day, a couple of weeks after Father and Saverio had returned from Java, Father was in bed recovering from influenza. One of his close friends, Autino, paid him a visit. Father offered his chum the exotic drink. Autino tasted the tea and then contorted his face in horrible grimaces, as if he had drunk poison. Mother and my sister Carmen burst into frantic laughter and then hurried to the kitchen to make Autino a good cup of coffee. When we were told about this incident we laughed too.

We all had a sweet tooth in our family. Sugar, being imported, was expensive. Ordinary people hardly paid any direct taxes in Italy. But whether they were rich or poor, everyone paid the indirect taxes levied on salt, sugar and tobacco, for these items were state monopolies.

We did not particularly fancy drinking tea, and to make it more pleasant to our palate, we used to put plenty of sugar in it for as long as the supply lasted.

24

Saverio tries to cure his baldness, but ends up being cheated. We move to a new flat. Damiano gobbles up a dish of aubergines

Saverio at this time was twenty-one. He hoped to find a cure to make his hair grow back. He consulted a few doctors, but they were unable to help, for there was no real cure for baldness. He would not take 'no' for an answer and, having noticed an advertisement in one of our national newspapers, he was jubilant. It appeared that a 'famous' Sicilian doctor had discovered a 'miraculous' remedy. Saverio could imagine – almost visualise – the wavy black hair which he once had growing again! Now he was prepared to spend extravagantly, if necessary, for the cure, so he parted with some of his hard-earned money for the hopefully 'miraculous' remedy.

Every morning, while wearing a kimono he had brought from Java, Saverio stood in front of our large mirror for about an hour. He ceremoniously and meticulously treated his scalp according to instructions. He applied a gadget which was like a large toothbrush and operated on a battery. It contained some needles which, with gentle electrical impulses, stimulated the scalp. Having done this, he vigorously rubbed in a lotion derived from exotic tropical plants.

Every day he examined the outcome of the 'miraculous' cure with a magnifying glass, hoping to discover something exciting. Although he could not notice the miracle yet, he stubbornly persisted, rubbing his scalp with additional vigour. He even begged the Lord, went to Mass and communion, hoping that the Almighty would answer his prayer.

After a while, having discovered that he was getting nowhere, he realised, much to his chagrin, that he had been cheated by the self-styled 'famous' Sicilian doctor. So he stopped the treatment altogether.

In any case, it wasn't really necessary, for he was an attractive young man and willing to get on in life. Baldness was not really a hindrance; many brainy and successful men were bald. For instance our beloved *Duce* was bald, and wasn't he doing well? Had he not succeeded in making us a nation of slaves? Besides this, quite a number of ladies had fallen in love with him; they admired his virility, his cocky manners and his dictatorial ways. It was calamitous that he, believing that he was always right, took decisions that ruined our country.

As long as Saverio proved to be serious, reliable, industrious and intelligent, he wouldn't have any difficulty in finding a decent and attractive girl willing to marry him.

Saverio was careful with his money. He had a couple of suits made to measure by a high-class tailor. He dressed well and spent the day going for strolls with his friends round our town. Being a businessman, he made new friends, with whom he went to Naples, which could offer a variety of amusements – they ate at restaurants, visited cinemas and theatres and some luxurious brothels.

This was the lifestyle of many young men who were looking for a little fun and had the chance of getting it. Saverio, after three years' absence from Europe, certainly deserved a little *dolce vita*.

When he and his friends did not go to Naples, they wooed attractive local girls, but there was no chance of any hanky-panky outside the blessing of holy wedlock.

Father spent a few thousand lire on us, buying us clothes and things we needed at home. One day he took Vince, Tony and me to the city and bought a wrist-watch for each of us. I was very proud indeed of my wrist-watch. Father paid eighty lire for it which I considered a small fortune. Having a wrist-watch made me feel important – superior to those boys who didn't have one. To make sure that my friends noticed it, I deliberately looked at my watch too frequently as if I were a busy executive whose time was very precious.

We did not have a radio yet. Father could afford it, but at times he seemed to lack imagination. The radio programmes were excellent: classical and light music, opera, news, plays, short stories, discussions and so on. They were often interesting, educational and recreational. But for the time being we were deprived of such a wonderful medium.

Having such a large family, Father and Mother came to the

conclusion that we needed at least a three-bedroom flat with a large kitchen, dining-room, two inside toilets and a veranda to dry our laundered linen and clothes.

Most flats at that time did not have bathrooms; only rich people had them. Whenever we needed a kind of personal spring-cleaning it was rather a ritual and an elaborate business ceremoniously supervised by Mother. She prepared a cauldron of water on our kitchen stove which was heated by blazing coals.

We certainly enjoyed that maternal treatment. My virgin sisters deserved greater respect, so they went through the bathing ceremony before their brothers.

We boys, especially me who had been a former pupil of Ciotto and had qualified as a street urchin, were not considered as pure as my sisters. Mother was probably afraid that, had we bathed before them, we could have contaminated the large basin in which we were bathing. Mother liked being there and assisting us. Deep in her heart she still considered us her little babies needing to be bathed by her. During this ritual we frequently engaged in affectionate bickerings, whenever she poured a bucketful of water over our heads or we carelessly spilled some water on the floor.

At the end of the bath she wrapped our wet bodies in a large linen cloth – probably a bed sheet – and helped us to get dry. This too caused a little friction whenever her strokes were too vigorous: 'Mother, you're hurting me!' She would take no notice and would start tickling me under my armpits, so our squabblings ended in outbursts of laughter.

After looking around for a few days, my parents found the kind of flat we needed. It was situated on the first floor of a building called *Palazzo Cardone*, at 228 Corso Umberto Primo, which was opposite the Piedimonte of Alife Station. The new home was about 400 metres away from Palazzo De Rosa, where we had been living for six years.

Our new flat was located in the best section of the town, where the buildings were not too old, had four or five storeys and where businessmen and the few professional people lived. A number of these buildings were constructed after the Great War and belonged to ex-emigrants who now lived in leisure with the income from the flats they rented out to tenants. They were very aware of being better off; they even flattered themselves that they were the new aristocrats of the town.

Living next to our new flat was a middle-aged couple: signor and signora Vivaldi. They had a boy and a girl who were both students and over seventeen.

When signor Vivaldi learned that we were going to live next door to him, he feared that we might interfere with his domestic tranquillity, as we were such a large family. Foolishly, he approached Father and tried to dissuade him from taking the flat; by doing so he irritated Father.

'Dear chap,' said Father, 'I don't need your advice. I know exactly what I am doing, and whether you like it or not, I am going to live there, because it's the flat I need for my family.'

Having said this, Father went straight ahead and paid for the rent in advance. He didn't give a damn about signor Vivaldi's selfish attitude. Our new neighbour, who had evidently forgotten his humble origins, seemed to be a very conceited fellow.

Father said that signor Vivaldi had been an artisan before the Great War. Like any other artisan, he had had to strive hard to make a living. He now worked in the state railways infirmary in Naples as a male nurse. He received a salary and appeared to be earning extra money. He seemed to be on friendly terms with doctors, and I had the impression that he was a doctor himself. People said that those running the infirmary were making money on the side, by issuing medical certificates to railway employees who feigned illnesses.

Regardless of signor Vivaldi's objections, we moved into our new flat towards the end of June, or at the beginning of July 1937. The flat was very spacious indeed and stretched from the front to the back of the building.

Our parents' bedroom was at the front, while our large dining-room was at the back. These were connected by a long corridor, where another two bedrooms, a toilet and a large kitchen were located. Our parents' bedroom had a balcony looking out on to the main road. The rest of the bedrooms, the kitchen and dining-room also had balconies, situated on the left side of the building and facing a block of flats. Our dining-room had a large balcony looking out on to the garden and a window giving a view into the courtyard.

Having so many balconies, Mother and my sister Carmen had a chance to communicate with our friendly neighbours, who always seemed ready for a chat.

'Good morning, signora,' Mother or my sister would say.

'Good morning,' replied the signora of the opposite flat.

'And how are you, signora?'

'Thank God, I'm well, but my *bambino* (baby) is a little indisposed; he doesn't want to eat.'

'Probably it's the hot weather, signora.'

'Yes, I think so, but if he carries on like this, I'll take him to the doctor; he might give him a tonic.'

'*Mammamia*!' (Dear me!) Mother would exclaim. 'This heat is a real nuisance. Lots of children seem to be affected by it. It hasn't rained for quite a long time. A little rain would certainly refresh the air. The farmers are very worried; they're afraid that if it doesn't rain very soon, their crops'll be ruined.

'By the way, signora, have you heard this morning's news? The man from the *municipio* (town hall) was going around, ringing his handbell; he was warning us that the water supply will be cut off till late this afternoon.'

'Really? I didn't hear a thing, signora; my baby was crying. Thank you, signora, for telling me. Now excuse me, I must dash to fill my buckets, pots and pans, else I'll be left without water.'

Topics for conversation like this reflected daily events. These housewives also talked about dreams, somebody getting married, sensational scandals, forthcoming festivities and so on.

We did not communicate with the Vivaldi family because of their unfriendly attitude towards us. They had two balconies facing the main road, one being at the centre of the building and next to our balcony. Whether it was summer or winter, they rarely stood on their balcony, especially if we were there watching passers-by. Whenever we met them on their way upstairs, downstairs or in the street, they ignored us and we naturally did the same. They deliberately avoided us as if we had a contagious disease. I personally resented their unfriendly manner which seemed so unnatural in comparison with the spontaneous friendliness of most people in the town. Nevertheless, we had to put up with the Vivaldis' despicable behaviour. Mother was especially cross with them, because their objection merely sprang from the fact that we were a large family.

Mother was extremely touchy if someone dared to sneer at us, for her family was sacrosanct. She would not hesitate to retaliate and give the rough edge of her tongue to anyone who chose to hurt her in the spot where she was most sensitive.

116

Our dining-room was spacious indeed: almost a small hall by itself. We used it as a parlour as well when we had visitors. Its large balcony was flooded with sunshine in fine weather and served us splendidly for drying our laundered clothes and linen.

To keep our place ventilated in summer, we left the windows and balconies wide open, and didn't care much whether our neighbours deliberately or casually noticed what we were doing within our domain. They were possibly mystified or amused when they saw us wearing the white silk, Japanese pyjamas and fanciful kimonos which Father had recently brought from Java. These garments were so cool and comfortable to wear and seemed to complement the aromatic tea we drank three or four times a day. We had created within our flat the atmosphere of a Japanese house, it seemed. Saverio, Vince and I usually went out in the morning and afternoon, but when we came back home, we were all agog to wear our cool silk kimonos and pyjamas.

That summer we did not go on a two-week holiday to a seaside resort as we had done in previous years, because Father and my brother Saverio were trying hard to make up their minds whether to return to Java – which was so hot and far away – or to start a business in Europe.

Occasionally Father and Mother, accompanied by some half-dozen of us, went to Naples on a shopping spree to buy those luxuries not available in the shops of our town. Going to Naples was rather a distressing business for Mother; she was not used to the deafening and ceaseless traffic of the city, so when we had to get across a main road, she was nervous and would shout: 'Wait! Wait! Waaait! The tram! The taxi! The motor car! The lorry!' – and so on. Her shouts were more frightening and confusing than the traffic itself!

Mother and most of the natives were not prepared to pay the price of goods on display. Tourists who were not familiar with our deeply rooted habit of bargaining were easy customers. For instance, a pair of shoes could be bought for twenty per cent less than the price shown by haggling. It would take hours and a lot of arguing to make even a few purchases. It was not an easy life for shopkeepers, especially for those who hadn't enough patience to deal with awkward customers. It was not unknown for them to become so exasperated that they either had a fit or a breakdown. It was not an easy life for most people who were poor or had a

117

limited income. It could be even worse for shopkeepers who couldn't get enough customers and were therefore in danger of going under.

The Fascist policy had created that miserable situation. A good government was supposed to use public money to expand industry, stimulate business, create employment and improve the standard of living. Mussolini preferred to spend our money to keep military barracks in Abyssinia and to build up our navy and air force.

As money was so hard to earn, people tried to get as much value out of it as they could. On the other hand, since there were too many shops and not enough customers, some shopkeepers were forced to reduce prices to tempt people to buy. By so doing, however, they were cutting one another's throats.

If Father or Mother felt peckish while we were in the city doing our shopping, we might go for a pizza. When a shrewd pizza shop owner saw us entering his shop, he would welcome us joyfully, expecting us to spend a lot of money. There were pizzas at various prices. A very simple pizza cost fifty cents; a more appetising one, a lira; a very substantial one, made with mozzarella and *provolone* cheese and ham, intended for gourmands, cost five lire or more.

One day while Father and Saverio were in the city, feeling a little hungry, they entered a pizza shop. Seeing that they were two prosperous-looking customers, the shop owner smiled radiantly. He then came forward, rubbing his hands, and courteously showed them to their table. *'Cosa desiderate, signori?'* he said obsequiously. *'Abbiamo pizze da cinque lire e dieci lire. Quale volete?'*

(What would you like, gentlemen? We have pizzas at five lire and ten lire. Which one do you want?)

The shrewd fellow did not mention cheaper pizzas, because he would not make so much profit on them, so he endeavoured to serve dearer pizzas to his well-off looking customers.

Aware of what the chap was up to, Father was annoyed. 'We'll have two pizzas of one lira a piece,' he ordered.

The man's mood suddenly changed – he became solemn and morose and dropped at once all the deference and courtesy he had lavished on Father and my brother a few minutes earlier.

'Give two one lira pizzas to these two men,' he shouted grumpily to his assistant. His impertinent tone angered Father and my brother, so they got up and walked out. The man looked at them dumbfounded, full of resentment.

118

'Eh, *signori*! Where are you going? The pizzas are ready!'

'Eat them yourself; we don't want them any more,' cried Father.

When we returned from our shopping spree, each of us, including Father and Mother, carried one or two parcels. There were in all about seven or eight of us, and as we walked home from the tram stop, we formed a small procession. Our curious neighbours, especially those who hadn't much to do, were always on their balconies or at their windows, looking at the people and the traffic passing by. They hoped to discover something interesting, although most of the time nothing happened there. However, when they noticed us carrying all those parcels, they were mystified and amused, and surely wondered how much Father had spent in the city that day, and how much would be needed monthly for a large family like ours.

While Father and Saverio stayed at home, they didn't mind spending extra on a treat, buying things that we needed and enjoyed, without being extravagant. I am sure that our neighbours admired Father for looking after us so well. Perhaps they even envied us for enjoying a decent standard of living, while many people at that time had to struggle extremely hard just to survive.

Seeing that we were growing up very fast, Father took a greater interest in us; he was getting closer to us and spending more time at home than he had ever done before. In previous years, when he came from abroad, he used to pass hours every day playing cards at the businessmen's club and losing a great deal of his hard-earned money.

During the summer of 1937 he bought a small machine and learned how to make noodles. When he was not arguing or quarrelling with Mother, he would busy himself for an entire morning and make excellent noodles, which we ate with fresh tomato sauce and Parmesan cheese and thoroughly relished. Being summer, he took a siesta in the afternoon. Later on he met his pals and went for a walk. When they had walked enough, they sat outside the businessmen's club, chatted among themselves or got into conversation with other groups.

We had a light evening meal about half past seven, followed by plenty of fruit. We usually drank a little wine with our meals; wine that we bought locally and which was of doubtful origin. Since we drank very little, it could not cause any unpleasant effects, even if it was adulterated.

At mealtimes we always made jokes and teased each other. Mealtimes were happy times. Provided that Father and Mother did not start one of their arguments, we enjoyed the family atmosphere. As each one of us had a nickname, we inverted its spelling, just to make it sound a little mysterious. We nicknamed one of my younger sisters *Patana*, thus by inverting its spelling it became *Anatap*. *Patana* is a Neapolitan term for potato. Father seemed amused by our tricks of speech.

I always teased my brother Tony, who was one year younger than me. He used to brag about having dates with his girlfriend on Sundays. This was purely a figment of his imagination. There was a girl, living not too far away, called Maria Palmieri. She was good-looking and about my brother's age. Tony, at that time, was about sixteen. He had a crush on Maria, and his mates were smitten by Maria's girlfriends. I doubt whether Tony had ever approached or spoken to her, yet he insisted that she was his sweetheart.

After mealtimes, when I was in the mood for talking and in high spirits, I stood up on a chair and teasingly addressed Tony: 'Maria!' I mimicked, 'My dear Maria! My sweet Maria! I sincerely love you. I am your faithful fiancé. Sorry I can't marry you now, I'm still too young. This autumn I am going with my father to France. I shall work very hard, become rich, then come back and ask you to marry me. I beg you on my knees to wait for me. Don't go out with other boys while I'm away.' Then I pretended to cry, saying: 'I can't bear the thought of you marrying anybody else!'

Father was amused at my improvisation and delivery. Tony and the rest of my family also laughed.

One Sunday in July 1937, Mother had prepared an aubergine dish for our evening meal. In the late afternoon she and my sister were on our balcony watching hundreds of our townsfolk going for their stroll on the wide pavement of Corso Umberto Primo.

Taking advantage of Mother and my sister being on the balcony, my nine-year-old brother Damiano crept into the kitchen to help himself to the aubergines. He found them so delicious that he was unable to stop eating them, so one by one he gobbled them up.

At mealtime we all sat at our long table waiting for the aubergine dish to be brought in. Mother had left it on the kitchen table near the stove, but it wasn't there! She was perplexed. Who could have taken it? She became suspicious and looked at us in dismay. However, she noticed that Damiano was missing. Where was he? One of my sisters found him under Mother's double bed. He was ill, his mouth was foaming and he had a painful tummy. Mother quickly took him to the pharmacist who gave him a remedy. He was sick for a couple of days, during which he seemed to have strange visions of animals and monsters wanting to gobble him up.

Damiano was quite a problem when he was a little boy. By the age of two or three he still had not learned to use the loo, so he relieved himself at random all over our flat, and my poor sister Carmen had to clean up his smelly mess. Because of this we nicknamed him *Cacasotto* by which we meant one who shits himself.

Father soon realised that we were no longer children; it was time that we started taking life seriously.

25

*Saverio's romantic involvement. Sala Tripoli and
the Golden Theatre. Father and Saverio intend to
start a business in France*

There was a family living opposite the building where we had our
flat, consisting of the parents, a son and two daughters. The older
daughter, Maria (Maria Andreozzi), was eighteen or nineteen and
very attractive. She resembled the Mona Lisa and had large brown
eyes and lots of sex appeal.

Saverio was about twenty-one at that time. As I mentioned
before, he had lost his hair three or four years earlier. Saverio fell
deeply in love with Maria. He spoke to her from one of our
balconies; it was balcony-to-balcony wooing. Saverio dearly wanted
to marry her. He had a little money, but not enough to get married
on and settle down, so he had to wait patiently until he was ready
to realise his wish. Having to go abroad the following autumn, his
future was precarious. He didn't have much to offer Maria except
a promise. Would she be willing to wait for him? And if so, for
how long? It was hard for her to say. Maria was really looking for
someone, even though he might be a few years older, who was
ready to get married and settle down right away.

From the age of fourteen onwards, my elder brother Vince had a
few girlfriends. The first was Teresa Cervicata, then followed Nina
Giandomenica and later Giuseppina Piscopo. Vince was quite a
Casanova. Owing to his sexual precociousness, he was ever ready
to plunge into the arms of Venus. I don't think, however, that he
got more than a few stolen kisses out of his romantic adventures,
for girls were generally schooled by their experienced mothers on
how to protect their virginity. It was highly regarded there, and if
a girl lost it and was poor, she would find it hard to get married.
It was likely that her parents would have disowned her and, if she

122

was unable to get a job, she would probably have ended up in a brothel. This was the worst thing that could happen to a woman. It did not matter how hard life was, a girl looked forward to getting married. Although she might have to adapt herself to a domineering husband, she would anticipate with pleasure a home filled with lively children.

Usually when girls finished primary school and were not too ambitious, those who were better off than others stayed at home and learned how to become good housewives. Their parents provided them with dowries, which were an incentive to eligible bachelors – young men with steady employment and income who wished to get married.

In 1937 I was seventeen and by no means an angel. In previous years, having frequented the company of rough boys, I had learned foul language, the facts of life and how to abuse myself. I was physically not as strong as Vince and not ruled by his strong sexual desire. Starting from the age of fourteen I would abuse myself every now and then, but after giving way to this impure act I would always feel remorseful. I was haunted by the thought that I was robbing my body of vital energy which I could have used for some worthwhile pursuit. I admired a couple of girls, but I neither chased them nor came into contact with them in any way. I was a little shy and too wrapped up in the company of my friends.

A beautiful girl was always an immense attraction and made my heart go pit-a-pat, but if I had approached her I would have felt embarrassed. How will she react? I used to think. What would I say to her, especially if she was not too inviting, or timid, or taciturn? I hated the idea of making a girl talk when she had no desire to do so. This feeling of constraint used to put me off. As I had occasionally experienced, she might bore me to death and make me feel sorry that I had ever approached her. I had no inhibitions whatsoever when I was with my pals; they were so spontaneous and easygoing, which made me appreciate the value of their friendship.

From early boyhood Mother used to tell us how poor she was when she was a little girl, and how we boys would one day earn a lot of money. We would become very rich, marry some princesses and live like princes, while my sisters would eventually marry princes and live like princesses. Brainwashed as I was by her extravagant predictions, I grew up with the idea that the most important thing in life was to make money – tons of it. As this was impossible to achieve in our poor and hopeless town, it was obvious that I would have to emigrate, sail across the ocean, explore the world and leave no stone unturned until I found a treasure trove.

I made new friends while I was frequenting the Sunday morning Fascist youth club. Occasionally the club organised excursions to Vesuvius, Pompeii or other localities not too far away; such activities helped me to discover new interests beyond the confines of our small town.

Going to the cinema was a cheap form of entertainment; even the poorest people managed somehow to squeeze a few cents out of their beggarly budgets and go to the cinema. If the performance was continuous, I could watch a film twice or more. I certainly got good value out of the one lira admission charge.

I remember seeing a glamorous American picture in the mid-thirties called *The Roman Scandals*, starring Eddie Cantor. This film showed a host of alluring, nearly naked women who were being sold in a slave market in Ancient Rome. This was too provocative and tempting for some boys; indeed, they became so excited that they indulged in masturbation.

I knew two boys, one called Berto and the other Brogio, who masturbated frequently and seemed to have no control over their sexual instincts. Even the sight of a girl's calf would turn them on – especially if she was sexy-looking. Neither of them looked healthy. Berto had developed a curved spine and was almost hunchback; Brogio's face was extremely pale. Most of the films I saw ended with lingering kisses.

Smoking was allowed in the hall, and when it was crowded clouds of smoke accumulated under the ceiling; the air was hazy and heavy and made breathing difficult.

We also had a theatre called 'Golden' which was about a stone's throw from the Tripoli Hall. The Golden Theatre performed Neapolitan comedies and variety. Most of the comedies were extremely passionate; they dealt with love, honour, adultery, revenge, and revealed certain aspects of the Neapolitan personality.

When the variety was on, attractive 'female stars', scantily dressed, sang and danced. Men in the audience with lusty eyes stared at the stars' near nakedness, their minds running amok with desire. They shouted wildly, praising the legs and bosoms of the voluptuous girls. They yearned to touch these temptresses, pinch their bottoms, fondle their breasts and go the whole way with them. In those moments of frantic excitement, they would have paid any price for the possession of their favourite dancer.

In 1935, when Italy attacked Abyssinia, economic sanctions were applied to our country. Mussolini reacted to this by replacing all the foreign names of businesses and institutions with Italian names. As a result of this our 'Golden Theatre' was renamed 'the Goldoni Theatre'.

While Father and my brother Saverio were staying at home, Father wrote to Uncle Pascal, who lived in France, asking him whether it was still a promising country for business. Uncle replied that there was some political instability and a lot of competition. Father maintained that France had rich colonies and so it was comparatively prosperous. He had also learned that one could easily make a living there so, without much ado, Father and Saverio decided to go to Rouen and start a business there, instead of going back to Java.

Uncle Pascal had married a French girl in the twenties and they had settled down in Rouen. They had two boys, Jacques, who in 1937 was about fourteen, and Moïse, who was two years younger. They both went to school, but neither Aunt Mary nor the boys could speak Italian.

Uncle was more enterprising and better educated than Father. In 1937 he was in his forties and still good-looking. He had combed-back wavy hair which was going grey, a wrinkled forehead, brown eyes and an aquiline nose. He spoke French fluently, but whenever he wrote a letter, Aunt Mary would check the spelling.

No doubt being an ex-sergeant-major helped him to become president of the Italian ex-servicemen's association in Normandy. On the occasions when he had to take part in some important French–Italian ceremony, he would wear spats, pinstriped trousers, *marsina* (tails) and top hat. With Italy under the Mussolini regime, he had to salute in the Fascist way, by stretching out his right arm. This, of course, displeased the democrats.

Uncle was ambitious. Apparently he wanted to become somebody, so he got involved in politics and made a number of influential friends, who were very helpful in times of emergency. He was also engaged in a textile business which he ran from home. He supplied suiting material to travelling salesmen and seemed to be doing well.

Soon after the Great War Normandy had been paved with gold for Italian immigrants. By 1937 the situation had changed drastically; there were now too many of them. Although the Italians were still regarded as ex-allies, as a result of the Rome–Berlin Axis established in October 1936, most French people hated Fascism and Mussolini. They now considered all Italians as Fascist supporters, and consequently no longer welcomed them.

A few months before departure, Father had met a middle-aged man whose name was Raffaele. He was in his forties, had a straight nose and was rather tall and slim. He was married to a nurse, but they were childless. As work was scarce and customers very few, he was unemployed and had to stay at home, do the cooking and rely on his wife's meagre income. She squeezed out of her hard-earned money a few coins to provide him with the cheapest cigarettes. These emitted a pungent, detestable odour whenever he smoked them. Being unemployed, he badly wanted to go to France, expecting to find work there.

Raffaele had been employed as a tailor's cutter in the rag trade and had some experience in mackintosh manufacturing. Father thought that he could be useful, so he proposed that Raffaele should go with him to Rouen, where they would start a small mackintosh factory.

26

*Father, Saverio, Vince, Tony and I are on our way
to France*

Since Vince, Tony and I had not done well with our studies, and
Father was not getting any younger, he decided by the end of July
1937 that we should follow him to France. We boys were jubilant
at the prospect of seeing a new country and meeting French people.
After all, they were better off than the Italians. It would not be
necessary to employ people and let them work on the premises;
instead we could use machinists who worked in their own homes.
They would collect the cut material, make it up into mackintoshes
and deliver them to our factory. An experienced machinist could
make two mackintoshes a day.

Father said that Vince, Tony and I were going to help to run the
factory, so he sent Vince on a four-week men's garment cutting
course in Naples, at a fashion school run by Professor Emilio
Capparelli. Vince, in his turn, would impart his acquired knowledge
to Tony and me, so we would be learning from him to make
ourselves useful in the business.

It was not easy for beginners to learn how the pieces of a
mackintosh – front, back, collar, sleeves and so on – fitted together.
However, with a little perseverance and Raffaele's help, we would
be able to make progress.

Uncle Pascal informed Father that he had found a suitable,
inexpensive place for our factory, with living quarters combined. It
consisted of a flat with four bedrooms in central Rouen, and it
seemed adequate for our purpose.

By tipping a few poorly paid bureaucrats, our passports were
ready in three weeks. So towards the end of September we packed
our suitcases, said farewell to our relatives and friends, hugged
Mother, our sisters and our two young brothers Giuseppe and

127

Damiano, and were ready to go.

'My God! My God! My children are leaving, going to a foreign country. Who'll take care of them? Why do they have to go?' Mother cried tearfully. 'Jesus, Son of God, my children are in your hands! Bless, protect and guide them.'

She knew that we had to go. We had to learn to face the world. We had to learn to be tough, industrious and earn money. By going abroad there was a possibility of our becoming rich. We could never do so by staying in our small miserable town.

Vince departed for Rouen a couple of weeks before his nineteenth birthday, otherwise our emigration officers would have stopped him from leaving Italy on account of his military service. He travelled in the company of one of Uncle Pascal's friends who, after holidaying in Naples, was going back to Rouen.

Vince arrived there after a wearying, thirty-hour train journey and went to stay at Uncle Pascal's house. While he was there, Uncle and his family went on a ten-day holiday to Calais and took Vince with them. Although he had learned only a couple of French words, he soon started chasing the local girls. He badly wanted to have a taste of French females, it seemed. While he was with our uncle at Calais he met a girl called Madeleine who became his girlfriend for a few days. It was – as Aunt Mary, Uncle Pascal's wife, told us – a very affectionate friendship. Madeleine had obviously grown very fond of Vince. Possibly he had given her a taste of his Italian masculinity.

Father, Saverio, Tony and I, with four heavy suitcases, travelled by taxi to Naples Central Station and caught an early morning train for Rome. Raffaele didn't travel with us, as he had some personal business to attend to; he said he would join us a couple of weeks later.

Tony and I were extremely excited for it was our first long journey. The steam train whistled, wheezed and puffed as it moved along. Later it reached a fantastic speed of about eighty kilometres an hour. Tony and I were thrilled and bewildered in turn; we had never before travelled at such a tremendous speed. The noise of the whistle and the vibration of the train were unbearable. This did not bother me, for I could never tire of watching the landscape from the window. There were fields, meadows, old towns perched on the brows of hills, sheep grazing on slopes, colourful rocks, dilapidated farmhouses, canals, a lake, one or two rivers and our blue Italian sky flooded with sunlight. The train screamed as if it were in distress. It dived furiously into a tunnel, emerged with the same impetus and then with seemingly augmented fury plunged into the next one.

The fumes and the smell of burning coal filled our nostrils. However, eager to discover new sights, I found it all entrancing and would let nothing upset my enjoyment of the journey. Unfortunately the passengers with whom we shared our compartment were all heavy smokers. There was almost no way to avoid them, so we just had to put up with their puffing and breathe the polluted air.

Our compartment contained eight seats. We shared it with four passengers. Italians don't need to be introduced; they easily engage in conversation, which may go on for hours.

'What a miserable life!' complained one of our fellow passengers. 'I can't sell my shoes in Naples. It's a very bad market, lots of competition and not many buyers. I have to go to Rome every day where I can sell my shoes, otherwise I wouldn't be able to survive.'

He paused a moment and looked round at everyone. 'I have a family of six kids, six mouths to feed, so I leave home very early in the morning and return late. I hardly have a family life, have I?'

'There's hardship everywhere, especially in the South,' answered another passenger. 'I've got a few acres of land. In a good season I can make a living, otherwise my family of eight kids would starve to death. A number of my neighbours are no better off; they can't afford to buy shoes and clothes to send their children to school, and have no money for doctors and medicine. This life is impossible, it's better to be dead.'

'The Romans live better than us,' said yet another passenger, 'probably Il Duce tries to keep on friendly terms with them. But I reckon the best place is North Italy; there are industries there. Those who work are better placed than we are in South Italy. We have become a colony of the North. They exploit us. They want our produce as cheaply as possible, but when we have to buy from them, we have to pay through the nose. Are we their slaves?'

This was the kind of conversation which would go on and on. Often it extended to other subjects, including those concerned with their private lives.

After more than two and a half hours travelling, the train reached the periphery of the Eternal City. I was wild with excitement at the sight of the aqueduct and other ruins scattered all over that area. I had the impression that I had been there centuries earlier. Was I the reincarnation of an ancient Roman or, perhaps, one of those lizards basking among those dilapidated stones?

Later, as the train came closer and closer to the city and I caught a glimpse of Saint Peter's Dome, I shouted frantically: 'Rome! Rome! Rome!' Our fellow travellers were startled and amused at my reaction.

'Behave yourself, son, we are not deaf,' said one of them jokingly. 'The Pope, the King and *Il Duce* might get scared.'

The train stopped at Termini Station before midday. I could still smell the smoke of the train on my clothes. The station was very crowded with people arriving and departing. A considerable number of tourists followed porters carrying their luggage. Some soldiers and officers were waiting for their trains. A noisy newspaper vendor was trying to sell the latest news. Trolleys loaded with food and drinks moved to and fro along the platforms.

As soon as we got off the train, Father hired a porter who carried our heavy suitcases to the baggage room. Our train for Paris was due to depart from Rome at 9.00 p.m., so we had seven or eight hours to spare.

While we were in Rome, it so happened that our cousin Jacques, Uncle Pascal's first son, was holidaying there as a guest of the Italian government. He was enjoying the annual summer holiday which the Fascists organised for the children of Italian parents who lived in France. This certainly was part of the Fascist propaganda; they made believe that they cared for the children of our emigrants. What about our starving children in Italy? As the number of children going on summer camp holidays was limited, those who were recommended were the lucky ones.

Father knew about the camp where Jacques was staying, so we went there by bus and obtained permission to take him away with us for the afternoon. Jacques, a boy of about fourteen, was in his *Balilla* (young boy Fascist) uniform and wore a badge on the left of his chest, on which was embossed the image of a ferocious-looking *Duce* – who had a helmet on his head and looked ready to challenge the whole world in combat. Jacques knew a few words of Italian, for he had learned them at the school for the children of Italian emigrants in Rouen.

We did not waste time, we had some refreshments and then went to visit Saint Peter's Church, the Forum and the Colosseum. I was much impressed; it reminded me of the ancient Roman history I had studied at school, and of the splendour of Imperial Rome.

Those ruins were evocative of the past and gave me a feeling of belonging. Entranced as I was, I would gladly have remained there in profound meditation but, like any other human being, I had to move on and do what God wanted me to do. Perhaps He wanted me to leave my country and face the conflicting and competitive world. Would I really become a rich man by doing so – or was all the fuss just a matter of scraping a living?

At about two o'clock we were feeling hungry, so we entered one of the countless busy restaurants, ready to devour a donkey. The smell coming from the kitchen was highly stimulating. We sat down at a table, the only one that was unoccupied. A waiter with a moustache – resembling our King Victor Emmanuel III – came forward and handed us the menu, on which several appetising Roman dishes and famous wines were listed. Father ordered a litre of white wine. We ate spaghetti, aubergines with tomato sauce and Parmesan cheese, stuffed roasted peppers, Roman cheese and fruits.

We were surrounded by the conviviality of visitors and customers who were so obviously enjoying their food. Everyone seemed to be laughing and conversing amicably. We heartily enjoyed our rather elaborate lunch and were also now jovially disposed. Father paid the bill which amounted to twenty-five lire (equivalent to about sixty old pence), tipped our King Victor Emmanuel III waiter and then we left the restaurant. By now it was about 4.00 p.m. and, as the sun was still high in the sky, we went to visit Piazza Di Spagna, the Trevi Fountain, Saint Mary Major, the Quirinale, the majestic Roman Cenotaph and Venice Palace from which *Il Duce* delivered his famous inflammatory speeches.

With so much happening in one day, we were feeling a little weary. Tony and I were not used to the dense traffic and glamour of a large city; we badly needed a rest to revive ourselves before embarking on the thirty-hour journey to Paris. However, we made an effort and so Father, Saverio, Tony and I accompanied Jacques back to his camp. By now it was well after seven o'clock. We had a light meal with a little wine at a restaurant near the station. The wine made Father almost tipsy and must have affected his judgement, for we only just had time to rush to the station, retrieve our luggage from the baggage room and hurry to the platform. Luckily we arrived there five minutes before our train's departure.

We should have got there earlier because the compartments were already packed, Rome being the starting-point of the train for Paris. Had we got there sooner, we could have settled down calmly. As it was, we had to struggle and force our way in. My heart was beating fast from running to catch the train. Gasping for breath, I sat on one of our strong suitcases in the packed corridor. Father, Saverio and Tony had to stand wherever they could. It was so uncomfortable, and it was all Father and Saverio's fault for leaving the train to the last moment. So for much of the night, we had to breathe in the suffocating cigarette-smoke-polluted corridor, hoping all the time that some passengers would get off the train somewhere along the route, so that we could take their seats.

The train sped north along the coast of the Tyrrhenian Sea, and after hours of jolting and shaking it reached Livorno (Leghorn) and Pisa in the middle of the night. Luckily a number of passengers got off, so we were able to sit down, make ourselves comfortable and try to doze for a few hours. By the time the train arrived at Genoa, we were able to sit together in the same compartment. Later on, while I was snoozing, I was shaken by a sudden violent jerk. I woke up and was dazzled by brilliant sunlight. The blue Ligurian Sea enchanted me with its vividness. It seemed to enchant the train also, for it shrilled and shrilled as if fresh vigour had been pumped into it.

We were sharing our compartment now with two middle-aged Italian couples who lived in Paris. They refreshed themselves with omelettes, *grissini*, ham, cheese and plenty of coffee from thermos flasks. Our snacks were modest in comparison. Not being hungry, we breakfasted on white coffee and bread rolls. At noon we lunched on bread and mozzarella and fruit we had bought in Rome. We also drank mineral water which we could buy from trolleys alongside the platforms.

I felt sad as the train moved away from the sparkling sea, on its way to Turin. Adieu Ligurian Sea, I thought. When will I be able to see you again? I could not get over my nostalgic feeling about leaving Italy, my beloved homeland. The train would soon approach the Alps, pass through short and long tunnels and reach French territory. This chain of thoughts weakened my resolve to live in a foreign country. I felt uncertain and confused now and wanted to go back home, to my *Bella Napoli*. I had not gone very far from home and already I missed my mother, my sisters, my friends and

132

even my small miserable town – yet I couldn't turn back and become the laughing stock of my friends, a gutless boy, a sissy. Whether I liked it or not, therefore, I had to soldier on, be tough, be a man ready to face a world of toil, stress and strife.

The train entered Turin station after ten. It was a fine sunny day and I could breathe the fresh air coming from the nearby lofty mountains. I didn't see much of the city from the train, except some new and old houses similar to those I had seen elsewhere. Groups of natives were in high spirits as they chatted and laughed, but their Piedmontese dialect sounded like Greek to me; it made me feel as if I were already in a foreign country.

The train stopped for half an hour and this enabled us to buy some food and fruit which we would need on our way to Paris.

At about eleven the train whistled and puffed its way out of the station, then on it went towards the French border. We refreshed ourselves with some fruit while our travelling companions had white coffee and biscuits. We didn't know their names, but since we had to travel many hours together, we were longing to make their acquaintance and have a chat with them. According to the labels attached to their luggage, the family name of one couple was Merlo, the other one Ferro.

'We'll soon arrive at Modane,' said signor Merlo, 'get your passports ready.'

'Beware of French immigration and customs officers,' said signor Ferro. 'If they smell a rat, they can be very fastidious and troublesome.'

'Yes, that is so,' signor Merlo confirmed. 'Last year, because of some drug dealers, the train stopped at Modane much longer than usual.'

We listened to what signor Merlo and signor Ferro were saying, but before we had the chance to engage in conversation with them, the train arrived at the border. Here a number of French passengers boarded our train, and customs and immigration officers began their inspection. Fortunately the checking of documents and luggage went smoothly – there were no suspect smugglers aboard – so after half an hour's stop, the train was allowed to depart from Modane.

We were in France now, travelling through mountain country similar to that on the Italian side of the border. High up, here and there, there were patches of ice, and the slopes were thickly covered with trees and undergrowth. Water gushed from rocks, tumbled down and gathered, forming into streams. Occasionally a lake came into view. Its smooth mirror-like surface reflected the mountain tops and the sky. At the edges of lakes there were often flocks of sheep drinking or grazing.

I gazed at the landscape curiously, endeavouring to discover something typically French, but nothing particularly foreign caught my eye. In fact, I thought that the Italian landscape was more colourful and picturesque. The French sky was partly cloudy and it made me feel downhearted. Were we going to the North Pole? I didn't find the French passengers particularly cheerful. Compared with Italians, they seemed gloomy and reserved. Father knew a few French words which he had learned when he was in Normandy, years before he went to Java. We would have to rely on him to ease our way in France.

At about 2.00 p.m. we arrived at Chambéry, where more French passengers joined the train. I was getting restless, looking forward to seeing the capital of the French Empire, an extremely exciting city – the Hollywood of Europe.

Our companions said: 'We like Paris very much. It's a lovely and lively city – full of life, even at night. We have been living there for many years and wouldn't like to live anywhere else. There's wealth and glamour there. The food's cheap and most of the people live very well. Paris is packed now with thousands and thousands of tourists who are visiting the International Exposition. It'll be difficult to find accommodation if you haven't booked in advance.'

I was listening carefully to what signor Merlo and signor Ferro were saying, and it stirred my imagination. Although we were still hundreds of kilometres from the capital, I could almost 'see' the Eiffel Tower. Signor Merlo and signor Ferro were just ordinary people who worked for a French-Italian company in Paris. They were very refined and looked prosperous.

Later, when the train arrived, I think at Chalon-Sur-Saône, Father bought some mineral water which he paid for with francs that signor Merlo kindly gave us in exchange for lire. We refreshed ourselves with the remaining food. Father said: 'We'll have a hot meal when we arrive in Paris.'

After 4.00 p.m. the train was on the move again and we were deep in the heart of France. By gosh, where am I? I thought. Among the Gauls? Many of them have Roman blood in their veins. What a pity they don't speak Roman or Neapolitan, or the language of Dante! That would save me the trouble of learning their language.

My brother Tony must have felt more or less as I had since leaving home. Father was used to long travels and staying away from his family, so probably homesickness no longer affected him. Saverio had already been away from home for more than three years, when he went to Java. Now he had left his attractive girlfriend Maria in Naples, the girl he was wooing, and probably did not know what to make of it. Whether he was going to marry her or not, depended on how well we did in business in Rouen. Tony didn't say much; no doubt he was too absorbed and marvelled at whatever he could see from the train window. Like me, he was interested in what signor Merlo and signor Ferro were saying.

Being tired, almost drunk with so many new experiences, I dozed, awoke, dozed and awoke again with a kind of blissful awareness. Was this the result of the prayers that Mother was saying for us? At about eight o'clock the train was past Dijon. It shrilled excitedly and was going faster now than ever.

'Our train is two hours late,' said signor Ferro. 'We'll arrive in Paris now, if all goes well, at eleven or perhaps at midnight.'

'I didn't sleep a wink,' said signora Ferro, yawning. 'This Jerking and jolting about is too much for me. I'm extremely tired and I'm very much-looking forward to getting home to my comfortable bed and resting for two whole days at least! I'll enjoy every minute of it.'

'Travelling at this time of the year, with so many people returning from-holidays, can be very trying,' agreed signora Merlo. 'We've been holidaying in Rome and its surroundings. We had a good time, but there were too many Blackshirts around, swaggering and shouting *Viva Il Duce*. They're Mussolini's fanatics. Even little girls and boys were wearing Fascist uniforms!'

'We have democracy in France and can criticise the government, but I had to be very careful in Rome,' said signor Merlo.

'The French democracy, I'm afraid, is corrupt,' argued signor Ferro. 'Besides, there are too many communists. The *Front Populaire* is dominant and alarming. They hate Fascists and rich people. Most of the workers drink too much, don't want work, or don't work hard, and then complain that they are poor.'

'If I spent my salary on drinks, I'd be as poor as they are,' said signor Merlo. 'The French politicians – Laval, Herriot, Blum,

Daladier and so on – are always quarrelling among themselves and unable to form a stable government; we have a new government every month. The politicians are also very concerned with the Germans who, having occupied the Rhineland in 1936, are now re-arming themselves. This is more or less the situation in France today. The Frenchmen seem to be confident in their Maginot line; they consider it impregnable and think it'll deter the Germans from attacking France.'

PART TWO

A YEAR IN FRANCE

27

We arrive in Paris. Signor Sorrentino invites us to dinner. We pay a visit to Michelino and later catch the train for Rouen

At last we arrived in Paris. It was about eleven o'clock. From the train window I could see colourful neon signs and nothing else in that moonless night. There was a stir now as passengers started removing their luggage from the racks. The train entered the Gare de Lyon and came to a standstill.

The station was all lit up and very crowded. Friends, wives, husbands and parents were either welcoming passengers or saying goodbye to them. We bade farewell to our travelling companions, then hired a porter who carried our luggage outside the station. Here, Father hailed a taxi which drove us to a small, clean and not too expensive hotel. We found a double room containing a large bed and two single ones. We had an inside toilet, a wash-basin, a shower and plenty of hot and cold water.

We had to spend the night in Paris because Father wanted to make contact with a couple of old friends who lived there. Besides, it was too late to go to the Gare Saint-Lazare and catch the train for Rouen. We had a quick wash, changed our clothes and went out for a light meal. It was well after midnight when we left the restaurant, but we didn't feel tired, for we were far too excited about being in Paris.

Father, aware of our excitement, took us for a stroll. He knew that in the vicinity of our hotel was a bar which Neapolitans frequented. The main streets, brightly lit up, suggested gaiety. Even at that late hour there were many people around. Elegantly attired couples, arm in arm, were perhaps on their way to nightclubs or going home. Women used a lot of make-up, I noticed. I saw a number of glamorous blondes. Were they film stars? Why not?

We were, after all, in the European city well known for film-making.

After ten minutes' walk or so we came to a bar where a group of Neapolitans were sitting at a table and chatting noisily. One of them recognised Father and walked towards us.

'Hello, Giovanni!' he exclaimed. 'How are you? Have you just arrived? Why so late?'

He shook hands with Father and us.

'You have a large family, haven't you? Your brother rang me up last week and told me you would be passing through Paris on your way to Rouen. Come, sit down and have a drink.'

We sat at a table near the men who were talking animatedly and each of us had a glass of beer. Soon Father and his friend were busily talking about the good old times. They mentioned their pals who no longer lived in Paris.

In spite of the late hour, several people came into the bar for refreshment. Saverio, Tony and I were listening to what the Neapolitans were saying, but did not get involved ourselves in their conversation.

Most of the Italians who settled in France, except for a few political refugees and Fascists, did not meddle in politics. They went there to work, make a living, and had neither the time nor the energy to devote to other activities. Some followed cultural programmes, just to keep in touch with their country. Their children usually went to French schools, assimilated French culture and grew up almost like French children, attached to the French way of living.

We left the bar after two, walked back to our hotel and were in bed by three o'clock. We slept for five hours. We got up and breakfasted in the hotel on large cups of white coffee and buttered *brioches* (buns). While eating we listened to the French news, coming from a wireless in the hotel lounge, without understanding a word of it.

It was a bright sunny day and the radio was playing popular French melodies such as 'J'ai Deux Amours', 'Un Reve D'Amour', 'J'attendrai', sung by Maurice Chevalier, Josephine Baker and Edith Piaf. I was no longer in my body. My soul had fused with waves of musical notes floating in the air all over that magical city. Those songs, and the enchanting way they were sung, made me fall in love with Paris.

140

1916. From right, front row: Grandfather Saverio and Grandmother Carmela. Back row:Uncle Cosimo and his fiancé. Uncle Cosimo died on the front in 1917.

1900. Grandfather Vincenzo, Mother's father.

Mother and Father when they got married in 1913.

Photo taken in 1916. From left: my sister
Carmela, Mother and my brother Saverio.

From right: Carmela, Saverio, Vincenzo,
Cosimo (me) and Antonio. This photo
was taken in 1923.

Photo was probably taken in 1926 at Castellamale (Pozzano). From right: Carmela,
Saverio, Cosimo (Me), Giuseppe, Mother, Maria and Vincenzo.

Photo taken in 1933, while we were holidaying at Gerolomini (Naples). From left: Carmela, Vincenzo, Cosimo (Me), Saverio, Antonio, Giuseppe, Maria, Fortuna, Immacolata, Damiano, Teresa.

Photo taken either in 1933 or at the beginning of 1934. First row from left: Teresa, Damiano and Immacolata. Second row from left: Giuseppe, Antonio, Fortuna and Cosimo (me). Third row from left: Carmela, Saverio, Maria and Vincenzo.

Patron saints of Secondigliano.

Immaculate Conception in the
Chapel of the Sacred Hearts.

Venerable Gaetano Errico,
founder of the Missionaries of the
Sacred Hearts.

We left the breakfast table at about nine o'clock. Father made a phone call to his close friend signor Vincent Sorrentino. He and Father had grown up together, played in the street and went to the same school. Their telephone conversation must have gone something like this:

'Hello, Vincent, it's me, Giovanni.'

'Oh! How are you, Giovanni? Pascal told me about you. When did you arrive?'

'Last night. I didn't ring you up because it was too late.'

'Did you have a good journey?'

'Not too bad. The train was about two hours late.'

'Sorry to hear that, but in a long journey delay can be expected. Where did you spend the night?'

'At a small hotel not far away from the station.'

'How long are you staying in Paris?'

'Till this afternoon. We'll have to catch the train for Rouen.'

'You said *we*, what do you mean? Oh, sorry, I forgot. Your brother told me that you were bringing your sons with you. Come and have dinner with me. You can come between midday and one, my wife and daughter will be very pleased to see you.'

'All right, Vincent, see you later. Now I'm taking my boys to visit the Eiffel Tower.'

Father bought some francs at a bank near the hotel. Later we travelled by Metro to Place de la Concorde. It was a very large square indeed, but we couldn't stay too long; we were on the way to the Eiffel Tower. Since there were too many tourists queuing up, we didn't go to the top of the tower. We went now to visit Les Jardins du Trocadéro.

At midday we caught a taxi which drove us to Sorrentino's house, where we arrived at about twelve-thirty, and with a good appetite, ready to devour a delicious and substantial dinner that signora Sorrentino might have prepared for us.

I reckoned that Sorrentino was more or less my father's age. Father was then about fifty. Sorrentino was of average height, stocky, had black hair with a left parting and a healthy complexion. He spoke calmly and clearly and seemed always to be relaxed and smiling.

Before emigrating to France, he had been a butcher who had had to work hard for his daily bread. Father had felt sorry for his dear old friend, so in the early twenties he had helped him by paying his railway ticket to France.

141

Being a newcomer and almost illiterate, he couldn't find work there, so he became a door-to-door salesman. He put aside some money, and with the help of his wife, he set up a shop near the Gare de Lyon. He supplied suiting material to door-to-door salesmen (*magliari*, as they were called in Naples). He knew exactly what kind of merchandise they wanted. If unscrupulous salesmen cheated their buyers, it wasn't Sorrentino's concern. He ran a shop, paid taxes and had a reputation for being a decent fellow. He also employed a couple of Russian refugees whom he found to be reliable workers.

As soon as we arrived at his place, he welcomed us with a radiant smile.

'Just in time, Giovanni,' he said to Father, 'my wife has prepared a good minestrone. It's what you need after a long journey.'

His assistants closed the shop for the midday summer break, which was from one o'clock to four.

'Come this way,' he bade us, and led us through the shop and a short corridor, where his lift was ready to take us to his flat, a couple of floors above his shop.

'My word,' I muttered, 'he has got his own lift! Only rich people can afford this luxury in Naples.'

Such ostentatious display, especially when I noticed his expensive motor car parked in his courtyard afterwards, made me wonder how prosperous Sorrentino was.

Father knew signora Sorrentino; her first name was Fortuna. Sorrentino, Father and she had played together when they were children. Saverio, being four years older than me, had already met Sorrentino and his wife when he was a small boy, but they were complete strangers to Tony and me.

As Sorrentino and Fortuna were childless, they had adopted a little girl whose name was Maria. In 1937 she might have been seventeen. She had been educated in France, so she was more French than Italian. She was plump, attractive, had long black hair parted in the middle and an oval face. She looked like a film star to me.

Fortuna was in her forties, wore a dark frock, had black hair twisted into a tight bun at the back of her head and a happy personality. She was a typical comely housewife. As a young girl, because she had a rather long neck, her friends had nicknamed her *Collo di pinto* (turkey-neck).

Fortuna and Maria were waiting for us outside the lift. They greeted us warmly and then led us to the dining-room, which was rather small but cosy. There was a rectangular mahogany table meticulously prepared for seven – the Sorrentino family and the four of us. Moreover there were two glass-panelled cupboards containing silver cutlery and china, wooden stands supporting flowerpots which adorned two corners of the room, Oriental tapestry on the walls, high-backed chairs, red velvet curtains at the windows and a chandelier hanging overhead. All the rooms had shiny wooden floors with fancy pink carpets in the middle. The flat had a luxurious bathroom and toilet and seemed fit for a king.

We sat at the table, with Father at the head and Sorrentino and Fortuna at either side, while Maria faced Saverio, and I was opposite Tony. Each of us had four glasses set in front of us, one for the aperitif, one for white wine, one for red wine and one for water. What a show of luxury! Tony and I were perplexed at the sight of so many glasses. At home we used one glass either for water or wine, and I am sure we did not need an aperitif to stimulate our appetite.

Father said grace and then we started our succulent dinner. We sipped the aperitif and afterwards ate hors d'oeuvres consisting of slices of salami, anchovy, celery, lettuce, salad tomatoes, black olives and *grissini* (bread sticks). Tony and I were shy. Since we were eating in the company of charming Maria, we felt that we had to mind our Ps and Qs. We slowed down our eating and tried to be as polite as possible – the proximity of Maria had suddenly civilised us! We didn't touch the food with our hands or make noises with our mouths – such as smacking our lips in the usual way while eating and drinking. In other words Tony and I suddenly became quintessential examples of good manners and gentility.

Fortuna cleared away the used plates and brought in a large porcelain soup tureen which she placed at the centre of the table. In it was a minestrone with a strong and very appetising flavour. We helped ourselves with a silver ladle. It was so delicious that Tony and I, bravely disregarding our shyness, went for a second helping. Maria was amused at our rather awkward manner; she probably came to the conclusion that we were not, after all, what we pretended to be, but just two common boys unable to control their animal instincts.

While we were eating, the conversation was reduced to a

minimum. Allusions were made to old friends and the general situation. After the minestrone we ate grilled fish with a dressing of parsley, olive oil and lemon. We drank white wine with the fish and red wine with roast beef. The dinner ended with dessert and coffee.

Sorrentino's dinner had been excellent, but Tony and I, having to behave like gentlemen, had not enjoyed it as much as the frugal meals we had at home.

'Giovanni, let me know how you're getting on with your business,' Sorrentino said. Then he went on, 'The situation isn't very good with this trouble going on between France and Germany, and France and Italy. I hope that things will improve. Anyhow, I wish you success in Rouen, and if I can be of help, don't hesitate to ask; I'm always your friend, remember.'

Having thanked signor Sorrentino and his family for their kind hospitality, we left their place after three o'clock. It was a sunny afternoon and we had about two hours to spare before catching the train for Rouen.

As I wished to visit an old friend of mine who was living in Paris, Father hailed a taxi that drove us to Rue Michel-Chasles, where my friend's brother had a shop.

My friend, Michelino, had emigrated to France at the end of 1936. He lived with his married brother and helped in his shop.

I had known Michelino since childhood; we were of the same age, and grew up together. His parents ran a delicatessen next door to the building where I was born. His mother, Concetta, and my mother were close friends. Her customers nicknamed her *La Rossa* (the red one) because she had red hair, and so did my friend when he was a little boy.

Michelino knew that we would be passing through Paris, but did not know exactly when. Luckily he was in the shop when we arrived. As soon as he saw me, he came towards me.

'Hello! How're you, Michelino?' I shouted happily.

'Come in, do come in,' said his brother cordially.

Father, my brothers and I went inside the shop. They were not too busy at that time of the afternoon. We exchanged greetings with my friend's brother whose name was Oreste. Father knew him well.

Oreste had a wife whose name was Lili, probably a diminutive for Liliana. She was from our small town too. They had been living in Paris several years and liked it. They were a little worried about the political situation, but did not take it too seriously. They offered us some coffee. We reminisced about those years when we were children, played games and had no worries. Unfortunately we could not indulge in tender thoughts, because we had to go back to our hotel, get our luggage, drive to the Gare Saint-Lazare and catch the half past five train for Rouen. We left the Michelinos, promising that we would see them again some time, either in Paris or when they might pay us a visit in Rouen after we had settled down.

We arrived at the Gare Saint-Lazare a few minutes before the train was due to depart, so we were able to sit in an empty compartment. Soon the train was on its way to Rouen, which was about 140 kilometres from Paris. I felt that the look of the countryside was dull and uninviting. It seemed so cold and strange after the warm south of Italy that it almost gave me goose-flesh. The train sped north-west, stopping at several stations and gradually filling up with French passengers. My brothers and I did not understand what they were saying, so we furtively examined them, observing their peculiarities.

The light of the day was fading away when the train pulled into the Gare Rive Droite (Rouen's station, situated on the right bank of the Seine). It was about seven o'clock. Uncle Pascal and Aunt Mary met us at the station and welcomed us with hugs. Uncle Pascal had an old Citroën with him but, as the car was too small for all of us and our luggage, we had to hire a taxi. Uncle Pascal led the way in his car to a small hotel near his home, in which he had booked a family room for us. He lived in Rue Cauchoise, near Place du Vieux Marché, the market where Jeanne d'Arc was burned at the stake in 1431.

Our hotel room was spacious. It contained two double beds, toilet and shower, and was very comfortable indeed. They even polished our shoes if we left them outside our room at night.

We breakfasted at the hotel on hot chocolate and *brioches* and had midday and evening meals at Uncle Pascal's house. Aunt Mary was an excellent cook – especially when she prepared stewed rabbit, which was one of her specialities.

Aunt Mary was in her forties, slim and energetic. She had fair hair, grey eyes and a rather small face with rosy cheeks. She kept her flat very tidy and her wooden floor well polished. She often scolded her fourteen-year-old son, Jacques, who was obstinate and moody. She had a preference for Moïse, who was younger than Jacques, but more obedient and of a happier disposition.

145

I had the sneaking suspicion that Aunt Mary was not too keen on having us for meals at her place, which meant extra work for her. No doubt Uncle Pascal had begged her to accommodate us in order to help us with our expenses. Had we gone to a restaurant, it would have cost us a great deal more than we were paying Uncle for our keep. Aunt Mary also had a grudge against Father. This was because of what had happened in Rouen in the twenties, while Aunt Mary was sewing a button at the back of Father's trousers. Unable to control his bowels, he had suddenly broken wind. Aunt Mary was revolted and screamed: '*Cochon! Cochon!*' (Pig! Pig!). Father found this funny and had exploded in a fit of laughter. This only served to exacerbate Aunt's revulsion.

Unable to communicate with her because she couldn't speak Italian, and owing to her lack of cordiality, I didn't feel at home while we were having our meals in her house. I sorely missed our warm family atmosphere, my friends and the Italian way of life. I felt sad, displaced, and I experienced for the first time the disadvantages of being in a foreign land.

28

Uncle Pascal arranges for us to rent a four-bedroom flat. We start a mackintosh factory. We spend some Sunday afternoons with the Elouards

Uncle Pascal arranged for us to take a four-bedroom flat in Rue Jeanne d'Arc. As one walked from the Gare Rive Droite, the flat was on the left side of the road – near the Hôtel de la Poste. Farther down the road – not too far away – came the old Rue du Gros Horloge. I don't know whether the Hôtel de la Poste is still there now, or was bombed during the Second World War.

Uncle drove us all over Rouen to auction sales, where we bought some furniture and two stoves to keep our flat warm. Moreover, we had to buy two new double beds, some more furniture, curtains, sheets and blankets and kitchen utensils. As soon as gas, electricity and telephone had been connected we moved into the flat. We had a French charwoman, the wife of an Italian, to do some cleaning three times a week.

Vince, Tony and I helped to clean our flat, which was dusty, before we moved in. All in all, however, it was in reasonably good condition.

Father and Tony went to the market two or three times a week. It was just an early morning market, not far away, where we could buy cheaply. There was plenty of fresh fish from Le Havre, a variety of cheese, poultry, fruit, vegetables and so on. Fruit came mainly from Spain. Basic food, including beef and stewing meat, was cheap.

We drank very light apple wine with our meals; it was made with the residue of apples which had already been pressed to make cider. We also drank beer or wine, especially when we had guests. We used to buy, like any French family, kegs of light apple wine, bottled beer and other kinds of wine, and store them in our small cellar. Every tenant had a cellar to store alcoholic beverages.

Raffaele, our designer and cutter, arrived from Naples a week before we moved into our flat; he had to sort out the equipment needed for our mackintosh factory. We bought two long tables, two electric cutters, two second-hand sewing machines, shelves, clothing material, lining, cotton, buttons and so on.

Uncle Pascal knew many people and had good business connections. Sorrentino furnished us with some of the textiles suitable for our production. In no time we found some skilful machinists, rolled up our sleeves and started work.

Raffaele, being the expert, was in charge. Vince, Tony and I were his assistants. Raffaele occasionally introduced a new pattern and, if it was suitable, we put it into production.

I learned to align the material by placing each length on top of the previous one, until I had formed a thickness of thirty or forty or more layers. This had to be done accurately, making sure that each layer was in line. The top one, which had already been marked with chalk, served to guide the electric cutter through the thickness of the material. We could even cut 100 mackintoshes in one operation. To cut linings we followed the same procedure. When the cutting had been done, the cut sections of material and the lining had to be separated and made into bundles. Each bundle contained front, back, collar, sleeves, lining and the cotton and buttons of each mackintosh. The machinists collected the bundles, stitched the pieces together, fixed the lining, and when they had finished they delivered their made-up mackintoshes. Saturday was pay-day. The machinists received a set amount for each mackintosh.

We produced good quality and not-too-expensive mackintoshes, which about a dozen salesmen sold for us. Some market stall owners were also interested in our product. We had made a good start; this was very encouraging and promising, and we kept our machinists fully occupied.

We worked six days a week. On Sundays we attended Mass in Notre Dame, Rouen's cathedral, which was not far from our home.

This cathedral in Rouen was built between the early thirteenth and sixteenth centuries. It is a Gothic building that was badly damaged during the Second World War and is a major tourist attraction.

We had our excellent Sunday dinner which Father prepared. He was quite a good cook. We dined at one o'clock and went out in the afternoon. From October onward it was almost winter there –

or so it seemed to us, coming from a sunny country as we did. The sky was mostly cloudy and the weather chilly.

Uncle Pascal introduced us to his next door neighbours, the Elouard family. The Elouards frequently invited us to Sunday afternoon tea during autumn and winter. They had four sons and a girl who was the baby of the family.

Monsieur Elouard was tall and slim, had grey hair, a long face and a pale complexion. He wore bifocals and always peered at his interlocutors. He spoke calmly and seemed to ponder over his words as if he were weighing them up. He had a tendency to be reticent, but, like English folk, he used to pass comments on the local weather, which was very similar to that in England. He was neatly attired in a dark-grey suit; a kind of uniform worn by most of the office workers. As he was in charge of a branch of an advertising company, it was customary, regardless of the hour? to offer a Pernod (an aperitif) when he dealt with a client. In consequence of this, even though he suffered from poor health, poor Monsieur Elouard found it extremely difficult to abstain from alcohol.

Madame Elouard was tall, slim and energetic. Her black hair was parted in the middle and twisted into a tight bun at the back of her head. She had dark smiling eyes, a soothing voice and really cared for her family. I thought she was exceedingly courteous, trying very hard at all times to please those who came in touch with her. She was inclined to agree with everybody by saying: '*Oui, oui, c'est ça*' (Yes, yes, it's so). Rarely did she say no.

The Elouards' sons, Jean, Paul and Daniel, were all over twenty. Paul and Daniel did not live with their parents; they worked in offices in other parts of France. They usually visited their mother and father at Christmas and at Easter.

Jean was about twenty-four. He was tall and slim and worked as his father's office assistant. Samuel, the youngest son, was about eighteen and still studying. Mademoiselle Denise, their only daughter, was fifteen and a student also.

Jean resembled his mother. He tried to teach us French by letting us recite or sing nursery rhymes. Mademoiselle Denise, although not physically attractive yet, had charming manners like her mother. When we went to visit the Elouards on those cold Sunday afternoons, Mademoiselle Denise used to say to me, 'Sit down here,' meaning beside her. 'Are you warm and comfortable? Have some cake! Do you prefer tea or cocoa?' If I made a mistake while she was teaching me how to play a game or speak French, she smiled and said, 'It doesn't matter, you'll learn.'

Monsieur Elouard and Jean were the breadwinners. I think they earned good salaries and could provide all the comforts for their family, and were even able to save for rainy days.

I remember, as if it were yesterday, the first time we went to visit the Elouards. I was wearing a new double-breasted striped blue suit which fitted well, a new pair of leather shoes and a grey *Borsalino* hat which Father had bought in Naples. I looked like a tailor's dummy. Aware of being elegantly dressed, I was feeling conceited and walked very stiffly, with head high and chest forward like a soldier on parade. Father and Saverio were amused by my self-important bearing.

Our flat was situated on the mezzanine floor of the building, just one flight of stairs – about fifteen or twenty steps – from the ground floor. The wooden steps had recently been polished and we were ready to go down. I placed one of my feet forward, but as the sole of my new shoe touched the floor, I slipped – suddenly my body was in the air – and then I fell on my buttocks and slid all the way down. The *concierge* (caretaker) heard the noise of my fall and hurried to assist me. Having made sure that I wasn't hurt, she, Saverio and Father helped me to my feet. I came to no harm, because I was wearing thick woolly underwear. My fall reminded Father and Saverio of one of the comical scenes in a Charlie Chaplin film and, once I had got over my shock, they couldn't stop laughing.

While we were visiting the Elouards, we met the Barb and the Millot families who lived in the same building as the Elouards and Uncle. They too were invited to the Elouards' Sunday teas.

Monsieur and Madame Barb had two daughters, Juliette and Nicole. Juliette was about seventeen and a student. She was blonde, had ringlets and blue eyes in an oval face. Her figure was very shapely. Nicole might have been thirteen. She was also blonde and looked like an angel. She wore a blue school uniform and a blue-brimmed hat most of the time.

We often played dominos at the Elouards' house, or a kind of hide-and-seek. When we did so Vince, who had set his eyes on Juliette, contrived to be near her and to fondle or even kiss her. No doubt she liked it, for she responded to Vince's amorous looks and touches with evident delight. Unfortunately such romance could not

150

last, for Juliette had to study and Vince had to work hard helping to keep our factory going.

Monsieur Barb, Juliette's father, was a customs officer with an itchy palm; he would do anything for money. He loved his food, his Pernod and a few drops of Calvados (a brandy made from apples). He was rather an awkward person and would have disapproved of Vince's amorous relations with his daughter; we couldn't afford to make enemies.

We worked eleven hours a day and six days a week. Being two years older than I was, Vince wanted to boss me. He wanted to do the most important tasks such as grading patterns for our production, taking orders and getting in touch with our customers. This gave him the chance to learn and practise his French. He passed on all the menial tasks to Tony and me. I resented his behaviour, because in many ways I felt that I was more mature and able than he was. We often had arguments because of his attitude, yet we had to carry on and do our best, otherwise our business would not survive among so much competition.

Soon after his arrival, Raffaele found a French lover and went to live with her. Had he already put aside his wife in Naples, who had to work hard to feed him while he was unemployed?

We had our evening meal, which was no less substantial than the midday one, at about half past seven. After this, all of us went for a long walk together. Father seemed to chaperon us; he probably feared that we might get mixed up with bad company, go astray and eventually cause the disintegration of our family. And if each of us went his own way, what would happen to the rest of the family – Mother, our five sisters and two young brothers in Naples? Who was going to look after them? Father wasn't getting younger and had put his trust in us; he couldn't do without our help and cooperation. Without solidarity our future would be grim.

Our evening walk started from Rue Jeanne d'Arc, then we turned left and walked through Rue du Gros Horloge. Having reached the cathedral we proceeded past it, then we turned right and sauntered through the Rue de la République to the end of the street. We turned right again and found ourselves in Quai P. Corneille. We strolled along the right side of the quay, where there were bars, coffee-houses, shops and restaurants. On the left was the Seine, where ships coming from Le Havre unloaded. Then they loaded up again and sailed towards the Channel.

151

People sitting outside bars and restaurants were entertained by lively musicians and singers. In wintertime, the outside area of a number of bars and restaurants was covered with canvas. Every now and then, as we strolled along the quay, we would stop in front of a bar or a restaurant and listen to the music. Occasionally, we met an old friend of Father's who would invite us to sit there with him and have a glass of beer.

Quai P. Corneille petered out into Quai de la Bourse. Between these there was a bridge, Pont Boieldieu, which connected the two banks of the river. We continued our stroll along Quai de la Bourse, and having reached Pont Jeanne d'Arc, we turned right, proceeded about one third of the length of Rue Jeanne d'Arc and were home.

Rue du Gros Horloge, the centre of the city, was always crowded. There were fashionable shops, bars, restaurants, and the red light district was not far away. There was also a small bar or coffee-house where lonely Neapolitans gathered for a little companionship. They earned what they could and lived for the day to keep body and soul together. They did not go back to their homes in Naples, because life would not be easier there, so they had no alternative but to stay in Rouen. Being illiterate, or almost so, and not knowing any French, they had no chance to improve themselves whatsoever.

For one reason or another, as the years went by most of them lost contact with their families and friends. Since their dreams of getting rich had not come true, disillusion and frustration had sapped their confidence. Of course, they still had memories to reminisce about; the sweet memories of those years before they left their beloved native land, when they could at least enjoy the company of their relatives and friends. And what had they now? No money, no hope and no motivation. The only consolation left to these misfits was to stick together. When they had a little money, they put aside their bitterness and squandered it by having a sumptuous dinner. They drowned their sorrows in plenty of wine, and later sought the embraces of the girls in nearby brothels. This was the only kind of joy they could get.

29

Saverio goes back to Java. Our paternal grandfather dies

My autumn in Normandy was very trying. As the days shortened, the weather grew dull and chilly and utterly depressed me. I had no idea what a long winter was like. In Normandy it could last about six months. In Naples, winter started after Christmas and was virtually over by the end of February.

We had plenty of food in Rouen and could have had three square meals a day, but I was emotionally starved and unbalanced. It was all work, eat and sleep with no fun whatsoever. Visiting our French friends was more like hard work than recreation, because I did not understand them. I dearly missed the joy of using my own language, the joy of being able to express myself and participate in various activities. No wonder I jubilantly welcomed the visits of some of Father's old friends who always had so much to say about past and present events. They had a knack of telling stories which entranced and relaxed me and made me feel at home.

Although my heart was heavy with discontent at being in a foreign country, I did not complain. I had to be a man of fortitude, do my work in the factory and help Father as much as I could. He had spent 30,000 francs to get the business started, and we had to work very hard to make it pay. We had at least to earn our keep and the money for the remittances Father had to send home. Otherwise how could we have survived?

I could tell that Father was feeling the weight of keeping his large family and that he really cared for us. When he was in difficulty or had to face an unpredictable outcome, he sought the Almighty's guidance. He had always seemed detached and lacked that warm touch that Mother had; he was unable to win my affection. No doubt the rest of my family must have felt the same,

153

but when we needed his support, he was solidly behind us.

My brother Saverio had been with us in Rouen for less than two months. He was interested in buying and selling, but unfortunately Rouen wasn't a favourable place for him; he thought he couldn't make a future there. On the other hand, he had no intention of joining our mackintosh business. Initially, production was promising, but later it slowed down. Saverio made up his mind to go back to Java, where he could easily make money, so towards the end of November 1937 he returned to Naples, stayed a few days there, and then sailed for Java.

His days in Naples, while he was waiting for the ship to arrive, were not happy ones. He was very worried, for his future up to now had seemed precarious. It was because of this that he had to end his romance with Maria. Besides, while he was in France, Maria had been seen in the company of a young man. Saverio had to make a painful decision to put her out of his mind; after all, he had nothing substantial to offer her.

Having understood Saverio's emotional turmoil, Mother tried to cheer him up with her best cooking. This seemed to help him get over his misery. He went out, met his friends and had a little fun. Did he really get over his troubles so soon? It was hard to say. He looked cheerful; he even bought a six-valve Phillips radio and played it at full volume, so that Maria, who lived in a flat about fifteen metres away from our dining-room, would hear it and get the message that he wasn't broken-hearted. Incidentally this happening was a blessing in disguise for my family in Naples; the blessing of having acquired a radio – a source of entertainment, education and daily news.

Christmas 1937 was now almost upon us. For Vince, Tony and me it was the first Christmas away from home, and we were wondering what to do about it. On 2 December we received a telegram bringing us the sad news that our paternal grandfather had died. He was over seventy-five. We went to Uncle Pascal's place that day to mourn the deceased.

Father and Uncle decided that they would not attend the funeral, because they were worried about their businesses and the political situation. Besides, a long journey to Naples and back would be too tiring. They sent money for the funeral, and the following day we

154

went to Mass in memory of our grandfather.

As I mentioned, Grandfather was poor and had a large family. He was born on 25 January 1862 and married about 1882. As I remember him, he was of medium height, stocky, had curly hair, a wrinkled forehead, grey eyes and a swirly moustache. He smoked a pipe and, winter or summer, always wore a waistcoat. He had a gold watch which he often took out of his pocket, held in his right palm and looked at with a certain concern, as if he had to attend to some urgent business.

Grandfather had no doubt learned to read and write. Even if he had neglected these precious skills, he was still able, when it was necessary, to sign documents.

Since he was poor and had a family of eight, he and his wife decided to take their last born, Cosimo, to an institute for unwanted children in Naples. So the family was reduced to seven – two boys and five girls. Grandmother never got over the shock of having been separated from her newborn baby; a sense of guilt seemed always to haunt her.

Grandfather had to struggle extremely hard to scrape a living. In late 1918, soon after the Great War, he was still running two businesses, fishmongering and coal-selling. He employed some of his daughters who were in their twenties.

Being a shrewd man, he made sure to keep on friendly terms with local authorities and influential personalities. When he needed a licence, a birth certificate, an identity card, or even a passport either for himself or for anyone he wished to oblige, he could speed up the procedures with presents of fresh fish or coal. Since the favours that Grandfather obtained cost him money, he exacted a fee for services rendered.

He gave up his businesses when Father and Uncle Pascal, having gone to France and prospered, were able to send a monthly remittance to their parents. Uncle Pascal bought a small one-bedroom flat for them, so that they could live rent-free for the rest of their lives.

Grandfather liked a glass of wine. After his frugal evening meal he used to drop in at the wine shop just a hundred metres from his house, where he met a few old pals. Wine then was very cheap. Although he was struggling hard to make ends meet, he managed somehow to squander a lira or two on his evening pleasure. He and his friends smoked, drank and chatted about their ardent youth, romantic affairs, the Great War, dramatic events and the town's coming celebrations. When he came home he was a little tipsy, causing Grandmother to grumble. She nagged him the following morning, but never went too far, for she was very tolerant, thoroughly forgiving and affectionate.

He was the undisputed master of his family. While he was still virile, he was occasionally unfaithful to his wife, and by so doing, caught a venereal disease.

He did not drink heavily because he could not afford it. The wine he drank was not always genuine, for wine shop owners would not hesitate to adulterate it, if it helped to increase their profit. As a result, he contracted cirrhosis of the liver. In spite of this, he was not able to give up the wine shop, so in the end the drink did it for him. He left his golden watch and chain to my brother Tony.

30

*Christmas Eve at Garibaldi's place. Christmas at
Uncle Pascal's. We meet the* compare

Having got over Grandfather's death, Father and Uncle Pascal
arranged that we should have our traditional Neapolitan Christmas
Eve dinner at Garibaldi's place. Garibaldi, the name of a great
leader in the movement for Italian unity, a person of courage and
stature, was being used derisively as a nickname for a small and
frail Neapolitan man.

Garibaldi came from the town where I was born. He was an
illiterate coachman and a lively character. In the early twenties he
gave up his job and went to join the crowd of Neapolitan travelling
salesmen in France. He was now in his forties, slim and about five
feet tall. He had black hair, a wrinkled forehead, bushy eyebrows,
a hooked nose and rosy cheeks. He was boisterous, garrulous and
ever ready for a contest of strength – provided that there was
nobody to challenge him, else he would safely back down. He met
a French girl, probably while wandering through Normandy; a girl
who, being almost a hippopotamus, was unable to find a husband.
Rather than remain a spinster, when Garibaldi came along, she
chose to marry him and have children. What a fine couple they
made; she was a mountain and he a foothill. People were curiously
attracted by such an odd sight. When they went to bed, had she
landed on him, she would have crushed him to death!

Madame Garibaldi was almost six feet tall and in her thirties.
She was blonde, had short hair, blue eyes and a round face. She
was quiet and not inclined to confront her dwarfish husband, so he
assumed that he was the head of his family and felt cocky about it.
They had two teenage daughters and a two-year-old son. Since their
marriage, they had been living in a three-bedroom flat in a building
near Rue des Charettes.

Garibaldi was a heavy smoker; he enjoyed his cups of coffee with a few drops of brandy and a couple of Pernods. Apparently he was not terribly fond of making love to his fat and gigantic wife. To gratify his lust he visited brothels, where he could find some alluring *cocottes* (prostitutes).

Being unaccustomed to long winters, we found December chilly and depressing, but the thought of the coming Christmas and New Year celebrations somehow helped to boost our morale.

At eight o'clock on Christmas Eve, we, Uncle Pascal and his family, Garibaldi and his family – thirteen of us in all – sat at the long table in Garibaldi's large dining-room. A candelabra hung from the ceiling and illuminated the place splendidly. The room was furnished with two walnut cupboards, and there were pictures on the walls. The thick brown curtains of the dining-room's two windows shielded us from the chilly air. The room was cosy and warm, and in its corners were pots with artificial flowers.

Father, being the oldest, said grace, and soon we started eating. We ate oysters with lemon dressing and a salad as an appetiser. Then we had spaghetti with clams, fish, an endive pie, nuts, dry figs, fresh fruit and Christmas sweets. We drank wine, coffee with brandy, and even a few drops of Calvados which was supposed to be a digestive. By eating too much we made a mockery of Christmas Eve. I could feel a weight in my stomach, but I was cheerful, elated and inclined to sing. We were all in a jovial mood, so we sang Neapolitan songs and later Christmas carols. We left for home before midnight. We went to bed, but with such a full stomach, I couldn't go to sleep. I tossed and turned and longed for the dawn.

When we got up on Christmas Day we had some *Maté*, a South American tisane which Father used to drink instead of coffee. This beverage was supposed to help our digestion, for we had more celebrations ahead. We dressed ourselves, wearing our best, and then went to the eleven o'clock Christmas Mass at the cathedral. It was packed; the Christmas service had attracted many visitors.

The town's dignitaries and members of local high society were present. The pungent odour of incense hit my nostrils. There was lavish display and luxury – many bejewelled women in expensive fur coats and elegantly dressed men. The illumination and splendour of the church and the lullaby music created an atmosphere of sanctity. It was so impressive that it made me sense a heavenly presence. The Gothic style – vaults, carved pillars, frieze, stained glass – dazzled me; I imagined that I was an angel with a long trumpet floating above the nave and announcing the birth of Christ.

My father was praying, probably saying a rosary, praying for his recently deceased father, for Saverio on his way to Java and for our business to prosper – else how could he support the rest of our family in Naples? Saverio was Father's tower of strength.

The Mass, which was sung, lasted over an hour. After a quick visit to the crib we elbowed our way out of the cathedral. The town's dignitaries and nobility had gathered on the square outside the church and exchanged Christmas greetings.

The weather was cold and the sky grey. We buttoned up our coats and walked through the fashionable and crowded Rue du Gros Horloge, where we bumped into a group of Neapolitans and said '*Buon Natale*' (Merry Christmas). They invited us for a drink, but we could not stop, so we pressed on. Having reached Rue Jeanne d'Arc, we crossed over and soon arrived in Place du Vieux Marché. We proceeded through Rue Cauchoise and reached Uncle's home at about one o'clock. We met Uncle's neighbours, the Elouards, the Barbs and the Millots, and said '*Joyeux Noël.*' Mr Barb, having had too many midday aperitifs, was more boisterous than usual. Mademoiselle Denise gave me an unexpected kiss which made me blush. Being a little confused, I did not return it. She was about two years younger than me and very kind, but since she was not physically attractive, I didn't particularly enjoy her kiss. Soon we left our friends and were ready for our Christmas dinner.

Aunt Mary had decorated her small dining-room with colourful balloons, festoons, tinsel and silvery stars which hung from the ceiling. A small Christmas tree, with tiny coloured bulbs switched on, enhanced the festive tone of the well-lit room. It was a family feast. There were Uncle, Aunt and their two boys, four of us and an old guest. We sat at the rectangular dining-table neatly prepared with plates, cutlery and glasses. The four of us sat at one side; Uncle, his family and their guest faced us. Raffaele, our designer and cutter, did not join us; he was celebrating Christmas with his lover.

I don't remember the name of Uncle Pascal's Christmas guest. Father and Uncle Pascal called him *compare*, which means godfather. He was in his late fifties and came from our Neapolitan

159

neighbourhood. Father and Uncle had known him since their childhood. He had worn spectacles for many years so they nicknamed him 'the *compare* with spectacles'.

Neapolitans are in the habit of having many *compares*, real ones and those of second or third degree. The latter can be *compares* of near or distant relatives. Sometimes Neapolitans use a description after the name, for example, '*compare* with spectacles', to distinguish one from another.

The '*compare* with spectacles' whom Uncle had invited at Christmas, was stocky, with greying hair, a wrinkled forehead, a small nose and a healthy complexion. He wore gold-rimmed spectacles, which gave him the appearance of a distinguished man. He attracted attention, especially when he narrated past events, for he had a natural gift of charming and soothing his listeners. Father said that he had a heart of gold and was an open and sincere friend.

Owing to his goodness, his relatives took advantage of him and tried to exploit him in every way: 'Uncle, we're running short of money! Could you lend us twenty lire?' They were always pestering him for money, or for something or other, and they never paid it back. As he was getting old and money was hard to earn, he became reluctant to give it away, so he had to learn to say no and to keep his relatives at bay.

After all, he needed to save a little for a rainy day, when he got old and feeble and had no state pension to support him. He had to go abroad and do what his expatriate friends did, namely be a travelling salesman. He was honest, earned good money and did not squander it. Being thrifty, he was able to buy a couple of old houses and rent them, but he did not get much, so he still had to work to exist. As long as he was healthy, he did not hesitate to go abroad, hoping to earn a little extra before he retired.

The *compare* loved staying in Rouen; Normandy had never disappointed him. He lived on the mezzanine floor, in a double room in an old building not too far from Uncle's home, at a very reasonable rent. He cooked, did his own laundry, mended his shoes and darned his socks. He went to work in small towns, about twenty or thirty kilometres from Rouen.

Uncle Pascal often gave a lift to four or five door-to-door salesmen in his car and drove them to localities well away from Rouen. He dropped each man in a different area where he would do his day's work. In the afternoon, Uncle picked up the men one by one and drove them back to Rouen. However, when the *compare* joined the men in the car, they made fun of him.

'By gosh, it stinks,' one of the men would shout. 'Who's let one go?'

'I haven't,' a second man would say.

'And I haven't either,' a third man would add.

'It must be the *compare*!' a fourth man remarked. 'Open the window, for goodness' sake! Let in some fresh air! I'll need a gas mask here.'

'Do you see, *compare*, what you're doing? I think you're constipated. Take a tumblerful of castor oil tonight; take it regularly, otherwise one of these days we'll get asphyxiated.'

He did not answer; he just listened, and even smiled at their saucy jokes.

On other occasions they teased him about his sexual prowess.

'*Compare*, you're looking younger and more virile today. I bet you slept with a girl last night. Was she blonde or brunette?'

'What are you talking about! Fancy the *compare* sleeping with a girl! At his age he is a *rammollito* (a soft one); nothing will turn him on. Usually men in their late fifties leave the girls alone and take to drink.'

'Do you mean that the *compare* is impotent?'

'He could be a *finocchio* (gay).'

'Well! If he's a *finocchio*, he'll need a boyfriend.'

The *compare* was not in the least offended; he let them talk, amuse themselves and laughed at their frivolous chatter, their humorous outbursts. After all, they didn't have many opportunities to do so. They had been in France several years but hardly spoke French, so they had to rely on one another for a few jokes, a little fun, a change from their normal tedious existence.

Uncle Pascal supplied the *compare* with suiting material, usually three metres a piece. Because he was old and a very close friend, Uncle gave him a discount.

The *compare* knew a few French words he had learned by chance, which he had to use every day to help him get along. Being an honest salesman he had some French customers. They liked dealing with him because of his reliability, looks and manner, and because he had told them that he had fought side by side with the French soldiers at Verdun during the Great War.

The *compare* seldom returned from work without having sold

161

something. When he came home, he did his shopping, washed the vegetables, had fish or meat and the other ingredients ready, and then busied himself preparing dinner, his main meal. He preferred to use earthenware pots, especially when cooking minestrone, and said that by doing so, it tasted better. While the food was cooking, he made his bed, swept the floor, washed his shirts or darned his socks.

He usually dined at eight o'clock; for him dinner time was the best part of the day. He had a good appetite and ate a large meal. He sat at his small dining-table and said grace for the good food in front of him. He chewed every morsel thoroughly, felt it in his mouth and savoured it before swallowing. Every bite was a joy, bliss, a gastronomic pleasure which he washed down with a gulp of wine.

At the end of the meal, he cleared the table, washed up and then was ready for his two-kilometre evening stroll. If it was cold, he wrapped himself up in a heavy coat, wore a sporting cap on his large head, lit a cigar and went out. He invariably walked through Rue Jeanne d'Arc and the quays where glamorous coffee-houses, nightclubs and restaurants were located, and where artists and musicians performed till late. As he moved along, he was absorbed in his thoughts. Every now and then he came to a halt and gesticulated with his hands. It appeared as if he was having a soliloquy, arguing with himself on some important issue. He also stopped for a while in front of the places of entertainment, listening to the lively music being played there. He returned home through Rue de la République and Rue du Gros Horloge. Every night, before going to sleep, he thanked the Lord for the blessings he could still enjoy.

Dinner on Christmas Day was no less substantial than on Christmas Eve. It would have been wiser to forgo Uncle's invitation and fast for a couple of days, but we couldn't do that at short notice, and besides Aunt Mary had spent hours preparing dinner. Uncle treated us to an aperitif to stimulate our appetites. We ate ravioli, capon with vegetables, an endive salad with seasoned peppers, cauliflower, anchovy, capers and olives, dressed with olive oil and vinegar. Then we had venison, aubergines and roast peppers followed by a choice of three kinds of French cheese, plenty of delicious wine, fresh fruit, nuts, Christmas sweets, a little liqueur and even a few drops of Calvados. It was an excellent dinner, but we had to be careful, take small helpings and not overstrain our stomachs.

It was not so with Uncle's guest, the *compare*, for he had an endless appetite and could eat like a horse. He really relished all the food set before him. Everything went, and he washed it down with several glasses of wine. His cheeks and the tip of his nose were pink from his extravagant feasting.

Almost at the end of dinner, the *compare* was still cracking walnuts and greedily devouring them. However, as he noticed Aunt starting to clear the table and put the bread away, he stated: '*Le noci si mangiano con il pane*' (walnuts are eaten with bread). He meant that walnuts are tastier if they are eaten with bread. What a nerve after such a large meal! Just sheer gluttony. Uncle got the message and begged Aunt to leave some bread on the table to enable the *compare* to continue with his feasting on bread, walnuts and wine. We were amazed, not believing our eyes at his capacity for eating and at his digestion.

At five o'clock we were still sitting at the table. Our cousins Jacques and Moïse recited some French Christmas poems. We all reminisced about our past Christmases and other dear memories. The *compare*, having drunk too much, was in a talkative mood – *in vino veritas* – and he was unable to keep secrets now. He smoked a cigar complacently and puffed smoke-rings into the air like a steam-engine. Uncle Pascal was a heavy smoker, so he and the *compare* were polluting the air. We had to open the windows a little, otherwise we would have choked.

The *compare*, smiling, radiant and at ease, with much gusto and sense of fulfilment, narrated some of his childhood stories which we found entrancing. Uneducated as he was, he had a flair for telling stories and was the focus of our attention. Later the Elouards and the Barbs joined us for a chat and some family games.

Boxing Day and the coming New Year's Eve were days of celebration, more or less similar to those we had already had.

On New Year's Eve we dined with Uncle again. Later the Elouards and the Barbs dropped in. Paul and Daniel, the Elouards' sons, who lived away from home, paid a visit to their parents and spent a few days with them. We saluted the New Year quietly, hugged each other and drank a few bottles of champagne. Later we left and walked home; it was a foggy and chilly night. Before we went to sleep our hearts flew to Naples where the New Year celebration, compared with that of Rouen, was boisterous, extravagant and even dangerous. Neapolitans greeted the New Year with firecrackers and by throwing out old pots, pans, plates and even chamber-pots from balconies and windows into the streets below. Wistfully we deeply regretted not being there to greet New Year the Neapolitan way, which had always meant a lot to us.

31

I get seriously ill. Formation of the Rome–Berlin Axis

January was very cold, cloudy and gloomy, but it did not snow. We could not get used to short winter days with little or no sunshine. We had to soldier on, learn to endure, be stoical and get on with our activities. We had enough work to keep us going, but we did not try to expand our business on account of the political situation – a kind of cold war. Hitler was bent on territorial conquests. He was inflaming his people, preaching nationalism and building up his war machine. Mussolini, an empty vessel, was making too much noise. He had been entrapped by his policy of cooperation with Hitler and by the establishment of the Rome–Berlin Axis in October 1936. From then on Hitler seemed to be in charge and was using Mussolini to achieve his own ends.

Being fearfully concerned at Hitler's attitude, the French were re-arming themselves and strongly relying on their formidable Maginot line. Civil war was raging in Spain. Our poor Europe was once again in what seemed to be a hopeless turmoil – tearing itself apart as it had done in those years prior to the Great War.

We hardly had any French friends, because we couldn't speak their language. French boys of our age were either students or employed. If employed, they worked six days a week. On Sundays they wore their best suits and went out with their girlfriends. Most of them danced in the afternoon and went to the cinema at night. They worked hard, were properly nourished, dressed well and behaved as dignified human beings. I simply admired their way of living. I envied them and yearned to enjoy their opportunities and freedom.

Father, Vince, Tony and I went for long walks on Sunday afternoons, and were in one another's company most of the time,

165

or with some Italian friends we had met at the *Casa Degli Italiani* (Italian Cultural Club of Rouen). We spent some winter afternoons at home, in the company of friends whom Father had invited. They were about Father's age and typical Neapolitan characters – very fond of talking about themselves, their adventures and experiences. They had been in South America as door-to-door salesmen and narrated grossly exaggerated stories in which they were protagonists. Their narrative was extremely good, entrancing, and we really enjoyed it. They had met girls, had been involved in romances, had confronted awkward ruffians and had almost been embroiled in fights or duels, but at the last moment everything had ended well. Of course, we weren't simpletons, so when their visits were over, we made fun of them, laughing for days at their incredible stories.

One of our visitors was known as Uncle Ciro. He told us that, when he was in his early twenties, he went in for a spaghetti-eating contest. Once he had boasted that he could eat three kilos of spaghetti in tomato sauce. Those who heard him took him at his word and dared him to do it. While the contest was on, punters betted among themselves. They stood by and were amazed to see him devour a mountain of spaghetti set on a table in front of him. Having eaten it all, he even asked for a crust of bread to wipe his plate clean!

Uncle Ciro, a salesman and an illiterate, had long since abandoned his wife and six children in Naples. Now he hadn't a worry in the world, except how to look after himself. He was always cheerful and ready for a joke, and did not seem to have any remorse whatsoever for his family living in abject poverty in Naples.

Being physically rather weak, I found the northern weather unsuitable. Our flat wasn't centrally heated; we had two coal stoves to warm up the whole flat. The bedroom where my brothers and I slept was cold. Although we had many blankets and I was wearing long johns, the sheets were icy, and I shivered for a while before I could get warmed up. In January 1938, I was affected by a stubborn cough, but I did not worry, I thought that it would eventually go. It did not, and when I coughed I felt very uncomfortable. I was spitting profusely, and the phlegm was rather dark, greenish or yellowish. I could not understand what my body was trying to tell me, so I was annoyed.

However, one morning in the middle of February, while I was coughing I had a haemorrhage – I coughed up blood instead of the

166

phlegm. I probably lost two glassfuls of blood. I was terribly shocked, and felt close to death. My father and brothers were alarmed and frightened. They rushed to our telephone and rang up Aunt Mary. She came at once. Father and Aunt hurried me to a nearby chest specialist who examined me through his X-ray apparatus. He found a couple of spots above my lungs and stated that persistent coughing had caused a blood vessel to burst and produce the haemorrhage. The doctor prescribed some drugs. I had to keep warm and needed absolute rest.

I lay on the divan in our dining room, which was comfortably warm, for about ten days. My brother Tony kept an eye on me. He massaged my chest morning and night with some pungent smelling liquid. He also fed me and helped me when I had to go to the toilet. I was on a diet of chicken jelly for a few days. Later, when I was a little stronger, I was allowed to get up, have a grilled horse steak for lunch and a very light meal in the early evening.

The first night after the haemorrhage was crucial. My heart was beating excessively fast; I feared that it would explode, that I was going to die. I yearned for Mother or my sister Carmen to be beside me. At such a crucial moment nobody except my mother or sister could be of real comfort. Thinking of them in these dramatic hours must have helped me to stay alive, to get over my crisis. It was a miracle; I think that I only just made it. I was very weak, bad-tempered and helpless; a little excitement would make my heart race.

My illness was costing a lot of money while I was being treated and during my recovery. My weakened body was responding to treatment, but progress was slow indeed. I was no longer coughing, but still spitting frequently, and the phlegm was as dark as a rainy cloud. No doubt Father and Mother were praying for me. What was haunting me was: would I ever be healthy again, normal like any other young man, or disabled for the rest of my life?

32

We spend Easter at Uncle Pascal's. Germany annexes Austria

Soon it was spring. When it was sunny, I wrapped myself up in woollies and a thick coat and went to the local park, which was about 200 metres long by 100 wide. I sat on a bench for a couple of hours, observed passers-by and appreciated the beautiful setting of the park. There were trimmed lawns with lots of flowers – multicoloured petunias surrounded by carnations, patches and rows of daisies, Saint Antony's lilies, sweet peas, scarlet geraniums, violets and pansies. There were also rookeries, trimmed hedges, shrubs, oaks, ashes, elms, horse-chestnuts, wild cherries, small palms and cypresses. An artistically designed fountain, right in the centre, threw jets of water high in the air, while quacking ducks splashed or swam in the pool round the fountain.

Quite a number of middle-class housewives frequented the park. Most of them were in their thirties. Dressed in elegant fur coats, they pushed prams and had one or two children walking with them. They sat on hired chairs, formed small groups and chatted animatedly. Their children fed or chased the pigeons, and when they got too excited or strayed, their mothers scolded them.

Poor, elderly people and others, who could not afford to spend twenty cents for the hire of a chair, sat on public benches. They either stared vacantly into the air or looked at passers-by. A few keepers patrolled to prevent damage by disorderly visitors.

When I felt a little better, if the weather was promising, I went for a walk along the Seine and looked at the barges sailing east or west. There were always cargo ships there; some of them came from French colonies. A number of seamen were Africans who, when they landed, squandered their hard-earned money in bars, where they met ladies of easy virtue. These women exercised their charms to inveigle their potential customers, making them spend and spend; later they sent them back to their ships with empty pockets, absolutely blotto. Those Africans who had white women for lovers had something to boast about; a sense of pride, a feeling of being equal to white men. It was not so in their native lands, where white men exploited them and treated them as inferior beings. Some of them put on their best clothes when they met white *cocottes* in places where they drank, danced and made love. No doubt they would have something important to tell their friends back home!

Continuing walking along the Seine in an eastward direction, after a while I reached a hill called Côte Sainte Catherine. There was a steep path which I climbed slowly, trying to avoid fatigue. Having reached the top, I found myself on a wide plain. The hill could have been as high as the Eiffel Tower. From it I had a magnificent view of the Seine and the city below, and of a waste area beyond the city. Quite a number of people went there; young people and lovers for romance, others to picnic or breathe unpolluted air, or contemplate the scenery. Boys went there to fly their kites; I went simply to lie on the grass and stare at the blue spring sky with fleecy clouds. There was so much life in that gentle and fragrant air all around me. Meanwhile I was being harassed, haunted by my lingering illness; I was barely half alive!

With the annexation of Austria to Germany in March 1938, the French were worried. This event did not make the life of the Italians who lived in France any easier. With our alliance with Germany, our country was irrevocably committed to Hitler's cause. Both France and Britain were seriously concerned about this political development, but were reluctant to make a strong stand.

We spent Easter with Uncle Pascal. In the afternoon my brothers and I went with the Elouards – Jean, Samuel, Mademoiselle Denise – and our cousins for a ramble in a forest about four kilometres from Rouen. There was a strange scent – a mixture of rotting fallen trees and crushed wild plants. We heard the twittering of unfamiliar birds and rested for a while on some tree stumps.

Later we explored part of the forest which was remarkably uniform. On our way back home we changed our route and bumped into crowds of young people dancing in the open to the sound of accordions. We stopped for a while, drank some apple juice we bought at a kiosk and watched the revellers waltzing. I was appalled. There was something erotic in the way the couples danced; they were too close together and moved their buttocks as if they were making love.

As we resumed our walk, we found ourselves in a rich area. There were small detached houses right and left of the paved road, surrounded by trimmed lawns, patches of flowers and trees in bloom. The architecture, so elegant and inspiring, revealed fine taste and the affluence of the occupants.

We spent Easter Monday with the same group as the previous day, picnicking at the Côte Sainte Catherine. We played games, sang French songs and our cousins flew their kites. We also met some Neapolitans there. One of them, called Carmine, a man in his forties, had his left arm in plaster. Carmine, a travelling salesman, lodged with a French couple. Apparently he flirted with his attractive hostess who was younger than him. On Palm Sunday, however, Carmine, his host, hostess, and their French friends went for a walk through the countryside and while doing so they came to a stile.

When Carmine was young, he was an amateur athlete and very proud of his jumping agility. Although he was middle-aged now, he was anxious to show off his dexterity and be admired by his hostess and her friends. Carmine mustered all his strength and ran to jump over the stile. Unfortunately his muscular reflexes deserted him, one of his feet hit the top bar of the stile and poor, daring Carmine tumbled over to the other side and fractured his left arm. His French companions were alarmed and dismayed at his accident, but surreptitiously they laughed up their sleeves at Carmine's foolish attempt.

Having returned from the outing, we had something to eat; afterwards Father allowed us to go to a cinema in the Rue du Gros Horloge to see *Naples a le Baiser du Feu* (*Naples has the Kiss of Fire*). This film was made in Naples, and its main actor was Tino Rossi. Because of its Neapolitan setting, we saw this film several times.

33

Mademoiselle Gisèle. A romantic tailor called Steve.
O signore *(man of leisure)*

Summer was imminent, but I was physically weak and could not shake off my illness. Healing was a very slow process indeed. However, I was making an effort to be useful by running errands for our factory.

One day at the beginning of June I paid a visit to Mademoiselle Gisèle, one of our best machinists, for some urgent work. She lived with her aged mother in an old building in a lane near Rue des Charettes, a street with disreputable bars, mostly frequented by negroes and prostitutes.

Mademoiselle Gisèle was a homely spinster in her thirties. She was tall, had dark hair, grey eyes and an oval face. Although still attractive, she showed the marks of her age.

I climbed a few steep flights of stairs to the second floor, which made me breathless, and rested a little before I rang the bell. She opened the door cautiously and then let me in. I had the shock of my life; Mademoiselle Gisèle was stark naked!

Transfixed, I couldn't believe my eyes! Having taken in her curves, I was excited – she turned me on! She had a beautiful body like one of those women painted by the old Italian masters.

I sat in a chair but could not stop staring at her. She came close to me and then sat on my lap. I had tremendous palpitations; I could feel my heart beating and was unable to speak. She started caressing and kissing me and placed my left hand on her breast. I was ready for her, but she was too exciting for my poor debilitated body; its distressing signals dissuaded me. Had I ventured into action, I felt that it could have been fatal for me. Mademoiselle Gisèle had apparently noticed my plight and stopped being provocative. She slipped into a dressing-gown, and I was out of danger. My blood pressure relented. Now we started talking.

'My mother is on holiday,' she said, 'she's staying with her sister in the countryside in the south of France. It's warm and always sunny there, especially at this time of the year. She'll be back here at the end of this month.'

'What about you; when are you going on holiday?' I enquired.

'Oh not till the end of July,' she said. 'I love the south of France and the countryside. Aunt Valerie lives there in a cottage not too far from the beach. Are you going to Italy this summer?' she asked me.

'I don't know. Father hasn't decided yet.'

I had not gone to her place for a striptease show or a social chat, and couldn't stay there any longer, so I said, 'Are the blue mackintoshes ready?'

'I've almost finished them. I'll deliver them tomorrow!'

'I must go now,' I said. 'Cheerio!'

I left her, but could not forget her amorous advances which I regretfully had to decline on account of my poor state of health.

On those summery Sunday afternoons in 1938, Tony, Henry, signor Novello and I went for long walks, exploring the vicinity of Rouen.

Signor Novello, five feet tall, came from Pisa. He was in his thirties, had black hair, dark eyes, bushy eyebrows and a round face. He taught Italian to the children of Italian parents. Being a bachelor and unable to speak French, he preferred our comparatively innocent company, rather than being alone. We obviously could not communicate at his cultural level, for we hardly had any education, so he adjusted himself to our simple way of thinking.

Henry was a boy of our age group, not yet twenty. He came from the same district of Naples as we did. He was just over five feet tall, slim, had dark hair with a left parting, a small face and a youthful complexion. He had been in Rouen for a few months and was helping his eldest brother Steve who was a tailor. Henry, back at home, was a passionate theatre-goer. He could get a seat for one or two lire in the gallery of a Neapolitan theatre. He learned parts of the scenes and some songs by heart. He told us what he had seen and heard at various shows, and frequently hummed his favourite tunes or sang a song. One day he told Tony and me that

172

his brother had a young French girl assistant called Gilda. Presumably she had Italian parents.

Steve was a bachelor in his late thirties. Gilda was at least ten years younger than him. Steve was not a self-denying chap and was prone to promiscuity. Perhaps he tried to control himself and exercise a certain restraint, but when he was off guard, he was unpredictable and could not ignore Gilda's sex appeal.

Sometimes, in his small workshop, while going through a narrow passage he brushed against her and apologised. Later, however, such occurrences became more frequent and deliberate and she did not object. Steve confidently took a further step, so he gradually became more bold and audacious, and in the end they became intimate. When Steve was in a passionate mood, he contrived to get rid of Henry by sending him on some errands, while he and Gilda made love on the sofa of his sitting-room.

Henry became suspicious; instead of going on an errand, one day he went to a coffee bar, drank a cappuccino and came back. There was absolute silence there. Suddenly he heard ecstatic murmurs, and he peeped through the keyhole. Although he could not see much, he knew exactly what Steve and Gilda were doing. Eventually Henry became jealous, so one day he lost his temper and remonstrated.

'You're having a lot of fun, aren't you?'

'What are you talking about, silly boy?'

'You know what I am talking about, you and Gilda are making jig-jig and I want my share, else I'll report your affair to Father.'

'Don't be so daft. She isn't a prostitute, is she?' said Steve. 'And be a good boy, else I'll give you a jig-jig on your knob.'

Henry had learned the word 'jig-jig' from some American seamen who visited Neapolitan brothels. I never asked him how he had settled his dispute with Steve. To avoid being blackmailed, I imagined that Steve bribed Henry with some presents.

Next to Steve's tailoring workshop lived one of his distant relatives called Rocco, whom Neapolitan friends mockingly nicknamed *O signore* (man of leisure). He was one of our townsfolk and in his forties. He had black hair, bushy eyebrows, brown eyes, a wrinkled face and pale complexion.

Rocco had emigrated to France in the twenties and was an

itinerant salesman. At that time he earned a lot, so he sent a monthly remittance to his widowed mother in Secondigliano, who had to bring up three daughters. He was a dear, thoughtful son, and his mother thanked God for that.

With a flow of thousands of emigrants to France in the thirties, the population of such salesmen increased enormously. Among the newcomers were a number of disreputable people who were a discredit to the trade. Because of this, Rocco's earnings gradually dwindled and he could hardly earn enough to keep body and soul together. It was a tragedy for his mother, for he was unable to send her any money. How could she and his three sisters survive in a poverty-stricken town? She wrote to him, begging him to find a means to help her, because he was the only son she had; how else could she and his three sisters manage? Had he been at home, things would have been different. Being abroad, he could not see or feel their difficulty. '*Lontano dagli occhi, lontano dal cuore*' (out of sight, out of mind). Perhaps also he had met a woman and lost his affection for his mother and sisters, and left them in the lurch.

In reality he had married a French woman in the early thirties. She presumably made him give up being a salesman which was getting him nowhere and, besides, it wasn't considered a respectable occupation. On the other hand, he did not have a trade and could hardly speak French; what would he do for a living? He and his wife came to an agreement that he should stay at home, do the chores and look after their little boy, while she would carry on working in her full-time domestic employment. Because of this arrangement, his frivolous friends jokingly hinted that he was a kept man wallowing in luxuries. They knew that he was under his wife's thumb, so they teasingly ridiculed him.

His mother and sisters did not give up; they wrote to him again and again, telling him that they were starving to death and that any help would do. He must have read their letters and felt uneasy, but he had no money to send them. He certainly was embarrassed, so he chose not to answer.

His mother and sisters continued pestering him, and when they got tired of doing so, they contrived a trick by sending him the following telegram: MOTHER CRITICALLY ILL. COME HOME AT ONCE. He was greatly shaken. His wife felt sorry for him, so she made an effort and paid for his return rail fare to Naples.

During his long journey he was in mental agony. A remorse

haunted him; his mother was probably already dead and he would not be able to see her again. One of his sisters met him at Naples station, and after she hugged and welcomed him she said: 'Dear brother, Mother is no longer dangerously ill. She had a heart attack about ten days ago. Our doctor told us that she was weak and probably would die. Thank God she seems to be recovering now.'

He was greatly relieved. Having arrived at home, he found his mother in bed. She was awfully glad to see him and shed a few tears.

While he was at home he spent the money, which he would have eventually disbursed for his mother's funeral, on food and things that his people badly needed. He rejoiced that his mother was getting well, but at the same time he became suspicious that he had been taken in, had been a victim of a plot, and this annoyed him immensely. He had made a long tiring journey to Naples, had been in anxiety, in distress, and spent almost all the money that his wife had given him; money that she had to borrow to enable him to go there. He reckoned that his mother and sisters had indeed played a cruel trick on him, and after about a week of staying at home, he was glad to get away, to return to Rouen and from then on he did not want to hear of his mother and sisters again.

34

The political situation is alarming

Vince had made a few Neapolitan friends of about his own age, and every Sunday afternoon he went out with them. Since their knowledge of the French language was not good enough to charm and conquer French girls, when they were under the pressure of masculine impulses, they visited brothels. In doing so, Vince probably did not take the necessary precautions, and one day he caught gonorrhoea. As he feared Father's wrath, he secretly tried to cure himself. Failing to do so, he was worried and confided in Uncle Pascal who in his turn informed Father. Naturally Father was not pleased, but he did not make a scene. He took Vince to a specialist, and he soon recovered. About ten years later, when Vince got married, his wife had no children. Was this Vince's fault? I suspected that when he contracted gonorrhoea, it might have affected his reproductive capacity.

Father wasn't too keen on staying in Rouen, for our work and life there had not lived up to our expectations. My brother Saverio didn't like the place and saw no future there, so he had gone back to Java; our business was not doing well, I became ill and Father hated the weather. Raffaele, our designer and cutter, was too fond of *la dolce vita* (a life of luxury and self-indulgence), and he had neither the initiative nor the creative capacity that we really needed to succeed. The political situation was alarming, making people restless. Hitler was getting more vociferous in his territorial demands and worrying France and Britain. These two countries sought an alliance in opposition to any German threat.

In July 1938 the British monarch, George VI, paid an official visit to France with his consort and family and reinforced the *entente cordiale*. The French President, Albert Lebrun, lavishly entertained the Royal Family with extravagant banquets, parades and displays. Such dazzling events were aimed at making some impact on the neurotic Führer, trying to dissuade him from bullying and taking too many liberties. France and Britain would not tolerate it if he went too far.

The political tension was worrying and disconcerting for us, for we were in a foreign country which disliked our government's policy. Father consequently made up his mind to shut down our business, before the situation worsened, and return to Java. We had received encouraging news from Saverio that business was still promising in that country far, far away from tumultuous Europe.

In August we went to a dinner organised by *La Casa Degli Italiani*. It was held in the countryside, about ten kilometres from Rouen. It was quite safe there tucked away from any political disturbance. There were more than 200 people, including women and children. The idea was to come together for a little celebration, so we gathered in a barn and had a three or four course dinner and a little wine. We also sang national songs and shouted, '*Viva Il Re!*' '*Viva Il Duce!*' (Long live the King! Long live *Il Duce*!). Did we really mean it?

Thousands of Italians in France did not bother to read newspapers and did not have the faintest idea of what Mussolini was doing. Necessity had compelled them to emigrate; they had to learn to adapt to life in a foreign country, to be prepared to face hardship, to be deprived of the comfort of close friends and relatives. Starved of their sacrosanct urge to express themselves, their natural source of love and happiness, our emigrants had the tendency to become morose, maladjusted and even insane. How could these unfortunates have loved their King and *Il Duce*? What had they done for their people whose living conditions were hard to bear? When these people shouted: 'Long live the King!' or 'Long live *Il Duce*!' it was no doubt sheer mockery.

35

Our brother Giuseppe dies

On the morning of 3 September, while we were at work, Uncle Pascal paid us an unexpected visit. Father had gone out on some business or other.

'Was your brother Giuseppe ill?' asked Uncle.

'We don't know, why?'

'I think he had an infection, and I'm afraid I have bad news.'

'Why, what's the matter?'

'I've just received a telegram from your mother. Your brother was dangerously ill and the doctor could not help him. I am sorry to say that Giuseppe passed away this morning.'

That was a severe blow which I couldn't take in. We had never had a death in our family and now Giuseppe had passed away. I was devastated, paralysed, could not speak. Suddenly I burst into a flood of tears; I could not accept that my brother, a boy of sixteen, had died. I thought that such a thing would, thanks to my mother's prayers, never happen to us, that we were invulnerable, and that our Venerable Gaetano Errico, the Immaculate Conception and the other saints would always protect us. Was Giuseppe's death God's will? I could not accept that. I was still too weak from my recent illness, and my heart was racing and bleeding from my brother's death. Was I going to die too and be with Giuseppe? I did not want to die; I had a strong desire to live. Besides, one death in our family was more than my parents could bear. Of course, our grandfathers had died, but they had at least lived three score years and ten. My brothers Vince and Tony, no doubt, felt the same. For Father it was yet another blow coming after a number of unpleasant events. He quickly rushed to the station, bought a ticket and immediately departed for Rome, and from there caught another train to Naples.

Giuseppe was born in 1922. He was at secondary school before he became ill. He belonged, as I did when I was sixteen, to a Fascist youth club called *Avanguardisti*. It was an organisation that had a tendency to brainwash teenagers with Fascist slogans. The boys paraded through our cities and towns singing Fascist songs and shouting 'Long live *Il Duce*!'

Giuseppe's funeral took place the day after he died. A group of his comrades in uniform, preceded by their flag, followed the hearse to the cemetery where one of them stood on a stool and made a short speech, praising Giuseppe's fervour for *Il Duce*. Towards the end of the speech, he raised his voice and shouted, as if he were reading from a roll-call, 'Arrichiello Giuseppe!' The rest of the comrades shouted in unison '*Presente*!' meaning the spirit of our departed comrade will always be with us.

Father did not arrive in time for Giuseppe's funeral, but he was able to pay his last respects at the mortuary, where in Naples a corpse is usually held for a day before it is interred. He spent a few days at home and then returned to Rouen.

Father told us that Giuseppe happened to have a boil under his nose a couple of weeks before he died. He and his friends went for a swim at a Neapolitan seaside resort. While he was bathing on that summer's day, he probably scratched the boil and so it became infected. Mother called Dr Borga, a local physician. He visited my brother, but failed to recognise the gravity of his sickness. He prescribed an ointment widely used to treat minor ailments. This was not only inadequate, but aggravated my brother's trouble – he was in pain and his head had swollen. Mother was alarmed and called Dr Gennaro Lupo. He stated that Giuseppe was gravely ill – he had blood poisoning. He tried in vain to save his life, but it was too late – Giuseppe was in atrocious pain; he was dying. Dr Lupo had to give him an injection for a peaceful release.

Dr Borga's negligence had been the cause of my brother's death. We felt that he had committed a crime and that his name should have been struck off the medical register. He wasn't devoted to his profession and spent several hours daily playing cards at the *Dopolavoro*, a smoke-filled club which ordinary people frequented.

Father thought of murdering him – 'An eye for an eye, and a tooth for a tooth'. Had he taken the law into his own hands, they would have put him in jail for a number of years. And how would we have managed without him?

Dr Borga felt a sense of guilt, so he contrived to approach

Father, trying to excuse himself and make sure that Father would not prosecute him. Had Father brought him to court, it would have taken years before the case could be heard and would have cost us a lot of money. Would all this bother have brought my brother back to life? What else could Father do? So after a while, he let bygones be bygones.

36

*We go into voluntary liquidation. Vince, Father and
Tony embark for Java*

Our business had been disappointing (for the reasons given earlier)
so, soon after the death of Giuseppe, we stopped manufacturing
mackintoshes and went into voluntary liquidation, selling our
equipment and domestic belongings. As we had not been in
business long enough, we suffered a considerable financial loss.
Raffaele, our designer and cutter, found another job and stayed on
in Rouen. Vince was about twenty. Had he returned to Italy, he
would have been liable for military service. However, Uncle Pascal
had a few friends at the Italian Consulate in Paris, so he was able
to get Vince's passport renewed. A few days later, having obtained
a Dutch visa, Vince was ready to sail for Java.

Father had a few thousand francs left. He bought some Italian
lire which could profitably be acquired on the black market. He
received 10,000 lire and had to hide them inside the soles of my
brother Tony's shoes, for money trafficking was illegal.

About the end of September 1938, we said goodbye to Uncle
Pascal, Aunt Mary, our cousins Jacques and Moïse and to all our
French and Italian friends, and then we left for Italy.

We arrived in Paris about midday. Tony and I were carrying three
heavy suitcases, but we had to wait a couple of hours at the Gare
de Lyon because our train for Rome was not ready.

Father and Vince parted from us; they had to catch a train to
Marseilles, from where Vince was to embark on the French ship
Athos sailing for Java.

Tony and I travelled third class and shared our compartment with
some English, French and Italian passengers. By the time the train
reached Turin, Genoa and Pisa, our travelling companions had been
reduced to three or four. One of them, an Englishman in his thirties,

181

spoke a little Italian and made jokes about Mussolini. He also showed us some cartoons which surprised and shocked us. Tony and I had no idea that foreigners would dare to mock our mighty *Duce*; we thought that he was above criticism.

Our journey lasted over thirty hours. We arrived at Naples at 1.00 a.m. and had to wait for a night tram, which took us as far as Capodichino military airport. We got off the tram and had to plod along with our heavy suitcases for about a kilometre. We often stopped for a breather and were almost collapsing with fatigue.

We were greatly relieved when we reached our family home, but the main door of the block of flats was shut. We knocked and knocked until the grumbling caretaker arrived. Having recognised us, he let us in and also helped us to carry one of our suitcases to the first floor. We rang the bell. Mother and my sister were bewildered – who could be there in the small hours? Hesitatingly and anxiously they came to the door, '*Chi è?*' (Who is there?) they shouted.

'*Mamma! Mamma! Siamo noi, Cosimo e Antonio.*' (Mother! Mother! It is us, Cosimo and Tony.)

We heard some unclear emotional utterances as Mother and Carmen hastened to unbolt the door. They let us in and hugged us. Mother started weeping, not only for the joy of seeing us but also because our coming home reminded her of our brother Giuseppe, who would never return. For me, moments like this are unforgettable; they always make me think of that priceless human touch that a family can give, especially one like ours. There were many of us; we had our little squabbles but at the same time we had great affection for each other. During moments of distress there was cohesion and solidarity, and Mother was the glowing heart of our family.

Our brother Damiano, aged ten, and our sisters, in their long white night-dresses, ran towards us and hugged us. It was a happy reunion, but we felt the absence of Giuseppe. It was hard to accept that he was no longer with us, so our reunion was a mixture of joy and sadness. Without doubt, Giuseppe's ethereal presence was there to welcome us; I could feel the vibration. Although he was with the Lord now, in spirit he would always be with us.

The room in which Giuseppe died was shut; it had been shut ever since. My sisters hadn't the courage to go near it; they were still too overcome by having seen him lying still in his bed surrounded by four long, thick, flickering candles.

182

Tony and I, to show how brave we were, swaggered into the room. Our sisters followed us and promptly made up the bed, which was double, so Tony, Damiano and I slept there. After this act of bravery, our sisters were no longer afraid of going into the room.

Father, having seen Vince off at Marseilles, travelled via Ventimiglia and arrived home one day after us. He spent about a month at home, during which time he made two bookings on a Japanese ship. And so in November he and Tony embarked for Java.

Father left me behind because I was still recovering from the illness I had contracted in France; he thought that I was not strong enough to cope with the tropical weather. Staying at home, I became my father's deputy, the man expected to make major decisions and to inspire my family. Although I was not confident, I was flattered and even conceited – but I hadn't the faintest idea how to play my part. I was also aware that Mother, being a strong character, would not hesitate to brush me aside and have her own way. However, when my opinion was requested, I did my best to be of assistance.

Being at home, I made some new friends who were students. One of them, Renato Giacometti, was about my age. He was just over five feet tall, had black hair with a left parting, bushy eyebrows, a dark complexion and was short-sighted. He was poetic and fond of literature. We went for long walks and talked about everything we could tackle. I knew a few words of French which I had learned during my stay in Rouen, so I could make some impression on my learned friend with my linguistic ability. I knew hardly any Italian literature, because I had not yet acquired the habit of reading.

Renato did most of the talking. At times he was eloquent and obstinate in his views. I listened and listened to him absorbedly, and most of the time, having nothing to say, I agreed with him. He was my lecturer and I his audience, and he was pleased with this tacit arrangement. However, when his eloquence went too far, I was wary not to contest him, for I feared losing his friendship.

As Renato had a gramophone, once or twice a week a group of students – Luigi Lupo, Antonio Barbato, Emilia and Delfina Papi, Maria Silvestri, Michela and Angelina Riccio and I – gathered at Renato's house and danced to music on records such as 'Santa

183

Mia', 'Maria Lao', 'Serenata del Somarello', 'Mare Perché' and other tunes. Renato's younger brother, Pasquale, and his two teenage sisters belonged to our group. Occasionally signora Papi, a midwife in her forties and mother to Emilia and Delfina, joined us. We had fun, innocent fun, and enjoyed the girls' company. We behaved in a gentlemanly way, refraining from showing sexual desires; kissing or petting was quite out of the question, or mothers wouldn't have allowed their daughters to dance with us.

I learned to dance through practice. I just followed the rhythm and did not bother taking lessons. Besides, I couldn't afford it, and my friends were no better dancers than I was. We all enjoyed each other's company and the friendly atmosphere. I was so confident of my dancing that I even helped my sisters and other girls to learn. They thought that I was a good tutor and an accomplished gentleman.

When, for one reason or another, we did not dance and had nothing better to do, we passed one or two hours at the *Dopolavoro* club. Since we had no money to squander on billiards or cards, we used the club mainly as a meeting place. We preferred going for walks in the fresh air and giving the glad eye to all the pretty girls we encountered. As we went along a footpath of our town or through a leafy lane, we indulged in idle talk and never ran out of topics. This was a kind of pastime in which we found pleasure and which cost us nothing.

PART THREE

PREPARATION FOR WAR

37

My pre-military service

On Sunday mornings, I was supposed to do my pre-military service, which was a Fascist scheme aimed at giving young men military instruction before conscription, but I did not always attend. A few local men acted as our officers. They wore impressive Fascist uniforms that made them feel that they were really somebody, as they swaggered round our town. Their uniforms, no doubt, cost them a small fortune. These men had been ardent Fascists since the famous march on Rome in 1922, and truly believed that their leader, Mussolini, was what our country needed; a strong man to put an end to our endless strikes, restore law and order, promote political stability, social justice and prosperity.

Mussolini achieved most of his policies by destroying the opposition; there was no justice whatsoever for the downtrodden population, who became poorer and poorer.

A few years before the Second World War, when someone took Saturday afternoon off work, this was known as *fare il sabato Inglese* (to do the English Saturday). Mussolini badly wanted the Italians to be at the same level as the English, so he introduced *il sabato Fascista* (The Fascist Saturday). However, this was a right that only those who worked for the government could enjoy. Private businesses, especially small ones, could not afford to give their employees Saturday afternoon off. If an employee insisted on the entitlement to have Saturday afternoon off, the employer would sooner or later find a pretext to give him the sack.

I am not quite sure whether the Fascist officers engaged in our pre-military training service received any remuneration. Probably they did it on an honorary basis, to demonstrate that they were supporters of the Fascist regime. By doing so they could win favours, get preference for promotion and an assured career in their regular occupations. Others helped themselves by exploiting every opportunity to further their self-interests. Some Fascists wore their uniform daily, which enabled them to travel freely on public transport and get some concessions elsewhere. Occasionally, I noticed Fascists in uniform doing their shopping.

Fruit and vegetable vendors seemed to feel uneasy in the presence of customers in uniforms. Then any haggling was kept to a minimum, done politely and with a certain deference, for vendors chose to be on good terms with any authority. If they displeased such customers, they might somehow run the risk of being fined. This kind of dealing enabled customers in uniforms to buy at a very reasonable price.

Nowadays quite a number of people have a tendency to be sentimental because of Italy's political instability on account of its proliferation of parties and the corruption which seems to be uncontrollable. They think that what Italy needs is a leader like Mussolini.

Mussolini's law and order was forced on us, as were all his decisions. Would any sensible person be willing to go back to Mussolini's time, when people had to work extremely hard, had hardly anything to eat, when there was no free medical service, no old-age pension or any kind of governmental financial assistance?

I went to Mass on Sundays merely to fulfil a Christian obligation. Often I escorted my elder sister. But when I went to Mass with my friends, it was an opportunity to look at the local talent, and so we rarely concentrated on the service. The Lord certainly wasn't pleased with us, but since we were so young and green, He probably forgave us.

Clito Zuccherini, a boy of my own age whom I met at the Fascist youth club when I was fourteen, became one of my closest friends. He was about an inch taller than me, well-built, had dark hair combed back, brown eyes and resembled an amateur boxer. As he worked six days a week at his uncle's shirt and pyjama factory, I usually met him on Sundays.

When I did not go dancing at Renato's house, Clito and I went either to the local cinema or to Naples. Sometimes other friends joined us, so we formed a group of four or five and strolled along the Neapolitan promenade which started at Via Partenopea and ended at a locality known as Margellina. After sunset, when the city lights were switched on, we visited a few brothels, browsing around, looking at naked prostitutes, a show costing us nothing. Many other boys of our age or older did the same. This was as far as we went, for we could rarely afford to buy sex.

As I had many sisters, Mother gave me some pocket money with the tacit understanding that if I felt in a randy mood, I could cool off by visiting a brothel. Since I was not promiscuous, I managed to visit a brothel only once a month or every two months.

When I made love to a prostitute, I always used a condom, being afraid of catching venereal disease. Had I not done so, I would have worried for a few days afterwards.

I did not take advantage of the privilege that Mother gave me, and tried to be as thrifty as possible, for I was well aware that in a large family like ours it was hard for Mother to make ends meet on Father's monthly remittance.

38

Carmen's fiancé

At the end of 1937, Carmen became engaged to an air force corporal doing a special course at Capodichino military airport, which was about one kilometre from our home. My sister was then twenty-three, and her fiance, whose name was Carlo Pizzorusso, was twenty-one. His family lived in a small country town called Trentola, about eight or ten kilometres from us. Carlo was about an inch taller than the average in Italy. He was energetic, well-built and intelligent. He had black hair with a left parting, bushy eyebrows, brown eyes and teeth as white as mother-of-pearl. He had a secondary school education and, like thousands of young men who were doing the same course, he hoped that one day he would become a regular air force officer. This occupation was well paid compared with most other jobs.

Carlo came to see my sister once or twice a week. He was allowed to see her only in the presence of my mother, for engaged girls in those days were usually chaperoned. If there was any kissing, it was done by stealth. When he was not on duty on Sunday, he was occasionally invited to dine with us.

Socially and financially we were better off than Carlo's family, and they were aware of this. Carlo's father, whose name was Dominic, was just a poor country tailor, struggling hard with his needle merely to survive. He had a wife and three daughters who helped him when he was too busy. If he wasted time charting with acquaintances and friends, who casually dropped in on his workshop during the day, it meant that Master Dominic had to work till late.

Dominic was then about fifty. He was of normal height, skinny, almost bald, with sparse grey hair at the temples. He had pouches under his dark, sunken eyes, projecting cheekbones and a cadaverous face, probably due to his late working hours, the quantity of black

190

coffee he consumed, the heavy smoking he indulged in and the amount of wine he drank. In spite of his appearance, surprisingly, when he chatted, his face livened up; consequently my mother nicknamed him *Morto Cazzuto*, which means, loosely translated, 'death warmed up' – or death from the neck up with a touch of vivacity!

Dominic and his family thought a lot of us because of our higher social status. To get away from their over-provincial environment, on some Sunday afternoons they visited us uninvited. We disliked this – what a nuisance it was – for we had to buy cakes, extra coffee and some vermouth to entertain them! Besides, they outstayed their welcome and made us very tired. Had we kicked them out, Carlo and my sister might eventually have broken off their engagement.

As I was my father's deputy, when our uninvited guests came I was unable to go out with my friends; I had to stay at home, forcing a smile and chatting to our naively inconsiderate visitors. I was bored to tears, for I became the target of Dominic's loquacity. He tended to harp on about the same subject, telling me again and again about his bravery and his narrow escapes during the Great War.

'Look,' he would say, 'we were doing very well on the front in 1917. We had advanced about eight kilometres towards Caporetto. Had we received some allied military help, we'd have knocked the Austrians out of the war. But with the collapse of the Russian Front in 1917, the Germans shifted some divisions from that front and deployed them on the Austrian one. So in October 1917 the Austrian and German Armies, after six hours of heavy bombardment, attacked and took us by surprise. General Cadorna, who was in command, did not expect an attack on the Caporetto front. The enemy rapidly overran us, penetrated our lines and cut off our communications. Our Second Army, being utterly isolated and disorganised, couldn't contain the enemy. We were on the run. *Si salvi chi può* (it is every man for himself). Our retreat was extremely chaotic. Being ceaselessly bombarded by Austrian and German artillery, we fled in panic.

'General Cadorna, to avoid the encirclement of other units, ordered retreat on the whole front. The poor, inadequate and muddy roads became heavily congested with every sort of military vehicle and with weary soldiers, keeping up what speed they could to

191

escape capture. The Austrian and German troops advanced more than a hundred kilometres; they occupied Gorizia, reached Udine and pushed forward as far as the Tagliamento and Piave rivers. We lost between 2,000 and 3,000 pieces of artillery, suffered 40,000 dead or wounded, and 250,000 of our soldiers were taken prisoner. Thousands and thousands of soldiers were on the run and were considered deserters. They were hunted down by our military police, and the captured ones, who were condemned by our military tribunals, were executed. General Cadorna blamed his soldiers for the Caporetto disaster.

'I, like any other soldier,' stated Dominic, 'amid the hell of explosions was severely shocked and terrorised; a number of my comrades were butchered, reduced to pulp by the enemy's fire, so I threw away my rifle and ran to save my skin. One or two people on the way gave me some civilian clothes, and this was a help. After several days of hitchhiking, I reached home, but the local *carabinieri* seemed to be waiting for me.

'I pretended to be mad, for I did not want to go back to the front and be massacred by the enemy. I was sent to the mental hospital at Aversa and kept under observation for many months. I shouted, cried, laughed, fasted, impersonated our King, the Pope, and did a lot of other silly things, just to convince doctors and nurses that I was insane. They were not quite sure about my mental state. Then, while I was still there the war ended. Later our King, Victor Emmanuel III, proclaimed an amnesty by which the deserters were forgiven, so I eventually recovered from my simulated mental illness and was discharged from hospital.'

Carlo, while engaged to my sister, asked to be sent to Abyssinia, our newly acquired empire. By doing so he hoped to hasten his promotion to sergeant (a regular), so that he could, as he said, get married and settle down.

During 1939, a few months before the Second World War started, he sailed for Italian Somalia, and from there he proceeded by military transport to his new destination, Addis Ababa. He and my sister kept in touch by correspondence.

In June 1940, Italy declared war on France and Britain. The Italian Army in Abyssinia could no longer receive military supplies from its home base thousands of kilometres away; how then could it defend our Abyssinian Empire? Consequently, when the British attacked, being adequately armed, they met little resistance. The

192

Italians, having no hope of winning, surrendered in May 1941 and were sent to prisoner-of-war camps. Months later, Carlo's parents learned through the Red Cross that he was a prisoner. A few years later, as a result of the Italian Armistice of 8 September 1943, Carlo was released, and at the end of 1944 he was back in Italy. He paid a visit to my sister and noticed that my family was hard up.

My father and my three brothers were in Java when the Japanese invaded. They were arrested and unjustly sent to a prisoner-of-war camp, so they were no longer able to send money home.

Carlo probably came to the conclusion that my family, being in serious financial straits, would never again enjoy their pre-war standard of living, and he wanted to have nothing to do with the poverty to which my family had been reduced, so he stopped coming to visit my sister, and the engagement was broken off. Carlo was gone for good.

39

Father arranges for me to go to Java. An emigration officer confiscates my passport

As I have already mentioned, because I was still recovering from the illness I contracted in France in 1937, I was unable to join Father and Tony when they sailed for Java in November 1938.

Father said, 'Listen, Cosimo, stay at home for the time being; it'll do you a lot of good. In six months from now, I'll send for you.'

Being at home, I tried to make myself as useful as I could. I also made some more student friends, whose friendship I found stimulating. I began to appreciate the value of education and wanted to go back to school, but I was eighteen, and at that age people rarely had a second chance. Besides, the prospect of going to Java and discovering a tropical country attracted me immensely. I would be able to work and perhaps become a rich man.

I did not have much to do just then, so I endeavoured to use the time diligently. With the help of my friend Renato, who was quite an accomplished scholar, I prepared myself for the examination of the intermediate school certificate, held in June 1939. It was a certificate that could be obtained at the completion of the first three years of secondary education.

My sister Mary, four years younger than me, was a promising student, so she was going through secondary education at a school in Naples. The rest of my sisters, not being interested in study, didn't do much. What a waste! Of course, they learned to do domestic chores which prevented them from becoming utterly useless. They dreamed that one day some young men with secure employment would come along and marry them. This was the traditional mentality of the majority of young girls in towns where female emancipation was still unknown.

At that time, with Hitler's insistent and disturbing territorial demands for Sudetenland and Danzig, and with the Italian invasion of Albania, European stability was seriously threatened. How much longer would Britain and France be prepared to tolerate Hitler's arrogant and aggressive attitude? It was hard to say.

In early spring 1939, Father sent me money to pay for my passage from Naples to Batavia, the Dutch East Indies. But when the Dutch East Indies became independent in 1945, it was renamed Indonesia, and Batavia was renamed Jakata.

Having had my passport renewed, I obtained a Dutch visa, and then I booked a berth on the Italian liner *Conte Biancamano* of the Lloyd Triestino Shipping Company. The liner was bound for Singapore. There I would board a Dutch liner sailing for Batavia.

Of course, I was extremely excited at the thought of a five-week voyage. I would be able to visit, if only for a few hours, a number of towns near ports where the ship was due to stop on its way to Singapore. I would meet travellers of many nationalities and, by using my limited knowledge of French, would be able to socialise with them. Besides, I would see the vast Indian Ocean under its blue or cloudy sky, and experience the lulling motion of the waves. Just thinking of the pleasure of such a voyage, it seemed like a dream. I eagerly waited for the day of departure which had been fixed for May.

I was bubbling with joy when the day arrived, glad to get away from a poor Italy at the mercy of the inflammatory Fascist campaign. Hitler and Mussolini seemed like two barking dogs, each trying to outdo the other; we all felt as if we were on the brink of disaster.

My mother, elder sister and eleven-year-old brother accompanied me to the dock by taxi. The ship, of average size and not too old, was anchored alongside the quay and scheduled to sail before midday. Its staff were busily dealing with passengers, checking their names and welcoming them aboard. I hugged my mother, sister and brother and, followed by a porter carrying my luggage, walked towards the ship. I showed my third-class ticket to an officer on the gangway. The ticket had cost Father about 6,000 lire, which at that time was a considerable sum, equivalent to the salary of a bank manager for six months. As soon as I stepped aboard, I was confronted by a mean-looking emigration officer.

'Show me your passport,' he said authoritatively.

195

I handed it to him. He peered at it carefully.

'I cannot allow you to leave Italy!' he stated.

'Why?' I enquired, bewildered.

'Because you'll soon have to do your military service.'

'Look here, officer, this is my doctor's certificate,' I said, as I handed him the document. 'I had a chest disease about a year ago and I'm still recovering from it. Last autumn, I went to be medically examined for the call-up and was deferred. With my physical condition, I doubt whether I'll ever be fit for military service.'

'Sorry, I can't help you, I can't let you go, you have got to do your military service!' he exclaimed stubbornly. Having said that, he confiscated my passport.

I was shocked, dumbfounded and extremely upset; I wanted to cry. Rage sickened me; I was so tense that I could not cry. I badly wanted to murder that man, get my passport back, and then make his body disappear by throwing it overboard. Listless and broken-hearted I disembarked, hired a porter and dejectedly trudged my way back to where my mother, sister and brother were still waiting to see me off. Had I been allowed to depart, they would have waved their handkerchief at me, while the ship was sailing away from Bella Napoli, that shore of passionate love and songs. My beautiful dream was gone, shattered, and this left me despondent.

Mother tried very hard to comfort me, but I couldn't shake off the rage and sadness that haunted and tormented me for quite a while. I cursed that emigration officer. He was surprisingly or perhaps deliberately too zealous, too punctilious in doing his duty, which made me wonder what he was up to. I had the impression that he was making a fuss for personal reasons. Since my passport had been renewed without difficulty, why should he have objected to my going abroad?

The trouble with me was that I was too young, too inexperienced, and I did not know how to handle him craftily. Had I placed a few hundred lire in his hand, I would no doubt have found him more reasonable and cooperative. In spite of the Mussolini regime, corruption was rife and some government employees resorted to any expedient in order to cheat the public and make some money for themselves on the side.

40

*The Second World War begins. The Germans attack
Holland, Belgium and Luxembourg. Signor Pasquale
Ragusa pays us a visit*

Having been thwarted by the over-scrupulous emigration officer
from sailing for Java, I soon overcame my resentment and carried
on with my tedious daily task of staying at home and being my
father's deputy.

Mother said: 'I'm glad you are here, at least we have a man
about the house to keep us company.'

This remark made me feel important, almost a man of substance,
even if I wasn't quite sure of myself. I would have felt a real man
if I had been able to earn some money and really help my family.

Meanwhile the political situation was getting worse, with Hitler
bullying and menacing, and Mussolini shouting from the famous
balcony of Palazzo Venezia (Venice Palace) to the crowd below.
The dictators made a lot of noise and inflamed their populace.

Mussolini busied himself by inspecting some detachments of his
'ten million bayonets'. He also showed his ally, Adolf Hitler, just
how fierce and impressive our Blackshirts and soldiers looked, and
how ready they were to shed their blood for their beloved *Duce*.

To assert and assess his popularity, Mussolini travelled throughout
Italy in an open car. All the towns along the route were extravagantly
decorated with our national flag. Ninety per cent of our population,
for one reason or another, did not possess the flag. The municipal
authorities distributed them freely, so that people would have no
excuse for not putting them on display while our mighty *Duce* was
driven by.

Secondary school and university students, urged on or organised
by Fascists, deserted their classrooms and lecture halls. Waving
flags and pennants, they marched through our main streets and

shouted: '*Guerra! Guerra! Guerra!* (War! War! War!) Did these irresponsible young men know what they were saying? Did they really mean it? They were just puppets whom the Fascists manipulated to create an effect. These foolhardy demonstrations were presumably aimed at putting pressure on Britain and France to give in to Mussolini's demands which were more or less: Nice, Savoy and Corsica ought to be returned to Italy. Corsica had been sold to France in 1768.

Nice and Savoy had been given to France in compensation for military help received against the Austrian Army at the battle of Solferino in 1859. Tunisia, Malta and French Somalia should be handed to Italy. There should be an end to the British domination of the Straits of Gibraltar, and to French and British domination of the Suez Canal. Italy should have equal opportunity with France and Britain concerning freedom of trade and manpower movement.

Britain and France, being rich countries and having colonial empires, were well aware that by waging a war they would have a lot to lose, so they were inclined to a policy of appeasement; at the same time they seemed to be determined not to yield an inch to the dictators' pressures. How would Britain and France manage? What was the alternative? Could they calm down the two dictators by making concessions? And would they be satisfied with them?

By going to war, Italy and Germany had little to lose compared with Britain and France. Italy's colonies were liabilities – a pain in the neck. We would really be better off without them. Germany, as a result of the Great War, had lost all her colonies and been reduced to dire poverty. In the Versailles Treaty of 1919, she had been treated too harshly, and now Hitler wanted to redress those wrongs and the humiliation inflicted on Germany.

Taking advantage of Britain and France's unwillingness and hesitation to aggravate the political situation, which Hitler undoubtedly considered a sign of weakness, on 1 September 1939, he went ahead and grabbed the free city of Danzig, later attacking Poland. This act of war set the whole of Europe ablaze in less than a year.

Soon our attention was mainly directed to the progress of the war. We were very concerned and spent hours listening to the radio. Although we were sorry for the gallant Poles trying to resist the Germans, since we were Germany's ally every German victory made sensational news in our national newspapers.

With the rapid German conquest of half of Poland, it appeared that the Second World War would not last long. The very efficient German troops advanced rapidly and seemed to be invincible. This made me wonder: Would our *Duce*'s 'ten million bayonets' be as efficient as the German soldiers?

The French, supported by the British, waited confidently behind their formidable Maginot line, ready to repel any German onslaught as they had done so heroically during the Great War.

Although Italy had declared her neutrality at the beginning of the war, there was a continual call-up of the reserve, many of whom were sent to our colonies.

I did not join the army at once, as a number of my friends had done, because I was still unfit; I had to wait for the following year's medical examination, which was due in January or February 1940.

Since the major West European powers were at war, we were extremely worried; we did not know what our country would do. We were seriously concerned about our father and three brothers in Java. We heard also that if Italy became belligerent, we would be subject to food rationing and would have to get used to black-outs.

Christmas 1939 and New Year's Day 1940 were not merry at all, and every kind of entertainment was subdued. Although there was no great loss of life due to the 'phoney' war, its shadow hung over us like a black cloud. We feared that sooner or later we would be dragged in too and have to face its consequences: killing and being killed; destroying and being destroyed. This was only to be expected in war; battles could not be fought without dead and wounded.

When I went for my military check-up in winter 1940, the doctor said that I was fit for national service. In a way I was proud to hear this, and content to be as able as my friends who were already in the army. Meanwhile I had to wait for my call-up which was due the following winter.

Now that Germany was at war, *Il Duce* continued to make his impressive speeches, but at this stage he was also praising the German military achievement in Poland. Meanwhile, demonstrations in Italy had somewhat subsided. Those gallant young men and supporters of *Il Duce*, who had in previous weeks so eagerly cried for war, realised the seriousness of the situation now that the war was on, and were no longer so enthusiastic about it. No doubt they were afraid of its hardships and of having to put their lives at risk.

At this stage, we were having difficulties with our monthly remittances, which came late on account of the war. Perhaps the Dutch were afraid of being dragged into it. Tension seemed to be affecting their banking and postal services, especially those connected with their colonies. It was likely that they had to concentrate their efforts on more pressing issues such as defence at home and abroad. As a result of the situation, foreigners living in the Dutch East Indies were finding it extremely hard to keep in touch with their overseas relatives.

At the beginning of May 1940, as the Germans attacked Holland, Belgium and Luxembourg, we were completely cut off from our father and brothers. Luckily, soon afterwards we had an unexpected visitor – signor Pasquale Ragusa. Signor Ragusa had left Java at the beginning of 1940. He had visited Singapore, Bangkok, Hong Kong, Shanghai and Peking at his leisure and later he caught the Trans-Siberian train on his way back to Italy.

Being eager for news from Java, we welcomed him with open arms, as if he were one of the family. He told us that our father and brothers were well, then he handed Mother some money on behalf of Father and tried to cheer us up by saying that the war would soon be over.

Signor Ragusa was a native of a town called Grottaglie, situated in the vicinity of Taranto. He was in his forties, stocky, had black hair with a parting on the left, brown eyes and a rather darkish complexion. He spoke slowly and clearly, and the tone of his voice was gentle and soothing. He had a tailor's shop in Java and had spent many years there, during which time he had accumulated substantial savings. He was a member of the Dante Alighiere Society. Although his education had only been at primary level, since there was nobody else available in Java, signor Ragusa ventured to teach Italian which was, strictly speaking, an honorary appointment. He taught twice a week after his daily work. As a result of his teaching, signor Ragusa assumed a professorial attitude, so the Italians resident in Java nicknamed him *Il Professore Ragusa*. He appeared to be an ardent supporter of *Il Duce*; however, in January 1940, probably tired of the tropical climate, or some other reason, he decided to go back to Italy. He bought some land there and hoped to find a spinster younger than himself with a good dowry. He could get married and become a member of the Italian landed gentry.

While signor Ragusa was visiting us, Mother asked him whether he would be willing to be my brother Damiano's godfather. He accepted, and a couple of weeks later he revisited us. On that day Damiano, signor Ragusa and I went to Naples Cathedral, where the confirmation ceremony took place. Later we returned home and sat at the table to eat a lavish dinner which my mother and elder sister had specially prepared. Signor Ragusa praised my mother's cooking highly and later, before the end of his visit, he kindly lent Mother some money, a loan that Father would eventually settle with Luigi, one of signor Ragusa's brothers still living in Java.

41

Italy declares war on France and Britain.
Graziani attacks. The British bomb Taranto.
Wavell counter-attacks

Between April and June 1940, the Germans had occupied Denmark,
Norway, Holland, Belgium and Luxembourg. The French and the
British, unable to contain the Germans, were in retreat on the whole
front. Three hundred thousand British and French soldiers were
evacuated from Dunkirk mainly in small boats, most of which
luckily reached the British coast. The French and British soldiers
left behind surrendered, while the Germans advanced rapidly and
without hindrance.

Mussolini, aware of an imminent German victory that could have
meant the end of the war, quickly set aside neutrality and declared
war on France and Britain.

Marshal Badoglio, Chief of Staff of the Italian Army, knew that
Italy was not ready for war; it would have taken years of preparation
and a lot of money to build up a modern army as good as that of
Germany. Mussolini reflected that since the Germans had almost
won the war single-handedly, the Italian Army would need to suffer
at least a few thousand casualties. This would enable him to
participate in the peace conference which, as he foresaw it, was
inevitable and imminent.

On 20 June, the First and Fourth Italian Armies, consisting of
450,000 men, attacked a French Army of 135,000. Fighting the
French in the Alps and trying to dislodge them was not an easy
task at all. Besides, the Italian Army, as Marshal Badoglio had
anticipated, needed a lot of preparation before launching such a
difficult attack. But Mussolini wanted quick action and success at
any price.

Hard fighting went on for five or six days, during which the

Italian Army suffered just under 4,000 casualties, including dead, wounded and missing. The French Army registered 229 casualties. The Italian Army paid dearly for the conquest of Menton – about three kilometres of French soil.

With the German occupation of Paris, the French surrendered and towards the end of June 1940, they signed an armistice with Germany and Italy.

Since I had been led to believe, through so much Fascist propaganda, that our army was very efficient and ready to conquer the world, I was very disappointed that when we joined the war we did not get quick action – conquests and victories – like the Germans. Unfortunately our army's performance was poor; we were doing nothing impressive or heroic as I had expected. I was utterly shocked, broken-hearted and could not sleep at night; our military machine was not only inefficient, but we were allowing enemy aircraft to raid us at their own will. Did we have no defence? What was our air force doing? Would we ever be able to display the military prowess to restore our confidence, capacity and dignity?

From the beginning of July onward, we had a tendency to believe that the British would surrender too. However, this did not happen. Although heavily bombed, the British bravely resisted the endless German blitz. They probably hoped that sooner or later the Americans would rescue them as they had done during the Great War.

Soon after the French Armistice of 24 June 1940, and the death of Italo Balbo, Italian Governor of Libya – the cause of which remains obscure – Marshal Rudolph Graziani took command of the Italian forces in North Africa. He knew that he was not ready to attack the British there, but Mussolini, eager for a victory, put pressure on him. So at the beginning of September 1940, Graziani reluctantly attacked. The British Commander-in-Chief was General Sir Archibald Wavell.

Luckily Graziani did not meet stiff resistance, so with light tanks that were no better than sardine tins, outdated artillery and other antiquated war material and resources, he invaded Egyptian territory. This army advanced as far as Sidi Barrani, conquering about 120 kilometres of Egyptian terrain. We all rejoiced in Graziani's achievement and eagerly listened to the news on the radio, waiting tor Graziani's next advance which, as we thought, would ultimately expel the British from Egypt.

Graziani, being an expert, knew how inadequate his forces were in reality, so he was cautious. Having reached Sidi Barrani, he ran out of steam and came to a halt. He did not have the resources in tanks, ammunition, fuel, water and other materials to enable him to press on, so he dug in and waited for reinforcements which did not arrive.

This hold-up of Graziani's advance lasted into October, but Mussolini again put pressure on the marshal who, lacking adequate armour, was not in a position to advance and take Mersa Matruh.

Marshal Badoglio disapproved of our Greek campaign: nevertheless, owing to Mussolini's pressure it began at the end of October 1940. Badoglio disliked Mussolini's easygoing attitude; he was taking great risks by venturing into two campaigns simultaneously with two ill-prepared armies. We poor Italians, with our scarce and outdated military equipment, were seriously committed on both the North African and the Greek fronts; with Mussolini's attitude and pressure, how could we avoid disaster?

The British badly wanted to destroy our sea power, without which we could not supply our troops in North Africa. For months they must have been preparing the plan for an air attack on Taranto Naval Base. This attack they carried out on the night of 11 November 1940. According to the Italian media, twenty British bombers successfully torpedoed the battleships *Littorio*, *Cavour* and *Duilio*, causing considerable damage and thirty-two fatalities. The *Littorio* and the *Duillo* were out of action for five or six months, while the *Cavour*, being an old vessel, was 'moth-balled'.

The Italian Navy had to keep a number of ships for military operations at our base of Taranto, but our defence was poor, and being inadequate, it could not prevent the British Air Force attacking our ships.

At the end of November 1940, Marshal Badoglio resigned on account of the Greek campaign. This was one of Mussolini's adventures with which Badoglio strongly disagreed. Besides, the campaign had not been planned properly. As a result, nine badly equipped divisions were deployed in Greece; Mussolini had anticipated they would conquer it in about two weeks. These divisions suffered heavy casualties and were on the verge of being repelled across the Albanian frontier.

Taking advantage of Marshal Graziani's long halt at Sidi Barrani, the British reinforced themselves with new and heavier tanks, aircraft, modern artillery and other weapons, and on 9 November 1940, they counter-attacked.

Graziani was taken by surprise. Bombarded by the British Navy, land forces and aircraft, he had to fall back. His inferior equipment and firepower could not stop the British who, under their Commander-in-Chief, General Archibald Wavell, and Commander of Desert Forces, Lieutenant-General Richard O'Connor, not only reconquered their lost territory, but penetrated deeply into the Italian colony of Libya. They quickly captured Sidi Barrani and Sollum, which had been temporarily occupied by the Italians, taking at least 38,000 prisoners, 237 guns, 73 tanks and about 1,000 trucks. The British losses were about 634 men, including dead, wounded and missing.

Having taken Sidi Barrani and Sollum, they crossed the border at Fort Capuzzo and entered Libya. Later, they attacked the stronghold of Bardia, which they captured on 5 January 1941. They took about 45,000 prisoners, 130 tanks and about 300 trucks. Afterwards they attacked Tobruk, which they occupied between 20 and 22 January 1941, taking 25,000 prisoners, 200 guns, 23 tanks and 200 trucks.

With the loss of Tobruk, together with the other losses, an entire Italian Army, the Tenth, had been destroyed. There were only four Italian divisions left in Libya. On 7 February 1941, the British seized Benghazi, captured another 20,000 prisoners and, pushing further, reached El Agheila, where they came to a halt.

This victorious British campaign had been a humiliating defeat for the easygoing Mussolini and the Italian Army. At the end of the campaign, the British Command announced the capture of 130,000 prisoners, 400 tanks and 1,200 guns. The British claimed 5,000 Italian dead and 500 British; almost 1,400 British wounded, and 53 missing.

On 8 February 1941, Marshal Graziani resigned and General Italo Gariboldi replaced him. One or two days after Graziani's resignation, General Erwin Rommel arrived in North Africa.

PART FOUR

ARMY EXPERIENCES

42

I join the army. My travelling companions

In January 1941, the British attacked our colonies of Eritrea, Somalia and Ethiopia which we could not defend, and by May 1941 they occupied them.

We were getting blows from everywhere, instead of delivering them; defeats instead of victories. Such disappointments were extremely depressing and were almost driving Mussolini insane. That atmosphere of defeat was seriously affecting our morale. Moreover, the black-out, rationing and black market all seemed to conspire to create an unbearable situation. The war was not as short as the *Duce* had initially envisaged, and for us Italians this was not encouraging at all.

Before Christmas 1940, I received a card concerning my call-up. On 4 January 1941, I had to report to the Garibaldi Barracks in Naples. I spent Christmas and New Year's Day with my family, but we had so many troubles and worries that we were not in the mood for the season's celebrations. While the war was on, we were constantly thinking of our father and brothers, earning the money for the monthly remittances they sent from the island of Java. Were they safe? What would happen to them and to us during this cursed war? Only God knew that!

Regretfully and with a heavy heart I left home and joined the army: an army of which I was not feeling proud; an army which was being defeated. Where were they sending me now in my poor physical condition? To fight a war which we appeared to be losing? A war where I would either be killed or end up in a prisoner-of-war camp? Such was my predicament.

On the appointed day of my call-up, I hugged Mother and my sisters and said goodbye to them. My thirteen-year-old brother Damiano came to see me off at the *Caserma Garibaldi* (Garibaldi Barracks).

As I entered the barracks, I noticed that there were hundreds of men about my age, herded into its courtyard, waiting for instructions to be sent to their eventual destinations. I had to wait four or five hours before they gave me an identity document and a railway voucher. I and another five or six young men had been assigned to a military school for training artillery officers, situated in a Piedmontese town called Bra, where we were to report the following day. I had a good look at my travelling companions, and was not pleased – most of them were illiterate and came from a poor section of Naples called *Quartieri* or from some miserable streets in the vicinity of Naples Central Railway Station. They were boys living rough, perhaps former street urchins – rowdy, argumentative and quarrelsome.

Towards the evening, a sergeant escorted us to Naples Central Railway Station, where we caught the eight or nine o'clock train for Turin. Since that train started at Naples, the five or six of us settled down in a compartment to ourselves and soon the train set off. My companions made a lot of noise; they indulged in vulgar talk about priests, prostitutes, homosexuals and so on. They also sang Neapolitan songs, for they were already feeling homesick for their *Bella Napoli*. I myself was feeling homesick at the thought of leaving my family and was already missing the company of more congenial friends. I was sad, desolate and very much concerned about the course of the war: our army was being driven back in North Africa by the mighty new British tanks and efficient artillery, and thus destroyed.

Our war against Greece was, so far, a failure; yet my travelling companions were quite unconcerned about the serious situation and the dramatic hours through which our country was passing. They chatted, told silly jokes and smoked, polluting the compartment and almost choking me.

The train puffed, spat, shrilled, vibrated and jolted. In spite of the shaking, smoke and piercing noise, I managed to doze for a few hours as the train sped north during the night. However, we had to be on the lookout, checking up on the progress of our journey, just to make sure that we would get off at the right station.

We arrived at Alessandria at about 4.00 p.m., but had to wait there at least an hour to catch the train for Bra, which was our destination. Coming from South Italy, we became aware of the chilly northern air, and not being dressed adequately, we were shivering. As the train for Bra was slow, it took us about two hours to get there.

When we arrived we were shocked to notice some snow. We weren't accustomed to it, for we seldom had snow in Naples. We expected to meet a picket at the station that would escort us to the barracks we had been assigned. However, there was no such picket, so a passer-by kindly showed us how to get to the barracks, about 300 metres away.

My rowdy companions, although tired by the long journey, were aware that in a few minutes they would be subjected to military discipline. They made an effort and began singing the triumphal march from *Aida* (Verdi's opera) as we walked towards the military academy, also known as the School of Artillery for Officer Cadets. Some townsfolk were startled; they looked at us in astonishment as if we were a gang of Martian invaders.

43

The Pellizzari Barracks

On entering the building known as the Pellizzari Barracks, I noticed a rectangular courtyard well over 100 metres by about 70, surrounded by arcades, living quarters, stores and offices. One of the guards escorted my travelling companions and me to a ground-floor room in the left wing, which contained a couple of desks and chairs. Two lieutenants seated at the desks interviewed the new conscripts.

When my turn came, I handed my identification document, which I had received in the military district of Naples, to one of the lieutenants. He asked me some questions concerning my education, my family in Naples and my father and brothers living in Java, and then assigned me to the Fourth *Someggiata* Battery. *Someggiata* means to transport by pack-animals. In other words I had been assigned to a battery of howitzers, which could be dismantled and carried on the back of mules through narrow mountainous *mulattiera* (mule-tracks). I was shocked, horrified at the thought of having to come in touch with mules. Until then I had known the word mule only as a derogatory term for a stubborn person.

The Fourth Battery had its quarters on the second floor of the right wing of the barracks. The orderly office (*fureria*), managed by a sergeant-major, was on the first floor. He had three soldiers helping him. My comrades, for one reason or another, nicknamed him *Pistacchio*.

Our quarters consisted of four very large double rooms that we called *camerate* (dormitories). A passage, like a corridor, right in the middle of our quarters, separated the left and the right sections of our dormitories. Each dormitory accommodated at least twenty-four soldiers.

The latrines were on the right, a couple of metres from our

quarters' entrance. Opposite the latrines was a large room with a long concrete wash-basin and taps and mirrors alongside the walls. There we shaved, washed ourselves and cleaned our greasy *gavette* (mess tins). Next to the washroom was a storeroom and then a room accommodating our sergeant-majors, Rossi and Langella. There was a large stove in the middle of our quarters, but I assumed that, on account of the war, we were not allowed to use it. Regrettably, we had to endure winter without heating facilities. We were not supposed to get used to comfort while our soldiers fighting on the Greek front were exposed to the cold. However, when all our comrades were inside, the temperature rose comfortably.

Each dormitory had two large windows; one looking on to the courtyard and the other on to the adjacent street. The lights of our quarters, as a war precaution, were dimmed, hardly giving any light. This made it impossible for us to read and write in the evenings.

Each soldier had a folding bed, a mattress, two sheets and three woollen blankets. At the head of the bed was a shelf, holding a rectangular wooden box about one metre long by half a metre wide and half a metre in height to store our clothes and other personal effects.

They gave me a bed in the dormitory to which the new conscripts were assigned. The *anziani* (veterans) who had already been there at least a year, spurred on by curiosity, paid me a visit during my first days. They made me feel a strange fellow still smelling of Civvy Street. They asked me personal questions: 'Where do you come from? What kind of work were you doing?' and so on. I could not avoid them, and to try to keep on friendly terms with them I had to satisfy their inquisitiveness.

Secretly I was scared, for most of them were rough and stocky and used to hard physical work. No doubt they were farmers or forestry workers when they were at home and used to handling animals. Of course, I had seen such characters before, but had scarcely come into close contact with them. Now that these rough boys were my comrades-in-arms, whether I liked it or not I had to get on with them. Since they had been there a few years, and had been subjected to hardship, they were inclined to be irascible and full of resentment. Unable to pass the knocks on to anybody else, they gave vent to their feelings by teasing and even scaring the newcomers, if the latter failed to humour them.

Their resentment was basically due to the fact that they had to work hard and did not even get enough to eat. Their pay, one lira per day, did not buy much in those days. These poor, rough, unhappy sturdy boys had a huge appetite; it was no use telling them that their rations were adequate, contained enough calories and nourishment to keep them in good health, when their large stomachs were not quite full.

Any recruit who did not humour the discontented veterans would most likely be bullied and have to endure spiteful tricks, especially when the lights went out after ten o'clock. Later on, while the recruit – the target – was sound asleep, a veteran who had a grudge against him would get up, tiptoe to the recruit's bed, seize the foot of the bed and with a rapid movement lift it up vertically and fling it against the wall, thus causing the mattress and the occupant to somersault. The unfortunate, shocked and angered, would start swearing, while the raider, having quickly returned to his bed, would secretly have a good laugh. The angered victim did not complain because he could not find the culprit.

The veterans guessed that I came from a different background from theirs, for I looked delicate, more of a student than anything else, as if I had never done any menial work, let alone hard manual labour. They maliciously seemed to enjoy the prospect of seeing me doing unpleasant tasks such as rubbing down the mules, cleaning the stables, carting the manure away, taking the mules to the drinking trough, or feeding them. Among my other tasks were learning to saddle and control the mules; taking them for long walks in the country; pulling their bits when they were stubborn; carrying a bale of hay on my shoulders – which weighed forty or fifty kilos – or cleaning the latrines which got all mucked up during the night.

Our latrines did indeed get all mucked up because some of the more uncivilised soldiers, who perhaps had no latrines in their homes, relieved themselves everywhere except in the right place. Early in the morning the latrines looked like a kitchen garden, with small and sparsely growing cabbages. The stench was appalling; we needed several bucketfuls of water to wash the muck down the drains, and had to use plenty of disinfectant to kill off the stench and germs.

Guard duties were demanding too, so the hard-pressed soldiers seldom had two or three free evenings a week.

Having heard the veterans mention their routine and complain about their hardship, I found this disheartening. My heart was still at home; my comparatively comfortable home where I did not have to do any hard or unpleasant work or put up with any rough fellows. I just wanted to run away from the barracks, but where? Our country was at war; our soldiers were being killed on two fronts, especially in North Africa, where the British had overrun our positions and penetrated deeply into Libya. On the Greek front we could not make any progress and were on the defensive. What had I to complain about? It was no use indulging in soft thoughts while thousands of young men were risking their lives on two fronts and enduring untold hardship. It was my duty to stay put and serve my country the best I could; after all, a little hardship would certainly help to strengthen my character.

44

My military service begins

On the third day after my arrival, a number of recruits and I were taken to a military store. They gave each of us a uniform, underwear, shirts, a pullover, two pairs of shoes (one pair to be worn for physical exercises), some cotton clothes for stable duties, and a rifle and bayonet.

By this time I had acquired some familiarity with the barracks. In the right wing, after the main entrance of the Pellizzari Barracks, was the officers' mess. Further on was an arcade in which were two staircases; the first led to the cadets' and soldiers' quarters – cadets on the first floor, soldiers on the second – the second staircase led to the infirmary. Under the arcade was also the sergeants' mess. In the left wing were the cadets' mess, the prison, the showers, the barber's shop and a staircase leading to the first, second and third floors on which were the quarters accommodating the *Reparto Autonomo* (Independent Section). This was made up of a detachment of sixty soldiers or more, who were employed as military store assistants, office workers, cobblers, members of our brass band and so on.

The commandant, Colonel Tricoli Corradini, and the second in charge, Lieutenant Colonel Enrico Fianchini, lived in the front section of the barracks. The administration was also located there.

At the back of the barracks was the infirmary which contained a dozen beds or more for soldiers and cadets who were only slightly ill; the serious cases were sent to a military hospital. On the ground floor, still at the back of the barracks, was the cadets' kitchen. Further back was an extension of the barracks. It consisted of a small building with a courtyard and an exit gate. This gate was called Porta Carraia; it was used by carts to get access to the barracks and by soldiers on their way to other military buildings.

Porta Carraia looked on to a small street. The right corner of this street, about thirty metres from Porta Carraia, led to the Trevisan Barracks which provided quarters for soldiers and cadets of the Field Battery.

In the Trevisan Barracks were a courtyard, a small soldiers' canteen, the soldiers' kitchen, our howitzer stores and a long concrete wash-basin with several cold water taps along a wall, where the soldiers could wash their mess tins and do their laundry. The soldiers gathered in this courtyard at mess time and queued up for their daily rations.

At the back gate of the Pellizzari Barracks was a street leading to the *scuderie* (stables), where mules and horses were carefully looked after. Not far away from the stables was a large square called Piazza D'Armi. This was the ground for various training exercises and for drilling soldiers and cadets for occasional parades.

La sveglia (reveille) was usually at six, but when we had to go out with our cadets for target practice five or six kilometres into the country, then we had to get up at four or half past four.

Within a few days of my arrival, I was fully employed. After reveille, we drank the ersatz coffee, which was served in our quarters and hardly sweetened. It tasted awful; it was a brew made from roast beans and barley. During the wintry mornings we longed for a hot drink and to put something in our empty stomachs, so we could not afford to throw away that unpleasant coffee substitute. It was supposed to refresh us, but it teased our stomachs, which yearned and screamed for a substantial breakfast, especially those mornings before a long march. Having nothing to eat sent my comrades mad with rage, so they swore and swore; we had to wait till eleven o'clock for our meagre rations.

Usually at half past seven we went downstairs and mustered in the courtyard in a long line three deep for the daily roll-call. Afterwards one of our officers, or our captain, would make a short speech about military discipline, behaviour or something else. Later we marched to our stables and took the mules outside to the trough. If the weather was promising we attached them to a long rail in the cobbled lane adjacent to our stables. The stables were very large and were divided into four bays; each bay held about twenty mules or more.

After we had taken the mules outside and fixed them to the rail, those on duty at the stables – three privates and a lance-corporal –

cleaned the stables and prepared the litter. The lance-corporal, in his private life, was usually an insignificant and almost illiterate peasant, but being in charge of three privates and the mules he behaved as if he were a general. He did not stand on ceremony, so he drove the three privates very hard. They wheel-barrowed the manure and the hay saturated with urine and dung away to the manure heap outside the stables and re-made the litter with new layers of hay. While all this was being done, we devoted our attention to the mules; we groomed them and had to make them look, as our superiors said, 'respectable'.

We were supposed to treat them and love them as we would treat and love ourselves. I certainly was not prepared to do that. I found the mules extremely hard to handle. I tried to be as gentle as possible, but they would not obey – I was getting nowhere. They did not understand gentleness or my pleas, begging them to cooperate. There was no way; they would only respond to brute strength, which I was not accustomed to and was not inclined to use, so I hated them, and was not in the mood to show them that I was the master. I would have preferred to go to the front than to deal with such stubborn animals.

The grooming of the mules had to be done every day. Each soldier took a brush and a curry-comb from a wooden box and started rubbing down the mule in his care. The rubbing down, which we called *brusca e striglia*, had to be done methodically, under the supervision of one of our sergeant-majors, and it lasted no less than an hour. He made us start from the head, neck, chest and the front legs. Later we rubbed the body and ended with the rear of the animal. This was the way the rubbing down had to be done and the soldiers had to follow the instructions. As the grooming routine proceeded, some mules became restless and whenever they were harassed by flies, they hammered the cobbled pavement with their hooves. A soldier had to be careful not to touch sensitive spots, else an irritated mule would promptly remonstrate with his hind legs.

I loathed stable duties and, as I have already said, I could not get used to handling mules, let alone hard physical work. Most of my comrades were strong; when they were at home they did more or less the same work that they were doing in their military service.

When I was on stable duty, the lance-corporal in charge, aware that I was not used to physical work, deliberately drove me very hard and seemed to enjoy it. When I came off duty, my back and the rest of my body were aching. I had to go to bed, but when I got up next morning, my body was still stiff with pain.

I disliked being in the army, because I found the work I had to do depressing. Had I been sent to the front, I would have fought for my country and died like a hero. There was absolutely nothing glorious or heroic in dealing with mules and doing stable work; for me it was an emotional agony, destroying my pride and ego.

As I said before, most of my comrades were peasants used to hard physical work. When they were at home they had to work very hard for a crust of bread. While in the army, a half-dozen of them or more wanted to get on, looking forward to promotion; something to boast about at the end of their military service in their relatively eventful lives. They were prepared to do anything to achieve their goal. Having been promoted to lance-corporal or corporal, they loved showing off their rank in a bumptious way.

Usually we left the mules outside during the day, but when it was too cold or rainy we drove them into the stables. Even if we had nothing else to do, we were not allowed to go back to our quarters and spend the rest of the day there; we could do that only during our free time. In bad weather we stayed in the stables in the company of the mules, which provided us with a source of natural heat. While we were there, one of our second-lieutenants, named Sanolla, lectured us on military discipline, or gave us instructions on how to use our outdated machine-guns and howitzers that had been captured during the Great War.

Our army must have used these outdated weapons in the Abyssinian war of 1935–36. Then it was quite safe to do so, because our enemies were disorganised, and their firepower, compared with ours, was insignificant. Surely we could not use our outdated weapons against the British Army in North Africa, for they were far better armed than we were. Besides, they were receiving US military help, because the Americans sympathised with the British in their fight against Hitler and Mussolini. No wonder, when the British counter-attacked at Sidi Barrani on 9 November 1940, they put us to flight.

At half past ten we returned to our quarters, had a quick wash and then the mail was distributed. At eleven the bugle signalled mess time. We were as hungry as wolves, so we rushed downstairs, marched to the Trevisan Barracks and queued up for the rations which we called *rancio*. Most of the time it consisted of a kind of minestrone, but not too thick; fifty per cent of it was water. Next they gave us a chunk of cheese or a pork sausage or stewed meat containing very little beef. They also gave us half a pound of coarse bread made of a mixture of wholemeal and corn flour. They gave us pasta or risotto twice a week instead of minestrone.

We usually ate our rations in the Trevisan courtyard or in the canteen which had a number of tables and chairs, but could accommodate no more than fifty soldiers. Those who had money sent to them by their relatives could afford to buy half a bottle of wine, soft drinks, cigarettes, writing paper and other items from the canteen counter. Soldiers who had to rely on their military pay could hardly buy anything. All those, from sergeant upwards, had their monthly salary, their own mess, enough to eat; they could afford to have a drink, go to the cinema and visit brothels. I just couldn't understand the mentality of our military men; our humble soldiers were treated as inferior beings. How could we win the war with leaders like that? The difference between a soldier and an officer was enormous. By comparison, even a sergeant felt that he was far above the lower ranks. As for the officers in their elegant uniforms, they were like a superior race.

We had our midday break till half past one, during which time we wrote letters, had a chat or rested. In the afternoon we either went back to the stables or to the training ground to learn how to use our howitzers. They were small 75/13 guns, mainly for mountain warfare. The length of the barrel was seventy-five centimetres and its diameter thirteen. The basic training consisted of learning how to dismantle the howitzers as quickly as possible and fix each part on the packsaddle of a mule. A howitzer was dismantled into six loads; one for each mule. A load could weigh about 100 kilos (200 pounds). It had to be lifted by four soldiers high above the body of a mule and cautiously attached firmly to its packsaddle. This operation was not always easy, for if the mule did not cooperate, it started kicking, and this could cause a serious accident.

When the weather was fine, we frequently took our mules for a long stroll in the afternoon; it was a change of scenery for them and us. We admired, especially in spring, the fields, meadows, slopes, wooded areas and flowers. We relished breathing the fragrance of freshly cut grass and loved hearing the natural sounds of the countryside. This long stroll in the fresh air always gave us an extra appetite which proved to be a nuisance, because we were unable to gratify it on our meagre rations. After the distribution of the rations, a number of our veterans (older soldiers), who were as hungry as wolves, often fought a pitched battle for the privilege of scraping the bottom of the *marmitta* (cauldron) in which the food had been cooked.

We had our afternoon mess at five or half past. After that, those who weren't on duty could go out and have free time till nine. By half past nine, we had to be in bed for the roll-call. A few minutes later, the bugle sounded *il silenzio* for the lights to go out. On Saturdays we could obtain a special pass to stay out till ten or half past.

Sunday was not a demanding day for those who weren't on duty. *La sveglia* was at seven. Having drunk our ersatz coffee, we and the soldiers of other batteries mustered in the courtyard of the Pellizzari Barracks, and later we marched through the town centre to the parish church, which could accommodate about 600 of us. The parish priest celebrated the Mass which lasted an hour, during which some of the soldiers received the communion. On returning to the barracks, we paid a quick visit to the mules, cheered them up with some refreshments and soon it was mess time – a ladle of stewed meat, plenty of watery soup, a loaf of bread and a cup of diluted wine.

The Sunday midday meal was regarded as a pure aperitif by my hungry comrades; but it was an aperitif without another course to follow it. They could have eaten a huge meal. What a disappointment for their craving stomachs! In the afternoon we were allowed to stay out till three. Many soldiers had no money, so they walked through the town aimlessly, just to while away the time and wear out the soles of their shoes.

Sunday afternoon mess was at five. We invariably had a couple of ladles of pasta and perhaps a handful of some seasonal fruit. Having feasted on this not very convincing meal, we went out again. Some made for the cinema, others hung about around the town and later visited brothels, where admission was free. They sat on chairs along the walls, and naked prostitutes paraded in front of them. The girls knew that most of these visitors had no money to spend and were there for a free show, so they teased them, called them softies, old men incapable of being turned on. I doubt whether these young men had this capability. Being undernourished, they hardly had enough energy to cope with the back-breaking military duties. Had any of them got excited and been unable to buy sex, what else could he do?

A few soldiers preferred to explore the countryside, doing a little scavenging here and there. They probably found some carrots or radishes, which they munched with relish to appease their hankering for food. When tired of walking, they returned to quarters and spent the rest of the evening singing old soldiers' songs, which enabled them to forget their grumbling stomachs and our own military setbacks. After all, we were in the Italian Army, and in spite of our *Duce*'s wrong decision, we did not want to lose the war.

Il Duce did not hesitate to put pressure on our capable military leaders such as Badoglio and Graziani. Generals, no matter how good they are, cannot perform miracles in modern warfare if they haven't got the means – sufficient firepower to destroy their opponents.

45

Injection day

At the end of February 1941, it was injection day for the new conscripts. We were taken to the infirmary, where each of us received a jab in his chest as a preventive measure against disease. On such occasions we stayed in bed for a couple of days, because the injection caused a temperature and swelling of the chest. Soon we were on our feet again and ready to resume our tedious daily routine. The injection had quite a beneficial effect, for in spite of fatigue and discontent, we managed to pull through and stay in comparatively good health.

The advantages of doing military service at the Pellizzari Barracks – an artillery academy – were that we lived in a proper building, slept on mattresses and between sheets, and had a hot shower once a week, so that we could afford, to a certain extent, cleanliness and comfort. Soldiers attached to regiments were not always housed properly and did not enjoy those few luxuries that we had, but their service and discipline were less demanding than ours. We had to work hard, stick closely to military rules and accept unquestioningly whatever we could get.

There were three or four soldiers in our battery who never had a hot shower or bath when they were at home. They seemed to be afraid of coming in contact with the water which was very cold except in summer, so they neither washed nor changed their underwear frequently. Soon we noticed that they were lice carriers. We nicknamed the lice *carri armati* (tanks), because they moved very slowly, like the clumsy and cumbersome tanks used in the Great War.

Soldiers who came off guard during the night had to rest for a few hours on a board, which was a makeshift bed covered with blankets. If they had to rest side by side with a lice-infested comrade, they would be infested too.

To exterminate lice, the authorities took a kind of ritual precaution. They assembled the lice carriers in a corner of our courtyard where cauldrons of boiling water had been installed. The lice carriers ceremoniously undressed and then consigned their infested clothes to the bubbling water. Next a barber cropped their hair. Afterwards these men had to scrub themselves with plenty of hot water and soap, and then they were given clean or new clothes. Their mattresses were eventually treated or destroyed. Our corporals kept an eye on them, making sure that they washed themselves properly and did not dodge the weekly shower.

We had half a dozen comrades in our battery who could neither read nor write. When one of them asked me, I always helped him with his correspondence. Frequently I had to guess what either his mother or girlfriend had written, for their expressions and spellings puzzled me. Also unable to read or write, the mother or girlfriend had probably asked one of their neighbours to write for them.

One of my comrades, Melillo, needed my services regularly; a service that was free of charge. He had a very romantic and affectionate girlfriend named Dora. She seemed to miss him badly and was eager to get the letters that I wrote for him. They enlivened her romance and made her almost as passionate as the Juliet she had perhaps seen at the cinema. Melillo had suddenly become her Romeo. She thought that military service was doing him a lot of good; he was being educated, becoming a poet and the Prince Charming of her dreams. Melillo wanted to reciprocate her romance when I wrote for him, but did not know enough words to express his feelings. He stammered, perspired, became all worked up and confused, which would get him nowhere, so he gave up the attempt and gave me a free hand to use my imagination. I promptly complied with his wish, but while I was writing, I would often let my fancy take over. On one occasion I started quoting from the fifth canto of Dante's *Inferno*, where Dante and Virgil meet Francesca of Rimini and Paolo who was her lover.

I quoted: *Amor, che al cor gentil ratto s'apprende* ... (Love, that by a gentle heart is quickly set aglow...)

Amor che a nullo amato amor perdon ... (Love, that excuses no one loved from loving...)

Dora was no doubt charmed and uplifted by these quotations, even if she didn't quite understand them!

On another occasion I wrote: *Dearest Dora. I love you so much that I cannot stop thinking of you. When I am tired, after a long march, I look at your photo and tiredness leaves me. When I am on night duty at the stables, amid the appalling stench of the mules' dung which takes my breath away, I imagine being with you in a garden full of perfumed flowers, and this revives me. Your image cheers me up, gives me courage and fortitude. How could I manage without thinking that you love me?*

When I read Melillo what I had written to his sweetheart, he was overjoyed, gave me a radiant smile and waited hopefully for her to reply. He was grateful for my help and often volunteered to make my bed while I was out. He even wanted to polish my boots.

'That won't be necessary,' I said. 'I'll do it.'

'It won't take me very long,' he would say. 'I've got to polish mine and will do yours at the same time.'

'All right, if you insist, please yourself.'

He made my boots shine like a mirror, but soon I found out that my tin of shoe-polish did not last very long. What was he doing with it? I discovered that he was using it to polish the boots of some comrades and charging them for the service!

46

Oath of allegiance. Rommel attacks

As new conscripts, we had to take an oath of allegiance to our King, by which we would become fully integrated into the armed forces. This was due to take place on 21 April 1941, which was the anniversary of the foundation of Rome. We spent a couple of hours daily at Piazza D'Armi, our training ground, where we drilled (square-bashing) for the forthcoming event. However, the drilling proved to be too strenuous for half a dozen of my comrades, who were unable to differentiate left from right. The poor chaps were utterly confused, so they needed extra training.

One of our sergeant-majors, Sergeant Rossi, tied a handkerchief on the right arm of each of them. This did not help to achieve immediate results, for these tardy learners still got it wrong. The sergeant became furious and shouted: '*Unodue, unodue, unodue*' (Left right, left right, left right), which is also equivalent to the British command: Left, left, left, right, left.

The poor learners were unable to follow the beat. When the sergeant shouted: '*Fianco destra*' or '*Fianco sinistra*' (Right turn or Left turn), they turned the wrong way and made him frantic with rage. He yelled hysterically: '*Cazzoni impappinati! Bischeri! Minchioni!*' (Confused cabbages! Stupids! Fools! Good for nothing!). But giving them undignified names did not always help to improve their performance.

Bystanders were amused at the sight of those poor clumsy soldiers, and at the sergeant's furious shouts.

The day of our oath of allegiance was warm and sunny. We made sure that our uniforms were spotless, no button was missing and our boots were properly polished. We were wearing white gloves for the occasion. All the batteries (Fourth, Fifth, Sixth and the Field Battery) gathered in the spacious courtyard of the Pellizzari

Barracks. Some civic and military authorities had been invited and our band played military tunes.

The barracks' commandant, Colonel Tricoli Corradini, made a speech: 'Artillerymen! Always remember our motto: *Sempre ed ovunque* (Always and everywhere). Remember that our artillery played a decisive part in the Great War, in which many gallant artillerymen fought and died for our King and country. At the moment you're doing your military service here. Should it happen that you go to the front, I'm sure that you'll be as brave as your fathers and ancestors who fought in past wars.

'As you know, our armed forces have suffered an initial set-back in North Africa, but now they have retaken Benghazi which the British had temporarily captured last February, and we are still pressing on.

'Here in Europe, the Italo-German forces have occupied Yugoslavia and Greece. This clearly shows that both Italian and German Armies are doing well.'

At the end of our commandant's speech, we conscripts took the following oath of allegiance: 'We solemnly swear to be faithful to our King and to his Royal successors, and to observe the statutes and other laws of our state for the inseparable well-being of our King and country.'

An officer standing on the rostrum who had a clear, projecting voice recited the oath, while we stood to attention. At the end of it, he shouted to us: 'Do you swear it?' Each of us repeated in a chorus: 'We do!' Soon after this we sang the national anthem and some Fascist songs, and then we paraded in front of our commandant and his guests. At the end of the ceremony, they gave us a special *rancio* (rations) which was slightly better than usual, and we were allowed to go out for the rest of the day.

Apart from what our commandant had just said about our military set-back, I was particularly worried because, during December 1940 and January 1941, news from our North Africa front had been depressing; all the Cyrenaica had fallen to the British. Then, in February 1941, General Erwin Rommel arrived in North Africa; he soon reversed the situation.

Rommel was in charge of the Afrika Korps, the German Army fighting in North Africa. Although the Italian General, Italo Gariboldi, was supposed to be the Commander-in-Chief and Rommel was formally under his authority, Rommel's real authority

227

was the Führer. Evidently he gave Rommel a free hand for action, and so the Italian general had to swallow his pride and cooperate with him.

On 13 February 1941, a few days after his arrival, Rommel attacked the British and, in less than two months, inflicted heavy losses on them, forcing them to abandon Benghazi and fall back as far as Sollum, on the Libyan–Egyptian boundary. The Italo-German forces seized all the territory, except Tobruk, that the British had occupied a few months earlier. Meanwhile Tobruk was under siege.

Winston Churchill, dissatisfied with the conduct of the North African war, transferred General Wavell to India. General John-Claude Auchinleck became the new British Commander-in-Chief in North Africa. Churchill yearned for a quick victory to convince the Americans and the rest of the world that Britain, being adequately supplied, had the military capability to win.

47

Naval battle of Cape Matapan

At the end of March 1941, a strong Italian naval formation was sailing south of the Peloponnese, in the direction of the island of Crete, when a British reconnaissance aircraft spotted it and alerted Admiral Cunningham at Alexandria. He quickly despatched Force A of the Mediterranean fleet towards the Italian formation. From Piraeus sailed Force B, under the command of Vice-Admiral Pridham-Wippel, which was also directed towards the Italians. Cunningham and Pridham-Wippel were in charge of the British formations. This included the battleships *Barham*, *Valiant*, *Warspite*, the aircraft-carrier *Formidable*, the cruisers *Orion*, *Ajax*, *Perth*, *Gloucester* and thirteen torpedo-boat destroyers.

Admirals Angelo Jachino, Cattaneo and Sansonetti were in charge of the Italian formation. Cattaneo and Sansonetti were under the command of Jachino. The Italian formation included the battleship *Vittorio Veneto*, from which Admiral Jachino directed the operations, and the cruisers *Garibaldi* and *Duca Degli Abruzzi*. It also included the cruisers *Fiume*, *Pola* and *Zara*, under the command of Admiral Cattaneo; and the cruisers *Trieste*, *Trento* and *Bolzano*, under the command of Admiral Sansonetti. Nine torpedo-boat destroyers escorted the Italian formation.

At dawn on 28 March 1941, the Italian cruisers *Trieste*, *Trento* and *Bolzano* and some torpedo-boat destroyers met the British Force B. This consisted of the cruisers *Orion*, *Ajax*, *Gloucester* and four torpedo-boat destroyers.

The opponents fought a forty-minute battle, during which no ship was seriously damaged. Suddenly the British formation, contrary to its expected aggressive behaviour, disengaged and retreated. Sansonetti, spurred by a sense of triumph, chased the fleeing adversary. This retreat of the British ships was, however, a stratagem designed to get the Italian ships within the range of the guns of Force A, and under air attacks of the aircraft-carrier *Formidable* which was also part of Force A.

Presumably the chase, after a while, made Admiral Jachino suspicious, so he ordered Admiral Sansonetti to end it. At this moment, Vice-Admiral Pridham-Wippel changed his tactics and in his turn started chasing the Italians. It is likely that the Italian formation fell within the range of guns of Force A in the vicinity of the Greek island of Gaudo, to the south of Crete. A battle ensued involving the Italian battleship *Vittorio Veneto* which exchanged fire with the enemy, but without success.

At about 11.00 a.m. six British torpedo-bombers, which had taken off from the aircraft-carrier *Formidable*, attacked the Italian battleship. It managed to dodge the torpedoes, but having become aware of the risk, Admiral Jachino decided to return to his base.

Admiral Cunningham, with a much stronger formation, was determined to scupper the Italian ships; he could do that if he succeeded in reducing their speed on their way back home.

At 3.00 p.m., torpedo-bombers attacked the Italian battleship again, but this time the battleship couldn't dodge all the torpedoes and one of them hit its stern, causing considerable damage. The ship was about 700 kilometres from its base. Flanked by six cruisers and eleven torpedo-boat destroyers, it sailed, regardless of the damage, at a speed of nineteen knots. However, towards sunset, with the approach of the night, Admiral Jachino felt safe and was looking forward to an uneventful return to base. Suddenly another torpedo-bomber attack was carried out while the Italian formation was steaming somewhere south of Cape Matapan. The cruiser *Pola* was hit and pinned down; its electrical system was put out of order, making it impossible for its sailors to operate the gun-turrets and return the enemy's fire. The cruiser was helpless and paralysed.

Admiral Jachino ordered the cruisers *Zara* and *Fiume*, and the torpedo-boat destroyers *Alfieri, Gioberto, Carducci* and *Oriani* to go to the *Pola*'s rescue. This was an unwise decision indeed, because Admiral Jachino did not realise that a powerful British formation, with three battleships and an aircraft-carrier, was not far away from the immobilised cruiser. Perhaps he imagined, as was usually the case, that warships would not venture to attack during the night. He also did not know that British warships were equipped with radar that would enable them to spot their targets in the dark.

The British battleships, which had pointed their guns towards the *Pola*, suddenly discovered that the cruisers *Zara* and *Fiume*, and the destroyers *Alfieri*, *Gioberto*, *Carducci* and *Oriani* all fell within their range, so the British immediately opened fire and hammered their targets mercilessly, setting them ablaze and causing complete annihilation and slaughter.

Quite a number of sailors were badly wounded or reduced to a bloody pulp. Others, unable to save their ships, dived into the sea, hoping to survive, but most of them were drowned. The cruisers *Zara* and *Fiume*, and the destroyers *Alfieri* and *Carducci* were seriously damaged and sank. During the night, the crew of the destroyer *Jervis* boarded the immobilised *Pola* without meeting resistance. Having transferred the crew of the *Pola* to their ship, they blew up the crippled ship. Three thousand Italian sailors perished, including Admiral Cattaneo and the captains of *Zara* and *Fiume*.

48

The Germans invade Russia

The war, so far, had not been favourable for us by air, land or sea. Had it not been for the Germans' support, we would have made no progress at all. They rescued us in North Africa at the beginning of 1941 and about two months later in the Balkans. We had nothing to boast about and could not forget our humiliation. We strongly relied on German successes. Had the Germans won the war, we would have rejoiced in their final victory and had a say in a following peace treaty.

On 22 June 1941, Hitler decided to attack the USSR by surprise. Again he did not consult Mussolini, who was his ally. He reckoned that in a couple of months his seemingly invincible army would defeat the Soviets. Of course, Mussolini had great confidence in the victorious Germans who had already defeated France, invaded Yugoslavia and Greece, and now were beating back the British in North Africa.

Although Mussolini wasn't being treated by Hitler on equal terms, he had no choice but to abide by Hitler's decisions. He even asked Hitler's approval to send an Italian Army to fight in Russia, helping the Germans to hasten victory. Hitler was not too enthusiastic about Mussolini's offer; he preferred that the Italians concentrated their efforts on fighting in North Africa, where reinforcements and material resources were badly needed. However, Mussolini insisted on sending an Italian Army to the Russian front to fight side by side with our German comrades. After all, weren't the Germans helping us in North Africa? And why shouldn't we reciprocate by helping them on the Russian front? Perhaps Mussolini badly wanted to show to the world that the Italian Army wasn't always in need of rescue by the Germans, but that it, in turn, was able to help the Germans fighting in Russia.

Hitler, to please Mussolini, accepted his offer. Mussolini asked his new Chief of General Staff, Ugo Cavallero, who had replaced Marshal Badoglio months earlier, to organise an Italian expeditionary force; this was under the command of General Giovanni Messe, and was allocated to a section of the Russian front between the Dniester and the Bug rivers. The Italian equipment sent there consisted of light tanks and artillery, weapons which were not as good as those of the Germans.

During their offensive of 1941, the Germans penetrated deep into Russian territory. Whenever they captured a Russian city, the newspaper vendor who came daily into our barracks shouted at the top of his voice, spreading the sensational news, which urged us to buy the newspaper. If I was in our quarters, I rushed downstairs and bought *La Stampa*, a national daily published in Piedmont. Good news was always in bold print. This helped to boost our morale and gave us hope for victory. We assumed that the Russians were no match for the Germans, and that they would eventually capitulate as they had done during the Great War. Our officers were optimistic; they were so impressed with the Germans' military progress that they called my class – the one called up for military service in 1941 – 'The Victory Class'.

However, there was no quick final victory in Russia, so the war dragged on and on; in spite of their tremendous losses in men and war material, the Russians bravely withstood the German pressure. Since the Germans were determined to defeat the Russians at any cost before the coming winter, they made a supreme effort and, on 1 September 1941, they launched a new offensive. This was intended to deliver the Russians a final blow, knocking them out once and for all.

On 2 December 1941, the Germans pushed forward as far as Khini, a town less than ten kilometres from Moscow. However, the Germans, utterly exhausted and lashed by a severe winter, couldn't go on any further. This was fatal; it clearly indicated that their campaign had failed to achieve its objective. How could they hold the conquered positions and fight back Russian onslaughts in that severe winter, without adequate supplies, or perhaps any supplies at all? This situation was caused above all by the lengthy lines of communication, where German trucks carrying supplies were exposed to attacks from the Russian underground movement.

The German offensive had failed – and that extremely cold

winter with plenty of snow and frost was against them. The Russians, on the other hand, being used to severely cold winters, and being adequately supplied, would attack the weakened invaders and give them a sound thrashing, the same treatment as they had meted out to Napoleon Bonaparte in October 1812.

The Italian Expeditionary Corps at the Russian front (CSIR), although ill-equipped, did their best when the Germans were vigorous, and victorious. The Italian position was precarious, and being a small army, they couldn't do much without strong German support.

49

*Our cadets. Captain Marzocchi is in command of the
Fourth Battery*

Our life in barracks went on as normal during the second six months of 1941. There was a glimmer of hope that the war would soon come to an end. We reckoned that if it was short, there wouldn't be any repetition of the horrors and huge losses sustained during the Great War.

Between 300 and 400 highly qualified students arrived at our barracks, at least once a year, to do a course that would enable them to become artillery officers. Sometimes the course was intensive; it was then shortened to three months. This meant that about one month after the completion of each course, a new one started. It also meant extra work for tutors, mules and soldiers. The soldiers often had to rise at 4.00 a.m. or 5.00 a.m. and get the mules ready for long marches to hilly areas suitable for target practice. Of course, they hated having to work harder than usual, and so they grumbled and swore, especially at mealtimes, for they did not get any extra food to recompense their effort.

I strongly disliked being a mule attendant. Luckily, after five or six months of doing various duties, I was asked to be an assistant in *fureria* (our orderly office). Two other soldiers and I assisted the sergeant-major, nicknamed *Pistacchio*, who was in charge of our office. I had to help to keep records of our daily services and of our equipment. We held a very detailed record of everything; even of the screws and nails used in our quarters. Once every two or three months, we made an inspection of our quarters, checking on the sleeping place of each soldier, his blankets, sheets, folding bed, canvas used as bedding, mattress, underwear, shoes, socks and so on. If something was missing, even a pair of shoelaces or a bedding hook, or if something had been damaged by negligence, then we would debit the missing or damaged item to the soldier concerned. He would not get his pay, which was one lira per day, until he had paid off the debt. Being employed in the orderly office was a full-time job, so I was exempted from doing guard duties and was rarely required to go on a march.

My mother sent me twenty lire a month by post, which was better than nothing and I tried to earn a little money by exploiting the black market. Having made friends in the town, I was able to buy cigarettes of good quality that were in demand by some of our cadets who came from well-to-do homes. I did not charge anything for my services, but they were thankful and tipped me. I also earned a little money by teaching basic algebra to the daughter of a baker named Mariuccia. He provided me with bread, some pocket money and an occasional meal. My extra income enabled me to go to the cinema twice a week and to have a snack during my free time outside the barracks. If I did not fancy my midday or after-noon rations, I passed them on to a hungry comrade who in return volunteered to wash my *gavetta* (mess tin) and make up my bed.

Captain Marzocchi Bruno was in command of our battery which consisted of about 110 men, including the sergeant-majors, second-lieutenants and lieutenants. The captain was an energetic man in his forties. He was rather tall, bald, had blue eyes, a sun-tanned face and a clear and resonant voice. When there were no target practices on, he came to the orderly office at 8.00 a.m. or 9.00 a.m. and dealt with daily reports and other tasks, then he followed his daily schedule such as tutoring officer cadets or meeting our group commander, Lieutenant-Colonel Salvo Calogero, to whom some of our cadets gave a nickname; they called him Zio Porco (Uncle Pig).

Captain Marzocchi promptly reproached us when he thought that we were being undisciplined or were malingering, such as feigning sickness to dodge duties, or simply to have a rest. This in military terms was called *fare il furbo* (trying to be clever), so he called us *lavativi* (slackers or scrimshankers). He also reproached us for being untidy, lethargic or for other misdemeanours.

When there was the possibility of going home on two weeks' leave, he said: 'Hard workers and those who have a good disciplinary record must have priority.'

236

Our captain was very intelligent and held in high esteem by his superiors. We regarded him with great respect and affection.

Lieutenant Pelle Mario was second-in-charge of our battery. He was in his early forties, had fair and curly hair, grey eyes, a straight nose and fair complexion. He looked delicate and refined; he was probably of noble descent. Apart from his uniform, he did not strike me as a military man, and I don't think he liked our mules; he would make sure that he wasn't too close to them. He was no doubt a learned man, and could explain to us in a few simple words how we should handle our howitzers or perform other tasks.

It is likely that our group commander, Lieutenant-Colonel Salvo Calogero, for one reason or another wanted to get rid of him, and so suddenly Lieutenant Pelle was removed and sent to the Russian front. What had he done? Was this a punishment? We soldiers were puzzled. A few months after his departure, we learned that an enemy shell had blown his head off.

Our two second-lieutenants, Sanolla and Villanti, were not highly qualified academically, so when they were on duty they spent most of their time with us, teaching us whatever we were supposed to know.

Our three sergeant-majors, Rossi, Langella and *Pistacchio* were regulars. They had served at our barracks for several years, and all of them were in their forties. Having to put up with a tedious kind of existence, they looked pale, withered, undernourished and on the point of breathing their last. As I looked at them they made me feel dull, tired, wanting to yawn, go to bed and sleep for six months. Poor chaps, what else could they do? They had to be grateful to be employed. Although their employment wasn't attractive, it was very hard to get and provided a comparative security; they were paid punctually, and when they retired they would get a state pension. Ordinary workers, who weren't state employees, weren't entitled to any pension whatsoever.

Sergeant-Majors Rossi and Langella supervised us when we groomed our mules, had to fix packsaddles on them or do any other menial task. If we didn't do our jobs properly, they scolded us and called us unpleasant names, but they would never venture to show us how a job had to be done. Both our sergeant-majors and our officers seemed to be afraid of getting their hands dirty.

In July 1941 I went home on ten days' leave, but my mother and my sisters, with no remittances coming from Father on account of the war, were extremely worried. The Italian government granted Mother a subsidy that was hardly enough to buy bread for her family. Fortunately she had some jewels and was selling them one by one in order to survive. In spite of their difficulties, they could still manage to buy some food, and so they were in relatively good health.

I did not enjoy staying at home; the thought that Mother was struggling hard to buy the basic necessities saddened me. If she had to feed me while I was on leave, my young brother and my sisters would have to eat less. I certainly did not want to be a burden to my family, so I yearned to see the end of my leave and go back to the barracks, where I didn't have to worry about my keep. Even away from home I couldn't silence my nagging thoughts about the hardship that my family had to endure, and all this because the Fascist government hardly did anything to help the helpless.

50

*Our barracks embark on a two-week target practice at
Dronero. Captain Marzocchi is promoted to major.
Captain Giustiniani becomes our new commander*

The officer cadet course ended in July. The new one, which was intensive and would last three months, was due to start in September 1941. The ex-cadets had been promoted to second-lieutenants and gone home for a short leave, and later they would reach their new placings.

At the beginning of August 1941, the batteries of the Pellizzari Barracks and those of the Trevisan Barracks – four batteries in all – embarked on a two-week target practice (*tiri*) in the vicinity of Dronero, about forty kilometres south-west of our barracks in Bra. The aim of these field exercises was probably to give us some experience of how the soldiers who were at the front lived and should behave when facing the enemy.

We travelled by train from Bra to Dronero, then marched about two or three kilometres to reach our campsite, which was located on a hill above the Moira Valley.

It was quite a job to get the mules into the wagons and to fasten them to some makeshift railropes; this was a job which some of our battery's veterans, who were used to handling animals, did with a sense of pride and satisfaction, and they certainly liked showing off their dexterity. Soon the mules were happily munching a generous portion of hay which kept them busy during the journey. We had no problems in loading the howitzers and whatever was necessary for our target practice. Being employed in the orderly office, I was not involved in other activities.

When we arrived at the campsite, we set up our tents – three soldiers to each. We got up at 6.00 a.m., drank our ersatz coffee and then were ready for the duties of the day. There was a route

239

march at least twice a week. Since I was exempt from the marches, I followed them in my thoughts; I could imagine my comrades perspiring and grumbling, as they drove the mules through rough, narrow, uphill paths, urging them on by pulling their reins, whenever the poor animals hesitated. The mules, no doubt, would have preferred to be free and able to wander from slope to slope, relishing whatever fresh and tasty grass they could find, instead of being forced to carry those hateful, boring howitzers.

My orderly office colleagues and I had to stay behind, preparing the daily rota and making requisitions for our battery's needs. During our midday break, we jumped into a tributary of the Moira River, which flowed alongside our camp, and sunbathed on its narrow and pebbly beach. Being in a bushy area, we couldn't see much of the open country, but we were able to hear the gentle soothing flow of the water when no gruff voices disturbed the atmosphere of that delightful place.

Having had the afternoon rations, those who were free of duty walked the two or three kilometres to Dronero, a small, typically Piedmontese town. Unfortunately it had nothing to offer soldiers who had no money, so most preferred to remain in the camp area and splash in the nearby stream. They tried very hard to catch a few trout, which would enable them to have a rare and luxurious supper. One of our sergeant-majors, who badly fancied a trout dinner, blasted the stream with a hand grenade and caused a fish massacre.

A number of soldiers explored the bush, looking for blackberries and sparsely-scattered fruit trees. Others walked about two kilometres and visited one or two farmers, where they bought *focaccia*, butter, milk and eggs. There were two or three poachers among us who were pillaging the orchards, helping themselves to the fruit. This caused the farmers to complain and to enrage our superiors.

Our group commander, Lieutenant-Colonel Salvo Calogero, a veteran wounded in the Great War, had risen from the ranks. He was in his forties and rather robust. He had slightly wavy greying hair combed back, a wrinkled forehead, grey eyes and a monocle, giving him the appearance of a person of distinction. He was very conscious of his authority and did not hesitate to show it in a rather ostentatious way, making his subordinates feel uneasy in his presence. I suspect that it was on account of his looks and attitude that a few of our cadets amused themselves by mimicking him.

Rumours circulated that when he was a major, his batman had had a love affair with his wife. Having become suspicious, he contrived to catch the lovers in bed, and so he shot his batman. As it was a question of honour, he got away with the murder without being penalised.

I remember vividly how once, while our cadets were firing the howitzers during a target practice, Lieutenant-Colonel Salvo was sitting in a camp chair that had been placed at an observation point some distance behind our guns. He looked like a general inspecting his battlefield. Later, as he examined the targets through his goniometer (an instrument used for measuring angles), he gave instructions aimed at adjusting the guns' optical instruments. Our Captain Marzocchi was stationed five or six metres behind our guns, and as he received his commander's instructions, he secretly rectified them. When the shots hit the target, our lieutenant-colonel was jubilant and ecstatic, and he joyfully wanted to share his moment of triumph with our captain for having carried out his instructions so scrupulously.

Credit was really due to our captain for having rectified the commander's instructions. So when he noticed that the commander was wallowing in false glory, he laughed up his sleeve. He knew exactly how to humour him, for he had set his heart on promotion. So he cleverly played on his superior's vanity, hoping to get a recommendation.

Lieutenant-Colonel Salvo frequently spoke to us, expecting us to behave decently. Now that we were in camp, he felt strongly that we needed his lectures.

'Soldiers,' he would say, 'you must respect the property of those who have given us permission to use their land. Be tidy, by which I mean don't make a nuisance of yourselves. Don't cause any damage and don't leave rubbish around; take it to the tip. Above all, don't relieve yourselves all over the camp; you know where the latrine holes are, so do it there – and bear in mind that poaching is a punishable offence.'

Though we were refreshed by the change of scenery while the camp lasted, by the end of August we went back to our barracks, carrying on with our wearisome routine.

Captain Marzocchi did not stay with us very long, for in autumn

241

1941 he was promoted to the rank of major and moved to a higher position. Later they sent him for one or two months to North Africa to acquire some knowledge of modern artillery warfare. This information was presumably to be included in our officer cadets' syllabus.

Captain Vito Giustiniani became our new battery commander. He, like Captain Marzocchi, was a regular. I think he came from a long line of military forebears; I heard someone say that his father was a general. He was about five feet six inches tall and of normal build, was almost bald, had grey eyes, a round face, gold-rimmed spectacles and a fair complexion. He seemed to be a *pignolo* (a fussy man), which made us wonder – what did he expect from us, a pound of flesh? We could not exert ourselves more than we were already doing on a bread and cabbage diet; we had already been driven to the limit. Did he not know that armies don't march on empty stomachs? Did he not know that the Romans, who were defeated at Trasimene in the year 217 BC, were sent out to fight on a chilly morning with empty stomachs? The Carthaginians, practical men, had a substantial breakfast before that fateful battle in which a Roman Army was utterly annihilated.

Captain Giustiniani had the tendency to be authoritative; he was always harping on about precision, efficiency and punctuality, the kind of talk we didn't really relish. It was very easy for him to express what his meticulous conscience urged him to say; after all, he was well nourished and healthy looking. My bored and dispirited comrades had only one wish: to go back home, work as hard as they could, have at least one square meal a day and be their own masters. They did not particularly fancy our new and over-exacting captain who, in their opinion, was not as good as Captain Marzocchi. They contemptuously nicknamed him *Pierino* (Little Peter).

Since Lieutenant Pelle had left us, quite a number of new lieutenants had joined our battery. Probably the army had too many officers and, not knowing what to do with them, they had to dump them somewhere. Most of the new arrivals were reserve officers. We had Lieutenants Lattuada, Eboli, Zattoni, Frontino and two others who were the youngest and in their early thirties. The older officers were highly qualified and except for Lieutenant Frontino, were used as tutors to our officer cadets.

The war seemed to be promising success, especially in Russia as the Germans pressed on. In North Africa the situation was changing.

On 18 November 1941, Lieutenant-General Cunningham, who had been chosen by the British Commander-in-Chief of North Africa, General Sir Claude Auchinleck, became the new commander of the British Desert Forces. Equipped with 700 heavy tanks, 600 field guns, 200 anti-tank guns, a huge mass of vehicles, other modern weapons, plenty of ammunition, an endless fuel supply and backed by 650 aircraft, Cunningham started the Great Crusader offensive against Rommel.

Rommel's armaments consisted of 400 tanks, of which 150 were obsolete Italian ones. He was unable to get reinforcements, which were badly needed on the Russian front. He could not hold the British, so he had to retreat and, by the end of December 1941, he had fallen back to El Agheila, the point of departure of his offensive of March 1941. The trouble with Rommel was that when he suffered a set-back, he always blamed the Italians. Perhaps he could not accept the fact that the Germans were not always invincible, so he had to find a scapegoat for his failures.

Of course, the Germans were good soldiers, and good soldiers help to win a war but, in modern warfare, firepower plays a major role. If an army can afford to maintain unceasing pressure on its enemy and quickly replace its losses, it will certainly win. Such was the situation during the Great War. Both the Great War and that of 1939–45 were wars of attrition, and the nations that had the backing of the wealthy Americans – which meant an endless source of war material supplies – would surely win.

51

The Japanese attack Pearl Harbor

On 7 December 1941, the Japanese attacked Pearl Harbor and simultaneously declared war on the USA.

Germany and Italy were members of the Tripartite Pact – Italy, Germany and Japan. This pact was signed at the end of September 1940. Now that Japan was at war with the USA, whether Germany, Italy and their allies liked it or not, they had to declare war on the USA, so the European war became the Second World War.

When our barracks radio broadcast the news that Mussolini had declared war on the USA, we were flabbergasted and received the news with great concern. Fancy our poor country declaring war on the rich and mighty USA!

The Japanese initially did well; they met almost no opposition, and this seemed encouraging for us, for they might help us to win the war. They attacked the USA by surprise and inflicted terrific blows. How far could they go? The USA, with its mighty industrial capacity, would soon recover, replace its losses and give the Japanese a sound thrashing making them feel sorry for their treacherous attack. With the USA on the opposite side, we stopped being optimistic and started doubting the outcome of the war.

The USA was averse to dictators like Hitler and Mussolini with their vicious bullying tendency, and must have felt that these two dictators were contrary to its policy and interests. The USA strongly sympathised with Britain; after all, they spoke the same language and had for years had special relations, so the USA decided to help Britain.

According to *The Daily Telegraph* of 31 October 1940, 20 January 1941 and 12 March 1941, the USA promised Britain more military help such as artillery, tanks, machine-guns, rifles, aircraft and ammunition. This clearly shows that Britain wasn't alone: she had the mighty USA supporting her, rescuing her in those crucial years.

On the Eastern front, the Russians were on the verge of being overrun towards the end of December 1941. However, now that the USA was at war with Germany and Italy, it boosted the Russians' morale, for they certainly would receive all the help they needed from the USA and repel their invaders. This probably explains why the Germans failed to take Moscow and knock the Russians out of the war during the winter of 1941–42.

Winter would not, of course, be a German ally; it was to be expected that the Russians, assisted by the USA, would reorganise and strengthen their army, and in spite of the extremely cold weather would counter-attack the weakened and weary Germans.

The start of 1942 wasn't a hopeful time because we knew that the Germans, on account of winter, couldn't start another offensive; on the contrary, they would be very busy defending their positions. And how could they do this if their supplies did not arrive?

At this stage, owing to equipment shortages, our campaign in North Africa wasn't faring well, so how were we to win the war?

Of course, our Japanese allies were getting on with their war, so we had a glimmer of hope in their final victory. In a few days they had invaded Guam, Northern Borneo, Mindanao, Lingayen Bay and Sumatra, had occupied Hong Kong and were still conquering more and more territory. When Mussolini plunged into the war, had our army been as efficient and aggressive as the Japanese Army, it was likely that we might have overrun the Mediterranean Basin, as the Japanese overran the Western Pacific.

52

Mother worries about my father and brothers in Java

Although life in the barracks was full of drudgery, being there meant we did not have to put up with the dangers of active service at the front. Every three or six months new cadets arrived to do the course, and this kept my comrades fully occupied with stable work, weekly marches and other demanding duties. We eagerly waited for the midday news on the radio. When the reader spoke with a clear and lively voice it meant that our army was doing well, but when he read with a dismal and muffled voice, it meant that our army was on the retreat. I heard someone saying that Mussolini censored the news, so that the bad reports wouldn't sound so dramatic and disheartening. For us soldiers, bad news meant that the dreadful war would hopelessly drag on and on, and cause untold hardship to our relatives and other people, especially those exposed to air raids.

My mother was extremely worried because she was no longer receiving Father's remittance. What had happened in Java, which was being invaded by the Japanese? My mother received a subsidy of five lire a day on account of my military service, but it was a drop in the ocean. During 1941 or 1942 our government granted Mother a subsidy of twenty lire a day. She spent half of this on the rent of the flat where she, my sisters and young brother lived; thus there was hardly any money left for them to live on. How could she manage to feed her family? She still had to pay for water, gas and electricity. She was compelled to sell whatever she could to keep the wolf from the door.

My sister Mary, who was about eighteen, had almost completed her secondary education. She applied for a position at the Meteorological Office in a locality some considerable distance from Rome. She was being trained for that particular work, which was to supply information to pilots and navigators. She had to live in a hostel for young women and received a small salary for personal expenses.

While I was employed in the orderly office, one of my colleagues, Musso Armando, became a close friend. He was about five feet ten and skinny, had fair hair with a left parting, grey eyes and a smooth face with clear silky skin. He came from Turin, had Piedmontese parents and was their only son. His father was a disabled veteran of the Great War and worked in the civil service.

Armando was good-looking and of a cheerful countenance. He hated being a common soldier; he had always dreamed of being an officer, wearing a smart uniform and catching the glad eyes of the girls. For one reason or another, he did not complete his secondary education. He was now feeling sorry for himself because he was just a private, was hardly paid, had to wear a dowdy uniform that did not attract the girls and, above all, he wasn't in a position to pass on the knocks.

In spite of his deep-rooted resentment, he was resilient, ever ready to crack a joke and have a good laugh. 'Laughter is the best medicine,' he would say. His sympathy lay with our wretched comrades, who had to toil hard for a crust of bread and some pitiable bits of pasta swimming in pools of watery cabbage soup. As for those famous fortnightly pay days, it was hardly worth being lined up in the courtyard for twenty minutes to collect a paltry fifteen fire. Had one of my comrades lost an article belonging to the army, even an article that had hardly any value, then its cost would be deducted from his pay.

Armando used his coupons to buy tobacco. He made his own cigarettes and smoked more than ten a day. His parents sent him some money regularly, so he wasn't really hard up. After five o'clock, he and I often went out for a walk, later had a snack or went to the cinema. He was inclined to be lecherous, ever ready to make love to any woman. Occasionally we visited brothels; there were three of them, but most of the customers were soldiers, so the brothels seemed very much like an extension of the barracks. They smelled of soldiers' uniforms and of their pungent sweat during summer. I didn't find the prostitutes attractive; they gave me the creeps, and I didn't understand how anyone could make love to such undesirable creatures. Evidently their customers didn't go there for romance, but merely to give free rein to their animal instincts. My friend's sexual urge was more demanding than mine,

247

and if he wanted a girl of easy virtue and could afford to spend five lire, he wasn't fussy. He told me that he disliked using condoms. I strongly disagreed with him and would lecture him about the risk involved, but it was no use, he just laughed at me.

The chance of a soldier finding a girlfriend was minimal, for soldiers came and went and so weren't considered eligible bachelors. Local girls were not interested in just having a good time; they were looking for someone they could marry, and if they were seen in the company of soldiers, they would risk losing their reputation and the opportunity of getting married.

Armando and I realised that if we did not complete our secondary education, when we left the army we wouldn't be qualified to get clerical jobs. Bearing this in mind, we decided that instead of going out when we were off duty, we would remain in the office three times a week and do some study by correspondence. But this wasn't always easy, for after a long day spent in the office dealing with one tedious thing or another, we were too tired and badly needed some fresh air and a little recreation. We went to the cinema and perhaps afterwards we would join our comrades and sing some sad army melodies before going to bed.

53

*Rommel reaches El Alamein. The Germans launch
their last offensive in Russia. Going home on two
weeks' leave. My friend Musso commits suicide*

Rommel started his last North African offensive on 21 January
1942. By 29 January, the Axis forces had taken Benghazi. On 21
June they seized Tobruk and by 1 July they had advanced as far as
El Alamein, about 386 kilometres from the Libyan border and 96
kilometres from Alexandria.

Rommel could not advance any further; he did not possess
enough tanks, guns, ammunition and fuel to embark on such an
over-ambitious enterprise. He had been promised reinforcements,
which never materialised. The Axis forces had to dig themselves in
and wait for the next developments.

Prime Minister Winston Churchill was not pleased with the North
African outcome; he wanted positive action, to kick the Axis forces
out of North Africa once and for all.

Major-General Neil M. Ritchie, who had replaced Lieutenant-
General Cunningham on 26 November 1941, resigned, as did the
Commander-in-chief, General Sir Claude Auchinleck. In August
1942, Lieutenant-General Bernard Law Montgomery replaced
Ritchie as Commander of the Eighth Army, and General Sir Harold
Leofric Rupert Alexander replaced General Sir Claude Auchinleck.

On the Eastern front, after the long Russian winter, the Germans
made their last effort; during 1942 they launched their summer
offensive, aimed at compelling the Russians to surrender.

During the previous year they had tried twice and had almost
reached Moscow, but the Russians did not give up. Now that the
USA was at war with Italy, Germany, Japan and their Allies, the
Russians, egged on by Britain and the USA, were stubbornly
determined to halt and defeat the Germans.

From August to October 1941, eighty per cent of Russian war industry was transferred eastwards. The Germans had overrun 300 Russian war production factories. Some salvaged factories were relocated as follows: 450 in the Urals, 210 in Western Siberia, 200 in the Volga regions and 250 in Central Asia.

In January 1942, the strength of the Red Army amounted to 6 million soldiers. During the winter months, the Ural factories had produced nearly 5,000 tanks, 3,000 aircraft, 14,000 guns and 50,000 mortars, and certainly the Russians had endless resources of fuel and plenty of ammunition.

Russia received American help, such as aircraft, for Russian aircraft were not of the best quality. Moreover, she received 427,000 motor vehicles, which included the magnificent 2.5-ton Dodge trucks, 2,000 locomotives, 11,000 freight carriages, 500,000 tons of track and 5 million tons of food.

Thirteen million Russian soldiers, including reserves, were equipped with winter boots donated by the USA. Wartime Russia survived and fought on American aid. So too did wartime Britain. With the backing of such a formidable ally, how could Russia or Britain lose?

With Rommel's advance to El Alamein, the war still seemed promising for Italy and Germany. Our barracks' commander, optimistic about our temporary military success, allowed us to go home on two weeks' leave. My turn came at the beginning of July and, after about a day's journey by train, I arrived home. I was very sorry to find that my mother, sisters and youngest brother had wasted away and become skinny. They worried too much about my father and brothers. Cut off from my father's remittances, they were endeavouring to exist on a government subsidy which was a pittance. Of course, there was plenty of food on the black market for the well-to-do.

The Japanese had occupied Java at the beginning of March 1942. Although the Japanese were our allies, we could not get news from my father and brothers. Were they free and well? We hoped that the Japanese wouldn't molest them.

Being at home for a few days, I couldn't be of much help; all I did was try to comfort my family. However, I was afraid that they had to feed me from whatever little food they had, so it really would be better for me and for them if I went back to the barracks; by doing so they wouldn't have to tighten their belts on my account.

As my family was far away from the fronts, they had not been subjected to air raids so far; for the time being they could at least have enough rest.

Should anything drastic happen to my father and brothers, who were the breadwinners, how would my family be able to survive? Mother prayed morning, afternoon and night, went to Mass every day and pinned the photos of my father, brothers and myself to the hem of the ornate dress of the statue of the Immaculate Conception, which was in the Chapel of the Sacred Hearts. She firmly believed that our Madonna worked miracles and would protect her dear ones, especially when they were likely to be exposed to danger. When Mother didn't get a quick answer to her prayer, she would rush into the kitchen, fetch the broom, and with its stick repeatedly beat the images of the Madonna and other saints. By doing so she thought that she would shake them out of their silence, urging them to act promptly and spare her the pain of her anxiety.

My two weeks' leave passed quickly and soon I was travelling back to Bra. While on the journey, I discovered that Mother had put little images of the Madonna, Saint Antony of Padua and the Venerable Gaetano Errico into the breast pockets of my uniform. I arrived back at the barracks around 20 July and got the shock of my life when I learned that my close friend Armando had committed suicide while I was on leave.

Armando had visited one of the brothels about a month before I went on leave. Then I quickly noticed that his mood had changed; he seemed worried and gloomy, but I did not question him. He went out alone during our off-duty time and was reserved and reticent. I thought that he had found a girlfriend. I observed that his hair was thinning; his eyes shone strangely and his facial expression no longer reflected his usual joviality. The truth was that Armando had caught syphilis. He could not forgive himself and was ashamed. He certainly could not keep such a shocking, worrying illness to himself, for he badly needed medical care.

Soon he had to confide in our captain and in his parents. This knowledge was no doubt a dreadful blow to them – the knowledge that their son, their only son, had caught such a ghastly disease. If it wasn't cured properly, it could cause serious consequences such as blindness, paralysis, heart problems and so on. He could even pass it on, if he got married, to his wife and children. I knew some Italian immigrants when I was in Rouen who had caught syphilis. Initially they were subjected to intensive treatment and later needed to have preventive treatment almost every year.

Armando feared that he would never be normal again, and would be a burden to the army and to his ageing parents. In his state of mind he was desperate, utterly hopeless, and came to the conclusion that he had ruined his life, so he decided to put an end to his misery. On an early July evening, he opened the battery safe, took a certain amount of money and a revolver and went out. He had his last supper, probably a substantial dinner at one of the best restaurants of the town. He might have drunk a bottle of wine to cheer himself up, and afterwards he went to the cinema. Later, instead of returning to the barracks, he visited a brothel, and must have stayed there till the small hours of the morning.

When the lights of our quarters went out that evening prior to his suicide, he was missing. Where could he be? Towards dawn of the next day, the officer on duty at the barracks learned that a soldier from our battery had committed suicide outside one of the brothels. A sergeant-major, accompanied by a couple of my comrades, rushed to the scene. Armando had shot himself in the head and lay in a pool of blood. The body was removed and taken to the local hospital. A few days later some of our comrades attended his funeral. He was secretly admired and had almost become a hero for having had the courage to take his own life.

252

54

Cadets and soldiers embark on ten days of hard marches

The new officer cadets arrived at the end of August 1942 for a three-month intensive course. In the middle of September all the batteries – soldiers and cadets – embarked on a course of hard marches, lasting ten days or two weeks. We travelled a certain distance by train, then every second day we marched about fifteen kilometres.

One of our orderly office colleagues and I went to these marches to perform various services that the battery required, such as getting rations for the cadets and soldiers, organising guard duties at the end of each march and arranging for those who needed medical care to visit our doctor.

Often we had to march along rough, deep and secret military paths, amid trees and thick undergrowth, putting our muscular strength to the test. I was not used to long and strenuous marches, and my boots were uncomfortable, so I had to make extra efforts to keep pace with the old sweats.

I really admired the mules; they carried heavy sections of our dismantled howitzers and climbed those steep, rough paths majestically. One false step would have spelt disaster; mules and drivers would have rolled down a slope and ended in a ravine.

What a relief when we reached the top of a hill and found ourselves marching for some distance across a plain and wooded area, with scattered chestnut trees. Later, as we descended the hill, we passed through one or two villages far away from anywhere, with old or dilapidated houses. I could see there was no agriculture, so how did those tough and healthy-looking peasants live? What were they doing there? Perhaps they preferred to live in those peaceful areas 'far from the madding crowd' and were quite content to do so without being subject to those desires which often drive 'townies' or sophisticated people silly.

After every four or five kilometres we covered, we had twenty minutes' rest. Towards midday we stopped somewhere, queued up for our rations, and grumblingly wolfed them down, for they did not satisfy our appetites. We dared not attempt to ask for more – as poor 'Oliver' had done – for there was nothing left except the bare *marmitta* (pot). A number of my hungry comrades scraped it clean, and afterwards the pot looked as if it had already been washed up.

We invariably reached a town to which we had been marching in the afternoon and stayed for the night in some state school or disused building that had the necessary facilities. We ate our afternoon rations and later, those who were off duty were able to go out, wandering through the streets of the town.

Most of the soldiers, being too tired, did not go out; they squatted on the floor of our make-do quarters and nursed their weary and aching feet. Those, who still had some energy left, sought solace in singing the usual tedious army songs, which lulled them to sleep on the bare surface of the floor.

The cadets' accommodation was no better than ours. Some daring cadets washed themselves in the chilly water of a nearby stream. Our officers, superior men, were provided with accommodation in the town's *locande* (inns), where they could get a decent meal, drink a bottle of wine and sleep in a comfortable bed.

The last march ended at Limone, which is a town about four or five kilometres from the French frontier. We found this town under a blanket of snow. We lodged for a couple of days in a camp consisting of wooden huts, which had probably been erected to accommodate soldiers or prisoners of war, while our army was fighting the French in June 1940. After this march, and the early experience of winter, we were undoubtedly glad to return by train to our comparatively comfortable barracks.

55

Montgomery attacks. Rommel falls back.
Avalanche cheers us up

When the Germans launched an all-out general offensive on the
Russian front towards the end of June 1942 – their last effort to
subdue the Russians – they occupied a number of cities and
encircled Stalingrad. We learned from the radio and the newspapers
that the Germans were making progress and hoped that this time
they would really succeed in defeating the Russians.

The situation in North Africa had not changed, but we were
certain that sooner or later something crucial would happen. From
August to October 1942, British reinforcements streamed to the El
Alamein front. These consisted of 41,000 men, 800 guns, more than
1,000 tanks, including 300 formidable Shermans that weighed 36
tons each and could outshoot any of the Axis's tanks, except the
latest Panzers of which Rommel had only 30. All the mighty
American war production was assisting the British, so what chance
had Rommel of winning?

On 30 August 1942, Rommel made his last attempt to smash the
Eighth Army and break through to Alexandria and Cairo, but
opposed by the solid and indestructible Sherman tanks, and blasted
by the air force, he was doomed to failure.

Having lost forty-nine tanks, he fell back to his point of
departure. This clearly demonstrated that Rommel had run out of
steam and did not have the means to apply any further pressure.

Aware of Rommel's weakness – inferior material strength – on 4
November 1942, Montgomery launched his mighty offensive at El
Alamein, determined to smash Rommel. The Eighth Army could
count on a two to one superiority over the Axis's tanks and in all
other departments too. The Imperial troops included Australians,
New Zealanders, Indians, Gurkhas and so on. The Eighth Army

255

was well supplied, while the Axis forces were suffering from critical shortages.

Rommel's supplies had to be transported from Tripoli, Benghazi and Tobruk, several hundred kilometres from the front, and so they were vulnerable to air attack. He was in a serious predicament indeed, for he needed 30,000 tons of supplies monthly, but he could get only one fifth of that amount, so how could he replace his losses? How could he reply to the enemy's firepower when he had no ammunition? How could he use his transport and his tanks when he had no fuel?

Taking advantage of the fact that the Axis forces were locked in a crucial battle, on 7 and 8 November, Anglo-American forces landed in Morocco and Algeria, thus squeezing the already outnumbered and collapsing Axis forces between two fronts.

The Eighth Army, after a few days of hard fighting, overran El Alamein and began its great push towards the west without meeting strong resistance.

The broadcast of this news worried us, especially those soldiers from South Italy; their cities and towns were now being bombed by Liberators, American aircraft based in North Africa.

As Naples is a port, it was blitzed ceaselessly by the Americans, whose aircraft frequently dropped their bombs at random, destroying houses and killing hundreds of civilians. Raid upon raid spread terror among the population and gave no respite to those who were digging, trying to rescue those unfortunates buried under the rubble. No wonder Neapolitans cursed the Americans for killing their relatives and friends; they also cursed our countryman Christopher Columbus for having discovered America.

As my family lived near the military airport of Naples, it was too risky to stay. Without giving up their flat, they moved out and went to Campobasso, a town in the mountains about a hundred kilometres north-east of Naples, which was free from air raids.

Our morale was very low indeed in December 1942. The man who came to sell *La Stampa* in the barracks still loudly proclaimed any German successes in Russia. I did not know exactly what to make of the war, for when I paid a visit to my civilian friend signor Raballo who listened to the BBC late at night, he confided in me that the Germans fighting in Russia were meeting stiff resistance.

My comrades, aware of our military set-backs, were disheartened and deluded. Now, whenever they sang the Fascist song *Vincere* (to win) they sang it derisively. When they came to the point where they ought to have said '*Vincere! Vincere! Vincere!*' they shouted '*Strincere! Strincere! Strincere!*' (to tighten). By this they meant having to tighten their belts and continue to make sacrifices, especially if we lost the war.

At this stage we were on the run in North Africa once again, and couldn't stop the well-equipped British Army. *Il Duce* must have realised that we couldn't do much to defend our country against the overwhelming superiority of the Allied forces, so how could he save us from a complete disaster? Our equipment was scarce and inefficient, and our resources depleted. Now, after about two and a half years at war, and not having the wealthy Americans siding with and supporting us as they did during the Great War, we were utterly without hope – only God could rescue us. Our air force had ceased to exist; our fleet had been savagely mauled; we had no tanks, no ammunition and no fuel. We had nothing left but our eyes, for shedding tears as we saw our homes destroyed by air raids and had to bury our dead.

Il Duce's dangerous game was up. It had started with our conquest of Abyssinia, continued with the forming of an alliance with the neurotic, untrustworthy and belligerent Hitler, and ended with the ruin of our country. *Il Duce* was finished and he must have known it. He no longer made his bombastic, flamboyant and flattering speeches. In spite of our tragic situation, he still seemed to have some hope in the Germans' secret weapons. Would these be able to turn our defeats into victory?

My listless and down-hearted comrades carried on disconsolately with various duties through those crucial gloomy days. Low morale was predominant and seemed to weigh heavily on their shoulders; they badly needed a shot in the arm, a bit of good news to revive them and give them hope. After all, the sun was still shining in the blue Italian sky and nature was performing splendidly, regardless of the conflicts of man – and wasn't God feeling sorry even for arrogant national leaders, who were unable to live in harmony, causing a lot of bloodshed and untold suffering?

We had a reserve lieutenant in our battery whose name was

Frontino. He was in his late forties, about five feet tall, rather thin and almost bald. He must have smoked no less than forty cigarettes a day and had a poetical disposition with a touch of irony and mockery. Militarily he seemed to be hopeless; probably his former superiors, not knowing what to do with him, had to dump him somewhere. Perhaps they might have sent him to our barracks to stimulate our sense of humour? His uniform was too large for him; he looked like a scarecrow. Surprisingly, he had a piercing voice which, although irritating, seemed to make up for his small stature. Undoubtedly he enjoyed making fun of my famished, depressed comrades. Having observed how weary and sluggish they were, every time they had to muster in the courtyard and did not go downstairs fast enough, Lieutenant Frontino shouted: 'The battery must come down like an avalanche!'

Such a demand was absurd and infuriating for my lethargic comrades, so they laughed and laughed sarcastically; they wouldn't have hesitated to murder him. Being weary and downcast, they were not in the mood to go downstairs at the speed of an avalanche, perhaps not even at the pace of a snail, for they had no enthusiasm left for serving our country on its way to ruin.

My comrades, to fight back, nicknamed Lieutenant Frontino, 'Avalanche'. He had a batman waiting on him, received a salary which enabled him to eat well, to have a comfortable room outside the barracks and also a girlfriend. My poor, almost unpaid comrades couldn't get enough to eat, and now they had to brace themselves for the worst thing that could happen to our country – and to them. Although demoralised, they still had to drag on with their dreary existence. They tried to get their own back on the lieutenant, so any time they saw him approaching, they nudged one another as they mumbled: 'Look! Look! Mr Avalanche is coming.'

56

A dignified Christmas dinner at our barracks

Our officer cadets, having finished the three-month intensive course, went home a few days before Christmas 1942. They spent two or three weeks with their families, and while they were there, they wore their brand-new second-lieutenant's uniforms and swaggered through their towns to be admired by acquaintances and friends and, above all, by the girls.

Parents wallowed in pride at having sons who had become army officers. This gave them something to brag about, a sense of dignity and respect, and raised them a little higher on the social scale.

The newly created officers were assigned to various military units. Lucky were those who were not dispatched overseas, where our military situation was precarious, dramatic – officers sent there were likely to be killed in action or taken prisoner.

Christmas was near; it was the second Christmas I was spending in the army. The commandant of the barracks, aware of the low morale of the soldiers, decided that we should have a proper Christmas dinner in the officer cadets' mess. In my experience, it was the first time we were treated as decent human beings.

At this stage of the war, we all – military and civilians – were deeply concerned and did not know what fate had in store for us.

Signor Pagliocchini, an old retired army officer, was in charge of the soldiers' kitchen. He fattened a few pigs and had them slaughtered three or four days before our Christmas dinner. Parts of the pork were probably distributed to all the officers in the barracks, and what was left over ended up in the pots in which our dinner was cooked.

Signor Pagliocchini was paternal and entirely devoted to his job; he tried very hard to please the soldiers. He stewed and roasted the pork with affection, for it was our main course.

Having learned in advance about the forthcoming Christmas dinner, our mouths watered at the prospect that we were going to devour mountains of succulent pork set before us. Were we to have an Epicurean banquet?

On Christmas Day, after Mass, we sat down at long tables that had been set with glasses, cutlery, napkins, jugs of water and even bunches of flowers. We sat facing one another, with great expectation and rumbling stomachs. A number of soldiers were acting as waiters. But as the food was served on each individual plate, my comrades stared at the portions in astonishment and horror; they were far too lean for their huge appetites.

'*Mammamia!*' they exclaimed, 'is this what we get? Is this a joke? Where's our sumptuous Christmas banquet? These small portions would not even appease the hunger of ants!'

Of course, we were dining like gentlemen and the food was being served by waiters wearing white shirts and bow ties. But this meant nothing to us, because we were hungry and yearned for something more substantial. On the other hand, had the food been served on trays placed at the centres of the tables, letting each soldier help himself, the greedy ones would have taken large portions, leaving hardly anything for the others. This would undoubtedly have caused wrangles, flying plates, punch-ups and bleeding noses, and destroyed the Christmas spirit.

Thank God we were still able to celebrate Christmas, while many soldiers at the front were either being killed or maimed, or going through untold hardship. The war news was so bad that we did not know if we would still be alive by next Christmas.

We ate a three-course meal, drank two glasses of wine each and soon dinner was over. However, my veteran comrades left the table with discontent; they were not convinced that they had actually eaten; they grumbled and said that they had been cheated, for that 'dinner' had hardly whetted their appetite. Such celebration was nothing compared with the substantial Christmas dinners they usually had at home.

I spent the rest of Christmas Day with my friends – the Raballo family. They were of great comfort to me. I ate the traditional Piedmontese Christmas dinner with them, washed down with plenty of Barbera – a typical light and delicious Piedmontese wine that made me forget for a while the miseries of the war.

Signor Raballo was a bespoke tailor in his late forties. He was almost bald, with a few greying hairs at the temples. He had grey eyes, a few wrinkles here and there and a fair complexion. He had two female assistants, both in their twenties, two daughters of school age and a boy who was the baby of the family.

Signora Raballo, a very devoted wife and mother, was a few years younger than her husband. She was a countrywoman by birth and a beautiful lass when signor Raballo married her. She worked very hard doing her chores and racked her brain as she tried to make the most of her husband's hard-earned money. She helped him with tailoring when he was too busy and she made her children's clothes. She had no time to take proper care of herself, so her face showed signs of her daily toil. Her large brown eyes were expressive and she combed her black hair back in a bun. Her pale face was delicately formed, with slender eyebrows and small nose and mouth.

She was gentle and had a ready affectionate smile, especially when her husband sang old Piedmontese songs boisterously at the top of his voice, while he cut the cloth and sewed the seams. He worked from 7.00 a.m., had about one hour for his lunch break, and then carried on till 7.00 p.m. He had to toil no less than eleven hours a day to provide for his small family.

When work was a little slack, he joined a group of his neighbours, who on late summer afternoons sat under a tree in the courtyard at the back of his shop. They debated the news of the war, complained about the cost of living and the black market, mentioned some of their domestic affairs and talked of other topics.

Signor Raballo listened and listened to what the others were saying, and if one of them had strong views, or was absurd or stupid, he did not argue; but when he was in his shop the following day, he told us about the absurdities or oddities he had heard. He also mimicked, with the tone of his voice and his gestures, those characters who had spoken off the top of their heads. We couldn't help laughing at his grotesque mimicry. One of the group, signor Rota, had never liked the Fascists and was pessimistic about the outcome of the war. Because of his views, we nicknamed him *Il Disfattista* (The Defeatist).

57

Surrender in North Africa. The Allied forces land in Italy. Mussolini is deposed. Badoglio takes over

A couple of days after the Anglo-American forces landed in Morocco and Algeria, landings which took place on 7 and 8 November 1942, the Axis forces, for strategic purposes, occupied Tunisia. The British, having taken Tripoli on 23 January 1943, continued their advance, chasing the Axis beyond the Tunisian border.

On the day the British took Tripoli, Mussolini appointed General Messe as Commander of the Italian First Army in Tunisia to replace General Gariboldi. General Messe had been Commander of the Italian Expeditionary Army in Russia – an army which, confronted by the advancing Russians, had ceased to exist.

Rommel was aware that he could not win. Known as the 'Desert Fox', perhaps he was eager to give a lesson to the freshly arrived Anglo-American forces? With this aim in mind, or to attempt his last military exploit, between 14 and 23 February he launched an attack at the Kasserine Pass which is 130 miles south-west of Tunis. He smashed an American division, which suffered 200 dead, 5,000 wounded or taken prisoner. The American Second Corps alone lost 183 tanks, 200 guns, 500 Jeeps and trucks, and a huge amount of ammunition.

Later, when the Anglo-Americans counter-attacked from the Algerian border and subsequently linked up with the British advancing from the south-west of Tunisia, the weakened and collapsing Axis forces were no longer able to contain the pressure, so their end was near.

On the European Eastern front the Germans, in spite of their supreme efforts during summer and autumn 1942, failed to break through, and suffered tremendous losses. The Italian Expeditionary

Army, fighting side by side with the Germans, was destroyed. Field Marshal Friedrich von Paulus surrendered at Stalingrad on 2 February 1943. What a tragedy – the Germans were in retreat on the whole front!

We could not conceal that all our hopes were gone and that our country now lay at the mercy of the Allies' intensified air raids. Hundreds of 'Flying Fortresses' – American aircraft, like flights of migrating birds above us – were the undisputed masters of our blue sky. Migrating birds are an awesome sight as they fly freely in the boundless sky, but those Flying Fortresses, en route towards our defenceless industrial centres, horrified us; for they were bringing death and destruction.

We often had to get up during those wintry moonlit nights, take our rifles with us and seek cover in the open country, about 300 metres behind the barracks. The following morning, yawning and weary-looking for not having had enough sleep, we discharged our duties with definite fatigue, and tried to make up for our lost sleep as soon as we were able to do so.

The newspaper man crept ghost-like into our barracks and sold very few papers. He did not shout; he had nothing to shout about when there was shocking news that reminded us that we were losing the war. He came quietly in and then slipped away almost unnoticed. The headlines were in small print, subdued and mournful. Anyone who read them could not help feeling uneasy or deeply disturbed, especially if they had relatives at the front during those crucial days. My comrades were solemn, no longer in the mood for cracking jokes. At mess time they had no intention of quarrelling as they had always done, while competing for bits of food stuck at the bottom of the kitchen pot. Bad news and worries had taken their appetites away.

Although *Il Duce* wasn't making many speeches, when he did, he was hysterical. He tried to offer a glimmer of hope by mentioning the German secret weapons and the Carthaginian or Punic Wars (264–146 BC). He said that during these wars the Romans lost many battles, except the last one. They were defeated at the battles of Ticinus, Trebia, Lake Trasimene and at Cannae, but they won at Zama which meant a great victory for Rome and the end of Carthage. And now, surely, the German secret weapons would enable us to win the last battle?

'Should the Allies attempt to invade our peninsula,' shouted *Il*

Duce defiantly, 'let them come, but I solemnly swear that they will be stopped on our beaches.'

I received news from my family staying at Campobasso, a town far away from the air raids. They still had no news from my father and brothers but, regardless of their financial difficulties, they seemed somehow to be surviving.

Tunisia was doomed as early as 4 March 1943. Hitler ordered Rommel home; he could not afford to sacrifice such an excellent general in a lost campaign. Rommel could be useful either in obstructing the Russian advance or in confronting an eventual Allied landing in France. Rommel handed over the command of what was left of the Afrika Korps to General Arnim, before he flew back to Germany. Arnim's task was to salvage what he could.

By the end of April the Axis had only seventy-six tanks left in North Africa and almost no fuel. On 8 May the Luftwaffe, confronted by 4,500 American combat aircraft, abandoned its Tunisian bases.

The Allies delivered the final blow by taking Tunis and Bizerta. The Axis, unable to continue fighting, surrendered on 13 May 1943. Some quarter of a million Axis soldiers, including their Commanders, General Arnim and General Messe, were taken prisoner. The conclusion of this campaign proved to be a great humiliation for Hitler, a disaster for Mussolini and untold misery for us.

We learned of the capitulation in North Africa with shame and dismay, and feared that the worst was still to come. We had a number of soldiers in our battery who came from Sicily. They were in tears at the thought that the Allies would at any moment land in Sicily and turn the island into a battlefield.

I myself was worried, for I had no confidence in what Mussolini said in his last speech, that we would stop the Allies on our beaches. How could we, when we were not capable of stopping them from bombing us and had no defences at all? We only had a few pieces of artillery scattered along our extensive coast and hardly any tanks or ammunition; our air force had long since ceased to exist. Besides, the Italians were unwilling to continue fighting a lost war, especially in our densely populated peninsula; such a battle would have endangered the lives of millions of civilians.

A month after the British and American forces kicked us out of North Africa, the British seized our Mediterranean islands of

Pantelleria (which was supposed to be an impregnable fortress), Linosa and Lampedusa. Since we had not succeeded in repelling the attackers there, even for a couple of days, what chance had we of preventing them from landing on our mainland?

A handful of Germans were determined to oppose an Allied landing, but to what effect? Only to cause more casualties and destruction, and to prolong our agony and theirs?

We soldiers in the barracks were utterly depressed, mourning this dramatic change in our circumstances. We did not know what to say. Our officers too had nothing to say; their silence was frightening and seemed to indicate that our country was in a serious predicament. Would God rescue us and prevent our country from becoming a battlefield, which would plunge us and our people into further misery?

The newspaper man, I suspect, was very patriotic; he stopped coming to the barracks to sell *La Stampa*. Perhaps he was fed up with bringing us bad news. Often during our midday break I stood by one of our windows looking into the barracks courtyard and stared at the Italian flag happily fluttering in the breeze. I smiled derisively and muttered, 'How can it do that? It ought to be ashamed; it ought to be flying at half-mast to mourn the misfortune of our poor country.'

We did not have to wait very long, for what we most feared actually happened. On 9 July 1943, the Anglo-American forces landed in Sicily, without meeting any resistance to speak of. What would the King say? What would *Il Duce* do? In view of this new situation, Mussolini asked to consult Hitler, so on 19 July the two dictators met in a villa at Feltre in the Dolomites. This was another humiliating meeting for Mussolini, during which he must have poured out his sad heart and asked Hitler for help against the invading Allies. But how could Hitler do that while the German Army was being defeated in Russia and under pressure from an imminent Anglo-American attack from the west? Hitler still had a fanciful hope of victory. He did not show Mussolini any concern about defeat; on the contrary, he insisted on a vigorous campaign by both Italy and Germany until victory was won.

While the meeting was on, Mussolini received a message that at that very moment the enemy was carrying out a heavy air attack on Rome. The Pope, our King and Mussolini himself were seriously shaken.

On 22 July 1943, Count Dino Grandi, a minister of state and a member of the Grand Council, had an interview with Mussolini at Palazzo Venezia (Venice Palace), during which he suggested that Mussolini should resign.

'I would resign,' said Mussolini, 'if we were losing the war. But the fact is that we are not losing the war; we are going to win it, because the Germans, within a few days, will launch a weapon that will reverse the situation. The rest we'll talk about in two days' time at the Fascist Grand Council.'

The Fascist Grand Council meeting was fixed for 24 July 1943, to deal with the grave situation and, above all, to cast a vote of confidence. *Il Duce* spoke for two hours, defending himself against allegations of misgovernment, abuse of power and misconduct of the war. He tried with his oratory to win the support of his ministers for his leadership and the continuation of the war; he firmly believed that the Germans, with their secret weapons, would win.

Later, one by one, all the twenty-eight members of the Grand Council had their say. They contested the argument fiercely, shouted and wrangled till well after midnight. The vote of confidence went as follows: out of twenty-eight members of the Council, nineteen, including Grandi, Federzoni, Bottai, Bastianini, Count Ciano (who was Mussolini's son-in-law), De Bono and De Vecchi, voted for Count Grandi's resolution that Mussolini should resign. Nine members were against it.

Mussolini left the meeting hall foaming with rage, calling those who had voted against him traitors, and was itching for revenge. Weary and feeling unwell, he arrived at home in the small hours of the morning. His dear homely wife Rachele, to whom he was unfaithful, had not gone to bed; she had waited for him. She sensed that some of the members of the Grand Council were not to be trusted; they were treacherous. She had suggested to him, before he went to the meeting, that he should have them arrested.

Mussolini's home was in Villa Torlonia. Rachele ran to meet him and soon perceived that he was overwrought. Having tried to soothe and console him, she asked: 'Have you had the conspirators arrested?'

'Not yet, but I surely will,' he replied.

In the morning, 25 July 1943, he went to his office as usual and

266

carried on with his work as if nothing had happened. He met various people, including the Japanese Ambassador.

On that same day the newspaper announced the fall of Palermo, and it was arranged that he would see the King in the afternoon. He had a late lunch at home, then put on his civilian clothes, which protocol specified for such an audience. Rachele felt uneasy.

'Don't go,' she said. 'I can smell a rat! The King is up to no good!'

Had he not consulted the King, what was the alternative? To flee to Germany?

He had had meetings with the King twice a week for almost twenty years, since he had become head of the Italian government, and the King had always agreed with him. Unhesitatingly Mussolini seized his briefcase, bulging with documents that crucial afternoon, and asked his chauffeur to drive him to Palazzo del Quirinale (Quirinale Palace), which, since 1870, had been the King's residence.

However, when the car stopped outside the main entrance of the palace, the chauffeur was surprised to notice the presence of many *carabinieri* in the grounds and the King coming down the few steps of the palace dressed in the uniform of Marshal of Italy. He had never seen the King greet *Il Duce* in such a guise before. But Mussolini seemed quite unconcerned and, after the greetings, he and the King walked into a cool parlour in the palace. Mussolini presented to the King the report of the Fascist Grand Council meeting held the previous night, and was trying to minimise the decision of the majority who had demanded his resignation.

The King said tartly: 'Dear *Duce*! Italy is in ruins, the army is demoralised; the soldiers have no desire to fight. You are, at this moment, the most hated man in this country, so the Fascist Grand Council's decision stands. I am your only remaining friend. Have no fear for your safety; I will make sure that you are protected. Marshal Badoglio will succeed you.'

The yellow and shrunken-looking Mussolini listened dumbfounded, and soon the audience, which had lasted only a few minutes, was over. Mussolini, accompanied by his secretary, gloomily walked down the steps towards his car. Half-way down, a captain of the *carabinieri* approached him, saluted and then said, 'Excellency! His Majesty has put me in charge of your protection.'

Mussolini objected, but the captain insisted that he must obey.

267

The captain escorted him to an ambulance a few metres away and stood by while Mussolini got in. The ambulance took him to an unknown destination.

58

The fall of Mussolini

25 July 1943 was a sultry Sunday. My comrades who were off duty
went out for a walk or to the cinema, or both. By ten o'clock we
were in our camp beds and soon the bugler sounded *il silenzio*. In
spite of having all the windows wide open, the heat was appalling;
we yearned for a little nocturnal breeze. I tossed and turned, but
couldn't get a wink of sleep.

My Sicilian comrades, having learned from the newspaper and
the radio that the Allied forces had taken Palermo, were worried
and feeling very low; their hearts were with their families back in
Sicily. Apparently there had not been any heavy fighting, but
communications had been cut off, so they could no longer get news
from home. Other comrades, indifferent to the serious situation and
the close weather, were soon sound asleep, dreaming perhaps of
Epicurean banquets, devouring succulent chicken legs, drinking jars
of wine and wiping their mouths with the backs of their hands.

About midnight our quarters were quiet; there were a few
sporadic snores and someone mumbled gibberish in his slumber.
Suddenly the sound of the bugle broke the silence. Was it the alarm
of an air raid or the reveille? The bugler, determined to wake us,
bugled again and again. I looked at my watch; it was about one
o'clock. Our quarters were soon alive with shouts, curses and
protests. My comrades were irritated by having been awakened at
that hour. One of our sergeant-majors strode noisily up and down
the corridor of our quarters, yelling with an irritating grating voice:
'Wake up! Wake up! Get dressed quickly and hurry downstairs.'

The batteries and the officer cadets from other quarters followed
suit. Soon the barracks became a hive of feverish activity and in a
few minutes we mustered in the courtyard.

Our captain stated briefly: 'A few hours ago, Mussolini resigned and has been detained. Marshal Badoglio has replaced him. We trust him, he knows what he is doing. Our alliance with Germany and the war continue. We are waiting for further orders from general headquarters. Go back to bed now.'

The sensational news about the fall of Mussolini was extremely disturbing and made me wonder. What would happen to us and to our country now? I could not go to sleep, but I was glad that our dictator had been booted out, and that the vain, pompous, worthless and hated Fascist regime had come to an abrupt end. This should have happened long before Mussolini's dictatorial and dangerous policy had led our country to ruin.

He was a dreamer. He prevented us from using our intelligence, human rights and liberty – and for what purpose? No doubt he flattered himself that he was the reincarnation of Caesar and had set his heart on re-establishing the Roman Empire. The fault lay also with the King who seemed to be quite complacent about Mussolini's policies. He let sleeping dogs lie. Did he not know about the appalling conditions of his people; people who, as a result of Mussolini's government, had been reduced to slavery? Our King did not care, and surely lacked insight, or he wouldn't have given Mussolini a free hand in governing Italy. Of course, he intervened when it was too late, when our country had been devastated. Perhaps, when he acted, he did it not so much as a result of our misery and suffering, but above all in an endeavour to save his crown.

The fall of Mussolini was hailed with tumultuous joy. People rushed out into the streets and at once set out to tear down Mussolini's statues and Fascist emblems. Fascist buildings and offices were ransacked. Documents, books, pictures, flags and so on were piled up in the streets and set on fire, while the crowds jubilantly stood by. All Fascist supporters went into hiding for fear of being lynched.

The police did not interfere – they let people who had been suppressed for over twenty years have a go, give vent to their hatred and savour the taste of freedom.

A state of emergency was declared all over Italy. We soldiers had to be at the disposal of general headquarters, so all leave was cancelled. We were sent to guard public buildings and railway stations, and had to patrol the streets during the curfew from 11.00 p.m. till 5.00 a.m.

We let the anti-Fascist demonstrations go on, provided that they did not go too far and, in collaboration with the *carabinieri*, we had to keep public order. We had to break up any groups of people we thought suspicious, or who made a nuisance of themselves.

We were carrying out our duties scrupulously; we hardly had any respite, but accepted the situation with resignation, hoping that it would not go on for ever.

During the state of emergency, I was on guard duty at the local railway station. My comrades and I had to inspect the arrival and departure of trains and their passengers, for we had to be ready just in case any Fascist supporters attempted to seize power. At peak times, we did not allow people to gather on the small square outside the station; we had to disperse them, keeping the square free.

While on duty we held our rifles in the firing position, with bayonets fixed; the chambers of our rifles contained live bullets, but nobody was going to shoot without orders. However, the people we dispersed, seeing our rifles pointing at them, were rather horrified.

I remember being in a sombre mood one night, while I was on guard duty at a local railway crossing, for I disliked being on guard, especially at night. A patrol of twenty or thirty men (they were officer cadets from our battery) approached the crossing. As they came closer I shouted angrily, '*Chi va la?*' (Who goes there?) with my rifle pointing at them. The patrol came to a halt. The men did not stir; they were afraid that I was going to shoot. The lieutenant in charge, one of my battery, recognised my voice and said the password. I opened the gate and let them through. The following morning, the lieutenant told our captain that I had scared him to death.

The arrest of Mussolini was kept secret. For safety reasons, they moved him from place to place. A number of Fascist leaders, to save their skin, sought asylum at the German Embassy. One of Mussolini's ardent supporters, Ettore Muti, tried to run away from his house, which was being guarded by the *carabinieri*. They opened fire and shot him. He became another hero who had died for the Fascist cause.

59

Italian Armistice, 8 September 1943.
The Germans occupy Italy. Our army disbands.
The Germans rescue Mussolini

Our officer cadets finished their course at the beginning of August and went home.

The Germans tried to defend Sicily, but were not able to resist the overwhelming pressure of the Allied forces, so by 17 August 1943, Sicily was firmly in the Allies' hands. According to the BBC, the Sicilians welcomed the Allies jubilantly, as they had done with Mussolini a couple of years before the war. Mussolini had nothing to offer them except toil and misery. The Sicilians hoped that the wealthy Americans would give them food, the chance to earn a few dollars and the possibility of emigrating to the USA.

With the fall of Sicily, it was obvious that the Germans would not be able to prevent the invasion of our peninsula. On 3 September 1943, the Allied forces landed in Calabria and were advancing so fast that we thought that they would soon conquer our entire country.

Badoglio's government decided that enough was enough, so they arranged that an Italian emissary should approach the Allies with the aim of concluding a secret armistice. The talks began on 17 August 1943, on a Portuguese island in the Azores.

With the rapid advance of the Allied forces, what were we going to do to fight them? We were certainly worried about the latest developments and so were the civilians.

As my sister Mary's saint's day occurs in September, I was thinking of her and the rest of my family, and the little celebrations that my family used to have on a saint's day. On such occasions before the war, we used to start the day by drinking chocolate diluted in coffee, and after the main meal, which we ate at midday, we had *sfogliatelle* (puffs) and a tot of vermouth. When there was a chance of a second helping, I quickly gobbled up my *sfogliatella* and waited greedily, hoping to get another. I remember that one day, as I bolted my portion too fast, it stuck in my throat. Mother promptly gave me a smack on my back, which enabled me to eject the stuff, else I would have choked to death.

That late evening of the 8th, as I lay in bed, I was assailed by a mixture of sweet memories and the sad realisation of the present situation in Italy. I could hear my heart moaning: *O mia patria, si bella e perduta* (Oh my fatherland, so beautiful and lost), which is a quotation from *Nabucco* (an opera by Giuseppe Verdi) and then I prayed: 'Lord! Don't desert us during these crucial hours. Save our country from further destruction. Save our people, our families. Save especially those in the south of our country, who have already suffered too much, and where war is raging now. Restore peace and stability in our country and throughout the world.'

Having said this prayer, I felt peace within myself, a peace beyond comprehension and was going to sleep. I was already dozing when I heard the bugle. Was it a dream? Then I heard it again and again. I looked at my luminous watch and it was about half past eleven. 'What's up now, an air raid?' I muttered.

Soon our quarters were astir. My comrades, still half-asleep and full of irritation, shouted, grumbled and swore.

'Wake up! Wake up!' cried our sergeant-majors. 'Hurry downstairs.'

This scene was identical to the one we had experienced a few weeks earlier, when we were told of the fall of Mussolini.

Our captain said with an emotional voice: 'The Italian government has signed an armistice with the Allies. This is no time for rejoicing; this is not the end of the war. We have a German Army in Italy, which is determined to fight the Allies at any cost, and this will not make our lives easier. Go back to your quarters now.'

We went back, but were greatly excited at the sensational news. There was undoubtedly a feeling of relief on account of the armistice, but also of anxiety and perplexity. Did this mean that we were going to be discharged from the army and could go home? My mind was in a turmoil, so I was awake for the rest of the night.

At dawn the following day, 9 September, we drank our awful ersatz coffee and afterwards were told to get our rifles and knapsacks ready for a long march. We hadn't the faintest idea where we were going. We were given emergency rations, consisting of tinned beef and unsalted biscuits; rations on which soldiers have to rely when fresh bread and cooked food cannot be obtained. Were we preparing for war? It seemed so.

Our marching column consisted of five batteries; two of them were horse-drawn batteries, which we called *artiglieria da campagna* (field artillery). In all, we were about 600 strong, including the officers. We had about 200 mules carrying our dismantled howitzers, ammunition, equipment and other indispensable material. The soldiers of the horse-drawn batteries were on horseback.

When we started marching, the streets were deserted, except for a few workers who had to catch early trains. As the long column – mules, horses and soldiers – moved along, my comrades and I were pensive; absorbed in troubled thoughts. Where were we going? To fight? To fight against whom? Our only possible enemies could be the Germans who would turn against us for having signed the armistice with the Allies.

The animals hammered the paved surface of the roads with their hooves, awakening the inhabitants. Half-asleep, they rushed to their windows and doors to see what was happening.

'Look! Look!' I heard someone say, 'Our soldiers. Where are they going?' They stared at us inquisitively, wondering what we were up to.

After a three-hour march, we reached a hilly locality. The sun was already high in the sky and we were very hot, hungry and thirsty. We unloaded our mules, assembled the howitzers and placed them in position. Did we have enough ammunition?

From our position, we could see the main road, which I reckoned was over two kilometres away as the crow flies, and presumably our target. It appeared to me that we were supposed to defend Bra, the town in which our barracks were located.

There was a lovely landscape around us under a cloudless sky. Moreover, there were verdant slopes and hills with a few scattered farms; tall trees, fields, meadows, orchards, and vineyards loaded with bunches of grapes ready for the vintage. A fragrant breeze skimmed over the grass and shook the leaves. Chirping and twittering birds enhanced the loveliness of the place. That spot, full of soothing sounds, delight and harmony, was a piece of heaven on earth. The cursed war had already destroyed beautiful landscapes in Southern Italy and in other countries. Was this the will of God?

Was God pleased for having made men who by misusing their free will were obliterating the artistry of His creation?

How long were we to stay in that firing position? It was hard to say. Having secured our mules to improvised rope-railings fixed to trees, we fed them. They also relished the mouthfuls of fresh grass they tore here and there. This surely was a treat for them, because they seldom enjoyed such luxury. Later we pitched our tents, allotting three soldiers to each one. Being in the open and breathing that fragrant air made us hungrier than ever, but the prospect of having to eat our dull emergency rations was not very inviting.

Since beggars cannot be choosers, we extracted the tinned beef and unsalted biscuit from our knapsacks and sat on the luxuriant grass. We opened the tins with our bayonets. I had to share my tin of beef with a comrade. The biscuits, which we called *gallette*, were so hard to break that we thought that they were part of our booty from the Great War. We crushed them with the butts of our rifles into small chewable fragments and stoically ate them. They were so dry that we had to wash them down with plenty of water. My word, what a dull meal! Still, hunger is the best sauce.

I tried to share my bits of biscuit with a few inquisitive birds, but they would not touch them; they seemed to look at me with contempt. I could detect a glint of superciliousness in their eyes; they would not stoop so low as to accept my beggarly offering. They were inhabitants of a luxurious environment which enabled them to pick and choose the best morsels.

It was about midday. We were talking about the armistice, but soon we learned that on that very day, 9 September, our King, his family, Marshal Badoglio and probably other members of his government had abandoned Rome. They had sailed from the ports of Pescara and Ortona a mare, and had landed at Brindisi, which was in Allied hands.

Marshal Badoglio had established his government there and was sending us radio messages: 'Don't cooperate with Germans and Fascists! Disband! Go into hiding and wait for the liberation!'

On the same day that we received the above messages the Allied forces landed at Salerno, which is south of Naples.

As a result of the flight of the King and Marshal Badoglio from Rome, a new situation was created, which worried us immensely. Would the military authorities give heed to Marshal Badoglio's messages and let us go? Since our leaders – the King and Marshal

275

Badoglio – had fled and left us in the lurch, what was the point of having our guns in position? What would the army do? Perhaps the only way out was to disband.

In the afternoon we were ordered to pack up and return to barracks. We broke camp, dismantled the howitzers, loaded the mules and marched back to barracks. We arrived there between 5.00 p.m. and 6.00 p.m., unloaded our mules, drove them to the water trough and afterwards to the stables. Having done this, we marched to the Trevisan Barracks and queued up for our afternoon rations, which consisted of a watery minestrone. It was just what we needed to wash down the pieces of biscuit we had eaten towards midday, which had stuck in our throats.

We were not allowed to leave the barracks on account of the awkward and chaotic situation; besides, most of us were too tired. That day, 9 September, had been very trying indeed; we had been on our feet since dawn, had marched no less than twenty kilometres to and from the barracks, and the quality of our rations had not been sufficient to boost our morale. Confined to quarters, we were getting perturbed and restless; we were learning from the batmen of our officers, who lived outside the barracks, that soldiers attached to several regiments and other barracks had already disbanded, for they feared being captured by the Germans.

Backed by tanks, the Germans were marching unopposed and brazenly grabbing control of barracks, military stores and other similar establishments. What were we going to do? And if we disbanded where would we go? Those with families in North Italy could go home. But what about those from South Italy who had to travel long distances? Could they safely go home while the war was raging there?

My comrades and I had spent at least two and a half years in the army. We certainly had not become rich on our miserly army pay of thirty lire a month, which could hardly buy anything; so how were we going to manage if while we were disbanded we had no money? Where could we go? I did not have to worry too much as I had friends who, in an emergency, would help me for a few days.

Although uneasy thoughts haunted us, we could not do much on the spur of the moment. On the other hand, there was nobody who could give us advice, for most of our officers were in the same difficulties as we were, especially if they had to support their families. It seemed to me that everybody had to rely on himself and use his own initiative and imagination. There was, of course, a decision to be made, but it had to come from the commandant of our barracks and his advisers; they should know how to safeguard our interests. Meanwhile we had to be patient. To run away might be too risky. We put aside such thoughts and waited for the following day, hoping that our commandant would make up his mind on what to do with us.

We were in bed by 9.30 p.m. as usual on that evening of 9 September, and the bugler sounded *il silenzio*, but I was restless; my mind was too active, so I could not fall asleep. I must have dozed for a few minutes. Then I heard something stirring in the courtyard. The noise gradually grew louder and louder. I looked at my watch; it was about midnight.

'What's going on?' I said to my comrade sleeping next to me, who had apparently had hardly any sleep. Then I rushed to the window and saw soldiers running away – it looked very much like a stampede. I heard hysterical and frightening shouts, doors banging, heavy footsteps in the corridor and hobnailed boots scratching the floor as my comrades got dressed in a jiffy, took a few belongings with them and ran. They tumbled downstairs in panic, as if our quarters had caught fire.

A soldier in the courtyard shouted alarmingly: '*Ugo! Ugo! Ugo!* (Hugh! Hugh! Hugh!) Hurry up! The sentries have gone! Quick! Be quick! Hurry up! *I Tedeschi! I Tedeschi stanno venendo!* (The Germans! The Germans are coming!) *Si salvi chi puo!* (Every man for himself!)'

As soon as I heard 'the Germans are coming', I was trembling – shaking like a leaf. I was so frightened that I wasn't fully aware of what I was doing, and my heart was racing. I got dressed at once in the dark, for the dim light of our quarters had not been switched on. I couldn't find my shoes or belt and everything seemed to be in the way. When I found my shoes, one of the laces snapped. This threw me into a fury; I had to get by without it. Then hurriedly, I grabbed my wooden suitcase containing my personal belongings, shouldered it and ran for my life through the unguarded back gate of the barracks. Cautiously I looked left and right, but no Germans were in sight, then I ran at top speed, keeping away from the main road. I stopped at every corner and had a good peep around before making further progress. Luckily the streets of the town were quiet, but I could detect the occasional footsteps of fleeing soldiers who scattered in various directions.

In less than ten minutes, I reached my friends' place and knocked at the entrance of the building. Someone opened the door, let me in and then called my friend signor Raballo. He was surprised and perplexed to see me at that late hour. Then he led me upstairs to the second floor and let me into his apartment. I briefly told signor and signora Raballo what had happened. Later they got a bed ready for me and went back to resume their slumbers.

I was far too excited to sleep, assailed as I was by many fearful thoughts. I listened and listened, but could hear neither any shooting, nor any sound of German tanks patrolling the streets. At 7.00 a.m. my friends gave me a large cup of white ersatz coffee and a couple of bread rolls, which was the usual continental breakfast. We put our heads together and decided that I should stay inside, in hiding, and wait for developments.

The Germans had not arrived. Had the previous night's stampede and pandemonium been a false alarm? By eleven o'clock there were notices posted all over the town, bearing the signature of the commandant of our barracks.

The notices stated: 'All the people who looted the military stores must return the goods at once. They will neither be questioned nor prosecuted. The soldiers who escaped must come back immediately or they will be regarded as deserters and executed.'

What should I do? I was frightened and utterly confused. The commandant had let us escape, but now he was ordering us to return to the barracks. After a moment of hesitation I decided that it would be safer for me to do so, then I slipped into my uniform and walked towards the barracks. As soon as I entered I was shocked. The courtyard was in an appalling mess; it looked as if hordes of Vandals and Huns had overrun the place. I could imagine a battlefield strewn with corpses and ruins. There were mattresses, sheets, blankets, items of underwear, trousers, jackets, coats, boots, socks, rifles, bayonets and other items heaped at the centre of the courtyard and scattered all over it.

A few pensive and dejected officers were around and stared gloomily at the ruins. There was a feeling of listlessness and apathy in the air, and the officers appeared to be reluctant to give orders. Nobody seemed to care! Did we still have a command? All was so weird and depressing! That sore and pitiful scene could have

278

moved our commandant and his officers to tears. Yet the flag on its mast was fluttering happily, as if nothing had happened. I stared at it and then laughed derisively – that flag had become a symbol of mockery.

Months earlier, the barracks had been a proud academy. Our officer cadets had paraded before Prince Umberto at the completion of their course and had sung patriotic anthems, praising King and country. On joining the army, we soldiers had sworn to be faithful to the King and to die for him. Now that our country was in serious trouble, the King, with his family and our new government, had fled and left us in the lurch.

On 10 September, the day after our King and government had fled, the Germans had occupied Rome and were seizing the rest of Italy – from Rome to the north of the country – without firing a shot.

I had been in the barracks about two hours and was feeling sorry for having returned. More than sixty per cent of my comrades were still at large.

Our captain ordered us to go to our quarters and to stay put. I don't remember whether the rations had been distributed; probably they gave us some stale bread and a little tinned beef, which was the emergency rations.

The kitchen had ceased to function. Utensils had been plundered and everything was upside down. I would not have been surprised if our howitzers had been stolen; they could have been melted down and made into pots and pans to be sold on the black market.

We were in our quarters exchanging views. We were well aware that soldiers elsewhere had disbanded and that German tanks were on the way, and could arrive at our barracks at any moment. If we did not run away, we would have to cooperate with the Germans, or they would regard us as enemies and send us to Germany as prisoners of war.

It was about two o'clock and we were either resting on our camp beds or talking. Suddenly there was a commotion followed by footsteps, shouts and banging.

'*I Tedeschi! I Tedeschi!* (The Germans! The Germans!) have reached the outskirts of Bra.'

The Germans were now about four kilometres from us, so the same scene of excitement and uproar as during the previous night was being repeated. Terror-stricken, I hastily shouldered my

279

suitcase once again and ran through the back gate. I very much feared that if I met a German patrol, they wouldn't hesitate to shoot me. Luckily I arrived at signor Raballo's house, but I was badly shaken.

Reviewing the events of the previous two days, it transpired that our commandant, having to face the actual situation, did not want to commit himself. Marshal Badoglio had ordered us to disband. How could our commandant and those officers who lived locally disband? They had their families, and where would they go? They could not leave their families behind and go into hiding. Had they done so, they feared that the Germans might have harassed their families.

Our commandant had to let us go, but he did not want the responsibility of ordering us to do so; he concocted a plot and an incident that would enable us to disband. Being aware that the Germans would not arrive during the night of 9–10 September, he contrived to withdraw the sentries from the barracks and to create a false alarm, warning us that the Germans were arriving. Such a warning would give us the chance to escape.

Those who ransacked our military stores during the night were civilians. I think they had been informed beforehand of what would happen, for they were on the spot with their trucks, ready to plunder our stores.

The following morning, 10 September, as the Germans still hadn't arrived, the commandant issued posters threatening those who had plundered the stores and the fugitive soldiers.

Looters were not easily intimidated by the commandant's threat; they cleverly disregarded him and did not return the plundered goods; they sold them on the black market and made a lot of money.

As for the commandant's threat, it was just a cover-up to demonstrate to the approaching Germans that he was unable to prevent desertion and pillaging.

All the soldiers disbanded, except a very few, who had perhaps nowhere to go and remained behind. They must have lacked the self-confidence to face the new situation and the challenge of fending for themselves.

The Germans took control of our barracks on the afternoon of 10 September. The soldiers who had stayed put had to reckon with their new masters.

Although the Germans were being defeated in Russia, they were stubbornly fighting on for their Führer, and were not sympathetic with those who would not cooperate with them.

A number of our barracks officers, including our captain, who were living in the town and had families, did not run away. But since they had no intention of cooperating with the Germans, they had to say goodbye to their relatives, and soon they were despatched to Germany as prisoners of war.

I couldn't go home. It was too risky to travel while the Germans were everywhere and ready to capture disbanded soldiers. Signor Raballo, for the time being, gave me hospitality and, since I had no civilian clothes and not enough money to buy them, he kindly lent me one of his tweed suits; a dark brown one, which was almost new, but a little large for my slim figure.

On 12 September 1943, we learned that a group of brave German soldiers, led by Colonel Otto Skorzeny, rescued Mussolini. He was being detained at the Albergo Rifugio (Refuge Hotel) on the highest mountain of Abruzzo called Gran Sasso D'Italia.

Mussolini had been detained since 25 July, when he had been forced to resign. From then on, for security reasons and to prevent him being rescued by the Germans or the Fascists, his place of detention had been kept secret and had changed frequently.

As long as the King and Marshal Badoglio were in Rome, only a very few trustworthy people knew where Mussolini was. However, when the King and Marshal Badoglio fled from Rome to Brindisi and were safely under the Allies' protection, they stopped worrying about Mussolini. They could not take him away with them to that part of Italy occupied by the Allies.

The USA, broadcasting on *The Voice of America*, had occasionally stated that if American soldiers had captured Mussolini, they would have placed him in a cage and sent him to America for public display.

Marshal Badoglio, the new head of the Italian government, could not prosecute Mussolini and let the King off scot-free, for he was responsible for having given Mussolini a free hand while he governed the country.

Now that the King and Marshal Badoglio had joined the Allies, if the Germans wanted Mussolini they were more than welcome to him. By this time, the Germans had some notion of where he was, so they organised a rescue party.

Those few *carabinieri* who watched Mussolini were there, more than anything else, to protect him from being lynched by those who hated him. When the German rescuers arrived, the *carabinieri* cooperated with them. They even stood side by side with the German soldiers as Mussolini walked towards the aircraft. They gave him the Fascist salute and shouted enthusiastically: '*Duce! Duce! Duce!*'

The Germans managed to fly him to Vienna. Hitler could at least use him to fight our partisans, which would eventually shed more Italian blood.

Having taken control of our barracks and the town, the Germans, tipped off by Fascist informers, started harassing and bullying people. They searched many houses, looking for disbanded soldiers, to prevent them from joining the partisans.

Because of the presence of Germans in the town, I did not feel safe. Besides, had the Germans known that my host was hiding me – a disbanded soldier – they could have harmed him. Soon I made up my mind and decided to move to a small rural area several kilometres away.

PART FIVE

COUNTRY LIFE

60

I am a disbanded soldier and make my way
to Bardo

At dawn on the fourth day after my escape from the barracks, 14 September 1943, I thanked signor and signora Raballo for their hospitality and then left. I sadly departed from Bra, the town where I had spent about two years and eight months doing my military service. I was carrying a small parcel containing a few personal belongings and some sandwiches. When I had found a place to stay, my friends would send me the rest of my belongings.

I started my journey on foot and walked cautiously through the back streets of Bra. I had to be on the alert, listening for the approach of vehicles. Had I bumped into a German patrol, I would have ended up in a prisoner-of-war camp.

It took me more than half an hour to reach the outskirts of the town. There I felt safer, for a number of back streets petered out into country paths and lanes. I preferred tramping along paths far away from the main road, where I could hear mooing, barking, cackling, crowing, chirping, twittering, the rustling of leaves and other natural sounds. When I was in the open country, the fragrance of the foliage, soil and freshly-mown grass made me drunk with delight; I almost forgot my fears and difficulties.

I was on my way to Bardo, a village near Rena, where my captain's batman Costa Biagio lived. Biagio (Blaise) was a farmer; he would surely put me up for a few days. His hospitality, I reckoned, would not need to last any longer, for I thought that the Allied forces, within a couple of weeks, would land on the Ligurian coast and expel the Germans from North Italy. Should this happen, I would be able to go home.

While at Biagio's farm, although I knew nothing about farming, I could try hard to make myself useful and earn my keep. All the

285

disbanded soldiers, who couldn't go home on account of the war, had somehow to find a means of survival.

As I walked to Bardo, the countryside enchanted me. I slowed down my pace to relax and absorb those beautiful surroundings. The blue sky, the sunshine, the irrigation canal with croaking frogs basking in the sun, trees, fields, meadows and orchards attracted me immensely. I felt my youth coursing through me and the overwhelming desire to live. There was so much freedom around me in that world of nature, yet deep in my heart I knew that I wasn't quite free. So far the dictates of human society had deprived me of freedom and made my life a misery. Whether I liked it or not, I had to conform to our vicious man-made world if I wanted to exist.

But now the splendour of the countryside in front of me was a relief to my aching heart, which longed for peace, harmony and brotherly love. I abhorred being hunted down, just because I was unwilling to support the continuation of a war that was getting us nowhere; it was aggravating the sufferings of our people and causing more destruction than it had already done.

I had covered about nine or ten kilometres and my stomach was rumbling, so I sat down on a stump and dug into the omelette sandwiches which my dear friend signora Raballo had provided for me. I was so famished, I could have gobbled the sandwiches down in one mouthful, but then it occurred to me that if I ate slowly I would relish every morsel and get the impression that I was eating a large meal; it was just a means of cheating my craving for food. While I was eating, a few inquisitive birds landed near me and seemed to be begging for a share of my paltry sandwiches.

I said tartly: 'Sorry mates, you must be joking! You have plenty of food over there in the fields, which are ready for harvest. And what about the juicy worms in that freshly-mown meadow? Buzz off, birdies! I can spare nothing for you.'

Having soothed the pangs of my stomach, I moved on in a south-westerly direction and stayed close to a narrow canal on my right, where the cultivated land began to slope gently towards higher ground. The rough and rutted path I was treading was hardly wide enough for two carts. To the right of the path, every now and then, I noticed dilapidated farms with scary barking dogs. There were quite a lot of vineyards laden with small black grapes ready for the *vendemmia* (grape harvest). On my left, there were empty sun-drenched fields, the golden corn ready to be gathered and meadows being mown.

Further afield, still on the left, lay the main road which I had to stay clear of for security reasons. While plodding along I noticed a cart, pulled by two bullocks, proceeding at a snail's pace, and advancing towards me. It was loaded with tree trunks, bales of hay and two grunting pigs. The carter himself, lulled by his jerking vehicle, was somnolent on that bright warm summer afternoon.

I approached him, feeling sorry about disturbing his slumber, and said: 'Please, is this the way to Bardo?'

He looked at me with sleepy eyes, surprised, confused and suspicious. 'Eh! Eh!' he mumbled, still half asleep.

I said again: 'Please, is this the way to Bardo?'

After a minute or two he appeared to have understood my request. 'Yes, oh yes, this is the way to Bardo, but you're going the long way round to get there. Keep walking close to the canal. Bardo I reckon is about six or seven kilometres from here.'

'Is it quiet there? Have you seen any Germans around?'

'No, I haven't seen any, but I've seen a few disbanded soldiers begging for food.'

'I'm disbanded too!'

'My God! I thought you were a German!'

I laughed, thanked him for showing me the way and then said, '*Arrivederci*.' (Goodbye).

Seldom did I meet people on my way to Bardo, but when I did, they stared at me with apprehension, because I, with my fair complexion, looked like a German. When I spoke I assured them that I wasn't, and I was there because I wanted to keep away from the Germans.

61

I meet the Boltis

Being very thirsty, I knocked at a rickety wooden gate that seemed to be struggling to stay on its hinges. Half a dozen nasty dogs, seething with rage, started barking, and a woman in her fifties, alarmed, peeped through a small window.

'I am thirsty, signora. May I have a glass of water?'

She gazed at me meditatively a few seconds, then smiled and said: 'Oh yes, yes, wait a moment, I am coming down!'

Later I heard her footsteps. She shouted at her angry dogs as she walked to the gate.

'Are you a soldier?'

'Yes, I am, I ran away from my barracks a few days ago!'

'*Mammamia! Che paura!* (Dear me! What a fright!) I thought you were a *Tedesco* (German).'

'About an hour ago, I met a man who told me the same thing. I am on the run because of the Germans. I have been walking since six o'clock this morning and I am going to Bardo.'

The woman was well over five feet tall and stocky. She was wearing a kind of headscarf fastened at the back of her head. I suspected she had lost her hair. She had a wrinkled forehead, grey eyes and smiled pleasantly in a motherly way. She wore a black dress, as did most of the farmers' wives in that part of the country. She opened the gate, which screeched, giving me goose-pimples.

'Come in! Do come in!' she said cordially. 'You must be very tired. Follow me. Let's go upstairs. Come, come this way, you need a rest and some refreshment!'

I entered the kitchen, which was about six metres by five. There was a long bench and a table alongside a wall leading to a small dining-room. On my right was a stove used for both cooking and heating, and on it was a large pot. On the other side was a dressing-table with a radio on it, and a few chairs. A calendar, some postcards, the image of a Madonna and a crucifix decorated the wall.

'Sit here,' said the woman smilingly.

I obeyed.

Then she shouted: 'Thomas! Thomas! Come here!'

Thomas, wearing farmer's boots, entered the kitchen.

'What's the matter?'

'This is my husband,' said the woman.

I got up and said: 'Pleased to meet you,' as I shook his hand.

Thomas was in his early sixties, of average height and rather stocky. He had white hair with a right parting, wrinkled forehead, grey eyes and was most of the time in a happy and contemplative mood. He was a real Christian, prayed for good weather and thanked the Lord, especially when the harvest was plentiful. He was held in high esteem at home; his sons and daughters had confidence in his judgement, so his decisions were final.

Thomas sat in a chair beside me. I told him what had befallen me since the recent armistice, which seemed to have started another war, with the Germans taking control of our country and causing us more hardship than we ever had before their arrival. While we were talking, Rose, the woman who had welcomed me at the gate, set the table and placed a large bowl of steaming minestrone before me. Its flavour was irresistible. I became incoherent and could no longer concentrate on our conversation. Thomas realised that I was hungry and so he stopped talking.

I grabbed the spoon and unhesitatingly attacked the minestrone. I had not eaten such a delicious minestrone for years. As Thomas was only a little hungry, to keep me company, he ate some *grissini* and sliced salami, which he washed down with a few glasses of his home-made red wine. He filled my glass again and again, urging me to drink. '*Bevete! Bevete!* (Drink! Drink!) this is light wine, wine of our vineyards, it will give you strength and cheer you up.'

I ate ravenously and drank several glasses of their refreshing and invigorating wine, which made me feel very warm and amiable. By the time I stopped eating, their daughters Agnes, Martha and Celia came into the kitchen. Agnes was the eldest.

'Two of my boys,' said Thomas, 'Giovanni and Francesco, were in the army as you were. They escaped and came home three days ago. They are now picking grapes in our vineyards, which are ready for vintage. Peter, the second of my boys, is in England; he was taken prisoner in North Africa.'

'Where do you come from?' asked the girls.

'Naples,' I replied.

'We know two *carabinieri* called Mark and Dino. Mark comes from Naples, and Dino from Tuscany. They usually come to visit us two or three times a week, but we haven't seen them for a week now; they probably don't know what to make of this armistice. They might have disbanded as you have done.'

I was there more than two hours and enjoyed their warm and generous hospitality. Having had a square meal, I was feeling stronger and more confident to face my precarious situation, so I thanked my host, hostess and the rest of their family and promised that I would visit them again as soon as possible.

'Yes, do come and visit us when you can. You are always welcome,' said the girls cordially.

I resumed my walk towards Bardo, which was about two kilometres from Codico; this was the name of the locality in which my newly-made friends lived.

The sun was still high in the sky. After the substantial meal and the delicious wine, I felt tipsy and my legs heavy. I plodded along cheerfully and pondered about the warm hospitality and spontaneity of Thomas and his family, and my heart glowed for them. With such friends I did not feel alone or forlorn, and I am sure that Italy was full of them. Even the poorest people were ever ready to help.

Although my new-found friends did not mention their surname, I had noticed some envelopes addressed to Thomas Bolti, so I deduced that I had just been a guest of the Bolti family.

62

*I arrive at Bardo. My friend Biagio gives me
hospitality. Biagio, his family and their activities.
I find it hard living on the farm*

I arrived at Bardo after five o'clock, and the day was pleasantly
warm and still young. My army boots and my trousers were
covered with brownish dust. It was a quiet afternoon, a quietness
that was occasionally broken by a girl yelling at her cows grazing
in a meadow, scythe grindings, chirpings, crowings and brayings.

I bumped into a countryman on a bicycle and said: 'Please can
you tell me where Costa Biagio lives?'

He looked at me and then stopped. 'What did you say?'

'Please can you tell me where Costa Biagio lives?'

'Costa Biagio, Costa Biagio,' he mumbled, scratching his head
and searching his brain. After a while he relaxed and said: 'Yes, oh
yes, I know where Costa Biagio lives!'

Then he turned round and, pointing with his finger, said: 'Walk
about five hundred metres this way, turn right, and after a further
hundred metres you'll get to Costa's farm.'

'*Tante grazie*,' (Many thanks), I said and moved on. A few
metres from the farm, I noticed someone unloading a cart. I
shouted: 'Biagio! Biagio!'

The man stopped working, looked in my direction and shouted
back: 'Hey Cosimo, I'm glad to see you; I'm glad that you have
been able to escape. I was worried; I was afraid that the Germans
had captured you. Have you walked all the way?'

'Yes, I have. I couldn't thumb a lift. Besides, it was too risky to
travel by the main road.'

'You must be very tired and hungry. It is sixteen kilometres from
Bra to Bardo.'

'I'm not very tired; it is very pleasant and invigorating to tramp

291

through the countryside, and I am not hungry either because about three hours ago I had a meal with the Bolti family – a farmer in Codico.'

'Oh, did you? Did you know them?'

'Of course not. They were just very kind to me.'

Without much ado, I told Biagio how I had met the Boltis and how lavishly they had entertained me.

'It's very peaceful here, tucked away from the trouble spots,' I said. 'I don't think the Germans would dare to stick their noses in here. And what luxuriant vegetation!'

'Well, summer is always like this here; we have plenty of grass with bumper crops every year and it keeps us very busy indeed; we have to work from sunrise to sunset.'

'Can I stay here a couple of weeks?' I asked Biagio. 'I think that the Allies will soon land on the Riviera and the war'll be over.'

'You can stay here as long as you like. We have got plenty of food; we'll manage somehow. Come and meet my family.'

In a couple of days, I had settled down nicely, and then Biagio began to show me the ropes; and what a life it was! We used to get up at dawn. Having had a hot drink made out of roasted barley, we went to work doing whatever had to be done; picking grapes, gleaning corn, loading or unloading hay, pruning trees, collecting firewood, mending fences and so on. I had never done hard physical work, so I used to get very exhausted; my back and the rest of my body ached. It was sheer slave labour for me, but I had to do it and suffer in silence. Had I protested, they would surely have looked down on me, laughed at me, considered me to be a softy, a sissy.

Having been born and brought up on a farm, they were physically conditioned to hard manual labour, so they were not affected by the discomforts that were afflicting me. If a man could not do a hard day's work, they would have regarded him as a weakling, a disgrace to the masculine gender, a loafer, a man not worth his salt – a man good for nothing.

I did not want to run the risk of injuring my pride. Although it appeared that I had been confined to a hard labour camp, I had to persevere and smile in spite of my aches and my unhappiness.

Born in 1915, Biagio was the oldest in the family. Daniele, his father, wanted to have more boys than girls, so he persisted in trying, but having had three girls in succession, he decided to give up. Boys for him were an assurance of family stability, for when he was old, they would carry on farming his land. Girls needed to have dowries and marry men who, as was the local custom, would keep their wives under their thumbs and be their undisputed masters.

Country people usually had large families, for when they were old, they needed the support of their offspring in order to survive.

Biagio was of medium height and skinny, but as strong as an ox. He had black hair combed back, grey eyes, a straight nose, projecting cheekbones and a long pale face. Looking at him, one could assume that he badly needed some nourishing food and a few bottles of genuine wine. Whatever amount of flesh stuck to his skeleton, it was firm muscle, steely ligaments and tendons. Biagio possessed Herculean strength; he worked hard and long hours without showing any sign of fatigue. He amazed me and I envied him, when my aching joints and my bruised back tormented me. 'Rome wasn't built in a day' so I certainly did not expect that my weak constitution could be transformed into a strong one overnight. I had to manage as best I could with my ineptitude as a farm-hand, and into the bargain I had to contend with an inferiority complex.

When Biagio and I were in the army, I thought that he had some kind of physical disability that made him unfit for ordinary military duties, so he became our captain's batman, which was considered a sedentary occupation. He had to polish the captain's boots and do whatever he, and perhaps his wife, asked him to do. In many instances he was also employed as domestic helper. He certainly would not protest, for our ordinary military duties were much more demanding.

Since Biagio, and other soldiers with the same farming background, looked forward to being employed as batmen, I came to the conclusion that this had nothing to do with their physical unfitness; they might just be malingering to avoid ordinary military duties and being sent to the front.

As food was being rationed, these soldiers employed as batmen bribed their officers with gifts of ham, salami, white flour, butter, fresh eggs, wine and so on. Usually professional officers had their families to support and couldn't afford to buy food on the black market; and the extra food, which they considered a luxury, came in very handy.

Having a batman who was a farmer in his civil life was very useful indeed. His officer would treat him on friendly terms. He would issue a weekend pass to him, so that the batman could go home, a home not too far away, and spend his time working on the farm. When he returned from his leave, he would bring some food supplies to his officer. This kind of tacit agreement, although immoral in principle, served the interests of both the officer and his batman; it was a case of 'you scratch my back and I'll scratch yours'.

If he could, a farmer would try hard to have his son exempted from military service, or have him do it in a locality not too far from home, so that when the land needed to be tilled, or at harvest time, his son could ask for special leave. With the shortage of manpower, while most able men were at the front, how could an unaided farmer grow the food needed to feed the armed forces and civilian population of our country?

Had one of the farmer's sons had a record of past illness, then the farmer, enlisting the help of a friendly doctor, could get a certificate stating that his son's case was chronic. The authorities, bribed with generous gifts, would be inclined to be less exacting and would acquiesce in the farmer's demand to have his son exempted from military service or else do it somewhere near home.

Biagio had four sisters who mainly did domestic work. They fed the chickens and ducks, looked after their five cows and two pigs, and helped on the land when asked to do so. All the girls, except Vera who was the baby of the family, were in their twenties and looked healthy. The main aim of each girl was to find a strong and hard-working husband, have a large family, be a good housewife and mother, and be willing to submit herself to her husband's undisputed authority.

During the first few weeks on the farm, I had difficulty in adapting myself to the farmers' way of living. They only fed and sheltered me, but I had to be thankful for that. Luckily I had saved a few lire while I was in the army, by earning some money outside the barracks. I could spend it now on whatever I strictly needed. My friend Raballo sent me those personal belongings I had left with him, and I returned the suit he had lent me. I had a few woollies just in case I had to spend the winter at Bardo.

I was sadly disappointed that the Allied forces had not landed on the Riviera as I had expected. They seemed in no hurry to see a quick end to the war, so they advanced from South Italy at their own pace, thus giving the Germans time to strengthen themselves by building the Gustav line across the peninsula between Rome and Naples.

The Germans turned Monte Cassino into a stronghold. However, the Allied bombers razed the sixth-century abbey to the ground in order to dislodge them. The opposing forces did not respect this most revered shrine, and we sadly shed many tears over its ruins.

I found living on the farm terribly tedious; a relentless physical life without any recreation whatsoever. We listened to the radio, which was under German and Fascist control, but their news, mendaciously inflated with their military successes, bored me. On the other hand, I seemed to have little in common with the people with whom I was staying. They spoke their dialect and, when they gossiped, told stories or chatted about other topics, I was completely cut off. I could communicate with them only when they made the effort to speak Italian, their knowledge of which was very limited indeed.

Although those country girls were physically desirable, they lacked the feminine qualities that usually attract men, inspire them, make them fall in love and write poetry, songs and so on.

There was the possibility of going to the cinema once a week in Rena, about a kilometre from Bardo, but it was risky; I was afraid that if I went there and suddenly the Germans arrived and combed the area, I would be trapped with the rest of the unfortunate young men.

63

A brief history of Rena. The Republic of Salò on Lake Garda

Rena, built on a small hill, had a position of dominance over the surrounding countryside. It was a prosperous rural centre connected with several villages including Codico and Bardo; those who cultivated the land were just small farmers.

In ancient times Rena, enclosed within square or rectangular fortifications, was certainly an important town and had several thousand inhabitants. But the Rena of the twentieth century was just a centre of rural villages. It had a castle dating from the Middle Ages and half a dozen old churches, indicating a strong religious influence. Today only two churches are centres of worship. The others have been closed for years and are badly in need of repairs; they are just historical monuments.

Rena, like any other Piedmontese town, has arcades enabling people to go for a stroll even in bad weather, but its population, including the inhabitants of its dependent villages, is less than 4,000. This is only half what it used to be in the sixteenth century.

In spite of the rationing, local people could get all the food they wanted from the countryside, and at almost normal prices. Besides, many of Rena's inhabitants possessed small plots of land on the outskirts of the town, which they used as vineyards, kitchen gardens, chicken-runs, pigsties and so on. The pigs provided them with lard, bacon, salami and an income from the ham and meat they sold to black marketeers. These visited country towns and villages to buy foodstuffs for their illegal trade.

Before the armistice of 8 September 1943, there was law and order. The farmers were under an obligation to give, as far as their means would allow, an annual quota of their crops, wine, livestock and other agricultural produce to their municipalities at an agreed price. This kind of arrangement was known as the *ammasso*. The municipalities stored the produce in silos and other buildings, and the authorities of the large towns used the produce gathered according to the basic necessities of their population, and of our armed forces.

Bakers obtained adequate flour supplies in proportion to the coupons they handed in, and so did butchers and other shopkeepers whose merchandise was subject to rationing.

The black market was illegal of course, and if a dealer was caught red-handed he would be penalised. This deterrent failed to take effect because the black market, in spite of its illegality, was well established, and no authorities tried earnestly to eradicate it.

Having fulfilled their obligation to the *ammasso*, farmers always had extra foodstuffs hidden somewhere, which they greedily sold to black marketeers and made a handsome profit. The black market was a godsend to the farmers; they had never had it so good.

Some farmers, for selfish reasons, found excuses to have the *ammasso* quotas reduced, but if inspectors became suspicious that the farmers were cheating, they had the authority to search the farms. Should they find food surpluses hoarded without justification, the farmers concerned would be prosecuted. However, the farmers knew how to mollify the seemingly inflexible inspectors by greasing their itchy palms, and this occurrence made a mockery of any attempt to stamp out the illegal practice.

At this stage, Rena was a quiet town where stray dogs lazed in the sun on the main square. If the sun was hot they moved away, still half-asleep, and resumed their slumbers in the shade of the houses, provided that a group of ragamuffins did not disturb them.

After the armistice of 8 September 1943, Rena became restless and agitated. The town's population had somewhat increased, because of the return home of disbanded soldiers, including some who, being unable to go home, had sought refuge somewhere around the town. Such a change could particularly be noticed on Fridays and Sundays.

Friday was market day in Rena. Farmers or members of their families took eggs, chickens, butter and land produce to the market, and with the proceeds they bought whatever they needed or were able to buy from the stalls. Those who had work to do returned home straight away.

On market days or on Sundays, villagers and peasants, dressed in their best, cycled to Rena to have a chance to meet acquaintances and friends. Young people hoped to encounter potential boyfriends or girlfriends. When some of the boys met girls they both seemed embarrassed and could find nothing romantic to say, so to break the silence they talked about their crops and animals, or just gossiped. This kind of country-bumpkin contact, although not particularly exciting, was a kind of rustic wooing and flirting, which often ended in marriage.

Of course there were bold and impetuous boys who, prompted by natural impulses, stole kisses. But the girls were on the alert for that; they would not yield an inch, for their virginity was part of their dowry, reserved for the men that they would marry.

At the end of Sunday Mass, the middle-aged gathered on the square in front of the entrance of the church and chatted animatedly. They gesticulated, shouted, cracked jokes, laughed, rolled cigarettes and smoked like chimneys. Those who had time to spare and were in a jovial mood went to an *osteria* (inn), drank a few bottles of Barbera and aired their views. The main topics for conversation were invariably crops, prospects for the coming harvest, how much a pig would fetch on the black market, German raids, partisan movements and so on. They always ended their social gathering by singing traditional Piedmontese songs. Anyone from another region of Italy, having heard those songs sung again and again, would be driven mad!

With the Germans' liberation of Mussolini, Hitler helped him to set up a government in a town on Lake Garda and called it the 'Salò Republic'. The Italians were not inclined to support such a government and so Piedmontese farmers stopped giving their produce to the *ammasso* altogether, as they had done in previous years, else it would have fostered the German and Fascist cause and prolong the hated and hopeless war. On the other hand, the Germans and Fascists did not have enough men to visit the farmers and coerce them into handing over their quotas. Had they done so, it would have provoked resentment, aggravating people's antipathy and loathing towards them.

During this obscure and chaotic period, law and order hardly existed, so unscrupulous people, thieves and villains had a free hand to please themselves.

Young men and disbanded soldiers had to be constantly on the lookout for German or Fascist raids; for they had no intention of fighting on their side.

Those who were farmers worked on their land and kept out of mischief. Other young men lived with their parents in Rena, but there were no jobs, except for a very few who were willing to adapt themselves to any kind of work. The unemployed had no alternative but to stay with their parents and wait for the end of the war. This was not always easy, for if their parents were poor, they had to tighten their belts in order to feed extra mouths. Young men needed much more than a meagre plate of polenta or minestrone; they needed clothes, shoes, a few cigarettes and some pocket money, otherwise their lives would be utterly dull and unbearable.

64

Rena and its villages. The parish priest worries about his flock

The villages around Rena were made up of a few dilapidated cottages. Walking along the rough and deeply rutted lanes, one often came across one or two stray cows, ducks or hens and was scared by the barking of hostile dogs on nearby farms. Each village had a small shop selling everything that peasants would need and could afford to buy.

Moreover, there was a blacksmith who also functioned as a carpenter and barber for customers who were not too demanding, then a miller, an inn and a small church without a priest. The inn was the heart of the village, where farmers and peasants dropped in on Sunday afternoons, gossiped, played cards and drank a couple of glasses of wine.

A Mass was celebrated in the village church every Sunday morning, so those who were unable to go to church in the town would have the chance to worship locally. Since the village was too small to support a resident priest, he came from one of the churches in Rena. He usually cycled to a village but, if it wasn't too far away, it was a good excuse for an energetic priest to stretch his legs and stride there; a brisk walk would refresh his mind and body, and give him a good appetite.

From Bardo's hillocks I could spot the slim, tall young priest striding along the rural paths to our local church. After Mass, which lasted about an hour, worshippers gathered outside for a natter, and later they walked home to their customary Sunday dinner – a *pastasciutta* (home-made noodles with sauce seasoned with bits of salami). They drank their table wine, and invariably finished the meal with baked apples or pears. Such a dinner was very appetising and filling indeed.

View of Secondigliano, 1900, with its main road (part of the ancient Appian Way), which goes towards Naples.
Photograph taken from the book *Secondigliano da Documenti Inediti* by Father Salvatore Loffredo.

Beginning of Corso Umberto Primo (now called Corso Secondigliano). The road goes towards Rome. This photo was taken in the early twenties.
Photograph taken from the book *Secondigliano da Documenti Inediti* by Father Salvatore Loffredo.

Early twenties. View of Corso Umberto Primo from The Great Coffee House, which is on the right. The road goes towards Rome.
Photograph taken from the book *Secondigliano da Documenti Inediti* by Father Salvatore Loffredo.

1900. View of Corso Umberto Primo from Barbato's Mill, which is on the left. The road goes towards Naples.
Photograph taken from the book *Secondigliano da Documenti Inediti* by Father Salvatore Loffredo.

Our parish church, 1900. Photograph taken from the book *Secondigliano da Documenti Inediti* by Father Salvatore Loffredo.

Victor Emmanuel Street in the early twenties or before. Photograph taken from the book *Secondigliano da Documenti Inediti* by Father Salvatore Loffredo.

Our Town Hall as it was long before I was born, and as it is today. This photo was probably taken in the early twenties or before.
Photograph taken from the book *Secondigliano da Documenti Inediti* by Father Salvatore Loffredo.

This building, with its entrance on Duke of Abruzzi Street, used to house the municipal administration before the Town Hall was built. This photo could have been taken in the eighties or early nineties.
Photograph taken from the book *Secondigliano da Documenti Inediti* by Father Salvatore Loffredo.

The rotunda and its surrounding obelisks (Field of Mars) was probably built during the nineteenth century. It was removed after the Second World War on account of traffic congestion.
Photograph taken from the book *Secondigliano da Documenti Inediti* by Father Salvatore Loffredo.

Chapel of St Antony at a large farmhouse called 'Scambia'. The chapel is near the pole.
Photograph taken from the book *Secondigliano da Documenti Inediti* by Father Salvatore Loffredo.

One of the chapels in our parish church - the chapel of the Virgin of Assumption. Photograph taken from the book *Secondigliano da Documenti Inediti* by Father Salvatore Loffredo.

Fashion in Secondigliano at the end of the nineteenth century. This lady, called Carmina, was the sister of the Venerable Gaetano Errico, the founder of the Chapel of the Sacred Hearts. Photograph taken from the book *Secondigliano da Documenti Inediti* by Father Salvatore Loffredo.

Coat of arms of our parish church, 1735. Cosma and Damiano are our patron saints.
Photograph taken from the book *Secondigliano da Documenti Inediti* by Father Salvatore Loffredo.

Emblem of the congregation of the Missionaries of the Sacred Hearts. The authorities first gave their approval for the formation of the congregation between the years 1832 and 1840. Photograph taken from the book *Secondigliano da Documenti Inediti* by Father Salvatore Loffredo.

Military parade at the Field of Mars in Capodichino, 8 December 1856, where an attempt was made on the life of the King of Naples, King Ferdinando II. Photograph taken from the book *Secondigliano da Documenti Inediti* by Father Salvatore Loffredo.

The Archbishop of Naples blesses the first stone of the Chapel of the Conception in Capodichino in the second half of the nineteenth century. Photograph taken from the book *Secondigliano da Documenti Inediti* by Father Salvatore Loffredo.

Photo taken in Secondigliano in 1957.   Photo taken in Australia in 1960.

Christmas party in London, 1992.

At a friend's in London, 1996.

The Boltis, who were a little better off than the other small farmers, had a second course on Sundays. It might be sizzling pork sausages or roast chicken with potatoes, onions and carrots, followed by a salad. There was never a lack of appetite in that fresh and invigorating countryside environment.

Rena's parish priest was quite an authority. He had been seriously worried for a number of years; he feared that religious faith in Rena and its dependent villages was at stake. Church attendance had dwindled since one of the two brothers who ran the coffee-house in the main square of the town had started a cinema.

The movies had had quite an effect on the life of the town; people had found them so exciting and entertaining that they had become addicted to them. They could see on the screen what was going on in cities and countries far, far away, and suddenly wanted to be part of that world; a wonderful world of achieved desires. It appeared that people there didn't have to work hard or didn't have to work at all, and yet they seemed to be wallowing in wealth. They could get anything they wanted at once, as if they possessed a magic wand. What a good idea to be able to live like that.

The average townsfolk and peasants had to toil extremely hard for a crust of bread. Going to church gave them spiritual uplift, consolation and strength to endure their miserable existence with equanimity. The movies made them restless, gave them hope, a stimulus, a desire to strive hard to improve themselves and get a share in the riches of the world.

Rena had nothing to offer them except a life of self-denial and poverty. Being devoted to religion meant having peace of mind and a promise that when they passed away, they would eventually be admitted to heaven. If they did not die prematurely, they would have to wait a lifetime before knocking at heaven's gate, of which Saint Peter, many Roman Catholics believe, is the keeper.

Supposing that he found out that their spiritual records were not in order, he might either confine them to purgatory or fling them down to hell. Wouldn't it be better if, instead of a life of deprivation and penury in Rena, they forged a new existence that enabled them to enjoy a few luxuries and a little of the lifestyle portrayed in the movies?

The parish priest was angry, shocked at the new attitude and behaviour of his parishioners, which had weakened their faith. Girls, who were members of the Legion of Mary, had always been a symbol of purity, but now they had been corrupted by the movies; by those amorous scenes showing alluring actors and actresses fondling one another and indulging in lingering kisses. Now only a very few girls were attending the Rosary and Benediction.

If people stopped going to church altogether, how could the parish priest manage? His livelihood depended entirely on the goodwill of his parishioners and benefactors. Collections at Mass had always been disappointing – a mere pittance – because parishioners ignored the fact that money had lost its value; they continued to offer a few coins on the collecting tray as they had done years before the war.

In the past, the church had inherited legacies from generous churchgoers, which consisted of a few acres of land, but the farmer who cultivated the land was rather mean, giving little in return. Therefore, the poor parish priest had to rely on his benefactors for his bread and butter, salami, wine and an occasional chicken. He thanked the Lord for having a middle-aged housekeeper entirely devoted to him. She lovingly prepared his minestrone, home-made noodles and so on. He fought a tooth-and-nail battle against that scoundrel who ran the cursed cinema, and had even endeavoured to have it shut down, but it transpired that those townsfolk who were under Satan's influence did not object to having a cinema there! The priest often gave vent to his bottled-up feelings when he delivered the Sunday sermon, and passionately shouted from the pulpit about the plight of one of his lost sheep.

'Dear brothers and sisters!' he would say. 'Our faith is being seriously threatened! One of our young girls has gone astray; she has been damned by the wicked movies. She was as pure as a white lily, then she started disobeying her parents, using make-up, smoking, going to dances and finally she eloped with a ne'er-do-well boy. She is pregnant now, and her good-for-nothing boy has deserted her, ruined her.

'Let's make an effort and get rid of the influence of the wicked movies; they put silly ideas into the heads of our teenagers and other inexperienced people, and will utterly destroy our morality. Young people need special protection; they can easily fall victim to satanic alluring snares. Satan is the deceiver; he is always ready to entice and damn us. Remember! If we pray to God daily, he will protect us, especially when we are exposed to temptation and in other difficulties.'

302

The sermons used to last about half an hour. The priest always mentioned the evil of malicious gossip, family arguments and how people were getting too greedy and failing to support their church; and how could repairs be done without substantial donations? He truly cared for the spiritual life of his flock and, in despair, he threatened to have the man who owned the cinema excommunicated.

65

Graziani is in command once again. I meet the
carabinieri *Mark and Dino*

On 9 September 1943, the Italian government surreptitiously
deserted Rome and fled to Brindisi, which had been occupied by
the Allies. Marshal Graziani for one reason or another did not run
away from Italy and, with the subsequent German occupation of
Rome and the rest of Italy, he must have found himself in an
awkward situation. He was old and perhaps not in good health and
secretly worried about what the future held.

Perhaps Graziani was unable to refuse when he was asked, and
so he agreed to help Mussolini by building a small army aiming to
fight anti-Fascist and anti-German partisans entrenched in the
mountains.

Having a leader once again, some Fascist supporters rallied round
him. Most of them were Fascists to whom Mussolini had given
fame and fortune before his fall, or they were simply employed by
the Fascist Party.

Reasonable men, whether they were ex-Fascists or not, would be
disinclined to support Mussolini once again; they could clearly see
that he, being under Hitler's influence, was on the losing side. At
this stage the Germans were in full retreat in Russia and even in
South Italy.

Mussolini needed men to enlist in his army, otherwise how was
he going to defend his Salò Republic? Perhaps only one per cent
of the disbanded soldiers enlisted in Mussolini's army having
nowhere to go or being unable to fend for themselves.

Since not enough able men came forward, the Fascists enticed
teenage boys to volunteer. They gave them twenty lire per day,
which was quite a lot for them. They dressed them up in combat
fatigues and armed them with German automatic rifles and hand

grenades, which the boys secured in their belts. These tender young boys looked tough, fierce and ready for action. They were called 'The Ettore Muti' formation or division. Ettore Muti was a highly decorated soldier of the Great War, a staunch Fascist and party leader. After Mussolini's fall, 25 July 1943, Signor Muti tried to escape, but the *carabinieri* who were keeping an eye on him shot him dead.

The Fascists used to parade the new formation through city and town centres, a display aimed at intimidating anti-Fascists and partisans. People nicknamed the formation *Sfegatati* (fanatics) and also *Sordomuti* (deaf and dumb) because these young soldiers behaved like robots, shooting and killing in cold blood when they were ordered to do so.

The number of partisans increased day by day; they freed many people in detention who were eager to join them. Men joined the partisans for various reasons; a few of them did it for love of their country, others to get some credit after the war, which would enable them to gain preference in securing civil service or other government jobs. In addition, there were those young men who were unwilling to adapt themselves to any kind of work and, if they did not mind living rough and taking some risks, they could sort themselves out by enlisting with the partisans.

The Germans allowed the *carabinieri* to continue in their duties; they needed them to keep law and order. Unfortunately only a few stayed on, the rest having run away.

The *carabinieri*, being few in number, could not do much and were in a precarious position. They were caught between two opponents – Fascists and Germans on one hand and partisans on the other – and had to strike a delicate balance. If they displeased either side, they could get into serious trouble. And who was going to protect them or save their skins when law and order hardly existed and it was a case of every man for himself?

I tried to stay away from Rena as much as I could; I feared some unexpected German and Fascist raids there. Often on Sunday afternoons I strolled to Codico, paying a visit to the Boltis. There I met the *carabinieri* Mark and Dino, who used to drop in for a chat while on patrol duty. On such occasions, the Boltis offered them a few glasses of wine. Mark had a crush on Martha, and Dino on Celia, the Boltis' fourth and fifth daughters.

Mark and Dino were both auxiliary *carabinieri*. As there was a shortage of *carabinieri* during the war, whenever there was a demand, ordinary soldiers could apply for the posts of auxiliary *carabinieri*. They also operated as military police.

66

Some background about Mark

Mark was born in 1916 in a suburb of Naples called Casalnuovo. He was about five feet nine inches tall, rather sturdy, had black hair with a left parting, black eyes and dazzling white teeth. Women found him very handsome and sexy.

During the Second World War he was in the infantry, but applied for the position of auxiliary *carabiniere* and was accepted. He had some basic training, and later in 1941 was attached to the Italian Expeditionary Corps in Russia, doing military police duties.

With the victorious Russian advance at the end of 1942 and the subsequent German surrender at Stalingrad in February 1943, the Axis forces were in full retreat on that front. The Italian retreat was chaotic, and a complete disaster; of our deployment of 229,000 men, only half survived the Russian onslaught and the severe winter. Here again it was a case of every man for himself.

Mark was one of the survivors. Cold, tired, hungry and under the constant threat of sporadic attacks, he trudged along through the deep snow for hundreds of kilometres. The retreat route was scattered with abandoned war material, bodies of dead animals and men who had perished of cold and fatigue during that cruel forced march, in which those who could not walk any further on account of frost-bite, weariness and sickness were left behind to die.

Mark thanked God when he reached safe territory and was able to travel by train, or any other means of transport available, back to Italy. He was saddened and shocked when he noticed the sorrowful state to which our country had been reduced. The cities had been bombed by American aircraft, part of Naples had been destroyed, people were starving and the black market was rampant. Still, the Italian misery was minimal compared with the sufferings he had experienced during the retreat in Russia.

Having returned from Russia, he was sent home for a short period of leave. Later he reported for duty at the *carabinieri* quarters in Rena.

Dino, Mark's companion in arms, came from a Tuscan farming family. He was about the same age and height as Mark, but stocky. He had black hair combed back, grey eyes, a bony nose and a rustic look. He had already been in Rena two or three months before Mark arrived.

The *carabinieri* were quartered in a small two-storey house overlooking the countryside and the hills. The ground floor contained the jail, the office and a couple of other rooms. The man in charge, a low-ranking marshal with a small family of two, lived in the flat on the first floor. A low-ranking brigadier, Albert, was the marshal's deputy and had his own room. Mark and Dino shared one bedroom.

The commandant of the *carabinieri* in a small town received the title of marshal, which was equal in rank to sergeant-major. A brigadier in the *carabinieri* was equal in rank to sergeant.

Mark and Dino carried out their daily duties together. Every day they patrolled their territory, which covered a radius of about ten kilometres from their quarters. With their rifles across their shoulders, they cycled to different localities. They passed through one or two villages, just to put in an appearance, since villagers were generally law-abiding people.

Every evening around ten, Mark and Dino were supposed to make contact with the *carabinieri* of the nearby town. When they were on duty in Rena, they had to keep an eye on black-market dealers and trouble makers. Taking advantage of the weak and ambiguous position of the *carabinieri*, there were those who set out to exploit the situation for their own selfish interest.

The *carabinieri* were regarded as German collaborators. Their job was to keep law and order but, being few in number, they couldn't enforce the law. On the other hand they were not keen to be committed to the German cause. They were expected to arrest disbanded soldiers and partisans whom the new pro-German government – the Salò Republic – considered outlaws, but they did not bother; if they knew that a group of partisans was in the town, they stayed put in their quarters to avoid confrontation. Should they meet them in the street, they contrived somehow to steer clear. They tried to protect decent people, but were unable to prevent crime and other offences.

The brigadier did the office work: typing, writing reports, keeping records, answering phone calls and looking after the administration. The marshal supervised and took major decisions. People said that he was an opportunist, for when Mussolini was in power, he appeared to be a Fascist sympathiser. Now he kept himself to himself; very seldom was he to be seen walking around the town and villages. Both the marshal and the brigadier had failed to complete their secondary school education, otherwise they would have been qualified to be officers.

67

Mark and I become close friends. He makes quite an impression on local girls. Mark's and Dino's recreation and boredom

Mark and I both came from small towns in the vicinity of Naples, and we soon became close friends. He trusted me utterly and told me all about himself. His parents were poor and had been very prolific; the Lord had blessed them with a dozen children. Almost all the inhabitants of his town were either tailors or shoemakers; Mark himself was a first-class shoemaker. His fellow citizens worked mainly for Neapolitan shopkeepers; they worked long hours, ate macaroni or minestrone almost every day, laughed at their jokes, sang Neapolitan songs and were happy.

Any time Mark had something important to tell me, he paid me a visit at Bardo. In that autumn of 1943, something was troubling him; he couldn't make up his mind whether to continue being a *carabiniere* or to desert the force.

'I would like to run away,' he often said to me, 'but as long as things don't get worse, I can carry on being a *carabiniere* till the end of the war. I have a comfortable room, which I share with Dino. We have an excellent cook and I like going on patrol through the countryside and chatting up a few peasant girls; although my pay is not much, it is sufficient for my needs. If I deserted the force, I would be on my own, I should find a hiding place somewhere and earn my living by making shoes, shoes made to measure. I could certainly make one pair a day and earn a lot of money, so that by the end of the war I could save enough to set up a shoe business somewhere and get married.'

'It sounds like a good idea,' I said, 'why don't you do it? The sooner you start, the better!'

'I don't want to do it yet. Being a shoemaker is hard work; I have to work indoors all the time and no less than twelve hours a day. I am still young, not thirty yet; I'm enjoying being a *carabiniere*, and my duties aren't too demanding. I've never had it so good! When I go back home, I won't be able to afford too much leisure time; it'll be a luxury. I'll have to work from dawn to dusk for the rest of my life just to keep the wolf from the door. At the moment, when Dino and I are off duty, we can sit down, play cards, listen to the radio and gramophone, have a chat, or perhaps visit the Boltis.'

'Well, if you like the way you are living now, carry on,' I said, 'but bear in mind that being a *carabiniere*, even on a permanent basis, you won't have much to offer. With your miserable pay you won't be considered an eligible bachelor. Only a poor girl on the verge of starvation would perhaps consent to marry you. Of course, being physically attractive is something, but it's not sufficient for a sensible girl; she surely would be looking for something more substantial. Fancy marrying a man just for being good-looking; she might run the risk of starving to death.'

Soon after Mark's arrival in Rena, the country girls quickly spread the news.

'Have you seen the new *carabiniere*? *Che bell'uomo!* (What a handsome man!); he resembles Rudolf Valentino.'

Almost every girl knew about Rudolf Valentino, that famous film star and lover whom girls had either seen in movies or read about in some magazine.

'The name of the new *carabiniere* is Mark, he is a *terrone*, comes from *terre da pipe* (volcanic lands) and has the Vesuvius fire in his blood.'

Terrone is a nickname that some supercilious people of Northern Italy contemptuously use to refer to those of Southern Italy. I have often noticed in London that some immigrants boast: 'I come from Northern Italy!' They think that they are a breed apart.

Before the Italian industrial revolution, the southern regions – the Kingdom of the Two Sicilies – were governed or misgoverned by foreign rulers. The King, the Church, earls and barons owned the land. They possessed vast areas, but much of it was uncultivated. They were exempt from taxes, lived in luxury and were despotic. The land, forests, water, minerals and the very bodies and souls of

311

their inhabitants were regarded as belonging to all-powerful landowners, or as their feudal property. Peasants were hard pressed, especially with taxes; they seemed to exist solely to please their domineering bosses.

With the unification of Italy in 1860, the central government devoted its attention to industrialising Northern Italy, because it was suitable for that purpose. Very little or nothing was done to develop the South and improve the livelihood of its people.

Farmers had to sell their produce for a pittance, but when they needed commodities manufactured in the North, they had to pay dearly for them. The South became virtually a colony of the North, a place where industrialists sold their goods, so the North prospered; many people could find employment and live comparatively comfortable lives relative to those of the South. Poverty in the South grew worse and worse as the years passed by; thousands and thousands of people were compelled to emigrate to avoid starvation. Secondary education was a luxury, especially for those living some kilometres away from the large towns. There weren't enough state schools, no public libraries and no other facilities whatsoever to help educate people. The economic difference was caused by lack of financial resources and by misgovernment.

The basis of the unification of a country lies in bringing its people together, making them feel that they are fairly treated and equal. In 1860 we had the unification of Italy but not of its people; they were very much divided, especially as the economic gap between the North and the South grew wider and wider.

Mussolini squandered our meagre wealth to conquer Abyssinia, a mere white elephant. He could have used the money to help develop the South. Had he done so, he wouldn't have had the time or the resources to embark on a devastating foreign policy, which culminated in plunging our poor country into Hitler's war.

As for the term *terre da pipe*, this was another contemptuous nickname that those of the North gave to Italians who originated from towns and villages near volcanoes – Vesuvius, Etna, Stromboli and Vulcano, all of which are located in the South.

Mark was aware that he had made quite an impression on the fair sex and felt very cocky about it. When the girls saw him for the first time, they couldn't keep their eyes off him and were eager to make his acquaintance. They found his smile, which displayed his dazzling white teeth, irresistible.

Mark and Dino patrolled their appointed district and did not harass partisans and disbanded soldiers. If someone committed a crime, the *carabinieri* intervened, but they did not bother much about minor transgressions of the law, for there were far too many. When they were on patrol, if it was too early to return to their quarters, they would stop at a farmer's house for a chat and a couple of glasses of wine, especially if the farmer had attractive daughters.

Farmers were interested in keeping on friendly terms with the *carabinieri*, for they secretly engaged in illegal trade by selling their surpluses on the black market. The *carabinieri* knew what was going on, but because of their weak and precarious position they let sleeping dogs lie; it was very much a case of live and let live.

Mark and Dino sought any opportunity to avoid boredom. They were no scholars and had hardly completed their primary schooling, which was the basic education required to become *carabinieri*, a position of trust and integrity. They were complacent and did not see the necessity to stretch themselves beyond their actual capability. When they were in the mood to make a mental effort, they read comics. If they preferred something less strenuous and more stimulating, then they looked with lustful eyes at illustrations of almost naked women in certain well-thumbed magazines which represented their 'library'.

Because of their attitude to learning, their literary progress had suffered a dramatic set-back since they left school. As a pastime, they often turned on the radio or played their gramophone, listening to some Neapolitan or other famous Italian songs, which stirred Mark's feelings for his *Bella Napoli* and made Dino long for his dear Tuscany decked in its summer splendour.

His carnal desire was too much for hot-blooded Mark; he could not repress it. He had quite a number of female admirers who gave him their sweet smiles and left it at that.

One day while walking beside Martha in a country lane, he suddenly grabbed her, held her tightly in his strong arms and gave her the benefit of a heady and lingering kiss that almost choked her. Martha was bewildered, shocked at his impetuous Casanova-like attack. Of course, she secretly liked it, but did not want to encourage him and fall under the spell of his ardent passion. She was not quite sure whether he was the man she would want to marry. Being a practical girl, she couldn't do that if he had nothing substantial to offer her.

313

Mark told me that when his sexual need was unbearable, he went to see his *maresciallo* (marshal).

'Signor Maresciallo,' Mark would ask politely, 'may I have a day off?' Mark shrewdly added 'signor' before the rank to flatter him, make him feel important and put him in a frame of mind by which he could get what he was after.

'What is the day off for, my boy?' the marshal would reply.

'I need it to clean my rifle, signor Maresciallo,' Mark would say with a mischievous and meaningful smile, 'it is getting rusty.'

'Surely you don't need a day off for that? Go and clean it straight away; it won't take you more than half an hour.'

Mark feared that if he didn't make love at least once a month, his 'rifle' would get rusty; he would lose his virility and become impotent. He couldn't do that, for women meant a lot to him; having to give them up would be like a death sentence.

The marshal wasn't out of touch; he knew exactly why Mark wanted the day off, but he seemed to enjoy teasing him, and in the end he would comply with Mark's request.

'All right my boy, go and clean your rifle, but don't get it mucked up, don't get it damaged; that would ruin your life.'

Mark cycled to Fossano, parked his bicycle somewhere and then travelled by train to the city of Cuneo. There were quite a few brothels, which afforded him a good choice. He always looked for the most alluring *commarelle* (prostitutes) and those who had most recently arrived. They would indeed obligingly help him to clean his 'rifle' in exchange for his money. These monthly visits to the *commarelle* enabled him to control the flame of his desire.

68

The Bolti family. Our Sunday events. Dancing in a barn

Thomas, the head of the Bolti family, was much loved and revered; they thought that God spoke to him when he had to make an important decision concerning the land and the welfare of his family. His faithful Rose, wife and mother, did the cooking with affection and devotion. She prepared simple but appetising meals, with vegetables and spices from her kitchen garden which she tended lovingly.

By now I had been Biagio's guest for over two months. The Allied forces, being held up by the Germans at Cassino, were in no hurry; they could afford to wait for the stubborn Germans to run out of war material and give up their hopeless and futile resistance. They were on the run on the Russian front, but would they be able to conjure up a rabbit from a hat by producing a mighty weapon at the last moment and obliterating the Russian and the Allied forces?

I was bored to death, forcing myself to be useful in exchange for my keep. At the same time I felt as if I was living in a foreign country, because my host and the other peasants spoke in dialect. Every time they talked, I stared at them blankly, trying to make sense of what they were saying, and was irritated: feeling tired, lonely and depressed. They knew that I was unhappy, but could not fathom why. It was true that I worried about my relatives, but their country manners and the difficulty of communication were really the source of my discontent.

We had a mild autumn in 1943. The days were getting shorter. After the grape harvest and the storing of the corn, the work slackened; we pruned trees, collected firewood, chopped stumps, mended fences, ate a lot of *polenta* (maize meal porridge), and in

315

general contrived to find something to keep us occupied and get ourselves ready for the winter.

Occasionally on Sunday mornings Biagio and I went to Mass at Rena. We walked along a bushy path full of ruts and bumps, which was often muddy. Then we crossed a narrow rickety footbridge, linking the banks of a small stream. We soon reached the town square of Rena and found ourselves outside the main church. At the end of Mass, which had begun at half past nine, Biagio met a few friends who were always ready for a natter.

Although I could not understand their language, nevertheless after a while they became my friends too. Towards midday we walked back to Bardo to our Sunday dinner, which usually consisted of home-made noodles with tomato sauce, followed by a few morsels of pork sausage. For our second course we might have an onion or spinach omelette or something else instead of sausage pieces, and invariably we drank a couple of glasses of wine with our meals.

On Sunday evenings, when I did not pay a visit to the Boltis, Biagio, his sisters and I went to a dance held in a dreary, dingy and smelly den, dimly lit by a few candles. We danced to the accompaniment of what I considered the tedious and discordant sounds of an accordion. Whether the tune, played by a self-appointed maestro, was harmonious or a mere jumble of notes, it was hard to say; peasants were not too fussy and couldn't tell the difference. They were there to dance and any noise made by a musical instrument would do, so they waltzed along, furiously bumping into one another.

The smell of cow dung from the nearby byres and the sweat and bad breath of the dancers made me feel quite unromantic during those rustic gambols, which those youths enjoyed immensely. Personal cleanliness was neglected, as they had to rely on their wells for water and be careful not to waste it. Having a proper bath was a luxury that peasants could not afford. I managed to have one once a month. Since there were no public baths, whenever I wanted one I had to book in advance at Rena's small hospital and pay for it.

69

*Our Christmas Eve party. Christmas Day dinner with
the Boltis. Giovanni and I share his double bed*

As Christmas 1943 was near, Biagio and I and a dozen of our
friends planned a Christmas Eve *ribotta* (carousal), which was to be
held in a hut attached to the farm. We arranged that each participant
should bring some food, such as wine, ham, salami, cheese,
grissini, nuts, pears and whatever else was available. On that
evening one of our friends brought some raw lean pork. He minced
it and garnished it with parsley, basil, garlic, onions, watercress,
capers and olives, and then seasoned it with salt, pepper, plenty of
virgin olive oil and lemon juice. I disliked raw meat, but that meat
salad was delicious, especially washed down with Barbera and
Nebioli wines.

Since there had been considerable snowfall in the middle of
December, the snow was by now two foot deep and the countryside
around us had been transformed into a huge iced cake.

Biagio's three sisters joined our party, so the hut was warm, cosy
and fairly crowded. We had many logs to burn and kept our old
stove blazing, roaring and crackling. Two kerosene lamps lit the
place, but we had to screen the windows with blankets to prevent
the light from showing outside. Several bottles of wine lay in a
corner, ready to fire our blood with their contents.

We sat around a table and wolfed down the raw meat salad;
which we relished so much that we licked our plates. Afterwards
we gorged ourselves with ham, salami and other foodstuffs, and
with every morsel we gulped a copious draught of wine, which
made us very friendly and boisterous. When we could eat no more,
we started singing popular Piedmontese songs at the top of our
voices, but our gruff shouting and disorderly singing could have
horrified wild beasts. This drinking and singing went on all night.

317

One of us, a stocky chap, stood up to sing solo, but as he sat down heavily on his rickety chair, a loud crash rang out and startled us; his chair had been reduced to smithereens. Luckily he wasn't hurt.

About 4.00 a.m., Rena's main church bell rang, calling the faithful to the first Christmas Mass, the Mass of the Nativity, which was due to begin at 5.00 a.m. Although we were tipsy, half a dozen of us decided to embark upon a pre-dawn excursion to Rena; after the orgy, we badly needed some fresh air and the Lord's forgiveness and blessing. We wrapped ourselves up in cloaks or heavy coats and trudged along a path, which was buried under the snow. The sky was cloudy and the temperature below zero, but the snow made visibility possible. In spite of this, we had to use our torches when the rutted path became tricky and slippery. A couple of my companions, while they were jesting, jostling and performing antics, fell down, but being cushioned by the snow they were unhurt.

Branches of trees, which weren't completely covered with snow, showed up eerily. We passed some detached cottages in which merry-making was still in full swing; their chimneys, ghost-like, smoked placidly in that windless night.

We arrived at Rena at 5.00 a.m. and went straight into the church, which was so spacious that it could hold a congregation of more than 600 people. It was one of the many Italian baroque churches that are to be found all over the peninsula.

As it was Christmas, the church was packed; all the pews were occupied and quite a number of worshippers stood at the rear. Many peasants huddled together in small groups; they had come from surrounding villages, were well wrapped in black cloaks and wore hobnailed boots – probably from ransacked military stores.

Some teenage girls, The Daughters of Mary, wore white veils that covered their heads and shoulders, and sang carols with their angelic voices. A certain amount of coughing, whispering and even snoring went on while the Mass was in progress. The incense had formed a misty film under the ceiling and was pungent to sensitive nostrils. My companions and I rested our backs against some marble pillars, but our minds were still befogged by the amount of wine we had drunk, so we were unable to concentrate on the ceremony.

Although the church was unheated it was not cold; whatever heat

318

was there had emanated from the bodies of the congregation. The warmth and odour of incense were soporific and made me want to fall asleep. At the end of Mass, the parish priest carried the figure of the newborn Jesus in solemn procession around the square outside the church. Later the parishioners queued up to kiss the figure of little Jesus. As my companions and I were almost at the end of the queue, when our turn came the figure smelt strongly of the garlic, tobacco, wine and liquor in which peasants and townsfolk had indulged before going to church.

We left the church after six, but it was still dark – perhaps the sun too had had a Christmas Eve party, and was now tired and unwilling to rise? Parishioners did not stop for their usual chat outside the church; many of them, having feasted till the small hours, were eager to go home and get some sleep.

We were feeling the effect of our exertions; our legs weighed almost a ton as we moved along. We would have liked to lie down in some sheltered corner of Rena and sleep to our hearts' content, but we had to walk back to Bardo, which was about a kilometre away, and to us it seemed to be at the end of the world. We had to summon up whatever strength we still possessed and walk, but were unwilling to do so. We tried hard, and as we made the effort we sang to keep the mind off our aching limbs.

However, our careless cacophonous rendering of the songs was not approved of by the dogs, which protested vigorously at our singing. We dragged along half-asleep and tottered at a snail's pace. Since our feet sank into the deep snow, we had to lift them vertically out of it before we could take a step forward. We stamped, panted, grumbled or uttered gibberish. The few birds twittering there were certainly startled at our clumsiness and clownish behaviour, and may have regarded us with a sense of shame and disgust.

Having trudged for what seemed an eternity, we came to a crossroads where Biagio and I parted from our staggering friends. Arm in arm for mutual support, we pushed along for a few more minutes and soon we were on our doorstep, noisily welcomed by Bill – Biagio's dog. I kicked off my wet boots and placed them near the stove in the hut where we had been feasting. Afterwards, still half-dressed, I sank on to my bed and soon was fast asleep. I slept from 8.00 a.m. till 1.00 p.m., when Biagio's father woke me up to remind me of my invitation to the Boltis' Christmas dinner.

I would have slept till next morning, but I could not forgo the Boltis' kind hospitality fixed for half past two.

I dressed in a jiffy, wearing the best clothes I could find in my scanty wardrobe, and then I rushed to Codico. The sky was still cloudy, but had brightened somewhat. It was snowing gently and the flakes danced like ballerinas in a choreographed ballet. The chimneys of nearby farms smoked calmly, as if they were exchanging Christmas goodwill messages.

I arrived at the Boltis' house just in time.

'Hello Cosimo!' shouted Rose Bolti, smiling. 'Are you cold? Warm yourself up with a glass of wine. Drink this, it is our best, we have just a few bottles; we drink it during Christmas festivities and at some other special occasions.'

I greeted the rest of the family, who had already gathered in the dining-room. We sat at a long table, Thomas Bolti at the head, me at the end, and Rose Bolti and her numerous progeny at each side. I felt the impact of that intimate familiar atmosphere, which I had not experienced since the last Christmas I had spent at home; an experience that also reminded me of my childhood, of those Christmases I enjoyed so much. Back then, my joy began long before the great event, and when Mother started doing the Christmas shopping, I got frantic with excitement. Christmas then was real to me, an event flooding me with an awesome happiness. My parents, brothers and sisters felt the same; we forgot our squabbles and skirmishes and were united more than ever.

White-haired Thomas Bolti looked like one of those patriarchs in the Bible. He said grace, and then we helped ourselves from a dish of ravioli, which was the first course of the traditional Piedmontese Christmas dinner. Then we ate stuffed capon with peas, onions and sliced potatoes. After this we had salad, nuts and a home-made cake. We drank plenty of excellent wine, and even real coffee, with a few drops of grappa (coarse brandy).

Dinner lasted over two hours. We talked about many subjects; we especially remembered our brave partisans in the mountains, exposed to hardship and risking their lives fighting Fascists and Germans.

On such a day Rose couldn't help noticing the absence of Peter, her second son, who was in a prisoner-of-war camp in England.

'Where is Peter now?' she said in an affected voice. 'Is he cold and hungry?'

She could not refrain from shedding a few tears.

'My God! My God! Is he safe and well? I always have a nagging headache. I cannot find peace without having news from him!'

'Don't get upset, Rose,' said her Thomas tenderly, 'our son is a strong boy and capable of looking after himself. The war will soon be over and our Peter will come back home. God has always been good to us. He has kept us in good health, blessed us with plentiful harvests, and He will take care of our Peter too.

'Millions of people are victims of this cursed war; many have lost their lives. Many have lost their homes and families. See how fortunate we are; we have a roof over our heads, we are now surrounded by our family and celebrating Christmas, so let's thank God for His protection and abundance.'

Rose stopped crying and calmed down. She probably realised that her worries about Peter were nothing in comparison with the sorrows of those who had been severely hit by the war and had little or no hope of recovery.

While we were still at the table, she looked around as if to assure herself of the presence of her large family. Then her motherly eyes fell on me compassionately, for I too was a victim of the war. I was almost stranded there, unable to go home, and my mother was surely worrying about me. I was overcome by emotion: which affected my appetite, but being resilient and in their warm company, I cheered up and resumed eating their tasty food and drinking their delicious wine.

After such a substantial dinner we were elated, cracked a few jokes and laughed uproariously. Later the girls cleared the table, did the washing up, powdered their noses and made themselves ready to receive their special visitors.

Mark and Dino arrived at six o'clock. They had had Christmas dinner with their superiors at their quarters. We danced to old tunes on the Boltis' gramophone till late and really had a thoroughly pleasant time. However, sometime after eleven, Mark and Dino made themselves ready to return to their quarters; they had to be back before midnight, so they walked to the farm gate accompanied by Martha and Celia, exchanged romantic farewells, jumped on their bicycles and rode to Rena.

As it was rather late to walk back to Bardo after Christmas

revelling, Thomas Bolti said: 'Cosimo, you can stay with us tonight, sleep with Giovanni; he has a double bed.'

Giovanni promptly agreed to his father's suggestion. He was the eldest son of the Boltis, about thirty, five feet ten inches tall, slim, had black hair combed back, grey eyes and a weather-beaten face. He had a steady girlfriend. While we shuffled along through the snow to our sleeping place, I asked him: 'How is your girlfriend, Giovanni?'

'She is all right. I meet her every Sunday,' he replied with a smile.

'Are you planning to get married?'

'Not yet, but I will after the war.'

'She'll be a lucky girl,' I commented.

'Why?'

'Because you are a good man, a good worker and as strong as an ox.'

'I have to be. Life is very hard. If I were a loafer, I'd have no future, no future at all, and life would be even harder, wouldn't it? And how could I make a living?'

Giovanni had a happy disposition. He smiled most of the time, which was probably due to the amount of home-made wine he consumed; he was not too fond of drinking water! He rolled his own cigarettes; he must have smoked ten a day. He also made cheese, mainly for home consumption. He was a jack of all trades; but he had to be, for small farmers could not afford to employ tradesmen. He was aware from gossip going round that he was a good worker, which meant he was an eligible bachelor in that rural area. As a matter of fact, he had made quite an impression on the girls of the village.

Giovanni's bedroom was in an old dilapidated one-storey building, which was about 300 metres from the Boltis' farmyard. As we stepped in, Giovanni lit a candle. It was a double room, sparsely furnished and with little to distinguish it, except the washstand with a cracked jug and basin.

He only spent the night there, so he did not bother to heat it. I quickly felt the impact of a chill creeping into my bones; it was like being in an icebox. We had taken two hot-water bottles with us to warm the bed. There were many blankets, but the bed seemed strangely uninviting. I undressed quickly, kept my pullover on and soon dived in. In spite of the hot-water bottles, the sheets were icy;

they caused me to shiver and my teeth to chatter. I regretted having accepted the invitation to stay for the night. Now the vision of Biagio's cosy bedroom in Bardo, which he shared with me, hovered alluringly before my mind; I badly wanted to run away.

Giovanni was used to the bedroom; he could not in the least fathom my predicament. He gave a long pull at a bottle of wine he had brought with him, which was his nightcap, and perhaps a kind of general anaesthetic to deaden the feeling as his body came in touch with those icy sheets. He blew out the candle and said 'good-night'. He was soon fast asleep and snoring loudly. I was shocked, and then aggravated by this irritating kind of lullaby; his snores varied from adagio to crescendo, and having reached the alto, they suddenly collapsed into a sort of pig's gruntings. This was followed by his breaking wind, which was similar to the roll of a drum. Breaking wind vied with snoring; it seemed as if they were in some prize-winning competition. I put my head under the blankets, hoping to escape the noise, but to no avail. I tossed and turned, and the hours of the night seemed to go on for eternity. I longed for dawn and was raring to run off to Bardo, to that double bed that I shared with Biagio. He was not perfect as a sleeping companion, but his nocturnal behaviour was moderate and not so nerve-racking and devastating as Giovanni's. Biagio's sisters shared a bedroom next to us; they were no angels, but their nocturnal noises were more ladylike.

Giovanni woke up at about seven and looked refreshed and quite innocent of his nocturnal crimes.

'Good morning, Cosimo, have you slept well?'

I really wanted to murder him. I feigned a smile and replied: 'Oh yes, yes, I have slept well indeed, but I dreamt that I was at the front and being bombed by the enemy. I was so infuriated that I bayoneted a couple of them.'

'Did you? What a peculiar dream you have had; you must have had a nightmare! Probably you worry too much about the war. I never dream anything, I sleep like a log.'

'Oh yes, I'm sure you do!'

'Come let us go and have breakfast,' said Giovanni cheerfully.

Still shivering and irritated, I badly needed a pick-me-up.

That morning, Saint Stephen's Day (Boxing Day), I and other members of the Bolti family were sitting at the kitchen table near the stove and eating a hearty breakfast. Rose was busily frying pork sausages and slices of bread; the flavour tempted me to make a pig of myself. I had already drunk a large cup of hot milk when she placed a plate with two sizzling sausages and some fried bread in front of me. I ate ravenously, as if I had not eaten for days, probably to make up for the cold and lack of sleep of the previous night. Rose filled my cup with hot milk again and again, and as she did so she asked me: 'Did you sleep well, Cosimo?'

'Oh yes,' I replied, 'but if Giovanni had not snored I'd have slept even better.'

Rose giggled. 'Did you hear, Giovanni, what Cosimo has said?'

Giovanni looked at me and then gave me a radiant smile; perhaps somebody else on a past occasion had already reproached him about his snoring.

After such a hearty breakfast, I was completely restored and had no hard feelings towards Giovanni; all was forgiven and forgotten! I was overflowing with energy now, and inclined to laugh and sing.

'Today is Saint Stephen's Day,' said Rose, 'you can stay here if you like, and go back to Bardo tomorrow.'

I would have liked to spend another day with them, but I dreaded having to sleep with Giovanni again.

'I would very much like to stay,' I said, 'but I promised the Costas, Biagio's parents, that I would dine with them today. Thank you just the same.'

70

Boxing Day with the Costas. A succulent cat

The Boltis regarded me almost as a member of their own family. They had rustic manners, but were sincere and meant well.

It was scarcely possible that Giovanni suspected that I resented his behaviour in bed. He was not infringing the law by snoring and breaking wind; this kind of behaviour was considered normal and tolerable in that unsophisticated environment.

Having thanked the Boltis on Boxing Day for their kind hospitality, I sauntered back to Bardo. It was a fine day; the sun was shining brightly in an azure sky covered with a few fleecy clouds and made the snow glisten like diamonds, which dazzled me. The canal alongside the cart-track flowed soothingly.

Martha and Celia, having to go to Mass at Codico's church, walked with me for some distance. The priest who said the Mass came from Rena and had just arrived. There were about half a dozen priests who lived in a monastery in Rena. They ran a primary school and also taught the first three forms in a secondary school. Having to rely on benefactors for their keep, they needed to strive hard to scrape a living. Since meat at that time was available only on the black market, they could not afford to buy it.

I was told that the Fathers had a ginger tom-cat and they fed him on vegetable soup, which was what they themselves ate. Of course, being a cat, he was able to vary his diet with some fresh meat when he caught a mouse, so he was well nourished, fat and complacent, and couldn't help looking at his owners with a sense of pity. They in turn seemed to envy him and were itching to teach him a lesson. Their desire for meat was so strong that it became an obsession. Any time they looked at their smug, fat and supercilious cat, they saw a roasted piglet, stuffed with a spicy, exquisite mixture, garnished with some delicious herbs and served with peas, young carrots, baked potatoes and onions. This caused their mouths to water. One day that very same devil who tempted Eve got the better of them, so they killed the cat and feasted on his carcass. Was the Lord pleased? Did He forgive them?

I dined with the Costas on Boxing Day. They invited some relatives to dinner, so we were quite a crowd. I was glad when dinner was over, for their Piedmontese dialect and never-ending trivial yapping got on my nerves. In the evening Biagio, his sisters and I went to a dance held in a barn, but the smell of cows, the poor music and that boisterous atmosphere did not interest me at all.

Irma, Biagio's second sister (about two years younger than me), had blonde hair parted in the middle and tied with a ribbon, grey eyes, an upturned nose, rosy cheeks and a fair complexion. She was a typical good-looking peasant girl with some sex appeal. She showed some interest in me, but our romance did not develop any further than furtive embraces and casual petting, which we both found stimulating. I honestly had no intention of getting married and hitching myself to her for life; my dream and hopes of building my future were not in Italy.

Although I loved my country, twenty-one years of the Fascist regime had done nothing but inflate us with vainglory, brought us humiliation, destruction and endless suffering. I was sick and tired of *Il Duce*, our King, our military leaders and other responsible people who in times of crisis blamed one another and left the population in deep trouble. What prospects did I have of making a living in my country, which had been laid waste? How could I and my countrymen get over our feeling of shame, humiliation and defeat? This was too much and couldn't easily be ignored and forgotten. A severe blow had been inflicted on our self-esteem and the image we had of ourselves as heirs of those legionary heroes who had fought and conquered.

71

*Very cold winter with heavy snowfalls. The starry
night sky entrances me*

In winter 1943–44 we had copious snowfalls and, because we were
near the Alps, the snow on the land usually melted only with the
coming of spring.

Since we didn't have much to do when it snowed heavily or was
extremely cold, we had to stay indoors, but not in our cosy kitchen;
that was a luxury that we could enjoy only at mealtimes. Besides,
we were not allowed to sit there while the women did the cooking.
Small farmers could not afford to heat every room of their houses
so their sources of warmth came mainly from their kitchen stoves.

To keep ourselves warm during our leisure hours, we had to sit
somewhere in the cowshed. Whether the cows liked our company
or not, it was hard to say; they did a lot of mooing and did not
hesitate to relieve themselves while we were there. Was this a kind
of protest? I found the stench appalling and almost unbearable, and
had to endure it without revealing my sense of discomfort.

It was customary for the women, during long winter evenings, to
sit in the cowshed, darning, knitting and gossiping till late. Often
our neighbours paid us a visit or just dropped in for a chat. If the
host was in a generous or friendly mood, he produced a few bottles
of wine, which helped to stimulate the conversation. In many
instances, those calling on us brought their own wine. Topics for
conversation were the latest events: German set-backs in Russia;
the landing of Anglo-American forces at Anzio; the Allied bombing
of Monte Cassino and Rome; Fascist raids, executions of hostages
and partisans; what the BBC and *The Voice of America* were
saying; and how much a calf would fetch on the black market.

Once or twice a week, after our evening meal, Biagio and I
visited our friends who were living in the neighbourhood. He lent

me a cloak, so we shuffled along through the snow to a farm beyond the crest of Bardo's hillocks. Our friends always welcomed us jubilantly. Later we and other visitors – no less than half a dozen of us – gathered in the host's cowshed or in his warm kitchen and whiled the evening away, eating *grissini*, salami, drinking Barbera and Nebioli wine, discussing the latest news and telling humorous stories to enliven our tedious wintry days. At about eleven o'clock, Biagio and I called it a day. We trudged along through the snow at that late hour – all was quiet there – but I could hear a whispering breeze and some occasional barking. From the hillocks round Bardo, I saw the countryside under the silvery moonlight and a brilliant canopy of stars. Frankly, all this amazed me; it possessed an awesome power only known to sensitive minds. Moon, planets and stars, in unison, sent forth a vibration that seemed to come from within our vast pulsating galaxy.

An eagle hovering above us might see, less than twenty kilometres away, the hills of the Tanaro river, where partisans lit bonfires at night to signal to Allied aircraft where to drop arms, ammunition, medical supplies and whatever else they could.

72

Germans and Fascists mount a night raid on Rena.
Biagio and I run away. Allied forces occupy Rome.
V-bombs fall on Britain

My *carabinieri* friends Mark and Dino told me of the growing
disturbances and discontent of some young men in Rena, where
boys, who were unemployed, were fed up with having to depend
on their parents. So a dozen or more of them joined the partisans
either for kicks or out of necessity, or because they thought that, by
doing so, they would eventually get some preference in finding jobs
after the war. They were not like the real partisans who operated in
the mountains, whose role was purely defensive, due to lack of
strength. Real partisans were ever ready for action and did what
they could to harass Germans and Fascists. They waited patiently
until their enemies had weakened, then they attacked and captured
or destroyed them.

Rena's partisans joined a detachment in the mountains around
Cuneo. When they were not under an attack, which often compelled
them to change position, they had food, wine, or perhaps even a
few bottles of brandy and other supplies either given to them or
dropped by Allied aircraft.

It is likely that Rena's partisans, having spent a few weeks in the
mountains, were not inclined to put up with that rough way of
living for too long. On the other hand the Allies did not seem to
be in a hurry to end the war, so it was hard to say how long the
partisans would have to stay in hiding. After a while, Rena's
partisans longed for their homes. They missed the contact with their
parents and friends, the hustle and bustle of Rena's market day and
Sunday morning town life. They decided to come back to Rena,
whenever they could, either for a short or long stay. If they brought
some money with them – presumably their partisan's pay, or money

they had come into possession of by fair or foul means – they were welcomed, especially if their parents were poor.

However, their comings and goings and their presence in the town, created an alarming atmosphere that worried both townsfolk and peasants; they feared that the Fascists might raid the district.

As a matter of fact, the Fascists did come round occasionally and search for partisans. During one of their raids, the Fascists bumped into a gang of partisans who were swaggering through Rena, and immediately shooting started. The partisans had to fight their way out to avoid being captured and executed. While they were exchanging fire, the partisans wounded one or two Fascists. Their comrades promptly retaliated by setting some houses ablaze.

One night in the spring of 1944, we were awakened by shouts, the crossfire of rifles and automatic weapons and the explosions of grenades. We rushed to our windows and noticed columns of smoke mounting in a crimson sky in the direction of Rena. We couldn't guess the scale of the attack and were afraid that the Fascists might extend their raid to our village. Biagio and I, who were disbanded soldiers, ran for our lives into the depth of the country, where we hoped that the Fascists wouldn't venture. Having covered some ten kilometres, we felt safe. We met half a dozen men our age, who were on the run too, so we tried to comfort each other.

At dawn the sun rose brightly in a cloudless sky. The trees were thick with new leaves and unripe fruit, and the fragrance of grass and flowers permeated the air. A farmer not far from us was already hard at work in a meadow. Every now and then he sharpened his scythe, gave a few swings at the grass, wiped the sweat from his brow and then swung again.

We sat down in a circle on a piece of land bordering a bushy ravine and talked about the night raid. We hoped to meet someone coming from that troubled area who might bring us some news about the latest developments.

While we were sitting there, one of our group told us that some men posing as partisans visited farmers and extracted foodstuffs and cattle from them, then sold whatever they had swindled from them on the black market.

The partisans had freed several criminals from jail because they needed men and assumed that they would fight in their ranks. Unfortunately a number of them, taking advantage of the lack of law and order, ganged together and engaged in illegal practices.

330

We also heard of a very sad happening: two men who were supposed to be partisans decided to pay a visit to some friends, an elderly couple with a daughter in her twenties, living in a small and isolated farm. They welcomed their unexpected visitors and gave them something to eat and a few drinks. After the meal, the guests attacked and killed their hosts in cold blood, then ransacked the place and set it on fire.

Farmers became criminals' targets at that time, for robbers were aware that they were making a lot of money on the black market and hiding it somewhere about their farms. Crime and murder in the part of Italy under German control were daily occurrences, and there was absolutely nobody who could stop them.

By noon we had been away from Bardo since 2.00 a.m. When we left we were in a state of panic and did not think to take food and money with us. Now we were about ten kilometres from Bardo and as hungry as wolves. I would have liked to have begged for a crust of bread, but Biagio was not complaining of being hungry, and this made me feel ashamed; ashamed of revealing my weakness.

I found an excuse to get away from our group squatting cross-legged on the grass; I wanted to have a look around to find something to eat. Luckily I discovered a kitchen garden in a secluded area, where I relieved the owner of a handful of small carrots which I gobbled up. About a few minutes later I rejoined my companions, without disclosing my pilfering.

While I was there, I noticed that one of our companions had caught some frogs which he had stoned to death while they were basking on the grass beside a canal. He had skinned them, had lit a fire and was grilling them. I was shocked and amused at the same time, and declined his invitation to participate in the subsequent repast.

In the late afternoon, we learned that the Fascists had departed from Rena. The population of the town were licking their wounds, getting over the shock and assessing the damage caused by the raid.

When people told us that the danger was over, we were greatly relieved, so Biagio and I started walking back home. We were hungry, our legs felt heavy and our sluggish muscles would not budge. Biagio noticed a heap of stones in front of us and said: 'I wish I was Jesus now, so I could turn those stones into loaves.'

We plodded along for almost three hours with great effort. As we came close to Bardo, we could imagine, almost smell, two plates of hot minestrone set in front of us. We were smacking our lips, devouring the food in anticipation and washing it down with a lot of wine.

The countryside was luxuriant and in full splendour under that warm spring sun, which gave me joy, but my joy was not complete and turned to sadness when I thought of my relatives in Southern Italy. How could they buy food if they had no money? And what had happened to my father and brothers in the island of Java, which had been occupied by the Japanese? Besides, I wasn't too sure of myself; there was always the possibility that I might be caught in one of those Fascist raids and killed.

Signor Costa's farm, just a few acres, produced mainly wheat, corn and grapes. Being spring, we were busy mowing meadows, sowing corn, pruning vines and doing other jobs, which kept us fully occupied. Biagio and his father, being the experts, did the mowing. I helped with the carting and storing of hay. Taking advantage of the irrigation system and the sunshine, farmers made hay three times a year: spring, summer and autumn.

The Allied forces at this stage had occupied Rome and had landed in Normandy. France was being liberated. Meanwhile the Germans had launched their first V-bombs (flying bombs) against Britain; these were the Germans' secret weapon and were supposed to give them the final victory. These bombs proved disappointing; they caused a certain amount of damage but did not worry the Allies too much, and were not helping Hitler and Mussolini to win the war. The dictators were doomed! Finished! On the Eastern front the fall of Sebastopol enabled the Russians to liberate Crimea and chase the beaten and disorganised Germans on all parts of the front.

73

The carabinieri *are in a precarious situation. Dino is shot dead and Victor replaces him. Their marshal is transferred and Albert takes over*

With so much happening in Rena and its vicinity, a startling and dramatic atmosphere had been created. This was due, above all, to the behaviour of some foolish partisans who swaggered around the town and its villages. They looked very fierce and impressive in their combat fatigues, with automatic rifles in their hands and grenades in their belts. If by chance they came up against German vehicles that happened to be in that area, a shoot-out would ensue. If a German soldier was killed, they retaliated at once by applying Draconian measures; that is executing ten Italian civilians for each fallen German.

The *carabinieri* were in a dilemma; they were between two adversaries – Germans and Fascists on one side and partisans on the other. If they pleased one side, they displeased the other. They had to be very careful not to commit themselves; they had to sit on the fence if they could, and stay there, for it was the only way for them to survive.

Mark was an easygoing *carabiniere*. He quite understood the precarious situation he and his colleagues had to face. He had no difficulty in adjusting himself to it. Dino was temperamental, too sensitive and impetuous, and had a tendency to over-react, to stick rigidly to his duty and to flaunt his authority. Mark often tried to restrain him – cool him down – in order to prevent a confrontation, which he and his companion in arms were supposed to avoid. Mark, however, was not always able to succeed in this, so one day while he and Dino were doing some investigations concerning a theft, one of the suspects swore at Dino – called him a parasite, opportunist and traitor serving the German cause. Dino lashed out and slapped the man on the face. This act was foolish indeed; that thug wouldn't be inclined to forgive him, and such an incident wasn't going to improve the *carabinieri*'s image with the public.

The marshal, the man in charge of the small quarters in Rena, in order to protect Dino from possible retaliation, acted promptly and had him transferred to other quarters far away from Rena. A month after his departure, while he was on duty in the new town, it seems that he got involved in another altercation. Probably as a result of the previous incident in Rena or maybe a new one, he was shot dead by a passing cyclist.

With Dino's death, Celia's dream of getting married and settling down in the beautiful countryside of Tuscany vanished. Malicious neighbours nicknamed Celia 'the widow' as if she had already been married to him.

Mark, Martha and Celia attended his funeral in Cuneo, where the *carabinieri*'s headquarters was located. Bills had been posted all over the town, saying that Dino had been treacherously attacked and killed by an outlaw, while carrying out his duty of maintaining law and order.

A military band, playing a lugubrious march, followed the hearse. Two small contingents, representing Fascists and Germans, were present at the funeral. At the end of the procession, a *carabiniere* captain delivered a speech praising Dino's qualities and the service he had rendered for his country, which was still at war. At the close of this address, the *carabinieri* paid their last respects to him by discharging their rifles in the air. His relatives had the coffin sent to their town and buried in the local cemetery.

After Dino's death, Mark visited the Boltis more often than ever; perhaps he feared that Martha, as a result of Dino's death and her sister's bereavement, would stop being his girlfriend. It would be too risky to be tied to a *carabiniere* who might get killed. However Martha, in spite of what had befallen her sister, did not break with Mark; she obviously was in love with him, the handsome man from Southern Italy, with the fire of Vesuvius bubbling in his veins, so she surrendered herself to the dictates of her heart.

When Dino was removed from Rena and transferred elsewhere, Victor succeeded him. Victor was in his twenties, well-built and as tall as Mark. He had black hair parted in the middle, dark eyes, a straight nose and a bronzed complexion. Being a professional *carabiniere*, Victor wore a navy blue uniform with silvery buttons.

He seemed to take good care of it; he obviously pressed his jacket and trousers frequently.

As Mark was an auxiliary *carabiniere*, he wore a grey-green uniform similar to that worn in the army. In appearance he did not look as smartly dressed as Victor, but the girls seemed to prefer him. This eventually made Victor jealous – he was puzzled, and couldn't understand the mentality of those girls; what did they see in Mark?

Victor was conscious of being from Northern Italy and a regular *carabiniere*, two reasons that caused him to feel secretly supercilious, so deep in his heart he regarded Mark as an inferior.

During the Fascist regime, anti-Fascists in Rena disliked the marshal of the *carabinieri* because he gave them the impression that he was a Fascist sympathiser and an admirer of *Il Duce*. Now the situation had changed: Mussolini had been kicked out of the Italian government, and with the help of the Germans he had become Hitler's puppet once again. If there were any Fascists who still supported him, or ventured to do so, sooner or later they would have no alternative but to succumb to the Allies.

The enemies of the marshal wanted to get rid of him, and he was aware of it. During July 1944, he and his family surreptitiously disappeared from Rena and nobody, except headquarters, knew where they went. Those who hated him welcomed the news of his departure jubilantly.

Since there was no other marshal available to send to Rena, his deputy, Brigadier Albert, replaced him. He came from Northern Italy, was slim, in his thirties and was almost six feet tall. He had greying hair with a left parting, and his wrinkled forehead suggested premature middle age. He had been in the *carabinieri* force about fifteen years, and had not completed his secondary school, but he was intelligent, willing and had initiative; qualities that enabled him to be promoted to brigadier before the Second World War. Soon after his promotion he married a girl named Clare.

During the war he was in a detachment of *carabinieri* near his home, but before the Italian armistice of 8 September 1943, he was transferred to Rena.

Albert was devoted to his work, but a few years after his marriage he felt the desire to widen his knowledge, so he started reading Plato and other Greek and Roman philosophers. He was passionately interested in Dante and Beatrice, and devoured all the books he could find about them.

335

As a result of his new interest, but having nobody at hand with whom he could share his passion for knowledge, he became an introvert and a dreamer. When he was not on duty, he indulged in contemplation; a sublime feeling would seize him and make his imagination wander through a heavenly realm of love, inspiration and perfection. Unfortunately, more pressing matters at hand, concerning human imperfections and frailty, would always break this enchanted spell and bring him back to earth.

74

Albert has a very attractive wife, Clare. Mark and
Victor fall in love with her

Clare, Albert's wife, was in her early thirties. She was an attractive
blonde, somewhat plump, a real come-hither girl and of average
height. Her well-brushed silky hair was parted in the middle and
cascaded over her shoulders. She had thin eyebrows, starry eyes, a
small snub nose and an oval face with rosy cheeks.

Was dreamy Albert, wrapped up in his philosophical and fanciful
world, paying enough attention to his charming wife? He had
known Clare since she was a little girl. They were from the same
village, had grown up together and were almost like brother and
sister. Albert had accustomed himself to watching her grow into
adult womanhood.

Men who set their eyes on Clare found her desirable, very
ravishing; a dish fit for a king.

Someone who knew the couple very well had told me that their
marriage had not been motivated so much by physical attraction as
by their mutual affection, a desire to live together and fuse into
one.

As a married man, Albert was lucky indeed; Clare was utterly
devoted to him. He was her husband and her lord to be served and
cherished. He didn't have the slightest doubt of her fidelity; she
was the typical wife of that period, whose body and soul belonged
entirely to her husband.

The new interests that Albert had developed, although an
emotional experience for him, created a gulf between him and his
wife, who was not in the least attracted by them. Though his new-
found intellectual pursuits caused him to neglect his sexual life, this
did not matter to him.

Clare was just a comely village girl who could read and write but had no great ambition. She wanted to be desired, loved, be a good housewife and have children. She did not wish to learn more than was necessary. It was unfortunate, that they, for one reason or other, found themselves unable to have children. Because of this, she concentrated all her attention on her husband and spoiled him. What did she get in return? Not much of an affectionate response.

Albert was always working, or wrapped up in his engrossing hobby, so his communication with his wife was limited to domestic problems and other strictly necessary things. This situation was compounded by the fact that her mental capacity didn't approach his. He was a completely changed man since their marriage; his intellectual bent seemed to have seriously interfered with his virility.

Clare had many admirers, but it seemed that the thought of being unfaithful to her husband or of wishing to separate from him on account of his lack of intimate responses never crossed her mind. Of course, now that the war was still on, she and Albert, like most people, had enough troubles in meeting the contingencies of everyday life.

Owing to the chaotic atmosphere and to the precarious circumstances of the *carabinieri* after 8 September 1943, Albert could not go home on leave regularly. With so many Germans, Fascists and partisans buzzing about in Clare's vicinity, she no longer felt safe in her own home, so she went to stay with Albert's mother, tucked away from the troublesome areas.

Soon after Albert took over the command in Rena, which consisted of two *carabinieri* and himself, he expected to be promoted to marshal. Why not? He was capable and experienced, so he deserved it. As commandant, he was entitled to married quarters, so he moved into his predecessor's flat. The cook, an elderly woman, fearing that the quarters might come under the partisans' fire, found an excuse for terminating her employment.

Towards the end of July or early August 1944, Clare arrived in Rena and was warmly welcomed by her husband, and by Mark and Victor. For such an important occasion, Mark made a Neapolitan pizza with fresh tomatoes, basil, oregano, garlic and olive oil. The smell of it permeated through the quarters and beyond, so nosy passers-by wondered: 'What are the *carabinieri* up to? Fancy having a banquet when so many people are struggling to get a crust of bread, and others are being burgled or murdered every day!'

Making a pizza was one of the two things in which Mark excelled: the other was making love. Whether he was a better pizza maker or lover, only an intimate lady friend could tell!

Once all the fuss of greeting, welcoming and celebrating was over, Clare soon settled down and started making a few alterations to make her flat look homely. It contained a spacious kitchen which could also be used as the dining-room, and since Albert, for one reason or another, did not employ a new cook, Clare decided that she would cook for her husband and Mark and Victor as well. At mealtimes they would eat together, as if they were a small family. Albert did not object to such an arrangement; with his passion for philosophy, he always seemed to be remote from the real world, so he let his wife take some of the decisions.

Mark and Victor helped with the washing-up and other menial tasks that Clare required. This arrangement was fine; Mark and Victor were greatly overjoyed at having a young and attractive woman doing their cooking – and what an excellent cook she was! They had always had an old cranky, grumbling woman in the kitchen, who wouldn't hesitate to nag them, but now that Clare, with her radiant smile, was there, this surely made a difference – mealtime for them was a really happy time and the main event of the day. They enjoyed the food, drank a couple of glasses of wine and cracked a few jokes, which made Clare laugh, so the table atmosphere was good-humoured and lively. Albert, being detached, did not completely enjoy the mirth of the conviviality.

Clare, a simple village girl at heart, loved Mark and Victor's easygoing ways and, above all, their pranks. At times the attention they paid to her seemed a little extravagant, but this did not worry her; on the contrary she cherished it. What else could she do in Rena? She did not know anybody there, the war was on and local people were not in the mood for social events. Mark and Victor were so far the only friends she had, and if they got too excited about her sex appeal, they could – and usually did when they were randy – work off their superfluous energies by visiting the whorehouse in Cuneo.

Albert, the dreamer, did not interfere with his wife's jollity. She was doing her chores and enlivening the atmosphere of the quarters, and Mark and Victor were discharging their duties scrupulously, so everything was fine, and would no doubt help him to get his long-awaited promotion.

339

Prior to Clare's arrival in Rena, Mark and Victor found their life in the quarters extremely boring; they preferred to be on patrol, where they met people, chatted up peasant girls and were in no hurry to return to their quarters. Now that Clare was there, they finished their patrolling hastily and, attracted by her magnetism, they bicycled like two madmen towards Rena. They yearned to be near her, hear her voice and laughter, and make violent love to her, even if it was only in their lustful thoughts.

The peasants, having noticed the sudden change in Mark and Victor's behaviour, were startled. 'What's the matter with the two boys; why are they in a hurry?' they wondered. Even Martha was a little bewildered about Mark, who was paying her less attention.

75

Bulgaria and Romania surrender. The Germans are in retreat on all fronts. Mark is besotted with Clare

By the end of August and the beginning of September 1944, the war went from bad to worse for the Germans. On the Eastern front Romania and Bulgaria surrendered to the Russians. On the Eastern front the Allies freed Paris and proceeded to liberate the rest of France, Belgium, Holland and Luxembourg. On the Southern front they reached Florence.

Although the Germans had unleashed the secret V1 and V2 weapons on Britain, these had had no significant effect on the outcome of the war.

The partisans, supported by the Allies, were getting bolder every day. They came down from the mountains and attacked the Fascists, who at this stage were extremely worried. Many of them, to save their skins at the last moment, defected to the partisans. Several *carabinieri* deserted their force; they either joined the partisans or went into hiding and waited for the war to end. Because of the dwindling number of *carabinieri*, Albert was busier than ever; there were so many pressing duties in store for him, which he had to discharge as best he could.

These tasks often compelled him to get away from Rena for a whole day, but he liked doing this kind of work; he felt like Sherlock Holmes. The inconvenience was that, when he was not at home, the population of Rena and its surrounding villages had to rely for protection on Mark and Victor who, in spite of their uniform, had no authority whatsoever. They were just two good-natured fellows, whose main aims in life were good food and sex.

Whenever Mark and Victor were left in charge of the quarters, patrolling either had to be curtailed or could not be done at all. Because of this and Clare's captivating charm, Mark did not visit the Boltis as often as he had done. Martha was puzzled, but he was always able to justify himself.

The newly created military situation in Europe indicated that the war would soon come to a conclusion. Mark was worried, pensive and couldn't make up his mind on whether to desert the *carabinieri* or to stay on. Clare seemed to have hypnotised him; he was finding it extremely hard to break away from her bewitching sexuality. He told me that she fancied him, how seductive she was, and of their secret mutual flirtation. Now he was just waiting for a chance to ravish her.

I saw Mark once or twice a week. In the evenings we frequently walked from Bardo to the Boltis' farm. He and I were more than close friends, almost brothers, so he confided in me all his private thoughts, without restraint. We both came from the Naples district, but were forced to stay in Northern Italy by the vicissitudes of war. We shared the same feeling of being tempest-tossed by unfortunate circumstances that compelled us to live temporarily in an environment we did not particularly enjoy. However, our Piedmontese friends meant well; we really could not complain, when we compared our quality of living with the appalling difficulties that many young men were having in other theatres of war.

Mark was completely ruled by his sexual desire; he would never miss an opportunity. Governed by this urge, he was ever ready to seek gratification when, where and however he could find it, without weighing up the consequences. He was too open and spontaneous, so whenever he had an affair, he could not keep it to himself. His Casanova-like vanity compelled him to brag about it, to talk too much; he wanted to be known as a seducer – a man irresistible to women. Of course, he ran no risks in telling me about his intimacies; my lips were sealed. I reproached him several times; told him that I wasn't pleased with his easygoing ways, asked him to be careful not to get mixed up in the lives of other people, let alone the intimate life of his superior. It would be too risky; he would be playing with fire. However, I was wasting my time; he never took my criticism seriously, but carried on unperturbed in his usual, self-indulgent ways.

That summer of 1944, the Costas had a plentiful harvest of excellent crops. By the end of September the wheat had already

342

been gathered in and stored, and we were under the hot sun harvesting the maize. In the evenings, after our meals, the Costa family, some of our neighbours and I sat down cross-legged in the farmyard and stripped the cobs. This activity, after a long day's work, was considered a kind of recreation or pastime, but I disliked it. I would have preferred to sit down comfortably and rest, and perhaps listen to the radio.

While we were busily stripping the cobs, my companions sang their usual Piedmontese songs to enliven the atmosphere, which bored me to death. We never went to bed before eleven, then we had to get up at six and start another day of slavery. Not being accustomed to such prolonged and back-breaking toil, my body protested; I was always tired out and had a nagging backache which I stoically endured.

I certainly earned my keep, but I think that I was considered a passenger; they had taken me under their roof just to oblige, but could have done without me. I quite understood my predicament, so when they offered me some pocket money, I declined; I told them that I did not need it for the time being. I still had a few lire that I had saved during the previous years.

Besides this, since I had been on Biagio's farm, I had earned a little money by giving some maths lessons during my spare time. As I used to be very good at maths, I set myself up as a self-appointed teacher and helped some boys with their algebra and geometry. I did not really exact a fee; I offered my help as cheaply as possible.

My romance with Irma, the second sister of Biagio, went on as usual, petting and kissing by stealth. These frolicsome spells somehow helped to alleviate my monotony.

The news that the Allies had captured Florence cheered me up; I thought that within the following month they would have liberated Piedmont, thus enabling me to go home and spend the coming Christmas with my relatives in Naples, assuming that they had been spared from the ravages of the war.

Unfortunately the Allied forces had once again been pinned down by the stubborn fanatic Germans at the 'Gothic line', which the Germans had formed across our peninsula north of Florence. I was disappointed that the war was still dragging on and on; perhaps the Germans thought that they still had a glimmer of hope of winning, in spite of their set-backs and tremendous losses?

343

76

*Mark tells me about his romantic progress with Clare.
Later they have an affair*

We were making wine in early October 1944 when Mark called on
me.

'*Ciao*, Cosimo,' he shouted exuberantly and with a mischievous
glint in his dark eyes. 'I'm making progress you know!'

'Making progress?' I said in bewilderment. 'Doing what?'

'With my hanky-panky; Clare and me, you know...'

'You bloody sex maniac, have you nothing else better to do,
instead of enticing a poor married woman to break her marriage
vow? Oh boy! Oh boy! You are looking for trouble, aren't you?' I
said in a matey way. 'Adultery is a deadly sin, you know.'

'You goody-goody, you sound like the parish priest of my town,'
Mark said smiling. 'And now listen, you just listen to what I have
to say. When Clare needs firewood for our kitchen stove, she
always asks me to chop some. Of course, I am only too willing to
oblige her, but I never chop too much of it, so she'll have to ask
me again and again, and this will give me the chance to see her
and get closer to her. If Albert is away when I take the firewood
into the kitchen, she offers me either a glass of wine or a cup of
coffee, if she has any. While I sip my drink, I tell her one or two
stories that have a sexual connotation. She enjoys them.

'Last week I mentioned the *commarelle* (ladies of easy virtue) to
her. She was a little puzzled; she couldn't make out what I was
saying, so I tried to be more specific, and when she understood she
exploded in a burst of frantic laughter. I told her that I used to visit
the *commarelle* regularly, but I had not been able to do so lately,
because I couldn't get a day's leave, and also because travelling
had become too risky. If I rode to Fossano and then travelled to
Cuneo, there was the possibility that I could get involved in a

shoot-out between Fascists and partisans. Since I had not been able to visit the *commarelle*, it was now as if I was starving to death.

' "How can that be, Mark?" said Clare. "You have many girlfriends, haven't you?"

' "Oh yes, I have, but there is nothing doing without marriage."

' "Poor, poor Mark," she said teasingly.

'Suddenly there was a knock at the front entrance of the building, so our conversation came to an abrupt end. What I have gathered is that she is willing and this gives me hope. I think that she is as willing as I am; all I need now is the right moment to set our passion on fire. My word, she has so much to give. What a waste! What a waste! Poor Albert! He is so absorbed in his work and study that he has absolutely neglected her. All work and no play makes Jack a dull boy. I can't get over it; is he impotent? How can he ignore the presence of such an attractive wife? I certainly feel sorry for her and will not hesitate to help her, to make her feel like a woman, a woman wanted, possessed and the object of someone's desire and affection.

'If I had to give up women, it would be the end of my life. I think Clare and I have something in common; we both love sex, and if she cannot have it, she's deprived of something very important to her.'

'I entirely agree with you,' I said, 'but I'm afraid that sex for you is rather an obsession. Sex is primarily an animal urge, but for human beings it is much more significant than that. Sex is a very powerful form of energy; an energy that we ought to use for something noble, worthwhile and constructive. You oughtn't to expend this precious energy on your lecherous pursuits. And I don't think that Albert is impotent; he seems to me to be an ambitious chap. He loves learning and wants to get on. Having developed an addiction for learning, he finds that gratifying. In other words, his intellectual interest is so strong that it has weakened his carnal desire.

'If I were you, I wouldn't be too sure of myself. You must watch your step, don't tread on somebody's toes, you might regret it and have to pay dearly for it. And if Clare or some other married woman turns you on, take a cold shower, it will help to cool you off and be rational. Always see what you are doing; look before you leap, else a fall might be fatal. You cannot pick and choose any woman who excites you, that's out of the question. We all have emotion and instinct. They are fine if we learn how to tame them. If we don't, we are at their mercy; they will drive us silly and destroy us.

'If a coachman cannot control his horses and lets them go their own way, it is likely that the coach will end up in a ditch or ravine, killing coachman and passengers.'

Did Mark take notice of my sermon? How could he! Young and full of the joys of spring, he believed in fixed and unalterable values that remained with him as long as he lived. Can the leopard change his spots?

When Mark left me after I reproached him, he must have wondered about my austerity and muttered, 'Cosimo must be a nut, I am not going to listen to his suggestions of taming my emotion and instinct. If I did, I would be like a monk; perhaps I should make a vow of chastity. *Il Duce* said: "It's better to live one day as a lion than a hundred years as a lamb." This motto suits me. And if *Il Duce* is not doing well at this very moment, well, it isn't my business, is it?

'Self-denial is not for me. I love sex, I love to live for the moment, to enjoy myself as much as I can, and then whatever will be will be. If I have the chance to make love to Clare, I will take it. And if it gets me in trouble, I will save myself by deserting the *carabinieri*.'

Next time I saw Mark, it was the middle of October. He had cycled to Bardo and was extremely excited.

'Cosimo! Cosimo!' he shouted. 'I have done it, done it.'

'Done what?' I exclaimed, pretending that I hadn't understood him.

'Clare and I, you know, have been having it off together.'

'You must be joking!'

'Honestly, it's true,' he said. 'It happened yesterday. Her husband went to a meeting at Fossano, which lasted the whole day. Victor had a day off; he had been invited to dinner by his uncle living at Trinita, so Clare and I were on our own. I was in my room reading comics and gloating over some nudes in an old magazine, when I heard Clare calling: "Mark! Mark! Are you there?"

'Of course I was there, and she knew it. I had to be there; I couldn't leave the quarters unattended, could I?

346

' "Would you mind coming into the kitchen at once, please, there is something wrong with the stove."

'I put aside the pornography that I was leafing through and had made me randy, and dashed to the kitchen. However, excited as I was, her request sounded to me like an invitation to sex – my heart was beating fast. The kitchen was a little smoky, but Clare was wearing a closely clinging dark gown and a blue jumper, showing her curves remarkably well. The blonde hair cascading over her shoulders made her look so ravishing that I was thrown into a turmoil. I forgot about her request; my burning desire flung me into a chaos of emotions. I felt as if the lava of Vesuvius was boiling in my veins.

'Without much ado, I seized her and covered her with my hot kisses. She did not resist my assault and returned my kisses just as fiercely and passionately as I had given to her, and later she yielded completely to me. We lay tightly embraced on the kitchen floor, abandoned in ecstatic murmurs. We remained there quite a while, until desire had thoroughly been sated, but I was insatiable, reluctant to release her from my grasp.

'However, she was afraid of an unexpected visitor, so we got up, she combed her hair, tidied her clothes and made a strong cup of coffee. I quickly fixed the faulty stove, which had a slightly dislocated pipe. Later we sat down, sipped the coffee and ate a few cookies.

'Clare felt a sense of guilt for having been intimate with me.

' "Albert is a good man," she said, "but he treats me as if I were his sister. When we are in bed, he says that he is too tired and so he goes to sleep. I badly wanted a child; we tried, but unfortunately without success. Perhaps, after the war, I might find a good doctor who can help me.

' "I beg you, Mark, to keep absolutely quiet about our affair, or else we'll both get into serious trouble." '

'Well, Mark,' I said, 'what you have done cannot be undone, but now, please, keep your trap shut. If Albert finds out, you never know how he will react. When I was in the army, I learned that one of our lieutenant-colonels caught his batman making love to his wife and shot him dead. Because it was a question of honour, the lieutenant-colonel wasn't penalised.

'If I were you, Mark, to be safe I would run away, join the partisans, or go into hiding somewhere till the end of the war. The

347

way things are going for the Germans and Fascists now, sooner or later they will have to surrender, and so the war will be over. I wouldn't be surprised if the war ended tomorrow, next week or next month.'

77

The romance doesn't last. The carabinieri *have to move
to Saliano. Victor deserts and Luigi replaces him.
Albert seems unaware of his wife's infidelity*

The affair between Mark and Clare did not last long; they must
have made love three or four times in all. As Mark was incapable
of keeping a secret and was boastful into the bargain, he let Victor
guess that something was afoot; Victor smelled a rat. He himself
fancied Clare, but Mark had pipped him at the post, so Victor
regretfully was the loser.

Victor secretly disliked Mark because he came from Southern
Italy, and women found him *simpatico* (handsome). Later, when
Victor was certain that Mark and Clare were lovers, he was
enraged, mad with jealousy, and could not accept the fact that Mark
had beaten him. He was itching for revenge, bent on giving Mark
a lesson by spoiling his romantic adventure.

Victor and Albert came from Piedmont, so Victor considered
Mark an intruder, almost a foreigner, and because he hated Mark,
he felt inclined to show some solidarity with Albert. He must have
approached him tactfully and dropped a few hints about his wife's
liaison. The affair came to an abrupt end and caused a certain
amount of distress to both the lovers.

This incident occurred at a time when Albert received orders to
shut down Rena's quarters and move to another locality. Because of
these simultaneous events, it was impossible to perceive Albert's
immediate reaction concerning his wife's disloyalty and entanglement
with one of his subordinates.

At the beginning of November 1944, Albert, Mark and Victor
moved to Saliano, a small town about fourteen kilometres from
Rena. The new residence consisted of a four-bedroom flat on the
second floor of an old building. It did not prove suitable as married

349

quarters for Albert and his wife, so Clare had to go back home, to live with Albert's mother, where she had been staying before she went to Rena.

Perhaps Victor felt uneasy at having informed Albert. Because of this and other personal reasons, he deserted the *carabinieri* and joined the partisans; it would enable him, at the end of the war, to rejoin the *carabinieri* and continue his career.

As Albert did not show any ill-feeling, Mark's anxiety lessened, so for the time being he put off his idea of running away. It was a case of wait and see; he would reconsider towards the end of the year.

Saliano had a small railway station about two kilometres from the centre of the town, which linked it with Cuneo and Turin. Most of the travellers, being black marketeers, carried large heavy suitcases.

Mark had a new colleague who had replaced Victor; his name was Luigi (Lewis). He was also an auxiliary *carabiniere* and from Southern Italy. Luigi was a little shorter than Mark. He had black hair combed from front to back, bushy eyebrows, a peasant face and was stockily built.

The war wasn't going well for the Germans and the Fascists; their attacks on the partisans had relented. The partisans, aware of their enemies' weakness, were getting the upper hand. At this stage there was a strong partisan influence in Saliano. A considerable number of townsfolk, having nothing better to do, were engaged in the black market and prospered.

The *carabinieri*, insufficient in number, could not keep things under control; they too had to make a living, so whenever they confiscated some foodstuffs they would turn it to their advantage. A black marketeer was not prepared to pay a fine to retrieve the confiscated merchandise, so the carabinieri kept it for their own use and ate comparatively well at the black marketeers' expense.

The new place in which Albert and his two subordinates lived was a hovel in comparison with their previous residence. It was an old building that they shared with the owner, an inn-keeper occupying the ground floor. He did not interfere or set foot inside the building, so the *carabinieri* were practically on their own. The front door, which admitted one person at a time, was left open during the day.

Inside the building was a spacious courtyard with two flights of wooden stairs climbing to the first and second floors, a few trees and a little undergrowth, surrounded by a rectangular dilapidated wall about two metres high.

The *carabinieri* had to buy and prepare their own food, for they could not get domestic help; nobody was seeking such employment. A would-be employee was aware that the *carabinieri* were in an equivocal position and, therefore, exposed to the danger of being attacked.

Mark and Luigi did their best to stay away from trouble spots and keep a low profile. They cycled or walked to Saliano railway station every day and met the arriving trains. If they noticed any suspicious travellers, they inspected their luggage. On the whole, they were not too harsh and brisk with black marketeers or anybody else. They often turned a blind eye and let quite a few traffickers get away – after all, how could people survive when work was hard to get?

Carabinieri and traffickers played their own games; there seemed to be a sort of tacit agreement between those who were supposed to represent the law and its transgressors. Since the traffickers weren't seriously harassed, they had no grudge against Mark and Luigi; they even regarded them as friendly.

Now that the *carabinieri* had settled down in Saliano, I did not see much of Mark. He cycled to Bardo and Codico, between fifteen and sixteen kilometres, when he was able to do so. Martha, his girlfriend, was not very pleased with this new arrangement, but it wasn't Mark's fault for having been transferred to Saliano.

The Costas, the people with whom I was staying, kindly lent me one of their bicycles, so I was able to visit Mark twice during 1944. On both occasions Albert was away conferring with his superiors on some urgent matters.

During my visits Mark fed me well with the foodstuffs he had confiscated at the station. He also called my attention to a heap of sand under a shaded terrace inside the building, which was about eight metres from their flat. Under that heap lay a couple of sub-machine-guns and some ammunition, which the partisans must have left somewhere. The *carabinieri* had taken them away and hidden them, because if the partisans had paid them a visit and noticed the weapons, they would have seized them.

At the end of each visit Mark gave me a small parcel containing ham, salami, bacon and other delicacies.

351

Since travelling in uniform was too hazardous, whenever Mark cycled to Bardo he wore civilian clothes. After his arrival, he and I walked to the Boltis who warmly welcomed us.

During one of our meetings, Mark said: 'I haven't heard of Clare since she went back home. I cannot forget her; I never had the chance to make love to such a beautiful woman before. What a splendid creature! She is a goddess – the best love affair I ever had. I miss her badly. I'm sorry for Albert, but she was worth taking the risk for. Now I am besotted with her; no other woman seems to be capable of turning me on. I must make the effort to free myself from this enchantment, from her influence, and be able to make love once again, before my rifle gets rusty. Sooner or later I may need to pay a visit to the *commarelle* in Cuneo.'

'You sex maniac,' I said, 'you and your bloody rifle. It'd be better if you had it cut off and became a eunuch. Haven't you anything better to say and do? At this very moment you may be in a mess without realising it. Be careful – keep an eye on Albert, the man you have wronged; pay attention to what he says and does; he may be plotting some kind of revenge.'

'What I've noticed lately,' Mark said, 'is that he doesn't like staying at Saliano, so he seems to be unhappy. It's hard to say whether his unhappiness is due to the fact that he has to stay at Saliano or to his wife's infidelity. So far he hasn't shown any resentment towards me; I have the impression that he either doesn't know or is pretending to ignore it. When we aren't talking about our duties, he seems gloomy and remote, and passes the time in the office, probably reading his books. We don't do much in Saliano; not that there isn't much to do. The way things are now with Fascists, partisans, criminals, anarchists and so on, it is complete chaos; therefore the less we do the better, if we want to save our skins.

'Our main duty is to be at Saliano station when a train arrives. We really don't bother too much, so we go there three or four times a day, just to put in an appearance. Besides, we don't like to interfere too much with the livelihood of the people; they have to make a living somehow, don't they?'

'Do you feel that you have settled down? Is there anything that is really troubling you?' I asked Mark.

'Yes and no,' he replied.

'Well, make up your mind, boy, the end of the war is near, we will soon be able to go home!'

'I think I'll stay at Saliano for the time being and see how things are,' said Mark wistfully. 'I really haven't much to complain about, I have a roof over my head, good food, plenty of wine and even real coffee. Of course, my salary isn't much, but it will do for the time being. I am a little worried about Albert; he seems a mystery to me. One never knows what is in his mind, and because of this, I'd be safer if I ran away.'

'If a doubt is haunting you, do not hesitate,' I said, 'quit tomorrow. What do you expect? You have grievously offended him, and his spirit may be raging to settle a score. Hurry up! Join the partisans! You might even get a medal and perhaps a good job for having supported them.'

Mark listened attentively to what I said, then he mused for a while and spoke: 'Yes, you're right, it'd be better for me and Albert if I went away. I'll take the decision shortly. And when I go, I'll let you and Martha know where I am going to stay.'

'That's fine, and contact me as soon as you can.

78

Rena's partisans ransack its silo

The local partisans stayed at home most of the time and acted with a certain restraint as long as the *carabinieri* resided in Rena; but now that the *carabinieri* had moved to Saliano, the partisans swaggered freely through Rena and its villages as though they were the new authority.

Before the armistice on 8 September 1943, as I mentioned earlier, food was rationed and farmers were under an obligation to give an annual quota of wheat and other crops to their municipalities. The municipalities stored the produce in silos. However, after September 1943, with the German occupation of North Italy, farmers stopped delivering their quotas, so the food rationing system broke down, and there was no authority that could force the farmers to continue to fulfil their obligations. The situation became chaotic and, as a result, food could only be bought on the black market.

Rena's municipal silo had remained untouched since September 1943. It contained thousands of tons of wheat, even while many townsfolk were on the verge of starvation.

A few days after the *carabinieri* moved to Saliano, the partisans broke into the silo and let the townsfolk help themselves; everyone was entitled to about 200 pounds of wheat. This was a blessing, especially for the poor, who unanimously acclaimed the partisans' action. They had plenty to eat now while their provisions lasted.

The partisans' decision to ransack the silo had been motivated not so much by brotherly love towards needy townsfolk, as by the gain they could net by such an exploit. They had loaded lorries with several sacks of wheat, which were presumably supposed to supply a detachment of partisans in the mountains, who were the real fighters for the liberation of Italy. These didn't get any wheat at all; it ended up on the black market, and the proceeds came in handy to line Rena partisans' pockets.

The days after the ransacking of the silo were happy ones for the partisans; they proudly swaggered through Rena and its villages, and were hailed as heroes by those who had benefited from their share of wheat. They certainly expected to be praised, and loved to wallow in vainglory. Now that they had made a packet, they indulged in idle talk and made *ribotta* (caroused). They passed the time feasting to their hearts' content while the money lasted, and were utterly oblivious to the fate of their comrades in the mountains, who at that very moment were fighting and dying for their country.

79

The partisans shoot Fred dead

There was an old and rather corpulent man in Rena called Fred (Federico). He was in his sixties, had grey hair, a wrinkled forehead, brown eyes and a florid complexion. He was greatly concerned about the presence of the partisans in the town. He was suspicious that these young men were not real partisans, but just a group of loafers looking for kicks and up to no good. Any time Fred met them, he remonstrated, criticised and even scolded them:

'If you're partisans, you shouldn't be here; you should be fighting side by side with your comrades deployed in the mountains. Being in this small town, you'll certainly make our life more miserable than it already is. We don't want you here! Stay away from us! Else Fascists or Germans will be chasing you all over the town and villages. We don't want to have our houses burned down, or be taken hostage. The sooner you go, the better.'

The partisans resented Fred's reproaches. They hated him and wouldn't have hesitated to do him in. They tried to stop him from blackening their reputation, by accusing him of being a Fascist and an informer for the Germans.

Towards the end of November 1944, a combined detachment of Fascists and Germans raided Rena once again. They were looking for partisans, but these luckily ran away in the nick of time. The raiders took hostages, assembled them in the main square and threatened to execute ten of them for every Fascist or German killed in action.

The partisans, being few in number, did not venture to attack, so in the afternoon, the raiders freed the hostages and returned to their base. Townsfolk, fearing the worst, were badly shaken and not pleased at all to see the partisans reappearing in the town.

Fred was indignant, and angrily confronted them, just to give them a piece of his mind.

'Listen, boys, why do we have to suffer and run risks on account of your irresponsible behaviour, which is causing us more harm than good; it is a discredit to the real partisans' name and movement.'

Having noticed that they were no longer welcome in Rena and its villages, the partisans were furious. Fred continued to rebuke them again and again that very day soon after the raid:

'See what you are doing, we are always agitated, we have lost our peace of mind. It's all very well for you to stir trouble and run away, leaving us in the lurch. We have had enough. Go wherever you want to go, but leave us alone!'

The partisans' leader, a man of quick temper and questionable reputation, was foaming with rage and could no longer tolerate Fred's reprimands and affronts.

'You bloody old fool, dirty Fascist and cursed spy!' he yelled hysterically as he drew his revolver, 'I'll shut your bloody malicious trap once and for all!'

Having said that, he fired twice and hit Fred in the chest. Fred staggered and collapsed. He lay still on the pavement in the square in front of the church, while blood trickled from his deadly wounds.

A team of partisans was present at the scene, and each of them in turn extracted his revolver and fired once at the corpse. This ceremonial procedure was meant to be a kind of execution.

When people heard firearm explosions, they were startled, bewildered and asked passers-by:

'What's going on? What is the shooting for?'

'The partisans have shot Fred!'

'What did you say?'

'The partisans have shot Fred dead!'

'Shot Fred! Shot Fred! *Mammamia!* What for?'

'We don't know!'

Several people rushed to the scene and clustered round the dead man. They crossed themselves, and with a sense of pity and incredulity stared at the poor man. Some had tears in their eyes, and knelt down and prayed. Most of them were perplexed; they just couldn't understand why friendly old Fred deserved such a death. He had been the heart of the town; the living personification of the town itself, an old man who sincerely cared for everybody's health and well-being, and the townsfolk would badly miss him.

Fred was a great gossip, ever ready for a chat and a lark. At least ninety per cent of the population did not buy a newspaper, but Fred was a reliable source of information on whatever went on in the town and its villages. Everybody was just too eager to hear what he had to tell, and he knew quite a few jokes, which he would crack on the spur of the moment to cheer and entertain his listeners. Now that he was dead they mourned a truly dear friend; life in Rena would never be the same again.

Fred's funeral was fixed for a couple of days after his death. Most of the townspeople, and quite a number of peasants and villagers, attended the service. The spacious parish church was packed; a large crowd, unable to get in, gathered in the square outside the church.

The parish priest delivered a vehement but solemn sermon in which he stressed repeatedly that Fred was a good-natured man who wouldn't hurt a fly and did not deserve such a violent death. He would have said much more; he would have torn Fred's murderers to shreds but, alas, he had to restrain himself from accusing and inciting people against the villains, for he loved life too much, so it was wise not to speak his mind and put his own skin at risk.

A long procession followed the hearse to the cemetery, and people mourned Fred for several days.

With Fred's murder, the partisans had gone too far in disgracing themselves. In fact, they hadn't got rid of Fred's influence at all, because now, as a dead man, he seemed to be more of a menace to them than when he was alive. People now looked on the partisans with a sense of shame, disgust and cowardice. They had not a single sympathiser left, so the day before the funeral, they surreptitiously crept out of the town. Fred's spirit was victorious; it had succeeded in stirring resentment in his people, which made the partisans feel uneasy and compelled them to leave.

80

Nina and Olivia, two saintly old spinsters

Nina had middle-class Roman Catholic parents. Her father worked in a small branch of a Cuneo bank. Her brother, two years older than her, became a priest and later a bishop, and her younger sister married a Cuneo lawyer.

Nina had had a secondary education. When she was in her twenties, she looked forward to getting married and having children, but was unlikely to find an eligible bachelor. Most young men in Rena preferred to marry peasants or village girls who had a dowry, girls with little education or perhaps no education at all, easy to handle and dominate.

Her parents died in their sixties. She and her sister inherited the house in which their parents had lived. Nina, left to fend for herself, and advised by her brother-in-law, embarked on a general hardware business.

When Fred died, Nina was an old spinster over ninety and the oldest person in Rena. She and Fred, born and bred there, were the living personification of the town; the salt of the earth.

Nina was skinny and sinewy, about five feet and seven inches tall, had grey hair combed back into a bun, grey eyes and a long face. She wore a dark, loose dress that hung like a sack on her square shoulders.

Winter or summer, she got up at five o'clock knelt beside her bed and prayed. As soon as she heard the church bell, she hurried to the six o'clock Mass, prayed fervently, and when the priest placed the Holy Communion on the tip of her tongue, she was ecstatic; she had received the Lord into her heart, the source of her dynamic personality and happiness.

After Mass she knelt for a while in front of statues of the Madonna, Saint Francis and other saints, where her lips quivered continually as she begged for their mercy, love and protection. Later, thoroughly gratified, she walked back home evidently with her heart full of Divine joy and ready to face another day, a day dealing with her earthy and matter-of-fact customers, very much interested in tangible things.

She lived in the old two-storey ancestral home, which contained three bedrooms and a large parlour equipped with solid, shiny walnut furniture. However, she spent the daytime on the ground floor, the front of which had been converted into the shop, with a kitchen at the rear.

Nina was well known for being deeply religious and for her honesty; people were only too pleased to do business with her.

When she returned from the Mass, she breakfasted on white coffee (ersatz made from roasted barley) and *grissini*, and by eight o'clock she stood, quite erect with her straight spine, behind the counter serving customers.

She worked long hours, darting from shelf to shelf, and drawer to drawer, almost as agile as a squirrel, looking for screws, nails, padlocks, pots and so on. She never showed any sign of the fatigue, bad temper or infirmity usually associated with old age. She managed her business efficiently, did not overcharge and lived thriftily. If something went wrong – a glass, cup or plate was broken, or there happened to be some other mishap, or she had to deal with an awkward, grumbling customer – she had the knack of minimising the mishap and putting the customer at ease.

'Don't worry,' she would say, 'it doesn't matter, it's an accident,' or, 'Take this, and if you aren't satisfied, I'll give you your money back.'

No adversity or set-back could ruffle her, and she had the ability to change a negative attitude into a positive one.

Nina had a live-in domestic called Olivia who also assisted in the shop. She regarded her as an adopted daughter. Olivia came from a poor family, living in a small town about eight or ten kilometres from Rena. When she was about seventeen she was glad to get away from home and start helping Nina, with whom she could at least get decent accommodation and a square meal.

When I met Nina for the first time, Olivia was in her thirties and a confirmed spinster. She was homely, had black hair combed back into a bun, brown eyes, rosy cheeks and a florid complexion. Her cheerful countenance was due to Nina's influence. Nina had to teach her from scratch – how to pray vehemently, be good-tempered, cook, do the cleaning, washing and mending; how to assist in the shop with a smile on her lips and be thankful to the Lord for her daily bread. Apart from the difference in age, the two women were like peas in a pod; they were both energetic, happy souls, and quite willing to share their happiness with all whom they met.

Having experienced the bliss derived from being a virgin like the Madonna, Olivia was completely fulfilled in her faith, and seemed to desire no more.

Had she married a man as poor as she was, she wouldn't have expected much from marriage, except untold hardship and a condemnation to slavery. Nina had been her salvation; a source of her new-found happiness which Olivia treasured so much and had painstakingly achieved. She would not be so foolish as to throw it away for the sake of a lousy marriage.

Nina and Olivia were absolutely devastated when they heard that Fred had been shot dead. They missed him very much now. He used to drop in for a natter almost every afternoon, when they weren't too busy. He was terrific, never ran short of news, and had kept Nina and Olivia well informed on whatever went on in the town and villages and about the war.

There was nothing but goodness in the two spinsters; it emanated from them and could be felt by all who came in touch with them. They basked in the light of the Lord; and by being attuned to Him, they lived in a self-made heaven on earth.

81

Mark is murdered; I strongly suspect Albert

Christmas 1944 was near. Early on a December evening, after supper, Biagio, two of our respective friends and I were sitting at the kitchen table, listening to the news, drinking a glass of wine and trying to organise a little party similar to that which we had had the previous Christmas Eve. And why not, especially now that the end of the war seemed imminent?

Signora Costa, Biagio's mother, was fattening a capon for our sumptuous Christmas Day dinner. And what a beautiful and dignified bird he was with his vermilion wattle and blue, reddish and tawny plumage! He had a very imposing posture indeed, and looked like a general inspecting his troops deployed for a battle. He had been castrated, deprived of his masculine urge and of the right to have heirs and father countless chicks. Now the day was near when he would be subject to the indignity of having his throat slashed to enable us to feast on his flesh.

While we were still in the kitchen busily chatting, Bill, Biagio's dog, started barking at an intruder. Biagio went to the door and saw Martha dismounting from her bicycle.

'Hello Martha! What brings you here?' shouted Biagio. 'Come in, come in.'

'Is Cosimo here?' asked Martha.

'Yes, he's here. Come in, do come in and shut the door, it's very cold today.'

'How are you, Martha?' I said cordially.

I noticed that she was puffing; she had probably been riding too fast. I also noticed a strange look in her eyes. Being too absorbed in her thoughts, she did not return my greeting.

'Cosimo! Cosimo! I've got bad news!' said Martha frantically.

'What did you say? Bad news? What is the matter?'

362

'Yes, yes, I have bad news about Mark! Mark has been shot!'

'Mark has been shot? Why, what happened?'

'Mark has been shot dead and taken to Cuneo's hospital. He was shot late last night at their quarters' courtyard, as he and Luigi returned from patrol. Luigi was wounded in the legs; nothing serious.'

I was dumbfounded, transfixed, thrown into a turmoil – I could not take in what Martha had just said. It was a tremendous shock, a real blow, and I couldn't get over it. Martha was terribly sad, mournful, so we tried to comfort each other; I had lost a close friend and she her fiance; the man she loved and was likely to marry.

Having recovered for the time being from the shock, she told me: 'I have just received the bad news from my sister Elena.'

Elena, a few years older than Martha, lived in Rena. She had married a businessman who dealt in poultry. He bought chickens that peasants sold to him on market day. He employed three or four women who killed the chickens, then plucked, gutted and refrigerated them. Every day he drove his van to nearby towns and delivered his merchandise to shops, hotels and restaurants. During one of his deliveries to a restaurant in the vicinity of Saliano, he had learned of the shooting in which Mark had been killed.

'Where is he now? What shall we do?' I asked Martha dejectedly. 'I want to go to Saliano and find out exactly what happened. He is my close friend and as he is from the same district as me, when I am able to go back home, I shall pay a visit to his people and tell them how he died.'

'If you go to Saliano, I'll come with you,' offered Martha.

'Well, if it is all right with you, do come, but I need a bicycle.'

'Don't worry, Cosimo, you can use mine,' offered Biagio kindly.

At about nine o'clock the following day, Martha and I started our journey to Saliano. It was not a very cold morning, and it was pleasant to cycle along the asphalted road in the midst of fields and meadows. The air was balmy – full of late autumnal fragrance. The only traffic we met were people riding on bicycles. Martha and I, absorbed in mutual sorrow, did not say much, but were eager to get to Saliano as quickly as we could.

We arrived there at about eleven o'clock. Albert, in charge of the quarters, appeared to be in a state of distress. He welcomed us and ushered us into his office, which consisted of a small room, with a desk, an old typewriter, a telephone, two filing cabinets, a shelf with two or three dozen books and four rickety chairs. A pungent musty smell, indicating decay, permeated the whole place.

Albert offered us a cup of real coffee and then sat at his desk. We were seated on two chairs facing him.

'On Monday night,' he said gravely (two nights before our visit there), 'Mark and Luigi went as usual on duty to Saliano railway station. They always come back home at about eleven o'clock, have a hot drink and then go to bed. Last Monday night, however, I was waiting for their return. Suddenly I heard the blast of an automatic rifle within this building, which startled and frightened me. I seized my revolver and cautiously rushed downstairs. My God! I was horrified to find Mark and Luigi lying on the ground. Mark had taken a full blast in the chest and died instantly. Luigi had been hit in the legs and was moaning. I immediately rang up our command, which sent along an ambulance. The two men were taken to Cuneo hospital, where Luigi is recovering. Mark's body is in the hospital's morgue. Shortly it will be taken to our barracks in Fossano, where friends and colleagues will be able to pay their last respects. The funeral has been arranged for this coming Friday.'

'Who shot them? And what for?' Martha and I asked simultaneously.

'We don't know yet. Probably black marketeers who don't like our presence here,' replied Albert hesitantly.

'How did the shooting happen?'

'Well, the firing came from the backyard wall opposite the entrance. Mark and Luigi entered the courtyard, and as they came forward, they were blasted off their feet. It appears as if Mark had been singled out – he was the real target. Whoever fired seemed to have a grudge against him and intended to kill him and spare his comrade, so Luigi got away with just leg wounds. Investigation is proceeding, but nowadays, with this chaotic situation, the chance of catching the culprit will be very slim indeed.'

We took our leave of Albert and later had lunch at a small restaurant. Its owner told us that the whole town was dismayed and mystified by the death of Mark, whom they called 'The handsome Neapolitan *carabiniere*'.

'Could they have been partisans who did him in?' asked Martha.

'I don't think so,' replied the restaurateur, 'the partisans are not interested in harming or killing *carabinieri* who mind their own business.'

After lunch Martha and I cycled to Saliano railway station and had a chat with the stationmaster. He knew Mark and Luigi very well. He too was amazed at the shooting and sorry for Mark's death.

'As far as I know,' he said, 'the *carabinieri* were two good boys, they never quarrelled with anyone. Occasionally they confiscated a little food, but on the whole they turned a blind eye and let black marketeers get on with their business.

We thanked the stationmaster for his information and, as it was getting late, we jumped on our bicycles and began the journey back home.

Martha seemed remote, wrapped up in her thoughts – for her romance had ended in tragedy. It was exactly what had happened to her sister Celia, whose boyfriend had been murdered five or six months earlier in very similar circumstances. Was this mere coincidence, a curse or just bad luck?

I too was rapt in my thoughts as I pondered over Albert's account of Mark's death, which made me suspicious. Who would have killed such a friendly fellow? Only someone who had a grudge against him and badly wanted to settle an old score such as a question of honour. Immediately my suspicions fell on Albert.

I knew about the love affair between Mark and Clare but had kept it to myself. Martha hadn't the faintest idea about it.

I tried to construe Albert's reaction and the following developments that culminated in Mark's death. When Albert found out that Clare had been unfaithful to him, he naturally was deeply hurt, but being a self-made educated chap, he could control and conceal his feelings. Evidently his heart was crying out for revenge to punish the man who had grievously offended him, and he was just waiting for an opportunity to get his own back.

So on that fateful Monday evening, after supper, Mark and Luigi as usual sauntered to Saliano railway station to discharge their duty. While they were away, Albert, taking precautions not to leave his fingerprints, may have dug out one of the automatic rifles hidden under the heap of sand outside the quarters, which I have mentioned before. He could have cleaned and loaded the rifle, and later gone downstairs and set it up in a shooting position behind a bushy spot at the back of the courtyard.

At about the appointed hour, when Mark and Luigi were likely to return from duty, Albert might have posted himself behind the rifle and waited; and as Mark and Luigi entered the courtyard he fired at them, making sure however to spare Luigi's life. Then he could have thrown the weapon over the adjacent wall, drawn out his own revolver and rushed to the scene, where the two men lay. Albert then rang up his superiors, who sent along an ambulance, which rushed the victims to Cuneo hospital.

After Mark's murder, there was a perfunctory investigation. The detective found the weapon and spent cartridges, and that was all. What else could they do? The country was in turmoil, murders were committed every day, and the scanty police force – almost non-existent – could not cope with the situation. Mark's murder and many others were soon brushed aside and forgotten.

My suspicion of Albert was so strong that I was considering taking legal action and putting him on trial – but how could I prove that he was Mark's murderer? Besides, I would need to hire a good lawyer, and a lot of money would be required to do that.

I really was sick and tired of everything. I desired nothing else but to go home as soon as the war was over, so I did not want to stir up trouble over Mark's murder. I had enough worries of my own about my people in South Italy and overseas and feared that, if something dreadful had happened to them during the war, I would not see them again.

On the Friday after Mark's death, Martha, Celia and I cycled a few kilometres to the *carabinieri* barracks in Fossano, where the funeral was taking place. Mark, dressed in his uniform, lay in an open coffin. He seemed to be smiling in his eternal rest, and this made me wonder; what caused him to smile while he breathed his last?

Martha, Celia and I stood a few minutes by the coffin and prayed. Several wreaths and garlands were lined up near the wall beside the coffin and the wall in the barracks' courtyard.

Albert was present, and so were a number of Mark's companions and the representatives of various authorities, paying their last respects to our beloved Mark. There was also a group of Fascists and another of Germans.

The funeral procession started at 2.00 p.m. We and all who had gathered there followed the hearse on the way to Fossano's cemetery to the sound of lugubrious marches played by a military band. When the mournful procession reached the cemetery, a *carabiniere* officer made a speech, praising Mark's loyalty and service and condemning the treacherous outlaws who had murdered him. At the end of the speech, about a half-dozen *carabinieri* stood to attention and paid their last respects to Mark by firing their rifles in the air.

As soon as the funeral ceremony was over, Martha, Celia and I returned to the *carabinieri*'s barracks, fetched our parked bicycles and rode back home.

A few days after Mark's funeral, I visited the Boltis. Martha was still in a state of bereavement and so were her parents, for they loved Mark and considered him a member of their family. They also pitied me for having lost a dear friend. I dined with them, and later Martha placed on the table in front of me some banknotes that were Mark's savings, and a wrist-watch that he had given her.

'Please, Cosimo, take these to the commandant of the *carabinieri* at the barracks in Fossano,' she said in an emotional voice.

'Why,' I said, 'this is not necessary. You can keep the watch and his savings as you have done so far; they are safer in your hands.'

She ignored my suggestion; she wanted to forget about him. Had she kept the watch and his savings, they would have reminded her of him and of his tragic end.

To comply with Martha's wish, I cycled again to Fossano's *carabinieri* barracks, where I had an interview with a Neapolitan lieutenant; he was a man of my district and I felt at ease with him. I handed Mark's money and wrist-watch over to him, and he made a note of it. I also confided in him about my suspicion concerning Mark's murder.

'What a strange story,' he commented. 'Unfortunately, because of the war and *carabinieri* shortage, I can do nothing about it. We cannot accuse and arrest anybody without a thorough investigation. I'll bear this in mind and give some attention to it in due course. I will eventually get in touch with you, but I advise you to keep quiet about it, else you might get into serious trouble.'

82

Christmas, and the end of the war seems imminent

Mark's recent death made quite an impact on me, so I wasn't in the mood to celebrate the 1944 Christmas festivities. I spent them quietly, partly with the Costas and partly with the Boltis. In a way we were elated, hopeful that the war would come to a conclusion, but my elation ended in sadness when I thought of poor Mark buried in Fossano cemetery, about 800 kilometres from his beloved Naples, never able to see his relatives again.

On the other hand, I couldn't just sit down and grieve all the time; all the grieving and sorrow in the world wouldn't bring Mark back to life, so when Biagio invited me to go out with him, I made an effort and joined him. We met our regular friends and, with the end of the war in sight, we saluted New Year's Day 1945 with a little celebration.

However, my heart wasn't entirely there, and nostalgia seized me. I was melancholy for having wasted the best years of my youth, and doing what? Being in the army and having to put up with endless bad news, whilst our country was being thrashed, humiliated and defeated. Whatever had happened to me was making me now feel old, in agony, disillusioned and depressed. What stopped me from being utterly overwhelmed by the effect of war was a faint hope that after it I would see better days – be born again.

I visited the Boltis regularly, and fairly often we talked about our beloved Mark, as if he were still with us. At the same time we were following the events of the war. The partisans were intensifying their activities; they were boldly coming out of their hiding places and harassing Fascists and Germans. During one of their raids, they had occupied Fossano's *carabinieri* barracks. As a result I lost contact with the Neapolitan lieutenant to whom I had delivered

Mark's money and wrist-watch. He had probably defected to the partisans. I also lost contact with Albert now that Saliano was virtually in the partisans' hands.

Hundreds of American bombers, like migrating birds, blasted whatever was left of our crippled Fiat industry. The Russian Army was advancing persistently, and so were the Allied forces from the Western front, and what was left of the great German Army (*Wehrmacht*) was being squeezed between the Allied and Russian Armies. On the Italian front the Allied forces had broken through the 'Gothic line' and reached La Spezia on the Ligurian Sea, and Ravenna on the Adriatic Sea. Having pushed as far as that, the Allied forces had to slow down because of the mountainous terrain.

83

A number of Rena's partisans are captured and executed

In November 1944, Rena's partisans, having murdered Fred and made a nuisance of themselves, fled the town and presumably rejoined their detachment in the mountains near Cuneo. They were supposed to stay put there, but seemed unable to do so and wandered from place to place.

One day in January 1945, the Fascists suddenly combed an area and trapped and captured nine of Rena's partisans. They executed seven of them and buried them on the spot. Two of them, for one reason or another, were spared the immediate execution and thrown in jail, to await execution later, or to be exchanged for Fascist prisoners held by partisans.

In view of these tragic developments, Rena's townsfolk had reason to believe in the supernatural; they maintained that the spirit of beloved Fred was taking revenge against those who had murdered him. Had the partisans stayed out with their fighting unit in the mountains, instead of stirring trouble in Rena they would really have served a noble cause and had the chance to save their skins. They were restless, wanted to please themselves, and so unthinkingly they took unnecessary risks. As part of the armed forces of free Italy, people expected them to behave decently, and not like selfish and irresponsible chaps.

The executed partisans had been buried in a common grave, and it was too risky to try to exhume them and give them a proper burial in Rena.

A requiem Mass was celebrated in Rena's church, during which the parish priest stressed from the pulpit: 'Seven of our young men are with the Lord, away from this world of toil, strife and endless misery caused by sinful men. We are all mourning them. They died prematurely because many men on earth haven't yet learned how to live peacefully, in harmonious coexistence, and to please the Lord. Let us pray for the bereaved parents, and may the Lord always bless and comfort them, Amen.'

When the Mass was over, one of the remnants of Rena's partisans made a speech on the square outside the church.

'Our partisans have not died in vain,' he shouted, 'but for a noble cause. They have sacrificed their lives for the liberation of our fatherland.'

I heard some townsfolk and villagers arguing and disagreeing among themselves with what the speaker had just said.

'Sacrificed! Sacrificed!' they muttered. 'They were humbug! A pain in the neck! Thank God for getting rid of them! The speaker has made heroes out of them, they were lazybones and up to no good. Let us hope that we'll at last enjoy a little tranquillity; days free from fear and anxiety. If there are no partisans here, we will have no Fascists or Germans raiding our town, will we?'

The Fascists regarded the partisans as traitors so, when they captured them, they either executed them on the spot or later in retaliation, or swapped them for Fascists whom the Partisans had taken prisoner.

The two Rena partisans that the Fascists had jailed were sons of prosperous farmers – the Italian landed gentry. When their parents learned that their sons were in jail, they enlisted the help of the parish priest and the town's authorities. These visited the prisoners and tried to bargain to get them released. Luckily they found a Fascist officer with an itchy palm interested in the deal. What was the good of being too exacting, vindictive and arrogant when the Fascists, at this stage, knew that they were going to lose the war? Having received a bag full of money, the officer concerned contrived to let the two prisoners escape.

The end of the war seemed very close. Fascists and Germans had quite a lot to worry about if they wanted to save their lives. They barely had any men, weapons or ammunition left for their defence, so they stopped raiding cities and towns.

Many young men of Rena and its villages, who till now had been in hiding or had kept a low profile, came forward claiming to be partisans. With this qualification, they hoped that, after the war, they would be able to find jobs in the civil service, post office, state railways and so on. The new, self-appointed partisans formed

371

squads. To demonstrate that they were truly members of the active patriotic movement, full of fighting spirit and capable of doing something worthwhile for the liberation of Italy, they set out to demolish old bridges that connected Rena to its villages. There was nothing heroic in destroying them, for most of the people who used them were peasants. Now they had to suffer the inconvenience of a detour, or try to get across to the other side the best they could. Apart from the hardship and annoyance that the peasants had to endure, there was no justification for such demolition, especially at this stage when Germans and Fascists were on the verge of surrender. A lot of money would certainly be needed to rebuild them; money that Rena's municipality did not possess.

84

Francis, a disbanded soldier, is murdered

Ferment, unrest, crime and violence were features of everyday life. Robbers and unscrupulous people, taking advantage of the situation, ran wild and pleased themselves, and who was going to stop them?

There was a disbanded soldier whose name was Francesco (Francis). He was in his twenties, of average build, had fair hair parted on the left, blue eyes and a fair complexion. Unable to go back home to his beloved Venice, which was firmly in German and Fascist hands, he stayed away and, like myself, went into hiding. He found accommodation at signor Nicola Cortese's farmhouse.

Signor Cortese owned a very small farm – just a few acres of good land. He had a wife and an only daughter, in her early twenties, whose name was Lucia. Wife and daughter did domestic chores, fed the chickens, collected newly laid eggs, milked their four cows, made the butter and helped on the land during the busy seasons. Since they seldom bought clothes, there was always a lot of mending to be done. This they did mainly during the long wintry evenings in their warm stable in the company of the cows.

Francis was a first-class shoemaker, able to make one pair of boots a day. As the farmers were making lots of money from the black market, most of them could afford to have boots made to measure. Francis took new orders every week but could not cope with demand; this meant that every customer had to wait about three months before his boots were ready.

Francis lived in a fairly spacious single room of the farmhouse, where he worked and slept. He had his meals with signor Cortese and family. Every morning he was awakened by the farmyard rooster. He got up early and stoked his stove in wintertime. Afterwards he drank a cup of strong black coffee with a few drops of brandy in it, rolled himself a cigarette, sat at his bench and eagerly started his long day's work. He happily cut, hammered and stitched the leather, while he was listening to his radio that kept him company and informed about the course of the war. He never ran short of tobacco, coffee or a good bottle of wine. Although he had a few drops of brandy in his coffee, he managed to stay sober while he worked. Before he knocked off, he looked at the pair of boots he had just finished with a sense of pride and complacency and thought of the money he would get for them. He was adding more banknotes daily to his accumulated savings, which he had hidden somewhere. After the war, God willing, he had the intention of setting up a shop in his beloved Venice, a thing he had always wanted to do.

Francis went to Rena two or three times a week to meet his customers and to buy whatever he needed for his trade. The basic materials such as leather and skin came from Bra, Fossano or Cuneo. At the end of his errands, he stopped at the local coffee-house for one or two drinks, but he felt so comfortable and relaxed while he was there that he lost count of them.

Towards nine, a little tipsy and with his torch in hand, he plodded his way back home, which was about two kilometres from Rena. He always took a short cut across a dilapidated footbridge that connected the banks of a narrow stream. He staggered along, often in pitch darkness during moonless nights, through a thick bushy area, before he reached the cart track with meadows and fields on either side. The dogs barked, hardly anybody stirred; perhaps most of the peasants were in their stables, chatting animatedly, while their women patched pants and darned socks. He always arrived home very late, dropped on his straw mattress and slept like a log.

By March 1945, Francis had been living with signor Cortese almost a year and a half and had saved a good deal of money. What was he going to do at the end of the war – marry Lucia and take her to his home in Venice? And why not, after all she had been more than a girlfriend to him.

Lucia, two years younger than Francis, was plump and blonde with long hair parted in the middle and falling over her shoulders. She had blue eyes, an oval face and a fair complexion. Although she had been born and brought up on the farm, having seen some movies at Rena's cinema, she wanted to get away from the cows, the barking dogs and the long, toiling summer days and live in a

374

large town. She loved the hustle and bustle of the city, the glamour of fashionable shop windows, market stalls, visiting cinemas and meeting lots of people. She would have her chance to achieve this if she married Francis. Good shoemakers usually did very well in large towns, and Francis could even become rich.

With this thought in mind, Lucia tried to please him. Whenever she had some spare time, she dropped into his workshop, kept him company and drank a cup of his coffee. She had sex appeal, which excited him, and with a kiss today, a touch tomorrow, in the end he succeeded in seducing her.

But as the weeks and months rolled by, she could discern that he regarded her just as a transitory romance, going nowhere. Now that the end of the war was imminent, Francis would leave her and go away as if nothing had happened between them. Signor Cortese was not a fool; he could sense what was going on and was not pleased with Francis's behaviour and indifference. He expected Francis to marry his daughter. By using his cunning and power of detection, he had a fair idea of where Francis kept his heap of banknotes and, if he decided to leave the farm without marrying Lucia, signor Cortese would not let him get away scot-free.

One day in March 1945, Francis went as usual on his errand to Rena. Afterwards he stopped at the coffee-house for a few drinks and stayed there until late. After that, he left and embarked on his two-kilometre journey back home. As he staggered along he stumbled. Every now and then he stopped, had a sip of brandy from a small bottle he carried in his coat pocket and then resumed his unsteady walk. He crossed the narrow wobbly footbridge that connected Rena to the countryside, but he did not go much further, and the following morning he was missing.

Towards midday, someone found him lying in the ditch of a bushy area beyond the footbridge with a fractured skull. The local doctor said that Francis had died between ten and midnight the previous day. He had been repeatedly hit on the head with a blunt object, probably a club or a stone and, as his wallet, which contained several banknotes, was missing, the motive for his murder was assumed to be robbery. News of the murder spread rapidly all over Rena and the surrounding villages. It was said that the murderer, knowing that Francis always carried a lot of money on him, had followed him and, having reached an isolated area, clubbed him to death and robbed him.

Many people were deeply disturbed; most of them knew Francis, he had made their boots, and they were perplexed.

'Who could have killed him?' they wondered. 'A poor disbanded soldier, far away from his home, who apparently had no enemies.'

The funeral service was arranged a few days after the murder and was attended by a considerable number of people. Signor Cortese, his wife and daughter were present at the service and acted for Francis's relatives who lived in Venice. They could not be informed, because after 8 September 1943 (Italian Armistice), they had lost contact with him and did not know where he was, or what had happened to him.

There was little attempt to make an investigation – considering the situation, with murders being committed every day, this would have been utterly impossible. Even after the war, owing to lack of evidence, Francis's murder remained unsolved.

Eventually, a few months after the end of the war, his relatives came and took his remains away to be buried in their local cemetery. They also took possession of his few belongings, but there was no money; his hidden savings had disappeared. Signor Cortese told them that Francis probably kept all his money on him or elsewhere.

85

*The partisans' uprising. Mussolini is captured and
executed. The war in Europe is over*

April 1945 was the month in which the Italian war came to a
conclusion. It had begun about five years earlier, when Mussolini
flamboyantly declared war on France and Great Britain. By the end
of April 1945, the Allied forces fighting in Italy had occupied
Genoa, Modane, Reggio Emilia, Bologna, Milan and had reached
the River Po.

General Raffaele Cadorna, Commander-in-Chief of the Italian
Army, collaborating with the Allies, sent out radio messages
ordering the Italian resistance to rise up against the Fascists and
Germans.

Mussolini could not escape his fate. He knew that his end was
near and lacked the courage to commit suicide. On 27 April 1945,
he attempted to flee to Switzerland and save his skin, but he was
intercepted and captured by the partisans. At this time his mistress,
Claretta Petacci, was staying, or hiding herself, in a room in the
Town Hall of Dongo, not far from the place where Mussolini had
been seized. One of the partisan leaders, Count Bellini, found out
where Claretta was and, as soon as she learned that Mussolini had
been taken, she begged Count Bellini to allow her to stay with him.

'Please! Please! Where is he now?' she implored with tears
welling in her eyes. 'Please! Please! For goodness' sake take me to
him! I love him! He is my life! I want to die together with him!'

'Do calm down, signora, don't get upset,' said Count Bellini, 'I
assure you that I have no intention of shooting him, but I have to
hand him over to the authorities.'

Mussolini and his mistress spent their last night in a farmhouse
near a town called Bonzonico. The following day Colonel Valerio,
who had always hated the Fascists, drove him and his mistress a

few kilometres away with the pretext of rescuing him. He stopped the car at the gate of a villa called Belmonte and ordered the couple to get out. Soon after that, as he levelled his machine-gun at Mussolini, his mistress tried to shield him by stepping between him and the barrel of the gun.

'No! No! Don't shoot *Il Duce!*' she protested hysterically.

'*Signora, si tolga di mezzo,*' (Lady, get out of the way), shouted the colonel who wanted to spare her.

'No! No! Don't shoot! If you shoot, you have to shoot me first.'

The colonel, being under pressure, could not afford to stand on ceremony, so he fired on both of them.

The corpses were taken to Milan and were shamefully hanged upside down for public display. The strutting dictator had come to an ignominious end.

On 29 April 1945, the German Army fighting in Italy surrendered, and by the beginning of May the war in Europe ended.

We all saluted the end of the war jubilantly. We were at last able to travel without fear of being harassed or molested by the Fascists or the Germans.

It was true that the war was over, but its cost had been very high and the visible and invisible scars were there, especially in the hearts of those who had been severely hit. Our army had been defeated, our morale shattered, people were unemployed and on the verge of starvation, sickness was rampant and our nation was on its knees, insulted and spat at. Some foreigners maintained that we weren't good soldiers, but we were indeed during the Great War, when we had adequate weapons to fight back at our enemies and were allied with the wealthy Americans. Then we had plenty to eat, our morale was high and we were confident of winning. Napoleon said: '*L'argent fait la guerre*' (money makes the war).

I was particularly dejected; my spirit had been crushed during five years of war, five long years of frustration, disillusionment and misery.

When I was a boy I had been indoctrinated at school with the belief that we Italians were invincible. When we were at war I was extremely shocked to learn that we were taking blow after blow instead of inflicting them; so where was our invincibility?

The war had ended, but I could not easily shake off the sad experience of my military service and emotional turmoil. It was an indelible experience that would remain with me for the rest of my

378

life. Although I was only twenty-five, I really felt ten years older, and this made me wonder – would I be able to find that zest for living that I had during the years before the war? I feared that those easygoing years of my early youth had gone for ever.

Now I had to put up with the stark reality of the present: a shattered Italy moaning and licking its wounds, our ruined economy and political chaos. With these afflictions in mind, although the war was over, I had no cause to be joyful and celebrate. I very much wanted to cry, but I couldn't. My heart was no longer tender and adolescent, it was full of rage and resentment – it had become a heart of stone. Had I cried, it would have done me a lot of good; it would have helped me to get rid of some of my bottled up emotions. My mind was full of tormenting thoughts that haunted me day and night. The situation was so hopeless and discouraging; it would take years of toil, hardship, deprivation and perseverance before our country would get back to normal.

Besides all this I was very worried about my relatives. I did not know whether my mother, sisters, and youngest brother in Naples, and my father and brothers in Java, were still alive; if they had perished during the war, I would have been left kinless and forlorn.

PART SIX

RETURNING HOME

86

It is time for me to go home. After a long, dangerous journey I arrive in Naples. My starving relatives have just survived

Rena's partisans, or what was left of them, returned home triumphant, draped in tricolour, as if they had single-handedly won the war.

Many young men, appearing to come from nowhere and having heard that the Fascists and Germans had surrendered, joined the partisans at the last moment, when the danger was over. They armed themselves with automatic rifles, which the captured Fascists had laid down, and swaggered through villages. These impostors and fakes, who a few days earlier had been hiding somewhere, wanted to impress and make us believe that they were among those men who had fought gallantly for the liberation of our country. Now that no Fascists or Germans were around, they pretended to patrol the countryside, searching for imaginary enemies, but all they could find there were a few barking dogs and cows happily pasturing in sunny meadows. They were mere opportunists, fooling around and hoping to get some recognition and preference in seeking jobs in the foreseeable future.

Those Rena partisans who had been executed by the Fascists during the war and buried in makeshift graves were eventually exhumed and brought to Rena. They were called by their surviving comrades 'Martyrs of the Resistance', given a solemn funeral and interred in Rena's cemetery. I heard someone muttering: 'Martyrs of Resistance, my foot! They were martyrs of their own foolishness, weren't they?'

Finally all the celebrations connected with the end of the war were over. It was time that Rena's life returned to normal – the quiet uneventful life of a small rural town as it had been before the war, when stray dogs slumbered undisturbed in the main square.

Unemployed people now left Rena and sought jobs in large towns. Undergraduates who were doing their last year and unable to complete their tertiary education on account of the war were treated generously and enabled to get their degrees.

The disbanded soldiers who had been staying with farmers and villagers were on their way home. The population of Rena and its surroundings had somewhat decreased; this was especially noticeable on market days and Sundays.

It was now time for me to bid farewell to my friends and acquaintances and embark on the wearisome journey to Naples, to look for my relatives with whom I had lost contact in September 1943. I wanted to go home, but I did not have the faintest idea how to get there, for the railway track had been bombed and badly damaged. There were a few trains in service, but they were used by Allied forces. Of course, there was the possibility of catching a train, but one had to wait a long, long time.

The trains went as far as they could, given the destroyed bridges, and if someone had to travel a certain distance, they did not know when they would arrive at their destination.

At last the day came for me to say goodbye to my dearest friends. I thanked them for helping me during the time I had spent at Bardo. I bid farewell to the Costas, the Boltis, a couple of my girlfriends and to all those I knew. Before I left I had a good look at the surrounding countryside, the hillocks of Bardo and the distant hills of the Tanaro river. My separation from these people and places was painful; part of me was there, and I discovered that I had an affection for what I was leaving behind, so I had to make an effort to tear myself away. I promised my friends that I would keep in touch with them, and if I decided to emigrate, I would pay them a visit before I went abroad.

I travelled by coach to Bra, the town where I was doing my military service and where my friends signor and signora Raballo lived. While I was there for a few days, I tried to gather some information on whether there was any chance of travelling to South Italy. I also met a couple of my ex-comrades-in-arms. I learned that there were trains from Turin to Liguria. From there I could continue my journey by hitchhiking on one or two lorries going to Rome, and then complete my journey to Naples by train.

I also learned that most shops in the South were empty, with nothing to sell because they couldn't get enough supplies from the North. Since I had some savings, amounting to a few thousand lire, I bought clothing material that I could easily sell at the end of my journey and make a hundred per cent profit. This would somehow enable me to help my relatives, who had been starving during the war.

Signor Raballo introduced me to three men who had to go to Liguria. Since I had to make the same journey, I joined them. Having said goodbye to signor Raballo and his family, I and my newly found companions travelled to Turin, where we had to wait a few hours before catching a train bound for Liguria. The train was packed, so we had to force our way in, and as I was carrying two heavy suitcases, it was a strenuous task; I had to do a certain amount of begging and shouting in order to get into the carriage.

Travelling in those conditions was very trying indeed – almost an impossibility. When the train pulled out of the station it proceeded at the pace of a snail and stopped frequently; every stop could last about half an hour or longer. This kind of travelling was so tedious – a heart-breaking task.

Along the route I noticed destroyed buildings showing the wounds of war; the decorated walls of what was left of a bedroom, dining-room and so on. Places that once had been happy homes filled with excited children were now just heaps of rubble, desolation and death – pitiful monuments to misery, reflecting the evil that wicked political people can cause.

My travelling companions refreshed themselves with wine, which was a kind of nourishment to them; I drank mineral water. We could buy sandwiches and drinks from station vendors.

The train took a whole day to cover about 200 kilometres. Having arrived at the northern bank of a destroyed bridge, it could not proceed any further. We got off and, carrying our luggage, we plodded along through ruins, then crossed a wooden makeshift bridge and reached the southern bank; but there wasn't a train waiting, and the chance of catching one was very slim. At this stage it was everybody for himself. I had to leave my travelling companions who had almost reached their destination.

It was almost midnight, I was alone, hungry and thirsty, and stumbling along a poorly lit deserted road, flanked by mournful war ruins. It all looked so eerie there; I could feel the palpable vibration of those who had been killed and maimed by the bombing. The anguished cries seemed to be all around me; perhaps parts of dismembered bodies were still buried there.

My vision and imagination of that desolate place gave me the creeps. Suddenly I saw someone. Where did he come from? Was he the ghost of one of those who had perished under those ruins? I was terrified; my heart was racing and I was on the point of leaving my luggage in the middle of the road and running away.

He stopped a few metres from me and lit a cigarette. 'Well,' I said to myself, 'if he were a ghost he wouldn't have a smoke, would he?' I plucked up courage, and as he came closer to me I asked him a few questions. He was a middle-aged man on his way home. He told me that in the morning there was a possibility that I could hitchhike on one of the lorries driving south. I was extremely tired, but hopeful that I would be able to continue my strenuous journey. I stumbled along another few metres to a corner where I discovered a group of people huddled together and waiting for dawn. I joined them. Most of them were about my age and had been stranded in the North as I was, and now they were on their way home. I supped on some stale bread and a little cheese, and quenched my thirst under a tap of local water.

These men were going to South Italy. Some were from Calabria and Sicily, and hoped that their relatives had been spared from the horrors of the war.

In the morning between five and six o'clock, an empty open lorry came along. The driver agreed to give us a lift to Rome, if we paid him approximately the same fare that we would have paid for travelling by train. We agreed and soon we were on our way to the Eternal City.

The lorry driver was doing brisk business. He often stopped and took more passengers until the lorry was packed. As there were no seats, we had to squat on the floor, but it was so crowded that we could not stretch our legs. I was very uncomfortable indeed.

The driver followed a route through the Apennines, probably to avoid the congested roads along the Tyrrhenian Sea. The road was a continuous winding one along hills and mountains. At certain tricky turns, I feared that if the lorry skidded a couple of metres it would end in a ravine. The road was in a bad state of repair, and the driver did not seem very reliable; he first accelerated and then suddenly applied the brakes, causing us to jerk and jolt tremendously, almost throwing us out of the lorry. It was an extremely rough drive, making it utterly impossible to rest. I personally was very worried and prepared for the worst, so I prayed ceaselessly for a safe journey.

We travelled all that day, and after hours of jerking, jolting and tossing, thank God, we arrived in Rome. It was about midnight, and I was utterly exhausted, hungry and thirsty and incredulous about having survived that long, rough and reckless drive. In spite of the late hour, I managed to buy some sandwiches and mineral water at a kiosk near the station.

Many passengers hoped to catch one of the early morning trains, which were invariably crowded. Unable to find a seat, they rested on the floor inside and outside the waiting-rooms. I too squatted on the floor and waited for the first train to Naples, which was due to depart at five o'clock. Since the train started from Rome, I managed to board it half an hour before departure, which enabled me to find a seat. By the time the train pulled out of the station there was hardly any standing room left.

My new travelling companions were of different ages; they spoke in their regional dialects and were talking about the losses that they had endured during the war and the arduous tasks they had to face now in order to make a living. All their comments and complaints were not too encouraging for me, for I had the uneasy feeling that, although I was going home, I wasn't quite sure whether I still had one. I was terribly anxious about my relatives, and hoped now that I would find them safe and well.

The train was slow and stopped frequently, because some rails were being repaired. After three hours of travel, I looked from the windows, searching for some landmarks. Only when I caught sight of the mountains near Vesuvius did I know that the train had arrived in Naples. I could soon hear the pulse, shouts and cries of that lively and boisterous city.

I got off the train at about nine o'clock, and the sun was shining brightly. The square in front of the station – Garibaldi Square – was a hive of feverish activity: stalls, trams, buses, fruit vendors, people gossiping and arguing noisily and gesticulating, pizza shops, the scent of ragout, aubergine with Parmesan cheese, or pepper dishes that restaurants were preparing for the day. A few alluring prostitutes, posted here and there, endeavoured to hook potential customers.

The part of the city round the port, which used to be densely inhabited, had been heavily bombed by American Liberator aircraft during the war and completely destroyed. They did a good job indeed; those who perished there had been 'liberated' by being bombed; spared the trouble of living, of having to put up with the post-war Italian misery.

I could not stand there for hours and mourn and meditate on that devastation; past was past and life had to go on. I and all those who had survived the hard knocks of the war would, with the sweat of our brows and endless sacrifices, rebuild Naples and the rest of Italy, which had always been admired by millions of foreign visitors.

I woke up from my meditative thoughts. I had to get to my home, which was about four kilometres from the station. Suddenly an idea popped into my mind. What about ringing up our family doctor? I rushed to the nearest telephone and rang the operator who kindly gave me the doctor's number.

'Hello, may I speak to Dr Lupo?' I asked.

'Dr Lupo speaking. And who are you? What can I do for you?'

'My name is Arrichiello, Cosimo Arrichiello, and you're my family doctor.'

'Did you say Arrichiello? Oh, yes, I know Arrichiello.'

'I am Cosimo Arrichiello. I was doing military service in North Italy during the war, and I am coming home now. Could you tell me anything about my family? Are they well?'

'As far as I know they are well, but we are all still a bit shaken about the war and struggling to survive!'

'I quite understand, doctor. Let us hope that things will soon get back to normal, and thank you very much for your information; I am greatly relieved.'

The good news of my family made me feel great; all the tiredness of a very, very long and wearying journey suddenly left me. I was brimming with joy, energy and inclined to sing. I was on the point of calling a taxi, but I could not afford such an extravagance; my family might need whatever money I still had on me. I seized my two heavy suitcases and strode about 300 metres to the provincial tram station.

After my phone call, Dr Lupo sent a message to my relatives, telling them that I had just rung him up from Naples railway station and was on my way home. They were jubilant and told the people living in the same building of my coming. My youngest brother and three of my sisters waited for my arrival at the nearest tram stop, which was a hundred metres from home.

I had hardly alighted from the tram when I heard my sisters shouting exultantly.

'Hey, Cosimo! Cosimo!' and at the same time they ran and hugged me. 'You're looking well!'

They tried to help me to carry my suitcases, but they were too heavy. One of our neighbours, a strong youngster, volunteered to carry one to attract my sisters' attention and win their admiration. While we were walking home, some women, who were happily chatting, interrupted their conversation, looked at us inquisitively and smiled.

As I entered the building, some of the tenants welcomed me. My mother and elder sister came to meet me. Mother was crying as she hugged me, while the people next door looked on.

Soon we were sitting indoors, and I was assailed by many questions: 'Where have you been? What were you doing?' and so on.

'While you were away,' said Mother, 'one day I was saying the rosary. Probably I must have dozed a little. Suddenly I had a vision; I saw you hiding somewhere and waving at me.'

Mother connected this event with our miraculous Virgin Mary in the Chapel of the Sacred Hearts, where she had pinned my photo during the war to the hem of the dress of the Madonna. She said that the vision was an assurance from the Madonna, that I was safe and well.

87

*Japan surrenders. We receive news from Father and
my brothers. Why were they interned?*

To get away from the Allied air raids during the war, my family
had gone to live temporarily in Campobasso, a small town situated
about a hundred kilometres inland from Naples, and sixty from the
Adriatic coast. They had not given up their rented flat in
Secondigliano, which was our permanent home.

Mother then received a meagre government financial assistance
on account of my father and brothers who, being in Java, were
unable to send money home.

With the Italian Armistice in September 1943, the new Italian
government fled from Rome to Brindisi, so our country's
administration was in turmoil. Because of this, Mother could no
longer get financial assistance which, although a pittance, was
better than nothing. Mother was compelled to sell whatever was left
of her jewellery and other things, including linen, blankets,
embroidered garments and other objects that were meant to be part
of my elder sister's dowry.

At the beginning of October 1943, the Neapolitans welcomed the
Allied forces jubilantly, especially the American Army. The starved
Neapolitans hoped that the Americans had brought them some
bread, but they were bitterly disappointed and even shocked,
because the first thing the Americans did was to introduce the
Amlira, which was their money of occupation – their spending
money. This made the Italian lira almost worthless overnight, so the
price of our food and commodities sky-rocketed, and even bread
became a luxury. Then what were our people going to do? How
could they live?

A number of audacious Neapolitans resorted to robbing the
Americans. Columns of American trucks carrying supplies sped

towards the 'Gustav line'; if for one reason or another the trucks had to slow down, daring Neapolitans would jump on to one of them at the end of a convoy and drop part of its load on the road. Accomplices standing by carried away the booty, which invariably ended up on the black market.

Another lucrative Neapolitan expedient was to get some American negroes drunk, and later sell them. A would-be buyer examined a drunk negro thoroughly, calculating how much he was worth, how much he could get for the clothes and shoes that the negro was wearing. Having agreed on the price and settled the purchase, the buyer carried the drunk negro to a side street, undressed him and left him there stark naked.

The American military police patrolling the town were quite aware of what was going on and did not make a fuss about it; they probably allowed this to go on to give Neapolitans a chance to make a living. They would remove the drunk naked negro, load him on to a small truck and drive away; later, no doubt, they must have had a good laugh about it.

The Americans with their *Amlire* were doing very well in Naples and all over Italy; they could buy anything they wanted and get value for money. Perhaps they deliberately let our people starve while the war was on; it would enable their soldiers with pocketfuls of *Amlire* to buy our various services cheaply and make it easier for them to enjoy the company of our girls.

If a girl accepted the company of an American soldier, it meant that he would take her for a drive in a Jeep and call her 'honey', invite her to an American canteen, where she would eat and drink and dance till late.

Of course, old-fashioned parents were not pleased with the behaviour of easygoing girls; they were more concerned with their own dignity and decorum than with their empty stomachs.

While the Americans stayed in Naples, they employed a number of people mostly doing menial tasks. Three of my sisters found jobs in an army laundry and my younger brother in an army kitchen. However, at the end of the war in Europe, most of the soldiers were sent either to Northern Europe or to fight the Japanese in Asia. Their departure from Naples meant that my sisters and brother and many other Neapolitans lost their jobs.

Now that I had returned home, I noticed that my family was in a bad state; they had been reduced to bundles of skin and bone.

This saddened me, and broke my heart. I wanted to help them, but how could I, when millions of people were unemployed and did not know where their next crust of bread would come from?

My family was pleased when I showed them the clothing material I had brought from North Italy. I managed to sell part of it, so we could spend the proceeds on food provisions which lasted us a few days.

Although the war in Europe was over, the Japanese were still fighting, so we could not get news from our father and brothers. We had not heard from them since 1940, when Italy declared war on France and Britain.

My younger brother and I had to do something to help our family. Taking advantage of the fact that shops, especially in some small country towns, were still running short of dress material and other merchandise, we set ourselves up as middlemen. We bought whatever goods we could from people who shuttled to and from North Italy and Naples, and sold them to shopkeepers. They had to comply with their new well-to-do demanding customers who had become wealthy by exploiting the black market. The previous generation of rich people, who did not look after their money and other possessions during the war, had been reduced to poverty.

Our activity of buying and selling enabled our family to scrape a living – to keep the wolf from the door. Later, when transport from North to South Italy and vice versa was nearly back to normal, shopkeepers could get their supplies direct from manufacturers and no longer required our services, so my brother and I were finding it extremely hard to earn any money.

With the dropping of the atom bombs on Hiroshima and Nagasaki, the Japanese surrendered, and by 15 August 1945, the war in Asia was over.

Towards the end of August, we received a letter from Father and ran wild with excitement; at the same time we were anxious to learn its contents. The letter said:

Thank God we are well now. We have spent about two years (from October 1943 to August 1945) in a Japanese prisoner-of-war camp.

On 5 October 1943, while we were having lunch, a Japanese truck came along and the soldiers took us away. We had to

leave our belongings behind, and the Japanese helped them-
selves to them.

There were about 8,000 prisoners of war in our camp, most
of them civilians, of whom several died of malnutrition almost
daily. Had we been in that camp a few months longer, we
wouldn't have survived.

We have no intention of leaving Java; we believe that it is
still a promising land that will enable us to prosper once
again.

Father inserted some British paper money between the sheets of the
letter; money he had presumably acquired on the illegal money
market. He told us that when the banks resumed functioning
properly, he would be able to send us a monthly remittance. The
good news from Father and our brothers made us forget the fear,
uneasiness and trepidation we had had about them during the war.
Although they had been subject for almost two years to starvation
and harsh treatment by the Japanese, thank God they were well
now and able to start again from scratch with their business
activities.

The Japanese had invaded Java at the beginning of 1942. They
had seized my father and brothers and put them in a prisoner-of-
war camp about a month after the Italian Armistice in September
1943.

The deposed Mussolini, in July 1943 (as I mentioned previously),
was kept under house arrest in a hotel in Abruzzo, but a couple of
days after the Italian Armistice, a group of German soldiers
liberated him. A few days later Mussolini set up the Salò Republic
in North Italy, then he raised a small army and continued his
alliance with Germany and Japan.

The Japanese regarded him as an 'ally', and all the Italians who
no longer supported him as 'traitors', deserving to be put away.

At this stage, in spite of the war, Father and my brothers had
been doing well with their business. It was likely that a half-dozen
of our countrymen, motivated by envy, jealousy or some other ill-
feelings, told the Japanese that my father and brothers and certain
other Italians were anti-Fascist. The accusers were mere opportunists;
they turned to being informers to show the Japanese that they were
collaborators, and so they would not be interned.

One of these suspect informers was a good-looking man in his

393

early thirties, very virile and fond of *dolce vita*. He was an unscrupulous and untrustworthy fellow who wouldn't have hesitated to sacrifice his mother for his selfish ends. His pursuits in life were money, alluring women and gluttony. He had set his eyes on the attractive wife of one of our countrymen, whose husband was an excellent pianist. Having had the pianist interned, he found his wife an easy prey, and as she wasn't the faithful kind of spouse, she did not resist her suitor.

With the internment, Father and my brothers lost their home, office, equipment, store room and the money that they kept in their safe because banks were not functioning. The only asset left to them was a building that had not been completed. When they were liberated from captivity, they sold the building to an American company, and with the proceeds they were able to start business again.

88

We learn that Uncle Pascal and his son Jacques
are dead. Contact with Father is back to normal.
Sukarno's rise to power

At the end of the war, we also received news from Aunt Mary –
our French aunt living in Rouen. She told us that her son Jacques,
our cousin, had died during an air raid on Rouen. Presumably this
occurred in the year 1944, when the Allied forces landed in
Normandy. Jacques was then no older than twenty-two. The raid
took place during the day, while he was on some errands in the
southern part of the city. He sought cover somewhere near the
railway station; presumably the Gare Rive Gauche, which apparently
was heavily bombed. Uncle Pascal died too, but in different
circumstances.

As I have already mentioned, before the Second World War
Uncle was an honorary president of the Italian ex-servicemen in
Rouen. He had been living in Rouen since he got married. He was
in business there and when Mussolini declared war on France and
Britain, he and his family stayed on. I know roughly what happened
to Uncle after France surrendered to the invading Germans in 1940,
and during their occupation.

Since Uncle's business prospered at that time, perhaps some
Italian anti-Fascists or his business competitors, for one reason or
another accused him of being a German sympathiser or collaborator.

At the end of the war, the French partisans arrested him, threw
him into jail and threatened to shoot him. They didn't give him any
peace, subjected him to endless pressure by interrogating him day
and night. He experienced terrible fear and did not want to die, for
he dearly loved his wife and what was left of his family. However,
constant coercion broke him down, drove him insane and caused
his death.

I spent the rest of 1945 and the beginning of 1946 with my relatives in Secondigliano. Contact with our father and brothers in Java was back to normal; they wrote to us once or twice a month, told us what they were doing and sent a regular remittance that helped us to keep body and soul together. They also mentioned their local political unrest, because the Indonesians were fighting for freedom from Dutch colonialism. However my father and brothers were not worried about the situation; they were confident that sooner or later there would be some kind of political settlement between the Dutch and the natives.

The Dutch had ruled their East Indies colonies for about 350 years. The natives had on several occasions expressed their desire for independence, especially in 1927, when a recently graduated engineer called Sukarno and his native elite founded the first major political party in the city of Bundung. Owing to Sukarno's gift for oratory, his party's membership was in no time more than 10,000 members. Soon after this achievement, Sukarno was arrested and imprisoned. Later he was released, but in 1933 he and his associates were exiled to a distant island, where they remained for almost ten years.

In 1942, when the Japanese invaded Indonesia, they met little resistance, because the natives regarded them as their liberators from Dutch colonialism. The Japanese freed Sukarno and his associates and allowed them to resume their political activity. The Japanese policy was to keep on friendly terms with the natives and exploit them for self-interest.

With the Japanese surrender to the Allied forces in 1945, Sukarno, still in charge of his freedom movement, declared his country's independence. The Dutch, however, were unwilling to grant it, and as soon as the Japanese quit Indonesia, the Dutch sent in their troops. They built an army and attacked the stubborn freedom fighters, trying to regain control of the country. However the United Nations intervened and after a series of round table conferences, the Dutch sadly had to give in to Indonesian demands; consequently, in 1949, the Republic of Indonesia was born and Sukarno became its first President.

89

*My father intends to start a clothing business. I enrol
at a fashion school*

I often went to Naples city, where I could not ignore the scars of
war. The rubble and ruins of destroyed buildings were scenes of
death and desolation. The atmosphere of the city, with so many
destitutes, unemployed and beggars around, was disheartening and
depressing. The merry people of *La Bella Napoli* seemed to have
gone for ever and to have left behind a dreary and appalling
sadness.

The sight of Vesuvius, the blue sea and the azure sky was still
there to alleviate the afflictions of mournful and hungry people. The
warm sun, giver of life, was shining brightly on those heaps of
rubble and ruins. Once there had been life, abundant life and joy,
now there was only dust and stones, stained with the blood of those
who had perished. Many Neapolitans, still on the verge of starvation,
went to the cemetery once a week to weep over the graves of their
dear ones who a few years earlier had been killed by American
bombers.

We spent Christmas 1945 and New Year's Day 1946 according
to our own traditions, but we were all adults now, the youngest of
my family being fifteen, so the Christmas and New Year festivities
had lost that feeling of innocent merriment and glamour that we
had experienced in the years before the war.

My old friends, ex-servicemen, having no prospects for the future,
were hopeless, worried and dejected. I felt exactly the same. I was
almost twenty-six; what was I going to do? People at my age usually
went to work, and later got married and started their families.

The Italian economy was shattered and seemed beyond repair,
and I was fed up with the whole situation in Europe. I was
extremely down-hearted and badly needed a change. I wanted to go

away somewhere, discover a peaceful and prosperous land, forget all about the war and its tribulations, and be able to smile once again. My only hope of salvation was to emigrate to Java and, with my relatives, to try to work and prosper.

They had in mind to start a new business importing fashionable goods mainly from Holland. The Dutch, who were still a colonial power in Indonesia, allowed businessmen to import, preferably from Holland, to enable them to stimulate their home industry.

With the prospect of going into the rag trade, my father and brothers suggested that, before going to Java, I should enrol for a design and cutting course in a good school of fashion in North Italy. Since I was unemployed and had nothing better to do, I promptly complied with their suggestion.

Towards the end of March 1946, I went to Turin and started training. My father and brothers paid my expenses. I had enrolled at an academy of fashion called 'Snob', directed by Professor Franco Musolino. He was dynamic, had a round face, dark eyes and complexion, and was of Calabrian origin.

I enjoyed that period of training, which lasted six months. I used to spend the whole day at school, absorbing the theory and learning, creating and designing. I took my studies seriously, and my teacher was very impressed.

I lived in a small bedroom, ate at a restaurant once a day and, every evening before retiring, I went for a walk with my schoolmates.

Turin, on the River Po, is a beautiful city. In that vicinity, the river is flanked by a park called 'Il Valentino'. I loved this city because people were courteous. It had an excellent tram service, good cinemas, theatres and cabarets. However, luxuries were not for me, for I had to be careful with my spending money.

While I was there, I kept in contact with my relatives in Naples and Java. I also visited my wartime friends in Bra, Codico, Bardo and Rena, localities about sixty kilometres away. I told them what I was doing in Turin and that I would eventually emigrate to Java, where I hoped to make a success of myself.

On visiting the Boltis I met their son Peter who had been a prisoner of war in England. He was captured in January 1941 at Bardia, where 40,000 Italians surrendered to the British forces. He had been in England for about four years, during which time he was allowed to work on a farm. Having returned home, he was finding it hard to get used to his own environment.

Agnes, the first daughter of the Boltis, who was in her thirties, was getting married to a farmer. Giovanni, the first of the Boltis' sons, had a fiancée and would soon take the plunge. Martha and Celia had new boyfriends, and their wedding days were not far away.

Martha asked me, 'Did you see Mark's relatives?'

'Yes,' I replied, 'I paid them a visit the week after I arrived home.'

Mark's relatives lived in a small town called Casalnuovo, which was not far away from my home. Mark, Martha's ex-boyfriend, as I mentioned before, was killed at Saliano in December 1944.

Casalnuovo was then a small town where everybody knew everybody, so it did not take me very long to find Mark's relatives. I met his parents, brothers and sisters. It was a large family cooped up together in a small flat in a dilapidated building. They were poor people existing somehow on bread and macaroni but, regardless of their poverty, they managed to be lively.

They already knew of Mark's death; they had received the bad news from local *carabinieri* at the end of the war. Unfortunately, they did not get the money and wrist-watch that I gave to Mark's lieutenant at Fossano a few days after his death.

My farmer friends had made a considerable amount of money on the black market during the war. Although glad that the war was over, they were much concerned now that life was gradually getting back to normal. The boom, their way of earning easy money, was over and they could not get very far with their accumulated money, on account of inflation. Now they had to face stark reality – working hard as usual just to make ends meet.

My friend Biagio Costa told me that the police could not find the culprits who had murdered Mark and Francis (the shoemaker). Albert, whom I suspected of Mark's murder, was missing. Farmer Cortese, supposed to have been involved in Francis's murder, was carrying on with his farming, and his daughter was helping him. Did he have a guilty conscience for having blood on his hands? A few years after my last visit to Bardo, while he was pruning some trees, a freak thunderstorm compelled him to seek cover under a mulberry tree, where he was struck by lightning. The peasants said that it was the scourge of God, or the spirit of Francis taking revenge.

90

*I become a teacher at the school, but it is very hard
to make a living. Having decided to emigrate, I get
myself a girlfriend*

I did very well at the fashion school, where I enjoyed making
patterns and creating novelties. It was mentally a very stimulating
activity, and I had a flair for it. At the end of my course, in
September 1946, the director asked me whether I would like to be
a teacher at the academy. Being enthusiastic and ambitious, I
wanted to give it a try, so I accepted.

He soon organised some short courses of fashion held in Naples;
each course lasted about one month. I was working very hard, but
could not make a living out of teaching. There were millions of
unemployed, who had no money to buy the basic necessities, so I
could not get enough people to enrol. Besides, it would have taken
me several years to get established. I was eager to work, earn my
living and get on, but not too confident that I could achieve this in
my own country, where everything then was so chaotic, pathetic
and distressing.

Without much ado, I applied for a passport. Having obtained a
visa, I waited for Father to arrange for my flight to Batavia, which
Sukarno, when he became the first President of Indonesia, renamed
Jakarta.

Aware that I was emigrating to an Asian country and did not
know when I would be able to return to Italy, I found myself a
girlfriend called Livia with the intention of marrying her as soon as
possible. I could marry by proxy and let her come to Jakarta, where
we could start our own family.

Livia was a friend of my sister Maria, who was studying at the
University of Naples. She was from a good family and a teacher, and
ran her private school consisting of about twenty or thirty children.

I disliked the idea of marrying a foreigner, so I had to abide by the old Italian saying: *Moglie e buoi dei paesi tuoi* (Choose wife and cattle from your own village); by doing so it would have been easy for both of us to understand each other and form a serene and harmonious family atmosphere. This was paramount for me after six years of turmoil, tribulation and misery. All I needed then was peace and tranquillity to help me to recover from past blows, and work intelligently and industriously for my future.

I was ready now to face my new life in Java – the tropical weather, the Dutch and Indonesian languages and their cultures. This certainly was a challenge; a great challenge that all those who emigrate have to overcome. Luckily I had a stout heart and great determination to prevail against any obstacle; nothing would discourage me from getting on.

The first six months of 1947 passed without any major events; I kept busy teaching fashion and creating new patterns. I also helped my five sisters make their own dresses and coats, which aroused admiration and interest. I was in demand; people were asking me to make up their garments. To a certain extent I did, but I was afraid to ask the right price, because my customers were not rich.

I loved art. I endeavoured to create something beautiful; I did not consider myself to be a common artisan, but an artist. If my customers or would-be customers wanted a novelty or style, they had to be prepared to pay for it, otherwise how could I make a living? How could I marry Livia and settle down?

Starting a fashion house or an *atelier* in Italy was out of the question because I had no money to do it; besides, poverty and political instability deterred me. But by going to Java, I would cut myself off from the European influence and artistic feedback. A tropical climate would sap my energetic flow, make me feel tired and tempt me to take things easy and avoid effort. Adieu to my artistic talent and career. I would vegetate, grow fat, have the possibility of making money and become utterly materialistic. Was this what I wanted? But since 'beggars can't be choosers', I had to be practical and take any chance that would enable me to earn my living and prosper.

While I was still at home I saw Livia no less than twice a week. I went to her home on Thursday and Sunday evenings. Her mother always chaperoned her.

Livia's mother, a saintly woman, was a widow in her sixties. She

401

went to Mass every day, and prayer was her strength. She was dear, kind and understanding, and always used to say: '*Chi si contenta gode*' (Who is contented, enjoys.)

As Livia was attending a teacher-training course in Naples once a week, I waited for her outside the institute, and when she came out at the end of the lesson we went for a walk to some quiet spot where I kissed her. This was as far as I went. Young men at that time did not make love to their girlfriends before they got married; it was just out of the question. Livia and I grew affectionate to each other, and I earnestly intended to marry her.

Days and months rolled by, I was eager to embark on my new activity in Java, but deep in my heart, a feeling of sadness haunted me. Why did I have to leave my country? Even if I was not able to live happily here, would it be easier to do so in a foreign land, especially in a tropical climate and Asian culture, where I had to learn two new languages? Would a better standard of living and the prospect of making money be worth the effort? Would it compensate me adequately for the sacrifice of leaving my beloved country, its lofty mountains, pleasant climate, azure sky, blue sea, my close friends, the delight of hearing and speaking my own language, listening to our music, songs, plays, short stories, the shouts of street vendors and so on? I had been accustomed to these things as I grew up among them; they were parts of my life and very dear to me. How could I brush them aside, tear myself away from them and go to live in a strange country without noticing the effect?

My last six years had been a time of anguish, frustration, delusion and hardship, getting me nowhere; years of exasperation and rage, almost driving me insane. We were at the mercy of our German 'ally' who had no respect for us on account of our poor military performance; and being unable to defend ourselves, we were exposed to raids by American bombers that attacked us at will.

I was fed up with our government, King and generals who had done nothing else but mess up our poor country. I utterly lost confidence in our leaders; most of them were self-seeking people who ruined our country.

At the end of the war we had new politicians: Bonomi, De Gaspari, Nenni, Togliatti, Saragat and many others trying to form a democratic government, but there were too many political parties, endless strikes, and squabbles in Parliament. All this wasn't at all encouraging for an ambitious young man wanting to get on in life.

402

It was all very well for me to have emotional attachment and a sense of belonging to my country, but I had to be adamant, brave, summon up my courage and break away, and let reason prevail over emotion. Now I had the chance to go abroad and must take it; the chance to work, prove myself, succeed, get married, and perhaps, eventually having saved enough for a rainy day, return home to my beloved country and live happily ever after.

91

Father books my flight to Jakarta. Signor Rossi's
grand hospitality

In September 1947 my father booked my flight to Jakarta with
KLM and sent me the ticket. I was to fly at the end of the month
from Ciampino Airport, Rome. At that time, travelling by air was
a luxury that only diplomats and the well-to-do could afford. This
was not the case for me. I had to fly because few ships were sailing
there, as most of the liners had been sunk during the war.

Before leaving Italy, I went to Turin, Bra, Codico, Bardo and
Rena once again. These places were peaceful, compared with
during the wartime years. I stood on the top of a Bardo hillock and
gazed at the landscape contemplatively. The sun as usual was
shining, and the luxuriant countryside, swarming with life, was in
full splendour. I had to break away from that enchantment, a spell
so penetrating and mystifying. Was that scenery real or just an
illusion?

Having stopped wondering, I realised that I was very much a
poor human being full of desires and expectations; one of the
millions of people roaming the earth and struggling for security and
existence. Soon I had to say farewell to my friends and promise
that I would write to them.

Finally the day came for me to go. My mother, Livia and my
youngest brother came to see me off at the central railway station
in Naples. The flight was scheduled for the afternoon of the
following day, which meant that I would have to spend a night with
a friend of my father living in Rome.

The train, an express, was due to depart from Naples at 10.00
a.m. Our taxi arrived at the station about twenty minutes early. I
did not have to worry about my seat; I had booked it in advance.
Having placed my suitcase on the luggage-rack, I spent my last few

minutes in Naples talking to my mother and Livia, who were standing on the platform. I had to make a great effort to conceal my sadness at leaving them behind; I felt as if I were still attached to my mother's umbilical cord, which I was reluctant to sever. Livia looked into my eyes earnestly, trying to discern my real feelings. At that very moment I knew more than ever that I belonged beyond doubt to both of them and did not want to leave; my heart yearned for their affection.

All this wasn't helping me to put on an act of bravery and controlled emotion, or lessen the pain of separation; a nagging thought kept creeping in and gave me no respite. Why do I have to go and leave things behind that are very dear to me? I knew quite a number of people who had made money, but were unhappy. Would I become one of them?

As the train pulled out of the station and my mother, Livia and my brother gradually vanished from sight, I was pensive and in emotional turmoil, unable to soothe my aching heart. I sat down and was quite unaware of the presence of the other passengers in the compartment. After a while, having caught sight of the panoramic countryside through the train window, it enlivened and almost cured me. I became rational; after all I wasn't on the way to the Tower of London to have my head chopped off, I was journeying to the Eternal City, which was the first stop on my way to Indonesia.

I arrived at Rome (Termini Station) at about 12.30 p.m. The station as usual was crowded and lively. I left my suitcase in the baggage room and then I was on my way to the address of my father's friend, signor Giuseppe Rossi. I did not have to go very far, for he had a textile shop somewhere near the station. I don't think he was very pleased to see me; most probably because his business was not doing well and he did not trust his partner. However, he invited me to dinner in one of the local restaurants, and later I spent the rest of the afternoon wandering through the city.

Signor Rossi originated from a small town called Maddaloni, which is one of the districts of the city of Caserta. This is about twenty-five kilometres from Naples. He was in his fifties, of medium height and rather thin. He had greying hair combed back, small dark eyes and a tan complexion.

Signor Rossi had been an itinerant salesman when he was in Indonesia. He had been there several years and saved enough money for a rainy day. Although illiterate, he met and married a well-educated mixed-race spinster (half-Italian and half-Indonesian) who had some money. She badly wanted to marry a white man, but there was a scarcity of them and many girls did not question their eligibility. So when signor Rossi came along, she must have seen in him her saviour, the man who one day would take her away from Indonesia to Italy, for she loved the Italian climate and culture.

As soon as they got married, she disliked his activity as a salesman, which she found undignified, so she endeavoured to change him. She set up a dairy business and, with her help, signor Rossi learned to manage it. Unfortunately a year and a few months after the Japanese invaded Indonesia, signor Rossi, like my father and brothers, ended up in a prisoner-of-war camp. At the end of the war in 1945, his wife sold her properties, and signor Rossi, his wife and children went to live in Rome.

92

*I go to Rome airport. After a three-day flight I arrive
in Jakarta*

Signor Rossi shut his shop at eight o'clock, while it was still
twilight. He did not take me to his home, which was in the suburbs
of the city. He told me that his business was for sale, therefore he
did not want to stay away from his shop for too long. He feared
that while he was away, his partner would enter the shop and
remove part of the dress material. Meanwhile, he slept in the shop
and hoped that it would be sold soon; he would then try to do
something else.

He invited me to stay for the night in the shop, if I didn't mind.
I certainly wasn't prepared for such a beggarly offer. My spirit
rebelled. Had I had enough money on me, I would have gone to a
hotel. But what else could I do? I had to swallow my pride and
accept his humble and undignified offer.

Having closed the shop that evening, he took me for a meal in
a small restaurant, where he met two old mates. We ate together,
but when the meal was over, he and his cronies started chatting in
their own regional dialect and reminisced about the good old days,
which meant nothing to me. I couldn't understand their lingo, so I
was bored, but for politeness' sake I had to beam, look interested,
even engrossed. I was greatly relieved when we left them and
strolled back to the shop. Although it was about midnight, life in
the fashionable centre of Rome was in full swing; those who had
the chance socialised until the small hours of the morning.

The air inside the shop, with so many shelves full of rolls of
men's clothing material, was not too salubrious to breathe. Signor
Rossi stretched some blankets on the shop's counter, undressed
himself, put on his pyjamas and lay down. I did the same. I wore
a pair of his pyjamas, which he kindly lent to me, but had to lie

on a layer of blankets spread on the floor. This reminded me of sentry duties during my military service.

I tried to be indifferent and almost forgave signor Rossi's meagre hospitality. I would soon forget about it, for I was going to spend the following three days in the company of congenial travellers, partly flying, and partly eating and resting at hotels while the aircraft was being serviced.

The excitement of my first flight made me restless; I tossed and turned on my hard makeshift bed but couldn't get a wink of sleep, and signor Rossi's endless snoring wasn't helpful at all. I waited patiently and eagerly for the first glimpse of the approaching dawn.

Signor Rossi and I got up before seven and had our continental breakfast of fresh bread rolls and white coffee. Since I had to be at the airport at one o'clock, I had a few hours to spare, so I went for a stroll. It was fine weather and the city was crowded with tourists as usual. I caught a bus that took me to Saint Peter's. I also visited the Forum, Colosseum, the famous Roman Cenotaph, which looks like an iced cake, and also Palazzo Venezia (Venice Palace), where there is a balcony from which Mussolini made his inflammatory speeches and plunged poor Italy into our sorrowful war.

Soon it was nearly midday. I went back to signor Rossi's shop, called a taxi and fetched my suitcase, which the driver kindly placed in the boot of the car. Having thanked signor Rossi for his not too agreeable hospitality and bade him farewell, I was soon on the way to Ciampino Airport, which was a good half an hour's drive from Rome. I arrived there at almost one o'clock, paid the driver, and then someone directed me to the KLM check-in. I had to wait half an hour or so, for the aircraft had not arrived yet. It was coming from Amsterdam and carrying mostly Dutch passengers on their way to Jakarta.

The aircraft landed at about two o'clock. It was a Douglas quadrimotor flying at the terrific speed of 300 kilometres per hour and carrying less than a hundred passengers. As I looked at it from the waiting-room, I was simultaneously scared and thrilled; I feared that if it crashed, my chance of survival would be almost nil. I had been through the war, exposed to many dangers, endured a lot of hardship, and thank God I was still alive. Being young and healthy, I wanted to live, and was now flying to Java, full of hopes and expectations and eager to achieve them. On the other hand, the flight would enable me to experience the thrill of being in the air and looking at various views of the earth from above, making me aware of the universe and the mystery of boundless space.

The passengers did not disembark, for the aircraft was due to take off shortly. Finally, it was time for me to embark, so I walked through a gate, showed my ticket, stepped a few metres along the tarmac and went aboard. A Dutch hostess, an attractive blonde, showed me my seat, which was near a window on the left side of the plane. The seat next to me was occupied by a Dutchman in his twenties and, like me, bound for Jakarta. I did not know a word of Dutch, but I had some knowledge of French and so did he. This enabled us to communicate.

My travelling companion was a Dutch government employee going to work in a new office in Jakarta. The rest of the passengers looked prosperous and dignified; they were rather tall, well-built businessmen, planters and government officers. Some had been on holiday in Holland and were now going back to their businesses or jobs in Indonesia.

The aircraft took off at about three o'clock while the sun was still high in the sky. I unfastened my seat-belt and looked down at the Eternal City.

'Goodbye, dear Rome! Goodbye, dear Italy!' I murmured, 'I am flying to a land far, far away and, God willing, I shall safely reach my destination. I haven't the faintest idea when I will be able to return. Goodbye, land of my childhood, of my happy carefree days in which I learned to love you! In spite of all my disappointments and bitterness during the war, I am finding it very hard to say goodbye. I had to leave, there was no other way. How could I have stayed at home without a job in the appalling post-war chaotic situation? I had to go; I couldn't stand it any more.'

As the aircraft was getting further and further away from the land of my affections, my attachment to home seemed to be growing stronger and stronger and causing me to indulge in too many tender memories. Had I remained in Italy and been lucky enough to find a job, I would have had to work like a slave for the rest of my life just for a pittance; my lifespan, I think, would have been shortened to less than three score years and ten.

But I was flying to Indonesia to work, and it was no use giving way to sentimentality. I had to be strong-willed, stoical, a man, roll up my sleeves and get on.

The aircraft was now flying over Corfu, and other Greek islands were in sight. As we flew east, the day was getting shorter and shorter. Soon after sunset, the Greek islands looked dark and eerie; they reminded me of the ancient history I had studied at school.

We arrived at Tel Aviv at about 9.00 p.m., but because of political unrest – Israel–Arab tension – the airport was under military control. While the aircraft was being serviced, a KLM hostess accompanied us to a restaurant where we had a meal. Hotel accommodation and meals were included in the fare.

Two hours later we were aboard, flying over Jordan and then Saudi Arabia. We passed the night resting in comfortable reclining seats. At sunrise we stared with amazement at the colourful desert beneath us and at the azure sky. Some oil wells, visible in the distance, were scattered over a vast area. They were operated, I was told, by people of various nationalities.

We landed at Bahrain for an hour or so. I was confronted with terrifically hot weather, making it difficult to breathe. This was my first taste of the tropics and I couldn't stand it; I was inclined to turn back, go home to my beloved Italian climate. How could I manage to stay in Indonesia? How could my father and brothers have managed to live there for so many years? It was possible that after a while I might get used to tropical weather as they had done.

While we were at Bahrain Airport, we were offered some refreshments. Later we resumed our flight, our next landing being Karachi.

Generally, the flight proceeded smoothly, but every now and then we had to put up with air pockets that caused a sinking feeling in the pit of my stomach. We flew over lands, mountains, rivers and seas, and their scenery changed continually.

We landed at Bangkok at about midnight and were driven to a hotel some distance from the airport; it wasn't very comfortable. We had a shower and later a meal. The beds weren't too inviting, the heat was suffocating and the ceiling fans weren't too efficient at alleviating my misery. I slept in a bed that had a mosquito net, but it couldn't keep all the mosquitoes out; they were persistent and annoyed me tremendously. I slept, if I had any sleep, with my socks on to protect my feet, but the socks, being dark, attracted mosquitoes that made a good meal of my blood. My socks stuck to my ankles where the mosquitoes had pierced my skin and gorged themselves.

We stopped at Singapore in the morning for about three hours, had a shower, a meal and a few drinks. My travelling companions drank beer and also brandy; most of them were heavy smokers, unknowingly driving nails into their coffins. I might have had a glass of beer or two, but usually I stuck to soft drinks.

On the whole the three-day flight was tolerable and quite an experience. I did not particularly fancy air pockets. Most of the time I chatted with the chap sitting next to me, or with someone else who could speak French and understand my attempts at the language. The food aboard was rather too rich for me; they served ham, bacon and lard sandwiches, which the Dutch seemed to relish, but in my opinion such fatty food wasn't suitable in a tropical climate.

Food was always served with beverages – soft drinks, beer or white coffee. Some of the Dutch, needing a boost or a pick-me-up, had tots of Bols, a Dutch brandy as strong as whisky.

Finally, we were almost at the end of the long flight. The aircraft took off from Singapore in the afternoon of the third day, and soon we were flying over a number of small and large islands. We caught sight of Borneo on the left side of the aircraft and Sumatra on the right, some native trawlers and a few steamers shuttling to and from the islands. The sea was calm and smooth under that scorching sun. I heard someone say that the temperature was usually no less than thirty degrees Celsius. This news did not particularly cheer me up, for I hated hot weather. I said to myself, well, I must do my best, try hard to get used to it as my father and brothers have done. I am not going there for a picnic, but to work, to sweat and hope that, with God's help, my efforts will be rewarded.

As we came close to the island of Java, I became excited; I had not seen my father and brothers since 1938. We had all gone through a hard time; they in the Japanese prisoner-of-war camp and me in the Italian Army. They had been away from Europe, sweltering in a tropical climate that can be hell for Europeans, with no hope of a reviving cool breeze. They had been there earning money – the remittances they sent us in Naples – a city with a pleasant European climate.

My father and brothers were not rich, but they had enough money to set up a good business that should in no time give us a satisfactory turnover.

I was no longer the teenage boy they had left behind in 1938; I

411

had gone through years of hardship and was now prepared to toil and get on; my future depended on how well I fared. Shortly, in about an hour's time, the aircraft would land at Kemaioran, Jakarta's airport.

It landed at about six o'clock, which was almost sunset there. I bade farewell to my travelling companions, alighted from the plane and soon caught sight of Father and my brothers. I was wearing a grey suit; they were dressed in white cotton trousers and shirts. We hugged each other, and they were extremely glad to see me. As they drove me to my new home in Jakarta, which was some distance from the airport, they assailed me with questions.

I couldn't ignore the sweltering heat and was seriously concerned about it. The Dutch had to be there because it was their colony. Other Europeans, like my family, were there to try their luck, but the constant heat had the tendency to wear them down, making any effort impossible and encouraging laziness. It had a definite effect on the minds and bodies of European residents; they found it extremely hard to exert themselves, so they had to rely on native servants for domestic chores and many other menial activities.

I often wondered why my family continued to stay in Indonesia after the war. Apart from the hot climate, there was the problem of political instability, for the Indonesians were pressing for independence from the Dutch, and were determined to get it.

My father and brothers had been away from Europe for too many years, and the heat and the prospect that they would once again enjoy pre-war material comforts and business facilities must have affected their judgement. They hoped that the Dutch and Indonesians would come to some agreement and settle their dispute amicably, and that the standard of living of the Dutch and other Europeans in Indonesia would be restored to the pre-war level. This would mean great comforts for them and slavery for most of the natives. However, the Indonesians had had enough of Dutch domination; they wanted to be their own masters.

When Father and my brothers came out of the prisoner-of-war camp, the Americans offered them the possibility of emigrating to the USA. Had they accepted the offer, I think it would have been the right decision in their own interests and that of our whole family. Life in Italy, in the immediate post-war years, was precarious indeed, and if we had taken the chance to settle in the USA, we

412

would have gone to live in a prosperous country with a suitable climate – but this was not to be.

I had arrived in Java, but my emotions were still greatly shaken on account of my experience of the war, which had left a scar that only time would heal. I was making a supreme effort to adapt myself and overcome my turmoil, but the tropical weather seemed to conspire to make my task harder. I needed to summon up all my strength to defeat my nagging feelings. Past was past, I must look to what lay ahead and make the best of it if I wanted to get somewhere. I had to bear in mind that there are no victories without casualties, and Java was now my new trial; the place where I could succeed or fail.

So far I have dealt with the first twenty-seven years of my life. I hope to write a sequel some time in the future, covering my experiences from the end of 1947 onwards, years I spent in Indonesia, Australia and Great Britain. They were years of great changes, with the Dutch colonials leaving Indonesia, the large-scale European emigration to Australia, and the emergence of the welfare state in Britain and other countries.

BIBLIOGRAPHY

In the course of my research I have read the following books:

Absalon, R.N.L., *Mussolini and the Rise of Italian Fascism* (London: Methuen & Co. Ltd, 1969)

Berto, Giuseppe, *Guerra in Camicia Nera* (Milano: Garzanti, 1955)

Bruce, Colin John, *War on the Ground 1939–1945* (London: Constable & Co. Ltd, 1995)

——, Colin John, *Chronicle of the Second World War* (London: Longman Group UK Ltd and Chronicle Communications Ltd, 1990)

Collier, Richard, *Duce! The Rise and Fall of Mussolini* (London: William Collins, 1971)

——, Richard, *The War in the Desert (World War II)* (Chicago: Time-Life Books, 1977)

'Freedom's Battle' in *The War at Sea 1939–1945* (London: Hutchinson & Co. Ltd, 1967)

Gilbert, Martin, *Marching to War 1933–1939* (London: Bracken Books, 1989)

Hibbert, Christopher, *Mussolini* (London: The Pan/Ballantine Illustrated History of World War ll, 1973)

Keegan, John, *The Second World War* (London: Arrow Books Ltd, 1990)

Laffredo, Salvatore Father, *Secondigliano da Documenti Inediti* (Naples)

Lucas, Phillips C.E., *Alamein* (London: William Heinemann Ltd, 1962)

Matanle, Ivor, *World War II* (New York: Military Press, 1989)

Montanelli, Intro & Cervi, Mario, *L'Italia Della Disfatta* (Milano: Rizzoli Editore, 1982)

——, Intro & Cervi, Mario, *L'Itatia Dell' Asse* (Milano: Rizzoli Editore, 1984)

Moorehead, Alan, *The Desert War* (London: Hamish Hamilton Ltd, 1965)

Overy, Richard, *The Road to War*, with Andrew Wheatcroft (London: Macmillan Ltd, 1989)

Pimlott, John, *World War II in Photographs* (London: Orbis Publishing, 1984)

Ryder, Rowland, *Oliver Leese* (London: Hamish Hamilton Ltd, 1987)

Silvestri, Mario, *Caporetto* (Milano: Arnoldo Mondadori Editore S.p.A., 1984)

Stern, Mario Riboni, *Il Sergente Nella Neve* (Torino: Giulio Einaudi Editore, 1953)

Daily Telegraph 'Record of the Second World War' (London: Sidgwick and Jackson in association with *Daily Telegraph*, 1989)

The History of World War II, Volume 3 (London: Orbis Publishing Ltd, 1972)

Young, Peter, *World War 1939–1945* (London: Pan Books Ltd, 1970)